Women's *Tanci* Fiction in Late Imperial and Early Twentieth-Century China

Comparative Cultural Studies
Steven Tötösy de Zepetnek, Series Editor

The Purdue University Press monograph series of Books in Comparative Cultural Studies publishes single-authored and thematic collected volumes of new scholarship. Manuscripts are invited for publication in the series in fields of the study of culture, literature, the arts, media studies, communication studies, the history of ideas, etc., and related disciplines of the humanities and social sciences to the series editor via e-mail at <clcweb@purdue.edu>. Comparative cultural studies is a contextual approach in the study of culture in a global and intercultural context and work with a plurality of methods and approaches; the theoretical and methodological framework of comparative cultural studies is built on tenets borrowed from the disciplines of cultural studies and comparative literature and from a range of thought including literary and culture theory, (radical) constructivism, communication theories, and systems theories; in comparative cultural studies focus is on theory and method as well as application. For a detailed description of the aims and scope of the series including the style guide of the series link to <http://docs.lib.purdue.edu/clcweblibrary/seriespurdueccs>. Manuscripts submitted to the series are peer reviewed followed by the usual standards of editing, copy editing, marketing, and distribution. The series is affiliated with *CLCWeb: Comparative Literature and Culture* (ISSN 1481-4374), the peer-reviewed, full-text, and open-access quarterly published by Purdue University Press at <http://docs.lib.purdue.edu/clcweb>.

Volumes in the Purdue series of Books in Comparative Cultural Studies include <http://www.thepress.purdue.edu/series/comparative-cultural-studies>

Li Guo, *Women's* Tanci *Fiction in Late Imperial and Early Twentieth-Century China*
Arianna Dagnino, *Transcultural Writers and Novels in the Age of Global Mobility*
Elke Sturm-Trigonakis, *Comparative Cultural Studies and the New* Weltliteratur
Lauren Rule Maxwell, *Romantic Revisions in Novels from the Americas*
Liisa Steinby, *Kundera and Modernity*
Text and Image in Modern European Culture, Ed. Natasha Grigorian, Thomas Baldwin, and Margaret Rigaud-Drayton
Sheng-mei Ma, *Asian Diaspora and East-West Modernity*
Irene Marques, *Transnational Discourses on Class, Gender, and Cultural Identity*
Comparative Hungarian Cultural Studies, Ed. Steven Tötösy de Zepetnek and Louise O. Vasvári
Hui Zou, *A Jesuit Garden in Beijing and Early Modern Chinese Culture*
Yi Zheng, *From Burke and Wordsworth to the Modern Sublime in Chinese Literature*
Agata Anna Lisiak, *Urban Cultures in (Post)Colonial Central Europe*
Representing Humanity in an Age of Terror, Ed. Sophia A. McClennen and Henry James Morello
Michael Goddard, *Gombrowicz, Polish Modernism, and the Subversion of Form*
Shakespeare in Hollywood, Asia, and Cyberspace, Ed. Alexander C.Y. Huang and Charles S. Ross
Gustav Shpet's Contribution to Philosophy and Cultural Theory, Ed. Galin Tihanov
Comparative Central European Holocaust Studies, Ed. Louise O. Vasvári and Steven Tötösy de Zepetnek
Marko Juvan, *History and Poetics of Intertextuality*
Thomas O. Beebee, *Nation and Region in Modern American and European Fiction*
Paolo Bartoloni, *On the Cultures of Exile, Translation, and Writing*
Justyna Sempruch, *Fantasies of Gender and the Witch in Feminist Theory and Literature*
Kimberly Chabot Davis, *Postmodern Texts and Emotional Audiences*
Philippe Codde, *The Jewish American Novel*
Deborah Streifford Reisinger, *Crime and Media in Contemporary France*

Women's *Tanci* Fiction in Late Imperial and Early Twentieth-Century China

Li Guo

Purdue University Press
West Lafayette, Indiana

Printed in the United States of America.

Library of Congress Cataloging-in-Publication Data

Guo, Li, 1979-
Women's Tanci Fiction in Late Imperial and Early Twentieth-Century China / Li Guo.
pages cm.—(Comparative cultural studies)
Includes bibliographical references and index.
ISBN 978-1-55753-713-3 (pbk.: alk. paper)
ISBN 978-1-61249-381-7 (epdf)
ISBN 978-1-61249-382-4 (epub)
1. Chinese fiction—Women authors—History and criticism. 2. Women in literature.
3. Narration (Rhetoric) I. Title.
PL2278.G86 2015
895.13'48099287—dc23
2015014480

Cover image: *Reading Books* by Yu Lan, Qing Dynasty. ©The Palace Museum, 4 Jingshan Qianjie, Beijing 100009, China. Used by permission.

To my parents

Contents

Editor's Preface

Chinese names follow Asian studies convention, where post-1950 names use the English sequence, given name + surname, and pre-1950 names use the source format, that is, surname + given name. In-text citations list names in the same sequence as the works cited to make it easy to locate corresponding works. Thus, citations will provide the first name listed in the works cited if sufficient, or both names will appear—in a post-1950s citation as

(Liu, Kwang-Ching, *Orthodoxy* 202) in-text and
Liu, Kwang-Ching, ed. *Orthodoxy* . . . in the works cited;

in a pre-1950s citation as

(Li Yü, *Xianqing ouji* 25) in-text and
Li, Yü. 閑情偶寄 (*Xianqing ouji* . . . in the works cited.

In-text citations for verse from the original scrolls are listed in the following sequence: *juan* (scroll or volume): *hui* (chapter), page number; thus, (1: 10, 234-55).

Titles of books and articles in Chinese and Japanese are translated in brackets after the title of the book in the original. If the book is not translated and published in English, its translated title is not italicized. If the text is published in English, its translated title is italicized.

Acknowledgments

My passion for conducting research on women's *tanci* fiction started in 2008, when Maureen Robertson, a leading scholar in late imperial Chinese women's poetry, encouraged me to pursue scholarly study in women's *tanci* novels as inspiring exemplars of "minor literature" in the pre-1900 Chinese literary tradition. In the early years of studing *tanci* novels, I received steadfast support from David Wittenberg, Steven Ungar, Linda Bolton, and Barbara Eckstein. This book could not have evolved without the generous help of Hu Siao-Chen, who supported my trip to Academia Sinica in Taipei in 2009 and in 2011 to conduct study on *tanci* and present research works. I am deeply thankful for Mark Bender, who offered substantial feedback on two of my conference presentations on women's *tanci* novels, respectively, in 2011 and 2014, and provided substantial suggestions to enhance the frame of this book.

I received crucial support and encouragement from Steven Tötösy de Zepetnek—series editor of Books in Comparative Cultural Studies at Purdue University Press who supported my manuscript and provided substantial advice for revising and preparing the book for its timely publication. Further, I am indebted to the theoretical trajectory of "comparative cultural studies" that underlies my own work and that has been developed by Tötösy de Zepetnek. My gratitude goes to Dianna L. Gilroy at Purdue University Press for her thoughtful suggestions as well as her careful and meticulous editing of the book in its copyediting stage. I am thankful for the two anonymous reviewers of the manuscript for giving rich and constructive suggestions for the revision of the book. Chapter 5 has been published as a refereed article in *Frontiers of Literary Studies in China*, volume 5, issue 4. While workshopping the book, I benefited from the insights and research rigors of Ban Wang and Russell Berman, as well as colleagues at the 2011 NEH Summer Seminar for College and University Teachers at Stanford University. In 2009, Garrett Stewart provided me an opportunity to workshop a book chapter through an Andrew Mellon Dissertation Scholarship at the University of Iowa.

Throughout the research and writing of this book, I have been constantly inspired by the pioneering research on women's *tanci* fiction by Taiwanese scholar Hu Siao-chen as well as mainland Chinese scholars Bao Zhenpei and Sheng Zhimei. My research has benefited extensively from Mark Bender, Wilt Idema, Ellen Widmer, and Maram Epstein for their inspiring publications, respectively, on performed *tanci*, women's *tanci* novels, and late imperial women's fiction. I am deeply indebted to Maureen Robertson's work on studies of women's *shi* poetry, Qingyu Wu's study of female rule in utopian literature, Grace S. Fong's work on women's *ci* poetry, scholarship by Dorothy Ko and Susan Mann on talented women's culture, Judith Zeitlin's research on the female ghost in late imperial fiction, Wei Hua's publications on Ming Qing female dramatists, Rania Huntington's study of the fox spirit, Ayling Wang's research on late imperial women's poetry, Joan Judge's work on women and media in the early twentieth century, Lingzhen Wang's scholarship on Qiu Jin, and Tze-Lan Sang's study of women's same-sex love.

While preparing this manuscript, I received support from many colleagues from Utah State University. I am profoundly indebted to professors Sarah Gordon, J. P. Spicer Escalante, and Gordon Steinhoff for reading various parts of the manuscript and giving very constructive feedback on individual chapters. My gratitude goes to Felix Tweraser, who warmly encouraged me to pursue this book project in its early stage of development. I am also very thankful for my department head at Utah State University, Bradford J. Hall, for his unwavering support for my research endeavors. I thank the College of Humanities and Social Sciences and Center for Women and Gender Studies at Utah State University for each providing two faculty research travel funds in 2011 and 2012 to support my research trips to Taipei and Shanghai to collect materials and expand research works related to the book manuscript.

Many colleagues contributed insightful suggestions and thoughtful questions for the book. Christopher Lupke encouraged me to present two chapters at the Annual Meeting of Rocky Mountain MLA. Laura Stevens, Jie Guo, Ping Zhu, and Mamiko C. Suzuki provided substantial comments on individual chapters. Audiences at annual meetings of the Association for Asian Studies and the American Comparative Literature Association gave rich suggestions. I am also thankful for the Gender Work Group led by Christy Glass at Utah State University, which helped me garner comments from fellow feminist scholars. I am grateful for the gracious assistance of the following institutions: Shanghai City Library, Fudan University Library in Shanghai, Hangzhou City Library, Zhejiang University Library CADAL Project, National Library of China, Peking University Library, Academia Sinica Fu Sinian Memorial Library, McGill Harvard-Yenching Library Joint Digitization Project: Ming-Qing Women's Writings, University of Iowa Library, and Utah State University Library. I am thankful to Beijing Forbidden Palace Museum for granting me the copyright for the book cover image. I am thankful for the extensive support from colleagues and friends including Ronald R. Janssen, Yiman Wang, Virginia Broz, Tianyu Chen, Ling Zhang, Jia Ning, and many others. Finally, I thank my parents and my family and relatives for their endless love and their constant support for my academic pursuits.

Introduction

This book-length study of women's written *tanci* in the late imperial to early modern period aims to contribute to the study of Chinese folk narratives. *Tanci* (彈詞), which means "plucking rhymes," is called so because "the verse sections of such long narratives are sung to the plucked accompaniment of the lute" (Hu, Siao-chen, "Qiu Xinru" 539). The concept of *tanci* includes two categories. One is the orally performed, seven-character liberatto that has been popular in the southern Yangzi River area for centuries. The second is *tanci* fiction, a prosimetrical narrative genre written in rhymed lines, composed chiefly for reading. In this book I focus on the second category, *tanci* fiction. My point of departure for this study is voice, a theme which I explore not merely as an affect of speaking established through women's textual maneuvers or constructed through patterns of oral narratives, but also as an act of acquiring social agency, of reinforcing one's subjectivity through speaking, of evoking the spirit of the past and embracing the present, and of finding empowerment and spiritual survival through one's own words. I address the value of reinstating *tanci* to its place in the heritage of Chinese women's narratives, as well as exploring *tanci* as an energizing and meaningful resource that exercises an intercultural and even global significance for a global audience.

Current scholarship on *tanci* encompasses research on orally performed *tanci* as a form of folk narrative and studies of late imperial women's written *tanci* novels which were composed for reading. Among researchers who approach *tanci* as an oral narrative form, Mark Bender, Vibeke Børdahl, and Stephanie J. Webster Cheng have investigated the genre of *tanci* in relation to folk ballads as well as the composition, revision, and performance of modern and contemporary *tanci* songs. Among the critics who focus on women's *tanci* fiction and its gendered readership, Hu Siao-chen considers late imperial women's *tanci* fiction as a form of écriture feminine which demonstrates resistance to patriarchal values. Ellen Widmer, in a comparative analysis of *tanci* and vernacular fiction, offers an insightful case study of the *tanci* author and editor Hou Zhi (侯芝) and the circulation and reception of her writings. In mainland China, Bao Zhenpei and Zheng Zhimei both provide historical studies of the *tanci* tradition as related to Chinese women's literary activities of the Ming and Qing periods. Maram Epstein and Ying Zou explore women's rewriting of Confucian orthodox conceptions of gender roles in *tanci* novels, and investigate how *tanci* authors negotiate with their prescribed gender roles and reimagine the domestic sphere as a site of feminine autonomy and self-empowerment.

Building on these critical studies, this book explores late imperial and early twentieth-century women's *tanci* fiction from the approach of comparative cultural studies. Women's *tanci* fiction is usually laid out in prosimetrical, seven-character lines and produced at the length of voluminous novels. In the Ming and Qing periods, governing-class women transformed *tanci* fiction into a unique medium of feminine expressions of loyality, filiality, and heroic aspirations. Such *tanci* novels, Hu Siao-chen argues, "can be thought of as the feminine counterpart to 小說 (*xiaoshuo,* vernacular fiction) in late imperial China" (Hu, Siao-chen, "War, Violence, and the Metaphor of Blood" 250). This study offers a diachronic vision of late imperial and early twentieth-century *tanci* and locates agency at the center of women's collective empowerment. It illustrates the intricate connection between literary *tanci*, its imaginary representation of gender roles, and the social environments that have contributed to such multilayered textual representations. I understand women's *tanci* fiction as a repertoire of tales that revitalize current discussions about the question of women as collectively reflected in diverse national, historical, and geographical domains. I explore the long-lasting values of *tanci* in the Chinese women's literary tradition, engaging this analysis of the genre in dialogue with studies on gender, agency, and voice in late imperial women's literature, such as criticisms offered by Ellen Widmer, Grace S. Fong, and Maureen Robertson. A study of *tanci* fiction opens up a space for the comparative investigation of conjunctions of nation building, gender, and representation, as Benedict Anderson, Joan Judge, and Tani E. Barlow vigorously investigated in the international milieu of women's studies. *Tanci* tales perform important cultural work around issues of gendered agency and freedom, and presage contemporary feminism's calls for an ongoing empowerment of women in a global context. The meanings of these late imperial and early twentieth-century works are contingent upon specific social and cultural landscapes as well as the historical negotiation by women of their social presence.

This book is a timely endeavor that addresses the increasing interest in Chinese women's late imperial and early modern fiction among a transnational audience. *Tanci* novels about women military leaders, artists, cross-dressers, and doctors depict women of various social classes with a vivid realism. Late imperial women inherited tales from the preceding dynasties and made them their own as they circulated, chanted, and rewrote what they had received. The expansive timeframe of this study designates women's writing of *tanci* as a continuous and proliferating process. Drawing on women's studies perspectives, this book increases scholarly access to *tanci* in the English-speaking world by offering translations and close analyses of important *tanci* works. Although the importance of many inspiring *tanci* tales is widely acknowledged by audiences in China, scholarship on these works is sparse. This book, containing my translation of selected passages from Chinese into English, offers English readers a comprehensive overview of *tanci* narratives and of their most significant textual scenarios.

Thanks to its combination of advanced scholarship with extensive translation, this study addresses scholars of Asian studies, Chinese folk literature, and women's and gender studies. It also serves as an introduction to *tanci* fiction and some of its representative texts for nonspecialists and scholars of East Asian literature and culture, folklore traditions, women's literature, and comparative literature. Close attention to the specific circumstances of the *tanci* authors' lives and times guards against a generalized positioning of feminine subjectivity. Thorough discussions of the emergence, evolution, and impact of women's *tanci* and the historical forces acting on the formation of the genre serve as the background for an investigation of cross-dressing, self-portraiture, and authorial self-representation, all of which are embedded in this literary tradition. Readers of this book may find the images of heroic women to be sources of intercultural sharing and appreciation, and perhaps will form a new generation of *tanci* readers who will preserve this genre for the benefit of the multilingual global community.

My research of *tanci* novels contributes to current scholarship by exploring key themes that gain symphonic depth over five novel-length late imperial and early modern *tanci* novels: 再生緣 (*Zaishengyuan,* Destiny of Rebirth; eighteenth century); 筆生花 (*Bishenghua,* Blossom from the Brush; nineteenth century), 夢影緣 (*Mengyingyuan*, Dream, Image, Destiny; preface dated 1843); 俠女群英史 (*Xianü qunying shi,* A History of Women Warriors; 1905); and 風流罪人 (*Fengliu zuiren*, The Valiant and the Culprit; 1926). The authors of written *tanci* passed on an enduring historical legacy by telling potentially emancipatory stories of cross-dressing, female chastity, self-portraits, and female citizenship. Women's *tanci* novels depict heroines who serve as repositories of feminine consciousness about moral propriety and imagine women's unconventional lives in and beyond inner chambers as cross-dressed scholars, female warriors, Daoist immortals, or even eminent ministers.

The historical audiences of women's written *tanci* consist of both male and female readers. However, the imagined audiences of these texts are identified by the authors as female readers in the inner chambers, with whom the stories are to be shared collectively or even chanted from person to person. A gender-specific audience, in this context, refers to a community of readers who share the same values, attitudes, interests, and preferences of this particular gender (Barwell 100). Ismay Barwell holds that a feminist aesthetic must be present in the structural features of the work (Barwell 64). As a narrative genre, *tanci* has been interpreted as a gendered genre with a female-oriented perspective. This alliance of *tanci* with feminine writing, however, needs more critical contemplation. In the study of feminine narrative features, "the desire for a unified aesthetic was misplaced because of the way in which it used universals to guide its search and to justify its hopes. From the existence of the social universals, it moved to the postulation of experiential universals and from there to the claim that women's art would reflect this common experience" (Barwell 64). That is to say, a universal aesthetic about women's narratives needs to take into consideration women's heterogeneous and specific experiences, as well as the social conditions that created these experiences.

This study of women's *tanci* fiction approaches anew the concept of a "female-oriented perspective" in several ways. A female-oriented viewpoint appropriates the narrative formulas of men's dominant literary genres and recycles these formulas in stories written by and for women. A female-oriented perspective writes for a female hypothetical audience and makes women's experiences of suffering, grievance, and aspirations sharable among an imagined community of women readers. A female-oriented perspective conceptualizes a narrative framework in which the heroines are endowed with mobility to exercise their talent and power as social beings outside the inner chambers as men's equals. The narrative point of view in such works creates and sustains an empathetic relationship between the women characters in the story, the authorial narrative self-identified as a female, and the targeted women readers. The authorial voice in a female-oriented narrative prioritizes a woman's freedom to speak on her own behalf. Narrative portraiture of women in such works maintain an affective and sympathetic relationship with the fictional heroines portrayed by the authors' brushes. A female-oriented perspective actively redefines normalized gender roles with an eye to exposing women's potentialities to transform historical and social customs in order to engender a world with better prospects for women.

This introduction explores how the genre of *tanci* endowed women authors and their audiences with narrative, bodily, and moral agency. These forms of personal agency, which came from women's experiences of writing and reading *tanci* fiction, speak to and reflect a broader cultural phenomenon of late imperial women's literary endeavors and achievements. For this purpose, the current study of *tanci* focuses not so much on making a gender-specific claim for *tanci*, but rather to reclaim the universal values and features of women's writing that this genre bears in common with late imperial women's literary works in general, and even with women's literature in a global context. The question at stake, therefore, is not so much whether women's written *tanci* belongs to a poetic genre or a fictional form, but rather how this traditional yet highly elastic genre brings new energy and perspective into women's literature today, how *tanci* finds new sustainability and survival in the modern period, and whether this highly adaptable narrative form can function as a medium for new ways of speaking for the socially disadvantaged.

A contextualized reading of late imperial women's *tanci* works invites a historical understanding of Chinese women's social status, which has been profoundly impacted by the Confucian system. The Confucian ethical and philosophical system, which has had tremendous influence on the culture and society of China, can be traced throughout many ancient and imperial literary and historical texts. Among these texts, the earliest is 論語 (*Lunyu*, *The Analects*), a compilation of statements attributed to Confucius by his students. During the Western Han Dynasty (206 BCE to 220 CE), the transformation of the Confucian philosophical system into state ideology took place. Modern critics have shown interest in how Confucian philosophy offered techniques for remaking and reproducing state and society using the model of a Confucian golden age (see Elman, Duncan, and Oom, *Rethinking*). The Confucian social system concerning gendered women's roles gives special attention to the principle of 三從四德 (*sancong side*), or Three Submissions and Four Virtues. The Three Submissions define women's subordinate relationship with their male family members. The Four Virtues refer to 婦德 (*fude,* womanly moral behavior), 婦言 (*fuyan*, womanly speech), 婦容 (*furong*, womanly bearing), and 婦工 (*fugong*, womanly work). Found in nearly all conduct books for Chinese women, these principles emphasized a woman's innate inferiority to a man as well as her domestic duty to serve her husband, his siblings, and his parents.

The renowned book of conduct 女誡 (*Nüjie*, Admonitions for Women) by Ban Zhao (班昭, 45-116 CE) opens with the chapter "卑弱" ("Beiruo," "Being Lowly and Weak"), which stresses women's submission to men. The author was one of China's earliest historians. She assisted her father Ban Biao (班彪, 3-54 CE) and brother Ban Gu (班固, 32-92 CE) in collecting historical data, and played a crucial role in the completion of the great history work 漢書 (*Hanshu*, History of the Han Dynasty). In her work, she defines the primary womanly qualification as "virtue," which means to "guard carefully her chastity; to control circumspectly her behavior; in every motion to exhibit modesty; and to model each act on the best usage; this is womanly virtue" (Tetsuzō 671). Womenly speech means to "choose her words with care; to avoid vulgar language; to speak at appropriate times; and not to weary others with conversation. These qualities may be called the characteristics of womanly speech" (Tetsuzō 671). These moral parameters constituted the ritual education of all women before marriage.

Such constraint of women's activities to the domestic sphere was reiterated in classical texts and didactic books. 詩經 (*Shijing*, *The Book of Odes*) says, "Women do not engage in public affairs, for if they did they would stop their weaving" (Deng Xiang 62). The exclusion of women from public affairs was a key principle that maintained the distinction between men and women in Confucian society. The ancient philosopher Guan Zhong (管仲) commented, "If women have a voice in people's affairs, rewards and punishment will not be reliable. If there is no distinction between men and women, the people will have neither integrity nor shame" (Guan 96). In the early ritual texts, plentiful evidence indicates women's subordination to men in domestic, social, and political life. Confucian ideology and didactic texts on women's virtue generated extensive discussion of the seemingly paradoxical relationship between women's virtue and their talent. A common phrase, "for women's lack of literary talent is a virtue," implied that in Confucian society, women were more likely to become notable for their virtue, whereas men were more likely to be acclaimed for their literary talent. The Confucian cult of women's virtue conceives a wife's relationship to her husband and his family as analogous to a man's loyalty to the emperor. Women's subordination to men reflects the so-called 五常 (*wuchang*), or the Five Constant Relationships that served as moral principles for the regulation of relationships in society. These five cardinal relationships include those between a father and son, an emperor and his subordinates, a husband and wife, older and younger siblings, and friends. Except for the relationship between friends, these relationships are hierarchical and reflect the power relationship between men and women.

Under the impact of these ideological concepts, later literary, historical, and philosophical texts offered differing definitions of women's virtue. Chastity, humility, modesty, and reserve in speech and devotion to housework constitute the main characteristics of feminine virtue in pre-twentieth-century China. 女論語 (*Nülunyu,* Women's Analects, eighth century CE) holds that "the foremost duty of women is to establish themselves to fulfill their proper roles," and "make themselves pure and chaste" (Tetsuzō 679). The book contains nine chapters on women's domestic duties on running the household and serving the husband's family, with not a single chapter describing women's intellectual life. Likewise, in 內訓 (*Neixun*, Domestic Lessons, early fifteenth century), Empress Renxiao offers twenty chapters of moral lessons for women. In the first chapter she defines women's virtue as "chaste and quiet, proper and constant" (Tetsuzō 769). After the seventeenth century, as more women engaged in writing and pursued "talent," debates about the propriety of such activities surfaced. A crucial example is a seventeenth-century text, 女範捷錄 (*Nüfan jielu*, Sketch of a Model for Women), written by a woman who repudiated the popular saying, "A woman without talent is virtuous." The author was the widowed mother of the Ming scholar Wang Xiang (王相). She states,

> With regard to the royal wives, humble concubines, and wives of common people in ancient times, none of them was unfamiliar with *The Book of Odes*. Does this imply that they were not virtuous? . . . Women should pursue knowledge in words and literature, and learn well the classics and histories, so that their fame will spread wide in their lifetime and so that their exceptional talent can be applauded by later generations. This is certainly the way it should be! (Tetsuzō 769)

Here Wang Xiang advocates the need for women's literacy, which serves as "a source of empowerment where women through the power of literacy become self-affirmative in their historical consciousness" (Rosenlee 8). The controversy between women's talent and virtue, however, persisted in later generations. In the eighteenth century, Zhang Xuecheng (章學誠) composed an essay to criticize his contemporary, Yuan Mei (袁枚), a poet who mentored women pupils and supported the publication of their poems. Zhang denounced Yuan for corrupting women's learning with entertainment and triviality instead of guiding them with the principles embedded in the ancient rites (Zhang Xuecheng 1: 128). Yuan Mei responded to Zhang, saying that women had been authors since the ancient times, adding that many famous song lyrics in *The Book of Odes* were composed by women (Yuan Mei, *Suiyuan shihua* 590). This debate laid bare the important question of whether or not women's speech should be considered a category of gender propriety as strictly defined by the Confucian cult of feminine virtue in the specific social context of the late Ming and early Qing.

The constraint Confucian society placed on women's speech was a dominant ideological principle that regulated women's literary activities. Women were cautioned to guard their talents of speaking and writing and to refrain from competing against others. The socio-ideological constraint on women's literary talent had been constant since ancient times, despite the fact that there had been several socially acknowledged women writers in individual historical periods. In the eighth century, courtesan poets Yu Xuanji (魚玄機), Li Ye (李冶), and Xue Tao (薛濤) actively participated in literary exchanges with male poets (see Ping Yao 26-53). Their achievements were such that even Zhang Xuecheng praised them, saying, "Their [literary] achievements could not be dismissed because of personal deficiencies" (Zhang Xuecheng 126). In a largely masculine literary tradition, these courtesan poets asserted their voices and visibility. Nevertheless, their marginal social status as authors made them vulnerable to criticism and attacks by conservative male scholars. Chen Zhensun (陳振孫, around 1183-1162), for example, commented that the courtesan poet Yu Xuanji was a most notorious woman who "disrupted the rites and corrupted social customs" (vols. 19, 29).

The contradiction between women's newly vigorous writing activities and the Confucian indoctrination of feminine virtues became all the more prominent in the seventeenth century. Supporters of women's literary endeavors, such as Ye Shaoyuan (葉紹袁, 1589-1648), asserted women's right to express their literary talents. Shaoyuan proposed the talent-virtue-beauty ideal for womanhood, which held that talent, together with virtue and beauty, are desirable components of women's achievements (Ye Shaoyuan, Preface, Complete Works). Parallel to this advocacy of women's talent were opposing voices from scholars who adhered to Confucian teachings for women. Lü Kun (吕坤, 1536-1618) suggested that proper education in the inner quarters should focus on classical texts, and that women should not compete against each other in poetic talent, nor should they take up singing or any other performing that could reduce their position to that of the lower-class entertainers.

These examples illustrate the universal belief that women should have family education in order to prepare for their domestic duties after marriage. Even if they were literate, running their households occupied most women's daily lives, leaving them little time to write. While the daughters of poor families depended on women's work for survival, upper-class women were also expected to perform these duties and set examples for their servants (Mann, "Women in the Life" 166). Late imperial writings by women include many personal laments about heavy domestic labor and the scarcity of opportunities for literary endeavors. Such obstacles to women's writing demonstrate both the suppression of women's writing by the patriarchal culture and the fact that women's self-expression in writing was a largely marginalized social practice in dynastic China.

Women's writing had long existed in China's literary history and had confronted many impediments. Among the many women writers in ancient and medieval periods, a handful of women poets was well known, such as Cai Wenji (蔡文姬, second century CE), Xue Tao (薛濤, eighth century CE), and Li Qingzhao (李清照, 1084-1155). The seventeenth century witnessed the expansion of women's education and the increasing visibility of active woman writers. The development of women's literary activity was especially marked in the Jiangnan regions, which encompasses several provinces around the lower reaches of the Yangzi River. In this period, the textile industry heavily contributed to the economic development of the area. Cities such as Yangzhou, Hangzhou, and Suzhou were marked by concentrations of rich merchants who boosted the local economy and expanded the need for entertainment. The social circumstances of these cities were characterized by their "nonconformity," "refinement of taste," and high levels of culture (Johnson 86). Poetry readings and gatherings of scholars became an indispensable part of social life, and subsequently a social trend of admiring women writers was cultivated.

These women authors of the time were recognized as 閨秀 (*guixiu*) writers, or talented writers of the inner chambers. The so-called 閨 (*gui*) refers to the inner quarters where women resided in the domestic compound. Many variations on the term "gui" appear in women's writings, such as 閨闈 (*guiwei*), or "inner room," and 閨閫 (*guikun*), or "women's bedroom." The word *gui* captures the Confucian ideological division between masculine and feminine, interior and exterior. It also indicates the patriarchal regulation of women's speech, which was not to be heard outside the inner quarters. A popular subgenre in traditional Chinese literati-verse is the 閨怨詩 (*guiyuanshi*) or lament poetry of the inner chambers, which is comprised of expressions of distress by neglected, offended, or simply unhappy women (Chang, Kang-I Sun, and Haun Saussy, *Women Writers* 14). In the late imperial period, educated gentry women transformed the inner chamber into a unique space that valorized women's voices. In this space, the dominant male literary discourse did not have absolute control. In the context of women's flourishing literary activities, the acutely interior quarters harbored multiple possibilities of a new feminine existence.

This division between the inner chambers and the exterior social sphere was destabilized in the late sixteenth century. Some women challenged the Confucian restrictions on women's speech and engaged in exchanges with other writers. Two prominent examples were Wang Duanshu (王端淑, 1621-1706) and Huang Yuanjie (黃媛介, seventeenth century). Wang was born into a high official family and was well-known for her expertise in poetry and calligraphy. Her poetry contains abundant evidence of her poetic exchanges with other women and scholars, showing her active participation in the literary scene of her time. Also known as a 閨塾師 (*guishu shi*), or teacher in the inner chambers, Wang became a professional itinerant teacher who provided literary instruction to women in the inner quarters. Another poet, Huang Yuanjie, traveled extensively, working as a teacher of women, and she had opportunities to make the acquaintance of famous literati poets who dedicated poems to her. These male poets included elite intellectuals such as Qian Qianyi (錢謙益, 1582-1664), Xiong Wenju (熊文舉, 1595-1668), and Mao Qiling (毛奇齡, 1623-1716). Another crucial aspect of the *guixiu* culture was the development of women's literary groups, such as the seventeenth-century 蕉園詩社 (*Jiaoyuan shishe*, Banana Garden Poetry Club), the eighteenth-century 隨園女弟子 (*Suiyuan nüdizi*, women pupils of the Sui Garden), and the 吳中十子 (*Wuzhong shizi,* Ten Women Poets of Wu).

The seventeenth century witnessed the recovery and publication of works by talented women. Other than governing-class women poets, during the late Ming and early Qing periods "there were at least twenty-three women playwrights who came from different social class and created a total number of over fifty-five plays in the form of 雜劇 (*zajü,* variety drama) or 傳奇 (*chuanqi*, romance play). Eighteen plays in its entirety and two in parts are extant" (Hua, Wei, "The Lament" 28). The surging print culture and the publishing industry in the Jiangnan region contributed greatly to the growth of women authors' readership (see Brokaw and Chow). Women's energetic participation in literary activities during this period imply that the inner chambers were not completely isolated from the social sphere and were open to the external world. Dorothy Ko suggests that the inner/outer dichotomy is "a relational category that describes a series of nested hierarchies whose boundary changes with context" (Ko, *Teachers* 273). The lives of late imperial women exhibit a degree of social mobility of women across established gender boundaries. For some women, this mobility relatively transformed the inner chambers into a space of gradual self-empowerment. Under this progressive social condition, *tanci* authors depicted cross-dressed heroines, who freed themselves from the family compound and entered the social and political realms that had formerly been men's privileged spaces.

The performed *tanci* songs took their origins in the oral traditions, and the name—*tanci*, or "plucking rhymes"—refers to a form of singing accompanied by instrumental music. The tradition of *tanci* performances can be traced to medieval China, where it manifested itself in various forms of storytelling. Although medieval oral traditions could have been sources of inspiration for Ming and Qing *tanci* writers, it might be fallacious to claim that *tanci* took its origin directly from these earlier oral traditions. The *tanci* form still awaits the rigorous examination of its origins that the 話本 (*huaben*, vernacular story), for instance, has received. (For the origin of *huaben*, see Hanan, *Chinese Vernacular Story* 28; Masuda 22-33; Wang, Qinghua 46). One of the theories considers the origin of orally performed *tanci* as predominantly a phenomenon of women's storytelling performance (Bender, *Plum and Bamboo* 153). Historical records from the sixteenth and seventeenth centuries document professional *tanci* performances conducted by blind women singers who performed this kind of storytelling as a vocation in public teahouses and professional studios. Early *tanci* performance was called 盲女彈詞 (*mangnü tanci*, blind women's *tanci*). Although both men and women performed *tanci* in public, women *tanci* performers suffered severe criticism for defying the Confucian restrictions on women in public activities. In 1860, male *tanci* performer Ma Rufei (1851-1908) denounced women's *tanci* performance as "amoral and appalling" (Zhou, Liang 75), comparing male mentors of women *tanci* singers to Yuan Mei, who was accused of corrupting women's morals in the inner chambers by teaching them to write lyric poetry. Despite controversies of this kind, professional women's *tanci* performances continued to develop in southern cities.

Another hypothesis holds that *tanci* originates from medieval chantefables, which evolved into *tanci* during the Yuan and Ming periods (Tan, *Pingtan tongkao* 35). This theory is supported by scholar Chen Wulou (陳午樓), who has studied the origin of *tanci* in Yangzhou storytelling, focusing on the "narrative communicatory situation" in the oral tradition (see Chen Wulou; see also Chen Ruheng). Mark

Bender offers an insightful analysis of the complex dialectics between narrative and dramatic registers. He stresses the "here-and-now" effect of the grammatical tense of verbs in *tanci* narratives, suggesting that the narrative passages and the dialogue are in a continuing "present" or neutral time (Bender, "Shifting and Performance" 181-97). Unlike written *tanci* targeted for reading, performed *tanci* must be explicit and immediately understandable for the audience (Lu Dan'An). Victor H. Mair and Mark Bender observe that orally performed *tanci* in Suzhou, or Suzhou chantefables, "has been especially influenced by the *Kunqu* traditions in terms of character roles, voice registers, and handmovements" (Mair and Bender 311). Professional *tanci* performances remain popular in modern South China. Today, at the Suzhou Pingtan School of Performance, special training is offered to cultivate the skills of professional *tanci* singers. In the southern cities of Shanghai, Suzhou, Yangzhou, and Hangzhou, *tanci* performances are regularly staged at tea houses and theaters. Men and women *tanci* singers' performances are also recorded, broadcast on radio, and staged in television series. With the development of media industries, the popularity of *tanci* as part of China's cultural heritage has expanded among ordinary audiences. Bender and Mair comment that such popular practices of using technology to "memorize" professional singers' performances propose new questions for scholars to reconsider the issue of orality in China (Bender and Mair 8).

Although *tanci* was later appropriated by talented women authors as a feminine fictional narrative, there were some written *tanci* works by men in the late imperial period and turn of the twentieth century. These male-authored *tanci* works can be considered in two categories. One is a cluster of men's *tanci* that arose in late Ming dynasty which were composed to offer accounts of historical events and characters, mostly circulated through oral tradition and thus also called 講史類彈詞 (*jiangshilei tanci*, or *tanci* that orally tell historical accounts). An important work of this school is 二十一史彈詞 (*Ershiyi shi tanci, Tanci* of the Twenty One Histories) by Yang Shen (楊慎, 1488-1559) (Zheng Zhenduo 358). Yang's work is also titled 歷代史略十段錦詞話 (*Lidai shilue shiduanjin cihua*, Poetic Remarks of the Abbreviated History of Previous Dynasties in Ten Lengths of Brocade).The work was composed in a blended form of traditional 詞 (*ci*) poetry, rhymed ten-character lines, and spoken parts between sections, which is very different from the later narrative *tanci* written mostly in seven-character rhymed lines. The content of this *tanci* contains a historical overview of China from the Prehistoric Xia era to the Yuan dynasty. Sheng Zhimei considers this work as *jiangshilei tanci* (*tanci* that accounts history), whose narrative is akin to that of a historical survey with commentary. A similar work is 明紀彈詞 (*Mingji tanci*, *Tanci* of the Ming Dynasty) by Zhang Sanyi (張三異) and his son Zhang Zhonghuang (張仲璜), which was much less influential in comparison with Yang's work. Stylistically, these works are more akin to historical narratives than to fictional storytelling.

Separate from *tanci* tales that transmit historical accounts, in the early twentieth century there emerged some short *tanci* tales by progressive men who appropriated *tanci* to depict heroic Western or indigenous women in order to instill Chinese women with patriotic passions or to inspire them into social activism. A pivotal work is 法國女英雄彈詞 (*Faguo nüyingxiong tanci*, Tale of a French Woman Hero; 1904). The author Yu Chenglai (俞承萊, 1881-1937) applauds the French revolutionary Marie-Jeanne Roland de la Platière as an exemplar for Chinese women. (Hu Ying, *Tales of Translation* 153-96) Yu claims that his purpose in utilizing the popular form of *tanci* was to advocate for the political and cultural movements of women. Such an activist inclination is also evident in 胭脂血 (*Yanzhixue*, Rouge Blood; 1908) by Zhou Shoujuan (周瘦鵑), who published the *tanci* under the pen name Qi Hong (泣紅, literally, "Weeping Blood") (A Ying, *Wanqing wenxue* 223-52). A later example is 二十世紀女界文明燈彈詞 (*Ershi shiji nüjie wenmingdeng tanci*, Twentieth-Century *Tanci*: Light of Civilization in the Women's World; 1911) by Zhong Xinqing (鐘心青). The book contains a series of short stories about Chinese women's awakening in the modern period. The first chapter depicts a reincarnated goddess, Ms. Picha from the United States, who dedicated her life previously to the liberation of black slaves in the Civil War. She now descends to the other side of the globe to free Chinese women from oppression and slavery. In 1915, Cheng Zhanlu published a collection of *tanci* tales, 同心梔 (*Tongxinzhi*, Heartlocked Cape Jasmine). The *tanci* depicts the widowed Qing poet Wu Jiangxue, who committed suicide when she was held hostage by a rebelling army. Cheng composed six stories about heroic women in China and the West, and the book's title, *Heartlocked Cape Jasmine*, suggests a unified conceptualization of women's identity across geographical, historical, and cultural boundaries. (For literati's reconstructions of Wu's life, see Hua, Wei, "From Private Life"). This text, together with the aforementioned short *tanci* tales, demonstrates that early twentieth-century male intellectuals found *tanci* instrumental for projecting a nascent feminine identity through transnational adaptation.

Women's *tanci* fiction constitutes a vital but infrequently studied literary innovation of late imperial women authors. These written *tanci* are voluminous books written mostly by upper-class women from the seventeenth century to the early twentieth century. They were written in a language very close to the traditional vernacular novel, or 章回小說 (*zhanghui xiaoshuo*, literally, fiction in chapters). The structure of these works consists of 章 (*zhang,* volumes) or 卷 (*juan,* scrolls), and their subordinate 回 (*hui*, chapters). The title of each chapter is a rhymed poetic couplet that summarizes the chapter's plot or events. The published versions of these texts also include extensive prefaces by the author or the author's friends, and, at times, poems dedicated to the author or to the fictional characters in the work. The texts were largely composed in rhymed, seven-character lines. This poetic structure is interspersed with dramatic dialogue, passages of straight narration, poems, and even verse riddles. Illustrated editions of *tanci* fiction in the first half of the nineteenth century include woodblock illustrations representing the characters and scenes in the story. The first half of the nineteenth century includes the 道光 (Jiaqing and Daoguang) reign periods of the Qing. Thanks to the steady economic development and common people's increasing interest in reading fiction and drama works, there was a rising demand for *tanci* works in the book market of the time. The audience for *tanci* at this time was comprised mostly of ordinary people rather than intellectuals (Sheng 74). Shorter *tanci* appeared in the early twentieth century in newspapers as serials or in journals. However, in the twentieth century only a few of the longer *tanci* works by pre-twentieth century women have been printed by publishers in mainland China and Taiwan.

The content of women's long *tanci* fiction portrays women's fantasies of dressing up in male disguise and enacting a "masculine" identity on the battlefield, in the examination halls, or at court. For the most part, the authors of *tanci* were upper-class women who were heirs to an extensive family education in poetry, history, and classic literature and who had a targeted group of women readers in the inner chambers where *tanci* narratives were composed, read, and circulated. Some *tanci* authors expressed a wish to expand their readership to lower-class women. The rhythmic nature of these texts made them fine candidates for performance with instrumental accompaniment, which allowed the works to be appreciated by less-educated women. The linguistically accessible and mobile nature of the genre made *tanci* an ideal choice for women writers, in comparison with other relatively male-dominated genres, such as poetry, drama, and fiction. The comparison of the status of *tanci* with canonic genres is reflected in many writers' statements. For instance, Tao Zhenhuai (陶貞懷, seventeenth century) says, "And why did I develop my story using the plucking rhymes? Because I wanted to incite people to moral effort. Now, those who cannot be regulated by means of the rites, may yet be moved by music; for those who cannot be moved by music, one writes plays; and those who may not even be reached by plays, may yet be awakened by plucking rhymes" (qtd. and trans. in Idema and Grant, *Red Brush* 724).

Despite the vigorous depictions of feminine desire in these texts, a large number of the authors claimed that they wrote *tanci* to entertain women friends and family members or to promote the moral integrity of their readers. Also, many writers emphasized their aptitude in womanly duties over their literary competence. Even the adventurous eighteenth-century *tanci* writer Chen Duansheng (陳端生) stated in *Zaishengyuan* that her book was about loyalty and filial relations. The disjunction between the moralistic tone of such authorial statements and the liberating and progressive potential of the texts reveals women authors' anxiety about censorship in publication, as well as their prudence in defining their literary competence as within the social regulations of women's literary activity.

The authorial statements in *tanci*, often distinctively feminine, have provoked scholarly discussions on gender identification and women's authorship as reflected in written *tanci* works. Ellen Widmer, comparing the *tanci* genre and vernacular fiction, suggests that *tanci* showcases a feminine authorship, constructed through female-voiced authorial comments in prefaces and head-of-chapter comments. Whereas most influential *tanci* by women in the eighteenth and nineteenth centuries are often the length of novels, the subject matter in *tanci* portrays women's fantasy about adventures outside the inner chambers, and thus makes *tanci* very different from domestic fiction as represented by nineteenth-century Victorian novels. Also, *tanci* authors' use of large amounts of poetry, a more conventional genre of writing, makes *tanci* appear as a genre "more properly feminine" than prose narratives (Widmer, "Ming Loyalism" 392). Hu Siao-chen, in her pioneering study, considers *tanci* a "feminine" form of poetic expression and suggests that literary *tanci* should be viewed in light of écriture féminine, a form of resistance against dominant masculine writings (*Literary Tanci* 2). Like Hu, Toyoko Yoshida Chen suggests that *tanci* authors appropriated the genre to challenge the Confucian orthodox ideal of womanhood, although they could not fully expose the inherent contradictions of the dominant social moral system due to their socialization in the prescribed gender roles (see Chen, Toyoko Yoshida, *Women in Confucian Society*).

Analyses by the above critics draw attention to the development of female consciousness in *tanci* by prominent women writers of the late imperial period, recalling women's self-fashioning and representation in other genres, including poetry, fiction, and drama. At least one more genre can be brought into the conversation: suicide notes. Grace S. Fong offers a comprehensive study of the representation of feminine consciousness in women's suicide poems in the Ming and Qing periods. Fong suggests that women's self-inscription in these poems, and their autobiographical prefaces, demonstrate an important form of female agency (Fong, "Signifying Bodies" 105-42). In the first half of the nineteenth century, women's *tanci* fiction reached its apex in development. With the flourishing of the book printing industry, many *tanci* novels were extensively reprinted, generating a wide impact on their audience. Also during this time, Hou Zhi (侯芝), the famous *tanci* writer and editor, completed her editing of major *tanci* novels such as 玉釧緣 (*Yuchuanyuan*, Jade Bracelets; late Ming), 錦上花 (*Jingshanghua*, Brocade Flowers; early nineteenth century), and 金閨傑 (*Jinguijie*, Heroines in the Golden Chambers; 1824). These printed *tanci* undeniably expanded the popularity of the genre among women readers of middle and lower social classes. The readership of *tanci* was correlated with the broad audience of public *tanci* performances. Chanted *tanci*, in comparison with written *tanci* fiction by women, were simpler in style and more explicit in language, with an aim to entertain the audience and to make the story understandable for people of less education and lower social class. In the early twentieth century, professional teahouses for *tanci* performances were prevalent in the southern cities of Shanghai, Suzhou, Yangzhou, and Hangzhou (Zhou Liang 232). Thanks to the more open social customs, going to the teahouses for *tanci* performances became one of women's favorite entertainments:

> In today's society, regardless of people's backgrounds, they are all fascinated with *tanci* fiction. For *tanci* performance houses, there are as many as several hundred in Shanghai. *Tanci* is mostly favored by women. They often sit in clusters, laughing and chatting, their feet resting side by side. When a singer at the corner of the room begins to sing the opening sessions, they all listen solemnly, with no one making noise. When the performance ends, they chatter and make gestures with their hands, take pleasure in discussing the stories, and even dream of the tales at night. The power of *tanci* is thrilling to such an extent. (A Ying, *Wanqing wenxue* 173)

When the introductory songs of performance-related *tanci* were adapted for radio broadcasting programs in the 1920s, the readership/audience of *tanci* was once again reconfigured. With the rise of China's radio broadcasting industry, numerous radio stations emerged in the southern cities of Shanghai, Hangzhou, and Suzhou. Some of these stations were exclusively women's *tanci* radio stations. From the 1920s to the 1930s, broadcasted *tanci* constituted an indispensable part of radio programming. At the crux of the question of readership/audience is how reading *tanci* may have empowered women's presences in the social and cultural landscapes of their times. As *tanci* continued to transform through new media and sending out new messages, these narratives perhaps could have recommenced an enabling process for women to embrace innovative social subjectivities.

How do *tanci* authors demonstrate agency as associated with the contextual background of Ming and Qing era women's writing? How does the authorial agency of late imperial women differ from men's authorial agency? And how does writing in a minor literary genre endow women authors with more power and the means to write and publish? A review of current scholarship on authorial agency provides a historically contextualized perspective of the readers of *tanci*. Narrative acts, in the Western fictional tradition, entail "telling a particular story to a particular audience in a particular situation for, presumably, a particular purpose" (Phelan 4). Authorial agency in the narrative is achieved through "the connection between voice and ideology: to listen to narrative is, in part, to listen to values associated with a given way of talking" (Phelan 43). Authorial voice plays a fundamental role in constructing the communication offered by the narrative. These theoretical discourses about "narrative voice" lend useful insights to the current reading of women's *tanci* works in late imperial and early modern China. The women authors' narrative voices frequently intervene in the *tanci* stories, lamenting their difficulties in writing, commenting on the interaction between the characters and the plot development, appealing to readers' empathy, and offering glimpses into the authors' inner worlds. In the opening and closing lines of *tanci* chapters, the authorial comments on literary history and women's hardships also provide rich possibilities for reading *tanci* both as fiction and as criticism, suggesting the diverse roles that the authorial narrator plays in the text.

Grace S. Fong, in her groundbreaking study of authorial agency in late imperial women's *ci* poetry, proposes that late imperial women authors can be considered "agents exceeding the family- or lineage-centered structure and momentarily or figuratively act in non-kinship defined roles, as friends, travelers, critics, artists, and connoisseurs, in which they make space for a degree of difference, of change or even of authority and autonomy" (Fong, *Herself an Author* 5). In writing, they open up alternative subject positions beyond traditional kin roles. The notions of agency thus account both for the action and the enactment of subject positions in the intersection between textual practice and social inscription that suggest instances and modes of self-empowerment in the Confucian ideological system (Fong, *Herself an Author* 5). Women authors, as Fong asserts, demonstrated their authorial agency by taking possession of literary genres and practices previously belonging to men, such as poetry, travel writing, and literary criticism. Amy Dooling, likewise reviewing women's authorial agency and the formation of women's new subjectivities in modern Chinese literature, offers an insightful discussion of the evolvement of progressive gender discourses in China in the first half of twentieth century (1-35).

Women's authorial agency in *tanci* is also intertwined with the debates that took place in imperial China about female talent and virtue. Ellen Widmer, in her study of Hou Zhi (1764-1829), a distinguished *tanci* author and editor, argues that Hou embodied and defied the common wisdom about the link between women's literary talent and early death, that is, that the most brilliant women sojourned only briefly on this earth and invariably died young (*The Beauty and the Book* 83). Hou confessed that her passionate pursuit of a literary career contradicted her father's belief that "lack of talent in a woman is a virtue," although she continued to indulge in study. Even though Hou was a competent poet, she feared that it would be difficult to achieve fame by writing poetry, hence her switch to *tanci*, a seemingly "lesser" genre, and one that would not evoke the Creator's jealousy as poetry did (Widmer, *The Beauty and the Book* 83). Similar motifs appear in the work of the gifted Zheng Danruo (鄭澹若), who turned to *tanci* because poetry, fiction, and drama were dominated by elite male authors. As these examples display, in the tradition of *tanci*, women's authorial agency is endorsed by their conscious choice of this genre as a less constrained, more liberating means of self-expression.

In comparison with female poets, novelists, or playwrights whose writing carved out a discursive space within the literati tradition, late imperial *tanci* authors took to narrative *tanci*, a female-oriented literary form, as a way of establishing their enunciative position in the elite literary tradition. Late imperial *tanci* authors endorsed their own value and literary capacity by exploring an alternate mode of self-expression, of which male authors had not yet taken control. This female-oriented narrative form provides women an organic structure that allows their voices and ethical concerns to be passed along to their targeted readers with efficacy and candor. Authorial agency in *tanci* implies not only the mobility that the often distinctively female authorial narrator enjoys in this unique narrative genre, but also the authors' conscious exploration and utilization of this narrative tradition to establish a feminine cultural legacy.

Tanci authors endorse women's social, moral, and narrative authority through storytelling, construing *tanci* as a source of female empowerment for readers. The authorial insertions and narrative portrayals of women espouse the traditional values of female chastity and filial piety. (Filial passions and self-sacrifice are likewise significant imperatives in late imperial Buddhist 寶卷 (*baojuan*), or precious scrolls which consist of prosimetric narratives on predominantly religious content that arose around the fourteenth century (see Idema, *Personal Salvation*; on prosimetrical narratives which combine prose and metric passages, and their connections with Buddhist lectures, see Mair, "The Prosimetric Form"; *Tang Transformation Texts*). In *tanci* fiction, many heroines value their filial duties to their natal families over their obligations to their husbands' families. While endorsing the traditional values of performing filial obligations, some women characters commit to virginity and decline marriage, devoting themselves to serve their aged parents. Maram Epstein offers a substantial reading of *tanci* heroines' filial values in 天雨花 (*Tianyuhua*, Heaven Rains Flowers) ("Patrimonial Bonds"). While female chastity offers late imperial women a way of resisting the marriage paradigm in these *tanci* tales, it also serves as a means of personal empowerment. Aside from portraying this personal dimension of moral rectitude, authors such as Zheng Danruo envision the responsibility of reforming social mores as resting squarely on women; by endowing women with moral agency, Zheng avoids typecasting them as social victims, portraying them instead as self-conscious social beings destined to execute their social and intellectual power for the benefit of the public. For the early twentieth-century author Jiang Yingqing, women's moral agency rests in their self-sacrificial devotion to national rejuvenation; such self-sacrifice includes living a single life. In Jiang Yingqing's text, women's celibacy is represented as a strategic choice that merges the personal with the political course of the nation.

Depictions of female chastity in *tanci* reflect the cult of women's chastity during the long historical period of imperial China. Since ancient times, didactic texts identified chastity as the most important principle for women to uphold. The Han didactic text 列女傳 (*Lienü zhuan*，Biographies of Exemplary Women; 16 BCE), authored by Liu Xiang (劉向), comprises seven scrolls of women's biographies, including biographies of chaste women of various social classes, such as wives and royal concubines, wives of high officials, widows of lower-class families, housemaids, and nurses. Imperial literature about exemplary women was edited and rewritten by both women and men to instill doctrines of feminine virtue and chastity in young girls and cultivate them as ideal wives, mothers, and daughters-in-law. The cult of chastity for widows became almost a religion in the eleventh century (Mann, "Widows in the Kinship" 37). Susan Mann comments that in the Ming period, "the court published detailed and explicit regulations for awarding imperial testimonials of merit to chaste widows, who—together with obedient grandsons, righteous men, and filial sons—were singled out for special honor, along with women who died resisting rape. In addition, under Ming law, families headed by chaste widows were exempted from the corvée labor tax" ("Widows in the Kinship" 38). These governmental policies encouraging widow chastity partially contributed to the cult of marital fidelity in the Ming dynasty.

In both history and the fictional space, late imperial women's potential emotional and moral agency is profoundly associated with, and sometimes made possible by, women's suicides. In the Qing dynasty, the female chastity ideal protected widows from downwardly mobile or forced remarriage (Mann, "Widows in the Kinship" 37-56; Elvin 111-52). Also, in late imperial vernacular fiction, women's suicide is sometimes manifested as an act of passion and self-assertion: female characters use suicide as a way of confronting adversities and endorsing themselves as agents of free will (Zamperini, "Untamed Hearts" 77-105). Similar scenarios recurrently take place in *tanci*, in which the heroines exercise their moral agency by vowing to maintain virginal celibacy and even resorting to suicide to reject imposed marriage. Female chastity, a moral principle frequently invoked in imperial China to regulate women's behavior before and after marriage, is dealt with in *tanci* from a female-oriented perspective. In the *tanci,* 榴花夢 (*Liuhuameng*, Dream of the Pomegranate Flower; nineteenth century), authored byLi Guiyu (李桂玉), gentry woman Fang Jingzi and her son fall into the hands of a bandit who attempts to rape her. In order to protect her chaste name, Fang commits suicide by throwing herself into a torrential river. Her chaste heart moves heaven, and she is eventually saved by a high official who used to be her father's friend. Fang's suicide attempt demonstrates both her moral integrity and her courage to resist the bandit's tyranny. This example both illustrates the late imperial cult of female marital fidelity and distinguishes the brave Fang from stereotypical, emotionally vulnerable female characters.

Rukang Tian divides chaste widows in late imperial China into three categories: "the virtuous ones who observed lifelong widowhood, those who committed suicide for the sake of marital fidelity at the death of a spouse or fiancé, and those who committed suicide preserving their chastity in refusing to submit to rebels" (Tian, Rukang 61). Chaste women's private practices of self-mutilation, mourning, and suicide demonstrate that "at the opposite pole of the regime of feminine virtue were women who provoked debate, not because of their private devotion to the principles of women's virtue, but because of their alleged public flaunting of those very principles" (Judge, *Precious Raft* 59). Women's acts of suicide and self-mutilation continue to inspire social debates about the Confucian regulation of feminine virtue.

In *tanci* fiction, not only do widowed women commit suicide to protect their names, but many unmarried young women also resort to killing themselves to prevent marriages forced upon them. In some Qing ghost stories, virginal suicide sometimes bestows supernatural powers upon the lifeless virgin, who returns from the dead to kill her would-be rapist and preserve her posthumous chastity (Huang, *Desire and Fictional Narrative* 261). In *tanci*, virginal chastity is highlighted as a way of women's self-assertion; as it is affiliated with the natal family, it is not fully subject to the husband's power (Epstein, "Patrimonial Bonds" 1-33). In *Mengyingyuan* (Dream, Image, Destiny; preface dated 1843), all twelve reincarnated flower goddesses reject imposed marriage by insisting on their virginal chastity (for images of flower goddesses in Qing fiction, see Yu, Dan 30-33). The text endorses this chastity as a moral virtue superior to the women's wifely duties, and endorses women's right to live lives outside of marriage. One heroine, the humbly born sing-song girl and female doctor Tao Xianbi (陶纖碧), refuses to be forced into marriage and takes poisonous medicine on the day of the wedding. Likewise, Princess Zhenyi is unwilling to be forcefully married and, together with her maid, kills herself by taking poison. Another reincarnated goddess, Zhou Miaohua (周妙華), falls victim to a scheme of a married man's wife and is forced into becoming a concubine. Unwilling to stoop to such humiliation, she kills herself with a sword. In the fictional world of *tanci*, women who commit suicide to preserve their chastity are often endowed with a posthumous moral power: self-murdered women are either granted a pleasant afterlife or rewarded with a title of virtue and piousness in the heavenly realm.

Not only did *tanci* authors depict female characters who insist on virginity; some even shared their heroines' determination. Sun Deying (孫德英), the author of 金魚緣 (*Jinyuyuan*, Affinity of the Golden Fish; 1865), was determined to live an unmarried life. In her youth, she spent much of her spare time reading without restraint, in order to indicate both her disregard of the conventional constraints on women's intellectual pursuits and her wish to live a life without marriage. Her parents could not succeed in persuading her otherwise and finally allowed her to live by herself in seclusion. Sun spent her life writing *tanci* and reciting Buddhist sutras. Her example, along with those of the many chaste heroines, celibate daughters, and loyal maidens in *tanci,* express the *tanci* author's impulse to endorse the upright and condemn the evil from a feminine point of view. In addition to female chastity, filial piousness and loyalty toward one's lord or country are widely portrayed in *tanci*. A prominent example appears in *Tianyuhua* (Heaven Rains Flowers). In the story, when the Manchurians break into the country and overthrow the Ming dynasty, Zuo Weiming (左維明), a high official, commands all of his family members, both men and women who have been honored by the emperor, to commit suicide. Such dedication to one's country is also portrayed in the later *tanci* 精忠傳 (*Jingzhongzhuan*, Story of a Filial Son). In this text, when the loyal General Yue Fei (嶽飛) is murdered by the malevolent prime minister Qin Hui, Yue's daughter drowns herself in a well (for a recent study of this *tanci*, see Zhang, Yu).

These examples are just a few cases from the vast repertoire of *tanci* works that illustrate women's attempts at suicide as a way of testifying to their virtue and filial devotion. In late imperial vernacular fiction, the act of suicide eliminates the invisibility of women and their deaths by forcing women onto the public stage in the role of dramatic heroines (Zamperini, "Untamed Hearts" 83). These heroines, by becoming agents of death, overstep the boundaries of their socially prescribed sphere of action to attain a moment of fame for the very first and very last time in their lives (Zamperini, "Untamed Hearts" 83). In *tanci*, a woman who commits suicide out of moral passion can be considered an agent of emotive power; her death brings about the climactic moment of the story, highlighting the heroine as an element of narrative agency. In the fictional realm, a woman's death serves as a means of rebirth; in the act of defending her moral integrity, the heroine is often rewarded by heaven with being rescued, and subsequently lives out the rest of her life under another name or cross-dressed as a man. The cult of chastity, which is predominantly a prescribed feminine virtue, is applied in *tanci* not only to women, but also to men. In *Zaishengyuan* (Destiny of Rebirth), the male protagonist, Huangfu Shaohua (皇甫少華), vows to live a celibate life while waiting for the return of his disappeared fiancée, Meng Lijun (孟麗君). Likewise, in *Xianü qunying shi* (A History of Women Warriors), several male characters insist on remaining unmarried and waiting for the return of their fiancées, who are in disguise and living as men. This appropriation and modification of the chastity cult in *tanci* foregrounds a feminine-oriented perspective, evaluating women's as well as men's moral propriety against Confucian ideological principles.

Cross-dressing, a recurrent theme in women's *tanci* fiction, reveals women's imaginative depiction of alternative gender identities. In dynastic fiction, drama, and poetry, there are numerous examples of transvestite men and women. In the Song dynasty poetry collection 樂府詩集 (*Yuefu shiji*, Anthology of "Music Bureau" Poetry), the well-known 木蘭辭 (*Mulan ci*, Ballad of Mulan) tells of a young woman who disguises herself as a man to stand in for her father on the battlefield and who later becomes a national hero (Guo, Maoqian 373-75; Edwards, "Transformations" 175-214). The emphasis of the original story is not placed on Mulan's intelligence or military skill, but on her faithfulness to her father, her loyalty to the country, and her preservation of her chastity among the crude soldiers. When she returns from the battlefield, Mulan declines the Khan's reward of an official position and returns to her hometown. In her chamber, she takes off her armor and puts on an old dress, suggesting a wish to live the life of a common woman. The legendary Mulan has undergone significant transformation and assimilation in Confucian society. In *tanci*, an allusion to Mulan serves quite another purpose; it reflects the authors' self-strategizing, not assimilation. *Tanci* authors attempt to rewrite the image of Mulan by inserting the story into their texts and endowing the allusion with new visions of agency. Mulan's filial devotion is thus appropriated as a cover that serves to legitimatize women's writing. Accordingly, the reiteration of the Mulan legend in *tanci* writings is often rendered with a double voice (Kwa and Idema, *Mulan: Five Versions*; Dong, Lan, *Cross-Cultural Palimpsest of Mulan*; Dong, Lan, *Mulan's Legend and Legacy*; Lai 77-107). Mulan's cross-dressing is "predominantly served to amplify the magnitude of her devotion to her father or her country because the transgression of gender norms places her in extreme physical and moral danger" (Edwards, "Transformations" 177).

In the narratives of cross-dressed women warriors, Siu Leung Li comments, "the representation of the woman shows several tension points where a complex negotiation between the empowered and empowering woman and an oppressive but posed-and-masked-as-natural male narrative is subtly played out" (Li, Siu Leung 106). In the universe of male writing, the cross-dresser's "subversiveness is continuously suppressed and rendered as a stereotype" (Li, Siu Leung 106). Li's criticism illustrates the paramount relation between the progressive initiatives of cross-dressing and the representation of it in a particular discursive practice, writings by literati authors. The legendary Mulan is not so much a woman as a substitute for a man, a son, and loyal servant of the emperor. Her image has often been constrained by a male-oriented overarching preoccupation with the connection between the state and its subjects/citizens (Edwards, "Transformations" 177). Things are quite different in *tanci*. In *Zaishengyuan*, the heroine Meng Lijun cross-dresses to flee from a marriage imposed by her family and thus denies her obligations to her family and fiancé. It is for her own sake that Lijun changes her dress and travels the world as a man. The plot is principally driven by the cross-dresser's desire to pursue a life in which she is equal to a man, which she can do only by "becoming" a man socially.

Tanci, by formulating a tradition of women's writing distanced from the world of male writers, allowed the vital manifestation of the transformative potentiality in women's cross-dressing.

Tanci authors' fictional reconfiguration and temporary transgression of conventional gender norms, however, is often limited by the characters' environments. Meng Lijun achieves prominent success as prime minister and contributes to the country with her outstanding intelligence; nonetheless, she cannot be exempted from inquisitions about her real sexual identity and, when exposed, is inevitably pressed to become the emperor's concubine. In a later *tanci*, A History of Women Warriors (1905), women's cross-dressing is presented as a more popular and pragmatic practice among heroines. Nonetheless, not all the disguised women characters succeed in concealing their true identities under familial and social pressure.

In cross-dressing tales, women's identities are often revealed when their bound feet are discovered. The early Qing perception of footbinding runs counter to popular modern assumptions: footbinding was still a valorized adornment and was the mark of womanhood; it was, says Ko, the most natural enactment of a woman's gendered identity (Ko, "The Body as Attire" 21). The dynastic perception of the body was primarily as a social body, which illuminates the significance of Chinese clothing as a social, moral, and ethnic marker (Ko, "The Body as Attire" 18; *Cinderella's Sisters*; *Every Step*). This perception concurs with the imperial Chinese notion of dressing as embodiment. For heroines in *tanci*, wearing a male disguise provides greater opportunity for bodily agency to travel outside the constraints of the inner chambers. Although the dominant literary tradition has largely classified *tanci* as a nonmainstream genre, the mobility and freedom of its cross-dressed heroines distinguish this narrative genre as a pioneering precursor of women's travel literature in dynastic China.

In *tanci*, heroines dress as men to flee from marriage and explore the world by performing a masculine role; as the narrative unfolds, women's cross-dressing also turns out to be a means of accomplishing heroic deeds without violating the Confucian regulations on chastity and virtue. Marriage is endowed with great significance in plot development, for as soon as the disguised woman's secret is revealed, she is given the choice of marrying either her betrothed fiancé or another man in an arranged marriage. To renounce marriage, some cross-dressed characters refuse to reveal their true sexuality. Many *tanci* authors also strategically delay the marriage event by arranging "mock unions" between the female transvestites and their sympathetic "sisters." In both Destiny of Rebirth and A History of Women Warriors, the mock marriages are so successful that even the cross-dressers' parents-in-law and handmaids are not aware of the truth.

The act of cross-dressing carries disruptive potential by reversing gendered codes for men and women. In the story 梁山伯與祝英臺 (*Liang Shanbo yu Zhu Yingtai*, Butterfly Lovers), the heroine Zhu Yingtai (祝英臺) dresses as a man to travel outside the inner quarters and study with a schoolmate Liang Shanbo (梁山伯) at a men's school. Zhu and Liang fall in love with each other. However, familial opposition forces them to separate. Later, when Liang dies from an illness,

Zhu commits suicide in front of Liang's tomb. Their spirits transform into a pair of butterflies and are never separated. The tragic myth has been passed down through generations via literary texts and traditional opera performances. The opera performances of this story, often conducted by all-women troupes in the southern areas of China, usually cast a woman cross-dresser as the male protagonist Liang Shanbo. Underlying the theme of true love, the textual and theatrical performances of the legend invite innovative readings of gender and sexuality on multiple levels of representation. For cross-dressed women, marriage challenges them to resume their socially prescribed gender roles as chaste wives, devoted daughters, and ultimately as caring mothers. In a *tanci* work 金魚緣 (*Jinyuyuan*, Affinity of the Golden Fish; 1865) by Sun Deying, the heroine Qian Shurong (錢淑榮) confesses to her parents her unwillingness to live the life of a woman.

> In this world, no one suffers so much as a woman. She is not allowed to make her own choice; she has to follow others in every matter. . . . Having understood my affinity with the ethereal life, I have not a shred of sentiment lingering in my heart. Unable to achieve fame in this world, I shall hide my tracks and conceal my path, and withdraw from mundane life. (qtd. in Sheng, 227; my translation)

Cross-dressing in *tanci* opens up a progressive reading of women's same-sex desire, an infrequently considered topic in pre-twentieth-century literature, except as regards the work of a few male authors. Examples of male-authored fictional portrayals of women's same-sex love include the sixteenth-century novel 金瓶梅 (*Jinpingmei, The Golden Lotus*), authored by Lanling Xiaoxiaosheng, and the play 憐香伴 (*Lianxiangban*, Cherishing the Fragrant Companion) by Li Yü (李漁, 1611-79). In women's *tanci* fiction, representations of women's same-sex desire celebrate a spiritual harmony among cross-dressed heroines and their feminine spouses via mock unions, or they create melodramatic irony by displaying unsuspecting women's infatuation with the beautifully disguised cross-dressers. Women's homoeroticism, whether poignant or comical, distorts gender boundaries and reveals cross-dressers as empowering characters who counterbalance patriarchal conceptions of sexuality. Tse-Lan Deborah Sang argues that premodern Chinese texts delineated social priorities that circumscribed and constrained women's love for other women. Although most late imperial male authors portrayed female same-sex intimacy within an ideal domestic structure, some, such as the early Qing author Pu Songling (蒲松齡), offered insight into the strength of women's spiritual love toward other women (Sang 64-65). Still, such portraits are often limited and frequently depict women as supernatural beings or immortals. In *tanci*, however, women's same-sex desire takes place outside of domestic confines and in the male world of action—and both the woman cross-dresser and her female spouse remain mortal. Women's same-sex intimacy in *tanci* thus provides an impetus for reconceptualizing women's homoerotic desires beyond the normative marriage system. Women's homoeroticism in *tanci* also differs from the modern, Western concept of lesbian love, as the female characters' affection for one another finds expression mostly on a spiritual level, as an idealized alternative to the heterosexual model, and does not lead to physical consummation (for men's depiction of lesbian love, see Wu, H. Laura 1-34; for the Western concept of lesbian love, see Zimmerman).

Although cross-dressing transcends women's prescribed gender roles, authors of *tanci* often insist on the moral competency of cross-dressed women by emphasizing their virginal chastity, their filial passion to serve their parents, their ingenuity in preserving their chastity by disguising themselves among men, or their courage in confronting evildoers in perilous situations. Depictions of morally upright cross-dressers are abundant in imperial literature. In the Tang *chuanqi* story of Xie Xiao'e (謝小娥), when the heroine travels with her family after her wedding, bandits murder her husband and father. To avenge them, she dresses as a man, searches for the bandits, and finally kills them. Xiao'e is represented as an ideal of intelligence and chastity, for by dressing as a man, she is able to march into the midst of the outlaws and to live with the servants and workers who do not notice that she is a woman (Ouyang and Song 36). In *Mengyingyuan*, a reincarnated goddess Ruan Lianqing (阮蓮清) is sold into an opera troupe while still a child. She disguises herself as a man to preserve her innocence and purity when she becomes an opera singer, a vocation considered as morally degrading and socially inferior to other professions. In *Bishenghua* (Blossom from the Brush), the heroine Jiang Dehua (姜德華) ventures to attend the imperial selection of palace maids in order to rescue her aged father from a political crisis, thus displaying her filial passions. She attempts suicide on the way to the capital city, but is rescued by a fox spirit who then assumes her form and takes her place as a royal maid. Dehua herself dresses as a man, passes the civil service exam, and subsequently is appointed a high official. When the emperor passes away, Dehua helps the palace quell a political upheaval, secures the throne of the new emperor, and is appointed prime minister, displaying both ingenuity and courage. To reward her vital contribution, the emperor endows her with the title The Female Lord of Loyalty, Filiality, Heroism and Valor. Similar scenarios can be readily traced in other *tanci* fiction, A History of Women Warriors and *Liuhuameng* (Dream of the Pomegranate Flower). In the former, the courageous swordswoman Wen Xiaxian (文霞仙) disguises herself as the spirit of General Guangong and rescues the endangered prince at night. In the latter, the military leader Gui Hengkui (桂恒魁), with her country in crisis, "abandons her rouge and powder at her vanity table, and picks up cap and gown to serve the court" (Li Guiyu 1).

In *tanci*, changing gender roles can even be presented as a moral reward for women's good deeds. In 娛萱草彈詞 (*Yuxuancao tanci*, A *Tanci* to Please My Mother-in-Law), the heroine Bimei Shuji (彼美淑姬), thanks to her extraordinarily filial and virtuous conduct, is given a chance to become a man by the heavenly emperor. Shuji accepts the offer, marries her own cousin, and later becomes a provincial governor. As presented in these *tanci*, the controversy over women's cross-dressing as a potentially disruptive and iconoclastic practice finds its solution when it is presented as an unconventional but effectual means of rewarding women's moral rectitude in a male-dominated social environment.

What approaches are available to the contemporary reader in interpreting these scenarios of women's cross-dressing in the context of late imperial China? Alphonso Lingis holds that "a body is a subject of and subjected to power and discourse" (286). The term "subjectification" here refers both to the making of the subject via discursive and nondiscursive practices and to the subordination of the subject to the power and discursive norms by which it is produced. In *tanci*, the subjectification of the female body is a subtle process in which gender and sexual consciousness negotiate the dominant discourses of the society and the nation. For Jiang Yingqing, the author of the 1926 *tanci* fiction *Fengliu zuiren*, the nationalist discourse of the early republican period provided the incentive for the developing pursuit of women's equality in education and work, and supported the early trends of 全球女權 (*quanqiu nüquan*, global feminism). Agency in the republican period, according to Jiang's depiction, could be achieved by women's actual participation in social affairs as members of the nationalist movement. This later *tanci* makes an important contribution by suggesting a more developed and open space for women to strive for self-actualization.

Aside from imaginative depictions of cross-dressed heroines, *tanci* fiction portrays myriad female knights whose valiant deeds reveal a legacy of feminine heroism. Some authors also retell stories of male heroes in their *tanci*. In 精忠傳 (*Jingzhongzhuan*, Story of the Loyal Son), the author Zhou Yingfang (周穎芳, ?-1895) renarrates the well-known story of the loyal hero Yue Fei (嶽飛), possibly to appeal to women readers in the inner chambers. From the female bandit leader Wei Yong'e (衛勇娥) in Destiny of Rebirth to the courageous female knight Wen Xiaxian in *A History*, *tanci* works depict many women knights and warriors. These depictions tend to represent women's fantasies about war and love, eliciting the readers' romantic or loyal sentiments or inviting humorous ruminations (Hu, Siao-chen, "War, Violence, and the Metaphor of Blood" 279). Often such heroic protagonists are women who disguise themselves as men and serve the nation with loyalty and passion. The anonymously composed *tanci* 安邦誌 (*Anbang zhi*, A Tale of Shielding the Nation; 1849) depicts Zhao Yueying (趙月英), a swordswoman whose "looks rival the legendary beauties Xi'Shi and Diao Chan, yet [who] fights with the courage of a crouching tiger and a soaring dragon" (Run Qin, qtd. in *Anbang zhi* 14). Likewise, in Destiny of Rebirth, heroine Huangfu Zhanghua (皇甫長華) surpasses her brother Shaohua in swordplay while practicing martial arts at home. Later, when her family suffers a political calamity, she becomes a leader in the "Army of Filial Daughters" and together with the female bandit Wei Yong'e (衛勇娥) defeats the invading troops of the vicious Liu Kuibi (劉奎壁), who schemed against the Huangfu family. Not only does Zhanghua possess wisdom and a grasp of military strategy, but she also deploys magic on her enemies and effortlessly defeats them on the battlefield.

Heroic women's ingenious employment of magic is a frequent scenario in *tanci*. In 天雨花 (*Tianyuhua*, Heaven Rains Flowers), heroine Zuo Yizhen (左儀貞) asks for her father's magical sword as a reward for her assistance with his work. When, later, Zheng Guotai usurps the throne, kidnaps Yizhen, and decides to establish her as empress, Yizhen uses her father's sword to behead him. Yizhen's remarkable deeds recall the example of Wen Xiaxian, a heroine in the later *tanci Xianü qunying shi* who avenges her father by beheading a family enemy and later rescues the prince in a moment of national crisis. If the symbol of the sword is often considered as representative of patriarchal phallic power, both of these stories reconfigure this narrative formula somewhat by portraying women's militant agency.

These tales of women soldiers and swordswomen display the creation of heroines of exceptional bodily agency. Women characters exercise their militant skills and power just as men do. Sometimes in *tanci,* depictions of swordswomen are entwined with the narrative scenario of cross-dressing. In *Xianü qunying shi*, cross-dressers Qin Ling (秦淩) and Su Zixiu (蘇子秀), as part of an attempt to become men's equals in physical strength and military skill, diligently study traditional swordsmanship. Moreover, fictional women who engage in acts of heroism often embody the ideals of devotion and loyalty to their elders, husbands, or country. In comparison with traditional women who suffer bodily torture and constraint, with their bound feet and heavy household labor, these heroines enjoy the bodily mobility to travel and to defend their country on the battlefield when summoned.

By creating exceptional female characters who travel and explore landscapes like men do, late imperial and early twentieth-century *tanci* authors reconceptualized the traditional domestic roles that Chinese women were supposed to occupy and mapped out a performative space for women outside the inner chambers. Women are presented as traveling heroines who flee from imposed marriage arrangements, seek political shelter and protection, or pursue intellectual careers of their own. Women as military leaders, doctors, female knights, alchemists, traveling students, or candidates for the civil service exam venture forth from the confining space of home to the vast terrain of the outside world. These roaming heroines in *tanci* reflect the authors' modification of Confucian ideological discourses regarding late imperial women's social and cultural identities.

Traveling women, whether fictional or historical, were unconventional figures in imperial China. Foot binding physically mutilated women and made it almost impossible for them to travel with freedom and ease in public as men did. Strict family discipline also forbade women to roam outside the household and imposed on them household duties from which even women of the gentry were not exempt. In imperial China, the ideological, symbolic, and physical gendering of space located men's proper place and function in 外 (*wai*, the outer sphere), while that of women was situated in 內 (*nei*, the inner sphere) (Fong, *Herself an Author* 85). Because Confucian gender ideology confined women's roles and responsibilities to the inner sphere, travel was less common for women, both of the gentry and lower classes (85). Female-authored travel writings from the imperial period are scarce; it is only in the seventeenth century that one finds significant signs of women traveling and writing. Grace S. Fong has examined rare examples of late imperial women's travel poetry, literary travel journals, and poetic records of women's sojourns, and proposes that these writings contribute to the study of women's agency, as the authors of these works assumed the subjectivity of travelers and transcended the constraints of social convention. Susan Mann also argues that late imperial women's travel accounts, like men's travel accounts, are coded to display their authors' virtue and learning. In the line of duty, following the proper principles of a daughter, wife, or mother, some upper-class women could move about free of scrutiny (Fong, *Herself an Author*; Mann, "Virtue of Travel"). Travel for self-acculturation, scholarly success, and business was mainly a privilege reserved for men. Women poets who were constrained by their circumstances resorted to writing imaginative journeys (Mann, "Virtue of Travel" 63). What Mann has termed "imaginary travels" function as an important theme in *tanci* stories, which often feature unconventional heroines who manage to escape marriage arrangements and follow the male elite's trajectory of studying, passing exams, mentoring students, taking official positions, and even defending the nation's territories on the frontiers. The current research on *tanci* fiction can be aligned with this scholarship on imperial women's travel accounts, as it draws attention to the multifarious literary presentations of women's journeys.

Perhaps the most famous traveling *tanci* heroine is Meng Lijun, the protagonist in *Zaishengyuan*, who flees her home to escape an imposed marriage and subsequently embarks on a journey while dressed as a man. Her exile from family calamity turns out to become a personal journey toward social achievement: she is adopted by an official under the name Li Junyu (酈君玉), passes the civil service examination, and is appointed prime minister by the emperor. If Lijun's journey represents a feminine adaptation of the travel formula often depicted in male authors' fiction, *Mengyingyuan* (Dream, Image, Destiny) portrays the female sojourn as one endowed with moral purpose (Zou, "Cross-Dressing"). In this *tanci*, twelve reincarnated goddesses travel throughout the secular world to redeem the upright and defend justice. The twelve individual heroines' journeys contribute to a collective narrative of women transforming social customs and empowering the weak through personal examples. In another work, A History of Women Warriors, cross-dressed women enjoy social mobility and become important military leaders. Privately, they also long to travel deep into the mountains to study alchemy and philosophy, in order to flee from the anxieties and constraints of the secular world.

The impulse of women characters to travel outside the boudoir took on a new meaning in the republican period, as it represented the nascent trend of pioneering women who studied abroad to empower themselves through knowledge. The well-known feminist martyr Qiu Jin (秋瑾), in her *tanci* novella 精衛石 (*Jingwei shi*, Pebbles of the Jingwei Bird; 1905), depicted a group of women who leave their home to travel to Japan to receive modern education, with the determination to reinvigorate their nation and to liberate women from social oppression when they return to China. *Tanci* authors' emancipatory desires and reformative initiatives are also prominently displayed in a later 1926 work, 風流罪人 (*Fengliu zuiren*, The Valiant and the Culprit), in which author Jiang Yingqing (姜映清) presents a modern adaptation of traveling heroines. In this *tanci*, the protagonist who goes to the United States to study medicine comes back to Shanghai to manage a hospital and later again embarks on a journey abroad to begin a new lifestyle as an independent modern woman.

To borrow Ellen Widmer's term, the text provides an example of the new *guixiu*, or gentlewoman, who, in the course of traveling to broaden her educational horizons—a necessity in the modern era—experiences anxiety about her new way of life, which poses a dilemma between marriage and career (Widmer, "Gentility" 21-45).

Roaming women's religious aspirations for a transcendental world are also powerfully portrayed in *tanci*. In Blossom from the Brush, the cross-dressed heroine Jiang Dehua is determined to pursue the world of the immortals. She ponders:

> Eliminating worldly desires, taking to pure meditations, ancient lives of the immortals are good examples for men to follow. Not to mention that I have the companion of Lady Xie, with whom I shall conceal myself in the deep mountains and live a couple's life. It is said that those who are determined will have their way; perhaps we may have our dreams come true and cruise the world on the backs of the mythical cranes. (Bao 221)

Such spiritual questing justifies female *tanci* characters' rejection of marriage and insistence on keeping their chastity. Characters like Jiang Dehua recall exemplary late imperial women pilgrims, whose motivation to travel was as much social as it was religious, for traveling was the only way they could get out of the house and meet others (Grant, *Eminent Nuns* 7). Accordingly, in late imperial *tanci*, traveling heroines like Jiang Dehua (姜德華), Meng Lijun in Destiny of Rebirth, and Han Xiangqing in 晝錦堂記 (*Zhoujintang ji,* Tale of the Daylight Hall) must disguise themselves as men to travel safely and conveniently. In contrast, *tanci* tales written in the early twentieth century, such as Pebbles of the Jingwei Bird and The Valiant and the Culprit, portray women who voyage freely, without having to disguise themselves as men, and who even study long-term in Japan and the United States. The travel trajectories of *tanci* heroines illustrate the expanding frontiers of women's social activity and the gradually broadening spaces in which women could test the limits of their gender roles.

The representation of traveling women is a vital aspect of the multilayered narrative form of *tanci* and contributes to the genre's unique literary, aesthetic, and sociocultural achievements. By invoking and reworking the travel genre models, *tanci* authors contributed to the development of late imperial women's travel writing and reconfigured women's subjectivities beyond the constraints of male-dominant social and cultural discourses. Through the eyes of these traveling heroines, the authors projected their imaginings of social, historical, and cultural landscapes in which women could strive for personal rights and freedom. Heroines on voyages evidence *tanci* authors' construction of unconventional female subjectivities; en route, these women are individuals with the freedom to decide their personal fates. In the authors' fictional constructions, these roaming women not only acquire agency and power, but they also create incentives for women readers of the time to reconceptualize their social and cultural universe.

The fact that some *tanci* authors' daughters also took up *tanci* writing provides further insight into the feminine tradition of producing and rewriting this narrative genre. For example, Zheng Danruo, the author of *Mengyingyuan*, was the mother of another *tanci* author, Zhou Yingfang (周穎芳), who composed 精忠傳 (*Jingzhong-zhuan,* Story of a Devoted Son; 1895), a story based on the loyal general Yue Fei of the South Song Dynasty. Both mother and daughter used the themes of loyalty and filial devotion as the thematic anchors of their tales; and in their own lives both demonstrated moral integrity when their personal fates intersected with tumultuous political situations. When Taiping Rebellion troops broke into Nanjing City where Zheng Danruo lived after her husband's death, Zheng, possibly to preserve her chastity, committed suicide by taking poison. Similarly, when Zhou Yingfang's husband Yan Jin (嚴謹), a provincial governor, was killed in a battle against the Miao bandits in 1865, Zhou attempted to commit suicide to preserve her chastity. After being rescued, she spent the rest of her life raising her son, serving her parents-in-law, and writing *tanci* as a way to dissolve her inner grievances.

The mother-daughter legacy among women authors is not unique to *tanci* narratives but belongs to a larger tradition of late imperial women's writing. A famous example concerns the playwright Ye Xiaowan (葉小婉, 1613-1657); her sister, the poet Ye Xiaoluan (葉小鸞, 1616-1632); and their mother, the poet Shen Yixiu (沈宜修, 1590-1635). The works of the mother and her daughters were anthologized by Ye Shaoyuan (Yixiu's husband and the girls' father) in the collection 午夢堂集 (*Wumengtang ji*, Dream of the Meridian Hall; 1636), as a sign of support for his wife and daughters. There are many such records of literary women and their daughters during the Ming and Qing. Current studies of the works of genteel women who wrote to and of their daughters, and of the daughters' corollary writings about their mothers, depict women's perceptions of their matrilineal existences within a largely patrilineal system (Hsiung 98). Most writings, due to contextual constraints, followed the patriarchal logic consistent with contemporary sociocultural norms, although some accounts do suggest the possible reconstruction of a feminine genealogy in the domestic sphere (Hsiung 98). The mother-daughter relationship in *tanci* affords contemporary readers an opportunity to reconfigure the "feminine genealogy" via a literary genre that addresses a largely female imagined audience and that is less filtered through male literary lenses. Perhaps because *tanci* offers a freer space of expression, women have depicted unorthodox women in these tales. Hu Siao-chen, in a study of 玉連環 (*Yulianhuan*, Linked Rings of Jade) by Zhu Suxian (朱素仙), offers a valuable analysis of images of alcoholic mothers, shrewd wives, and celibate daughters. However, such extreme mothers and daughters are minor characters who serve as the heroines' doubles and add to the diversity of characters in the story ("Unorthodox Female Figures" 311-24).

In *tanci*, the mother-daughter legacy is often constructed by the authors as an emotional bond between themselves and their targeted readers. Many authors proclaimed that they wrote *tanci* to entertain their mothers or mothers-in-law; their filial affection was their major motivation for writing. In 娛萱草彈詞 (*Yuxuancao tanci*, A Tanci to Please My Mother-in-Law), the author Ju Daoren (橘道人) claimed that her work, as its title suggests, is just "a book showing my filial love to my mother." Modeling her *tanci* on the didactic 孝經 (*Xiaojing*, Book of Devoted Children), she hoped that her *tanci* would help her mother-in-law pass time, dispel her worries, and lighten her mood. In this way, late imperial women's writing of *tanci* was legitimized by the authors' conscious and purposeful endorsement of filial love and female virtue. Also, motherly love provided moral support for *tanci* authors. In Destiny of Rebirth, author Chen Duansheng comments that she could take up the writing brush in her spare time between household tasks, thanks to her mother-in-law's encouragement.

Some *tanci* novels were coauthored by a mother and daughter. The late Ming *tanci* work 玉釧緣 (*Yuchuanyuan*, Jade Bracelets; 1693), which was written by anonymous author(s), provides abundant textual evidence of a mother-daughter coauthorship; witness the opening lines of chapter 31: "The daughter applies the writing brush to compose exceptional lines; the mother, holding the jade pen, writes unusual words." This coauthorial relationship suggests that women's *tanci* writing may have been a familial and collective tradition in the inner chambers. More frequently, *tanci* authors acknowledge their intellectual indebtedness to their mothers, who, themselves educated through family learning, took on the role of scholarly mentors to their daughters. The authors' intellectual inheritance from their mothers bespeak a private, discreet, and multifaceted legacy of women's writing in the inner chambers. *Tanci*, therefore, may expose women's psychological traits and ideological values more effectively than other literary genres (Hu, Siao-chen, *Cainü* 9). When considered in Ming and Qing family fiction, the mother-daughter relationship in *tanci* manifests the impact of the 母教 (*mujiao*, mother's education). In the culture of the imperial period, motherhood represented domestic power and authority, as mothers were responsible for educating their daughters and supplying moral support for them. In *tanci*, motherhood is evoked to demonstrate the daughter-writers' filial affection as well as to proclaim the author's moral legitimacy: it is for entertaining her mother or mother-in-law that the author takes up her writing brush and thereby acquires the agency to write.

Thematically organized and historically contextualized, this book contains six chapters, covering five principal *tanci* works from the eighteenth century to the early twentieth century. The first chapter, "Envisioning A Nascent Feminine Agency in *Zaishengyuan* (Destiny of Rebirth)," studies the acclaimed eighteenth-century *tanci* text by Chen Duansheng. The unfinished text depicts a female protagonist, Meng Lijun, who is forced to disguise herself as a man to escape an imposed marriage, and later successfully passes the civil service exam and becomes the prime minister of the country. Enjoying greater social freedom and prestige, Lijun refuses to revert back to her feminine identity and will not marry her former fiancé, Huangfu Shaohua. The tale comes to an abrupt end when Lijun's true identity is revealed to the emperor, leaving Lijun the choice of becoming the emperor's secret concubine or being executed for deceiving the royal palace. The disguised heroine, mimicking masculine demeanors, actively takes part in constructing her image by drawing on seemingly incongruent gender roles. Cross-dressing foregrounds the heroine's power to appropriate and circumvent Confucian ethical codes, codes which promoted the subordination of women in both the inner quarters and the public sphere. This exceptional *tanci* holds a place of prominence in late imperial Chinese literature because of its revelation of the troubled relationships among gender construction, narrative agency, and women's identity. The multilayered textual representation of Lijun manifestly disrupts conventional attitudes toward gendered identity, yet also exposes the social and practical challenges of such temporary and often imagined transgressions, which must be exercised by incarcerating the feminine and borrowing the male subjective position. Chen's *tanci* illustrates an imaginary feminine autonomy, represented by the disguised Lijun, displaying Chen's endeavor to carve a space for self-expression in the face of socially and politically enforced silence.

Chen Duansheng's *tanci* inspired multiple *tanci* authors to either compose sequels or re-edit her texts to meet the moralistic demand of mainstream readers, some of whom remained skeptical of Lijun's adventurous character. Continuing this exploration of the cross-dressing narrative convention, chapter 2, "Disguised Scholar, Fox Spirit, and Moralism in *Bishenghua* (Blossom from the Brush)," examines a later *tanci* novel by Qiu Xinru in the nineteenth century. Qiu emulates Chen's strong autobiographical narrative statements and adapts the theme of cross-dressing. However, Qiu relies on the formula of the fox spirit and female immortals to provide moral justification for her heroine Jiang Dehua, who disguises herself as a male scholar. In contrast with Lijun, who risks her own life to protect her sexual identity and determinedly rejects the return to marriage, Qiu's heroine Dehua, after also achieving phenomenal success in her career, reconciles with and marries her fiancé, and withdraws from her eminent position as prime minister. This ostensible reconciliation rewards Dehua with a series of royal awards and honors, but also paves the way for her reconfiguration of the orthodox family relationship in the inner chambers after her marriage. An exemplar of feminine virtue and filial passions, Dehua utilizes her intelligence and resourcefulness to harmonize relationships between wives and concubines, to assist her husband to take concubines and acquire more siblings, and when summoned by the emperor, to protect the royal family and suppress rebelling forces at a time of national crisis. Qiu's retelling of the cross-dresser's tale disguises the author's own ambitious undertakings with a didactic narrative convention, and by resituating the heroine back in the inner chambers, suggests the possibility of women acquiring autonomy within the traditionally defined domestic sphere.

If Chen Duansheng and Qiu Xinru both present women's predicament between imagining alternative female subjectivities and rigid moralistic self-reflections, Zheng Danruo's *Mengyingyuan* (Dream, Image, Destiny; preface dated 1843) elevates such concerns to the level of ethical self-reflection. Zheng was born in a county of Zhejiang province in the early nineteenth century. She established her fame as a *tanci* author after writing *Mengyingyuan*, which stood out with its erudition, splendid style, and refined diction, and consequently brought about a transformation of *tanci* fiction. Zheng's husband was the head official of Hangzhou when the rebels broke into the city in 1860. Probably to preserve her chastity, Zheng committed suicide by taking poison. *Mengyingyuan* is written in a distinctive first-person voice that makes ready use of commentary on the narrative, requests for the audience's sympathy, and moments of authorial self-appraisal. In chapter 3, "Ethics, Filial Piety, and Narrative Sympathy in *Mengyingyuan*," I study how the metatextual nature of this *tanci* sheds new light on the key theme of the authorial voice. The term "authorial voice" is applied here in part to propose a narrative conception of women's agency as portrayed in the specific genre of *tanci*, and to draw parallels between *tanci* and women's voices in other genres, especially the lyric poetry of the late imperial period. Tactfully advocating moral integrity by rewriting mainstream moral codes of filial piety and chastity, Zheng outspokenly distinguishes her *tanci* from other popular *tanci* of love and romance, while lending credence to her right to a personal voice. Evoking and transforming the late imperial cult of 情 (*qing*, feelings and emotions), the text includes sympathetic identification as a form of emotive affinity between the narrator and narratee, the raconteur and the fictional character. This notion of sympathy, situated in the late imperial context, empowers the author's literary presence and involves the fictional characters and the readers in reflection and affective responses.

Continuing this study of Zheng's *tanci,* chapter 4, "Gender, Spectatorship, and Literary Portraiture in *Mengyingyuan*," centers on the use of portraits that offer verisimilitude to their viewer. In the text, women's points of view are represented through their making and viewing of portraits and through their writings concerning portrait scenarios in literature. Late imperial male intellectuals approached paintings of women as voyeurs and connoisseurs of feminine beauty. Alternatively, imperial women had a tradition of making their own portraits as well as making statements about their ideals through these painted images. Talented women, many of whom were skilled in painting, even composed poems for paintings of their female friends. This chapter reconsiders examples of men's representations of women in portraits and women's self-representations. Portraits of and by women reflect distinctive points of view in gender representation and grant the reader pluralistic possibilities for spectatorial agency, that is, multiple prospects for viewers to evaluate, respond to, and dynamically interact with the painted images. Zheng reprises late imperial literary representations of the "painted beauty," but also transforms these scenes by rewriting them from a feminine perspective. Her text modifies male literati's narratives by transforming images of women from passive objects for male connoisseurship to active agents who evoke dynamic spectatorial responses. The inner chambers embody the fictional space and the actual locale of the audience, where the paintings can be viewed by their private eyes. The text's endorsement of women's spectatorial agency gives a strong impetus for the critical evaluation of *tanci* as provisional works that can broaden and deepen contemporary studies of gendered identity and spectatorship.

The vital achievement and everlasting influence of the above pre-twentieth-century *tanci* works anticipated the continuing growth and success of lengthy *tanci* novels by women in the early twentieth century. The last two chapters of this book consider itinerant heroines in modern *tanci* fiction, with a goal to extend the historical framework of this study to the modern era by analyzing two stylistically and thematically dissimilar *tanci* novels written, respectively, at the turn of the twentieth century and during the interwar period. Chapter 5, "Cross-Dressing as a Collective Act in *Xianü qunying shi* (A History of Women Warriors)," revisits the tradition of women's cross-dressing in a 1905 *tanci* novel that has not been studied in current scholarship. The authors were three sisters who adopted the pen names of Yonglan (詠蘭), Youmei (友梅), and Shuzhu (書竹). Resonant with previous discussions of the progressive potential of women cross-dressers, this chapter examines multiple examples of women masquerading as men, comparing the presentation of cross-dressing with precursor narratives. In contrast with the heroines in the previous *tanci*, most women cross-dressers in this text do not revert back to their feminine identities, but continue to conduct their lives as men's social and political equals. These women's actions question and even controvert Confucian ethical discourses about virtue and chastity. Cross-dressed women are depicted as erudite scholars and heroic warriors who uphold the good, punish the evil, and valiantly save the country at moments of national crisis. The stories of these women dressed in men's robes illustrate the intersecting themes of nation and gendered identity, providing a counternarrative to the Confucian male-centered nation-state discourses. The extensive reconfiguration of the gender hierarchy in the text presents a more optimistic vision when it comes to imagining possibilities for women to exercise their sexual, social, and political power.

The last chapter, "Illustrating A New Woman in *Fengliu zuiren* (The Valiant and The Culprit)," analyzes a text by Jiang Yingqing, whose portrayal of the modern woman in 1920s and 1930s Shanghai exemplify the extended development of the *tanci* tradition in the late imperial period. Identifying the notion of agency as the core of women's empowerment, this chapter explores how Jiang's depiction of the "modern woman" recapitulates previous authors' concerns with women's autonomy and social agency, portraying women's self-conscious exploration of their social roles as teachers, doctors, lawyers, and journalists. The heroine in Jiang's *tanci* has traveled to the West and come back to work as a doctor. With an ambition to contribute to the good of her people, she declines a marriage proposal by the male protagonist, who later is yoked to a conventional marriage arranged by his family and abandons his personal ambition. This forward-looking initiative reflects social and cultural discourses about women and work, featuring women's self-empowerment through their intellectual undertakings and pursuit of social freedom in 1920s China (See Keshi 25; Hua Erxi). Unlike traditional *tanci*, which portray women's imaginative freedom as achieved by cross-dressing and taking on men's social roles, Jiang's work, through its appraisal of the vexed relationship between gender and modernization, reflects on women's identity and gender relationships in light of the new possibilities of women's societal roles. If prior *tanci* novels offered rich possibilities for women acquiring social agency through cross-dressing and exploring the world beyond the domestic sphere, Jiang's *tanci* offers reflections on the particular dilemmas for women who encountered an evolved and complicated social situation during this transitional historical phase. Jiang's work both inherits the legacy of precursory *tanci* and speaks to the evolving social discourses about women's consciousness at the turn of the twentieth century.

Chapter One

Envisioning A Nascent Feminine Agency in *Zaishengyuan* (Destiny of Rebirth)

The heroine of *Zaishengyuan* (Destiny of Rebirth), a *tanci* written by Chen Duansheng (1751-1796), is Meng Lijun, a daughter in a gentry-class family in the southwestern province of Yunnan in the early fourteenth century. To escape from a marriage imposed by the emperor and remain faithful to Huangfu Shaohua, to whom she was originally engaged, Lijun cross-dresses as a man the night before her wedding and flees from home, leaving a self-portrait of her true self as a keepsake for her parents. Later, having taken the civil service examination, Lijun ranks first among all the candidates and is appointed prime minister by the emperor. As a successful and handsome young "man," Lijun is favored by the emperor, who arranges for Lijun to marry Liang Suhua (梁素華), the adopted daughter of an eminent official. It happens that Suhua is actually the daughter of Lijun's former wet nurse Su Yingxue (蘇映雪) and has changed her name after being adopted by the Liang family. Since Suhua and Lijun had grown up together as sisters, the mock union between them, with Suhua's complicity, passes as a happy marriage. Lijun's fiancé, Huangfu Shaohua, is also selected to be an official. Ironically, his mentor is none other than his own betrothed, the cross-dressed Lijun. Love-sick, Shaohua takes Lijun's self-portrait from her parents' home, unaware of Lijun's identity. Shocked by the likeness between the prime minister and the portrait, he confronts the minister and questions "his" identity. Shaohua reveals his suspicion to his sister, who is the empress, as well as the emperor's mother to reveal Lijun's true identity. At a palace banquet, the empress dowager gets the prime minister drunk and has "his" boots taken off, revealing Lijun's bound feet and exposing her real identity. It happens that the emperor intersects with the maid who had taken off Lijun's lotus shoes, and thus hears the secret. Lijun is then pressed by the emperor to become his concubine, under threat of execution. In the last scene in Chen's text, Lijun, enraged by the injustice and suffering damage from the wine, becomes seriously ill and spits blood. Although the direct cause of Lijun spitting blood remains ambivalent, the text implies that the heroine's collapse might be the result of both alcohol damage and heightened stress about the revelation of her real sexuality.

Chen Duansheng was born in Hangzhou, a city of rich intellectual and cultural heritage. Located in the center of the urban Jiangnan region, south of the Yangzi River, Hangzhou was home to many semicloistered women from the gentry who left rich records of their accomplishments. The women's literary culture of the time was manifested in their own works and in elite male authors' writings on and perceptions of these talented women. Chen Duansheng's family looked favorably upon women's education: her grandfather, the famous scholar Chen Zhaolun (陳兆倫, 1701-1771), proposed in the essay "才女說" ("Cainü shuo," "On Talented Women") that women's learning would enable them to better assist their husbands and educate their children, and that education in classics would augment women's virtue (Chen Yinke 15). Chen's family also had frequent contact with the scholars of the time. Her sister Chen Changsheng (陳長生) was a disciple of the renowned scholar Yuan Mei (1716-1797). Both published poetry collections: Duansheng's was titled 繪影閣集 (*Huiyingge ji*, Collected Poems from the Huiying Chamber) and Changsheng's 繪聲閣集 (*Huishengge ji*, Collected Poems from the Huisheng Chamber). The title "繪影" ("huiying," depictions of images) suggests Duansheng's precise imitative strategies in characterization. Although the original text of this poetry collection is lost, critics suggest that some of the poems might have been embedded in the introductory poems to the chapters of Destiny of Rebirth (Chen Yinke 25).

Among current scholarship on this *tanci*, Mark Bender's doctoral thesis in 1995 offers a substantial analysis and translations of exerpts of *Zaishengyuan*. Bender's research, in addition to a formalistic analysis of the text, extends the study of the novel to its broader sociocultural context by discussing modern adaptations of Meng Lijun's story in Suzhou *tanci* performances (see Bender, *Zaisheng yuan*). Hu Siao-chen, in her book-length study on *tanci* published in 2008, situates Chen's *tanci*, along with several other *tanci* before and after Chen's work, as constitutive of steps toward the establishment of a late imperial and early modern women's narrative tradition in China. Framing her reading of Chen's *tanci* in the context of the vast "reading community" of *tanci* consisting mainly of women, Hu states that Chen's work is composed for an "imagined" readers' community including elite women readers in the inner chambers (Hu, *Cainü* 6). Hu argues that Chen's choice of focusing on Lijun's cross-dressing accentuates the heroine's incongruity and conflict with social orthodoxy in the Confucian society; additionally, Chen's refined narrative strategies and structure contribute to an unprecedented aesthetic achievement in the *tanci* genre (Hu, *Cainü* 6). Ying Zou, in her 2012 essay on this *tanci*, traces the cross-dressing tropes in the text and traditions of *tanci* fiction, and suggests that these tales of women disguised as men reflect the "limitations of feminine authority," citing Nancy Armstrong (Zou, "Cross-Dressing" 147). Zou further proposes that Chen's work, rather than representing a feminist tale in the modern sense, suggests that the author conceded to traditional moral values and that female "agency is represented . . . by participation in the constitution of norms" (148).

These readings of Chen's *tanci* offer nuanced and situated interpretations of Chen's work in the tradition of late imperial Chinese women's written narratives, and emphasize this *tanci*'s cultural specificities in representing feminine identities in contrast with modernist, feminist interpretations of cross-dressing and gender performance in the Western context. This chapter, in answering to and resuscitating research works on Chen's *tanci*, endeavors to expand studies of the work. Continuing current scholarly dialogues on Chen's *tanci*, this chapter further interrogates and renegotiates the modern/pre-modern theoretical paradigm underlying the critical positioning of women's *tanci* fiction. Whereas Chen's depiction of female cross-dressing indeed creates a different incentive than modern and contemporary feminist discourses on gender performance, Lijun's story projects imaginary transgressions of dominant gender roles for women in the orthodox Confucian society and plants seeds of women's individual empowerment. When contextualized in the tradition of historical and literary women's cross-dressing in pre-twentieth-century China, Lijun's tale epitomizes a legacy of female autonomy and power, and it bears social and historical relevance to today's audience beyond native Chinese communities. Rather than relying solely on a feminist critical stance in deciphering the texts, or entirely rejecting such a perspective, this study suggests that Chen's *tanci* inspires readers to formulate a new theoretical language for interpreting feminine identities as represented in non-Western, untranslated, and understudied women's narrative traditions. Continuing Hu Siao-chen's inquiry into the work as part of a burgeoning feminine narrative tradition in late imperial China, this study explores the narratological resonances between Chen's *tanci* and other dynastic storytelling genres, including women's poetry, fiction, and drama. This comparative narratological approach to Chen's *tanci* can be instrumental in revealing both the ethical and aesthetic values of Chen's tale, values that carry its cross-cultural resonance to audiences of women's literature in China and beyond.

According to Chen Yinke's study, Chen Duansheng's mother was born into a branch of the Wang family in Zhejiang province (15). The Wang family was prominently wealthy and also paid serious attention to literary studies. Chen's great-great-grandfather Wang Sen (汪森) built a family library and frequently welcomed literary scholars. Due to their distinguished literary achievements, the Wang family enjoyed fame and official titles (119). Coming from such a family, Chen's mother might have been well educated in literature. As *Zaishengyuan* reveals, Chen's mother divided poetry rhymes for her and her sister to practice writing. Similar evidence of motherly education in literature are available in Chen Changsheng's poetry collection *Huishengge ji*. The death of Chen's mother might also have been a reason why Chen stopped writing for a long time. Zhang Dejun points out that Chen's work became extremely popular in Zhejiang and the Southwest province, possibly due to the fact that her maternal grandfather Wang Shangyu (汪上堉) governed Yunnan province. During his governance Wang was diligent in his service to the local people and was commemorated in temples. Chen's father Chen Yudun (陳玉敦) and her cousin Wang Ruyang (汪如洋) were both appointed officials in Yunnan province in the late 1780s. It was also possible that Chen's *tanci* text was brought to Yunnan by Chen's maternal family to prolong the family influence in the province. This discovery about Chen's maternal family reveals the possible influence of family learning on Chen's literary career and further illustrates how women writers' maternal families could continue to play supportive roles for their literary endeavors and the dissemination of their writings.

This family background may have played a crucial supportive role in Chen Duansheng's ambitions as a writer. Although her solitary existence almost relegated her to obscurity, traces of her life are evident in autobiographical statements embedded in *Zaishengyuan*. Before her marriage, she finished the first seventeen *juan* (sections or volumes) of *Zaishengyuan*. Her marriage to a lower-level official, Fan Tan (范菼), had an important impact on her literary pursuits, as several years into the marriage Fan Tan was involved in a political scandal concerning the civil service examination and was banished to the frontier region of Xinjiang (新疆). The identity of Chen's husband has provoked controversy among scholars (see Li Kaixuan, *Jisu*). However, Chen's writings show that she was left alone to support two children and her parents-in-law and had little time to continue writing. Her husband's scandal also forced her to retreat from intellectual exchanges with other women. Her forced silence is dramatically juxtaposed with the imaginary autonomy of the gender-bending heroine of *Zaishengyuan.*

Although *Zaishengyuan* was one of the most influential and extensively reprinted *tanci* works, several previous pieces popularized the genre; one such *tanci* is the seventeenth-century *Yuchuanyuan* (Jade Bracelets), which provided the story from which Chen's *tanci* developed its own plot as a sequel. Though the authorship of *Yuchuanyuan* remains unknown, the chapters' introductory poems and the epigraph of the book suggest that the authors were a daughter and a mother, the daughter being the main author (Bao 87). *Yuchuanyuan* recounts the story of a young man, Xie Yuhui (謝玉輝), and his sister, Xie Yujuan (謝玉娟), who exchange identities. The male protagonist Xie cross-dresses as his sister in order to rescue his fiancée, whom the emperor has selected as a royal attendant. Correspondingly, his sister disguises herself as her brother to take the civil service examination, as a result of which she is selected as a top candidate and becomes an imperial official. Although the text portrays a striking subversion of male and female gender roles, it ends with the hero reverting to his real sexuality and marrying several women characters. Yujuan ultimately discloses her cross-dressing to the emperor and then marries a royal heir.

Chen's *Zaishengyuan* adopts this narrative frame, relating the tale of Meng Lijun, the cross-dressed reincarnation of Zheng Ruzhao (鄭如昭), who was Yujuan's sworn sister and also the second wife of Xie Yuhui in *Yuchuanyuan* (Jade Bracelets). The title, *Zaishengyuan* (Destiny of Rebirth), suggests this intertextual bond between the two *tanci* and that the characters are reincarnated to fulfill their destiny in the sequel. The two works, though, have fundamental differences. Jade Bracelets portrays a central character who disguises himself as his sister to save his fiancée from the inner palace. The work ends with the polygamous marriage of Yuhui to his fiancée and several other women. *Zaishengyuan* restructures the story around the cross-dressed heroine Lijun, who repeatedly denies her feminine identity to postpone the marriage event. Lijun's fiancé Shaohua plays the role of a constant "spouse," ironically reverting the Confucian code of women's chastity with a representation of male "widowhood."

Lijun is modeled on Yuhui's concubine Zheng Ruzhao in *Yuchuanyuan*. Zheng is wrongly accused of adultery by Cao Yanniang (曹燕娘), another of Xie's concubines. Indignant at her husband's unjust treatment of her, Ruzhao takes a vow of celibacy, abstaining from intimacy with Yuhui; she swears that if they are at all acquainted in their ensuing lives, she will never again become Xie's concubine. This unsettled relationship between Ruzhao and Yuhui serves as the backdrop for Lijun's romance with Shaohua, foreshadowing her refusal to become Shaohua's wife in a polygamous marriage. The author effectively transforms the discontented Ruzhao into the central character of Lijun, perhaps to compensate for Ruzhao's slighted feelings in the original story. As the tale unfolds, however, the cross-dressed Lijun acquires self-sufficiency as a "man," thanks to her exceptionally successful performance. When Lijun's ability to exercise social, political, and intellectual power surpasses Shaohua's, Lijun is no longer harnessed to a marriage with a predestined spouse.

Chen's adaptation may suggest an authorial desire to reinvest in and morally elevate several of the minor characters in Jade Bracelets, particularly the women—to see them pursue their unfulfilled desires through another round of worldly encounters. For example, Lijun's bosom sister and "wife" Su Yingxue is based on the humble and lowly born Chen Fangsu (陳芳素), one of Xie Yuhui's concubines in Jade Bracelets. In contrast to the less developed original character Chen, Su Yingxue is portrayed with liveliness and psychological depth, and she demonstrates a heroic spirit by performing a number of extraordinary deeds. In Destiny of Rebirth, Yingxue stands in for Lijun on the night of marriage and ventures to assassinate the bridegroom Liu Kuibi, who, defeated by Shaohua in his initial attempt to court Lijun, attempts to murder Shaohua and falsely accuses Shaohua's father of betraying the emperor while he was fighting against the invading Koreans. If Su Yingxue, as a surrogate of Lijun, represents the ideal of feminine chastity and self-sacrifice, her role is also transformed gradually after she is rescued from suicide by the Liang family, takes on the name of Liang Suhua, and marries the cross-dressed Lijun, who is now the prime minister. Meng Lijun and Liang Suhua's mock marriage, as their surnames imply, refers to the legendary couple Meng Guang (孟光) and Liang Hong (梁鴻) of Eastern Han (25–220 CE), illustrating a cross-dressed Meng Lijun playing the role of the ideal husband Liang Hong. The poet in exile Liang Hong and his wife Meng Guang were a couple in the first century. Everyday when Liang returned from the field, Meng Guang would prepare a meal for him and serve the bowl level to her eyebrows, to show her esteem for her husband. The expression "serving the bowl level to one's eyebrows" was then passed down as a synonym for an ideal couple who treat each other with respect (Liu Xiang, *Xu Leinü zhuan* 2: 8, 10a-b). The relationship between the protagonist and the other characters is suggestive of an extensive pattern of gender displacement and reversal.

Like Su Yingxue, another elevated minor character in Jade Bracelets is Liu Yanyu (劉燕玉), who rescues Shaohua from her brother Liu Kuibi's plan to murder him, and, admiring Shaohua's talent, is secretly betrothed to him. Liu Yanyu is, in the original story, Cao Yanniang, who is overwhelmed with jealousy of the other concubines and cannot ascend to heaven after her death. In Destiny of Rebirth, heaven grants Cao the opportunity to repent her wrongdoings by serving as Shaohua's wife and performing virtuous deeds. In contrast to her precursor, the invidious and slanderous Yanniang, Yanyu is depicted as a devoted daughter and a chaste and kindhearted wife. When the newly wedded Shaohua vows three years of celibacy in order to wait for Lijun's return, Yanyu accepts his decision with no complaint, devoting herself to her filial duties to Shaohua's parents. By reinvesting in these minor characters, and by transforming the mistreated Ruzhao into a cross-dresser of free will, Chen's *Zaishengyuan* remodels the power relations between the characters and overturns the subjectivities of the shrew and the virtuous, the powerless and the powerful, the female and the male.

Shifting the historical background from the Song dynasty in Jade Bracelets to the Yuan period, Chen's *tanci* includes an extended depiction of the formerly marginalized women characters and transforms the male protagonist. The male cross-dresser in Jade Bracelets, Xie Yuhui, is reborn as Shaohua, with a twin sister, Zhanghua. Readers of the original tale may suppose that Chen has split Xie into two characters, with Zhanghua as the female "other" of Shaohua. Whereas Shaohua is an idealized, gallant hero, Zhanghua represents the heroic and potentially transgressive aspects of Xie. Outstanding in both literary talent and military skills, she assists her father in official duties and takes a soldier's role in the battlefield. The narrator applauds her exceptional aptitudes: "Riding a horse herself she thrusts forward into a thousand enemies, with two steel blades she can fight against ten thousand soldiers. In tranquility she takes the needle and does embroidery in the perfumed chamber, in leisure time she takes a ride on the grassland." When the Huangfu family is falsely accused of betraying the emperor by the perfidious Liu Kuibi, the elder sister Zhanghua protects their mother from the family peril and flees into the wilderness. She befriends the cross-dressed Madame Wei Yong'e, who governs a group of male rebels in a mountainous area. Together the two openly claim disobedience against the emperor. Zhanghua even organizes a woman's troop called "孝女兵" ("Xiaonü bing," The Army of Devoted Daughters), claiming that her militarism is justified by the rescue of her parents (477-81). When Liu Kuibi (劉奎壁) leads a royal army to suppress the "rebels" led by the two women, Zhanghua, who masters Daoist alchemy, defeats Liu's army with her magical powers and captures Liu alive. In comparison to the effeminate Shaohua, Zhanghua is notably superior in knowledge and military intelligence, showing a heroic spirit through her open and sometimes radical challenges against tyranny. Zhanghua's transgressive character is largely justified by her devotion to her parents. When the emperor finds out the Liu family's plot against the Huangfus and redeems the honor and official title of the Huangfu family, she leads the rebels and surrenders to the emperor, and becomes the emperor's concubine. The author foreshadows Zhanghua's fate, saying, "A daughter like this from a general's family is truly unrivaled; she surely deserves the fortune of marrying into the royal family."

The intertextuality of *tanci* creates a symbiotic relationship between stories. The alignment of *tanci* texts with prior texts also reflects the oral traditions in which *tanci* originated, for every story follows a previous story and anticipates its continuation in a subsequent narration. It is through this process that *tanci* has developed its own durability as a narrative tradition. Destiny of Rebirth preserves the traditional oral storyteller's technique of opening and closing a tale with poems. The first chapter of each volume begins with an introductory poem, which is followed by the main story, written mostly in seven-character rhymed lines, with intermittent vernacular prose passages.

In these introductory poems, the author recurrently alludes to her writing brush as the "brush of vivid colors," a reference to literary and artistic talent. This allusion is frequently evoked by literati poets to foreground their talent and depict moments of lofty thought and poetic rapture. The "brush of vivid colors" alludes to the male poet Jiang Yan (江淹, 450 CE-589 CE). In his youth, Jiang dreamed that he was given a magic brush with five colors, with which he wrote many splendid poems (Li Yanshou 1: 209). Chen Duansheng's use of the image asserts that she is endowed with a talent equal to that of literati poets, as in this chapter opening:

> In tranquility I sit by the studio window, contemplating the past,
> At times I collect scattered thoughts to compose new lines.
> The brush of vivid colors makes thick ink strokes,
> Enlivening delicate insights, eliciting astute ideas.
> The subject of the book is filial devotion and loyalty,
> My humble self composed the comments in the opening poems.
> Since my devoted audience hopes to hear more after
> reading the previous work,
> I shall write this work as a sequel and enjoy it with them. (1: 1, 2)

In another chapter opening she writes, "Without reserve I consecrate my spirit to the brush, / and infuse my passion and thoughts entirely into the book. / . . . May the three-inch pointed brush in my hand / Bring into being / Countless events in Destiny of Rebirth" (14: 53, 531). The brush metaphor also reflects the visual quality of Chen's writing, as brushes were used for both painting and writing. How do *tanci* facilitate a specific form of imagination and desire—for the author, the characters, and the women readers? What does the narrative lens of *tanci* reveal about late imperial women's conception of selfhood? These questions invite a reading of Destiny of Rebirth beyond that of *tanci*, and draw attention to the "cultural and social function" of women's writing as "a technology of self-inscription and communication" which is well-displayed in other literary genres of this period, such as Qing women's poetry (Fong, *Herself an Author* 144). In Chen's *tanci*, authorial insertions set the stage by communicating the author's emotion, locale, and time of writing, and contribute to the pluralistic presences of the author, her upheavals of thoughts, and her passionate longings (Berg, "Female Self-Fashioning" 238-89). The author's narrative self-portrait endows her presence with a certain independence and autonomy, declaring her transcendent perspective in a timeless historical background. It is through this narrative frame that the author portrays the evolvement of Lijun from a genteel elite woman to a heroic protagonist who performs as man's social and political equal with great success.

The scene in which Lijun paints a self-portrait, which may be compared with similar examples of women making and viewing portraits in late imperial China, provides useful material for considering the relation between portraits of women and their gendered spectatorship as well as the ironical relationship between women and their painted images. The trope of women painting self-portraits is recurrent in theatrical and novelistic narratives of the late imperial period, and is particularly associated with the theme of women's artistic agency. In this scene, before leaving home to escape the arranged marriage with Liu Kuibi, Lijun leaves her parents a portrait by copying an image of herself as seen in her mirror:

> Lijun stands up, facing the mirror,
> And rearranges her make-up and embroidered dress.
> Gazing at the mirror, she lets out a sigh at times,
> Thinking to herself that she has to change her girl's appearance soon.
> No longer will she sit by this window and put flower pins in her hair,
>   beneath the tree, on a spring morning.
> No longer will she sit near this warm stove,
>   and put on the sweetly perfumed clothes.
> From now on, she will travel in wind and rain and stop at roadside inns.
> From now on, she will be a lonesome one riding across mountainous regions.
> "I am a fledgling swallow that loses its nest and is chased by arrows.
> I am a damaged flower petal fallen from the tree and drifting in the wilderness.
> Once I change my appearance and leave home,
> When will come the day of my return?"
> This refined girl looks into the mirror, with sorrows surging in her heart;
> She strives to bestir herself, though her sleeves are wet with tears. . . . (3: 10, 280)
>
> [Lijun looks into the mirror and compares her reflection with the portrait.]
> Cloud-like hair rolled up in a fine coil,
> A golden hairpin parting the hair at one side of her forehead.
> Face fresh as a lotus flower bathed in jade-like dew droplets,
> Eyebrows two willow leaves carrying spring mist.
> Adorned with plum flower petals, her brow is all the more lovely.
> Rarely do words depart from her cherry-like mouth.
> Almond-shaped eyes, gazing attentively, reflect the limpid light of
>   autumn waters.
> Snowy complexion is nicely set off with crimson blushes.
> Bright pink skirts hide her gentle footsteps;
> A dark cape hugs her pale blue shirt.
> Dark sleeves softly conceal her fair wrists;
> The skirt sways slightly to reveal a lotus foot.
> Her elegant manner outshines many,
> Truly incomparable among those of her generation.

Lijun examines the portrait,
And cannot but sigh for her misfortune.
"Many times I have seen beautiful women.
None of them can rival this painted image.
Can it be that my appearance is not as stunning as the painting?
Is it much lovelier than my real person?
If the image truly resembles myself,
I shall take the lead among women and rise to the top of the world."
Turning to her maid Ronglan, she asks if the image resembles her,
Or is the image even more attractive?
The maid leaps in joy
And says, "This painting is a triumph,
For the eyes, the eyebrows and even the attitude are all identical,
Not to mention the stature, as slender as my mistress's.
If you really want to compare the image and the person,
My mistress is certainly more spirited."
The talented girl, upon these words, is finally convinced,
And then spreads out the painting on the desk to ponder it again. (3: 10, 280)

At this moment, the portrait functions as an extended screen through which the woman interacts with her projected image, as well as the very surface that activates and meets the gaze of the viewer/reader. Lijun's gaze at the mirror is a secondary process of identification, a process through which the subject is anxiously in search of a self-image. This search is not gratified, for the image mirrors the subject's discordance with reality. The portrait is modeled on her feminine appearance, which is about to be changed. The poised woman's body is inadvertently caught in a moment of anticipation and indeterminacy. "The lotus foot" refers to Lijun's bound feet, a fetishized sexual symbol of women in the late imperial period. Rearranging her make-up and embroidered dress, Lijun is hesitant to accept the drastic change into men's clothing, comparing herself to "a fledgling swallow that loses its nest," "a damaged flower petal . . . drifting in wilderness." Her gaze into the mirror brings sorrow and a fear of loss.

Accompanying the woman's gaze at her own image in the mirror is a reflection of the subject's split sense of self. Her tears reflect her anxiety and fear at the threshold of the unbearable outside world. Lijun's gaze into the mirror corresponds to a transitional moment between the imaginary and symbolic registers of her subjectivity. She is both the active agent looking at herself, and the elusive image which is being looked at. In this narcissistic moment, the subject is entranced with the captivating image of the self. Lijun is caught up in the discrepancy between her own internal desire or longing to stay in the "perfumed chambers" and the necessity to confront a world of vicissitudes and danger on her own.

To make a self-portrait, the artist needs to fix his or her own image in a certain symmetry and bridge the difference between the body felt from within and the image perceived in the painting. Lijun's self-recognition takes place when the maid assures Lijun about the evident resemblance between herself and the painting. Lijun's girl's hairdo and dress in the portrait betray her resistance to the parents' arrangements for her marriage, even though the painting was made to demonstrate her devotion to her parents. The notion of women's filial devotion carries multifaceted meanings in the late imperial period. Hu Ying, regarding married daughters' filial devotion at the turn of the twentieth century, notes that the language and sentiments of such devotion facilitated a substantial expansion of women's rights. Hu considers filial devotion a gendered category and argues that it plays an important role in expanding what a literati daughter can claim as an intellectual inheritance, in providing legal documents for a daughter's right to legal inheritance, and in offering a conduit for women's participation in political changes (Hu Ying, "How Can a Daughter" 234-69). The protagonist exploits the irony implicit in her self-exhibition: she is at once the artist and the object of the artist's gaze. Employing the mirror as a tool of a reversed gaze, Lijun shifts her "gaze" from the "window" to the "flower pins in her hair," from the "warm stove" to her "sweetly perfumed clothes." This reversed look sets the visual structure in motion, by now positioning Lijun with the readers, allowing both parties a refracted look at the inner chamber. The text thus invites the readers to become active participants by "seeing" Lijun through reading.

The image of the protagonist is remarkably dramatized in the visual narrative underlying the text. Lijun is an active agent of looking, whereas the authorial position is that of a detached and disembodied eye with the vantage necessary to see the subject as she is. Compelled to achieve a likeness between the image and the person, Lijun relies on the portrait to mimetically represent herself with accuracy. Yet for the woman artist, the mirror/portrait trope here is not a symbol of desired objectivity, but a medium for self-representation and endorsement.

On top of all this, and markedly in control of what the readers see, Lijun also shows her literary talent by composing a poem on the portrait itself.

> What's the use of sighing in regret, when a grave calamity
>   befalls a person?
> How can I allow my purity to be eroded, like a flawed jade?
> No longer will I cling to my parents for shelter from upheaval;
> To preserve my chastity I shall exile myself to terrains remote.
> A paper kite with a broken string, I will float away with no destination.
> With a handbag of gold jewelry, I can travel to places distant.
> Today I leave this painted image of myself, hanging it up on the wall,
> For I would change this feminine coif into an official's coif. (3: 10, 100-01)

The poem, and the painting of which it is a part, travel through the story. First, Lijun flees from home, leaving her self-portrait and the poem for her parents. Then Lijun's fiancé Huangfu Shaohua, who thinks Lijun has already passed away, asks for the portrait from Lijun's parents and discovers Lijun's secret cross-dressing by reading the poem. In late Ming and early Qing visual culture, poems composed on paintings reflected "a dialogic relation" between the painted image and the observer who composed the poem on the painting (Mao, "Gu Taiqing" 56). While poems composed about paintings can be used by the viewers to reconstruct details of paintings that have been lost (Mao, "Yige qingdai" 56), poems inscribed on the paintings likely served to enrich the viewers' experience of interacting with the painted image. In Lijun's case, her portrait draws attention to her status as a talented woman of artistic and literary accomplishment. The poem on the portrait is an exemplar of a mirror-text, which foreshadows the progression of the plot and adds tension to the narrative.

In portraits, the woman's body becomes marked, valued, and preserved in the form of brush strokes. Judith Zeitlin notes that the so-called 美人圖 (*meiren tu*) or beautiful woman portrait in the late Ming drama of the sixteenth century is affiliated with the body, in that the painting is also a material object, a hanging scroll (Zeitlin, *Historian of the Strange* 138; also see Li, Xiaorong, "The 'One Hundred Beauties' Genre" 617-53). Destiny of Rebirth invites an investigation of the theme of "portrait narratives," foregrounding the visual trope of Lijun's self-portrait as a lens for considering issues of identity and subject formation. The heroine's speculating gaze at her self-portrait reveals the gulf between visual mimicry and the character's subjectivity (on mimicry and self-representation in response to the gaze, see Silverman 201). Despite her expectation of making an image that truly resembles her person, Lijun is frustrated in her first attempt to paint the self-portrait:

> Her heart full of pain,
> Lijun wonders how to depict her *real image*.
> "If the painting does not resemble the person,
> I should not bother to take up the brush.
> Alas, Meng Lijun, Meng Lijun!
> You are so beautiful;
> Why do you have to suffer so much misfortune!
> If the painting cannot be made satisfactorily,
> Doesn't this predict an ominous future for my trip?
> If the trip cannot realize my wishes,
> I would rather
> Hang myself on the day of the wedding!" (3: 10, 99)

The 真容 (*zhenrong*), or real image, is used in late imperial literature to refer to a portrait of a person. Interestingly, the term carries a great deal of irony itself, for the assertion of women is always in the absence of real women. Compelled to achieve a likeness between the image and the person, Lijun relies on the portrait to mimetically represent herself. Also, for the woman artist, the mirror/portrait trope here is a potent medium for self-representation and endorsement. One may surmise that for genteel women authors, the self-portrait exposes their desire to acquire an extended life after death: the painted image is complementary to their written words, for their disadvantaged literary status does not allow them the possibility of being remembered by their writings.

In contrast to the male literati's voyeuristic appreciation of feminine beauty in imperial China, women had a tradition of painting their own portraits and making statements about their ideals through these painted images. Some women also composed poems for their friends' paintings. Men and women's different gendered points of view have led to contested interpretations of the woman's image in literary writings (for men's scopophilic pleasure in fashioning women's voices in literati poetry, see Robertson, "Voicing the Feminine" 69-72; for a discussion of the male gaze in 詞 (*ci*, lyric poetry), see Fong, "Engendering the Lyric" 107-44). A portrait scenario that exemplifies the troublesome relationship between portraits and women's self-representation is associated with the famous and possibly fictitious courtesan poet Feng Xiaoqing (馮小青, 1595-1612), who insisted on having a "real image" of herself painted before she died of tuberculosis at seventeen (Xu Zhen 1: 1-36). In her leisure time, Xiaoqing enjoyed gazing at her reflection in the lake, often becoming engrossed in an imaginary dialogue with herself. In one of her well-known poems, "怨" ("Yuan," "Regret"), she writes: "With fresh make-up I rival the beauties in the portraits, / Knowing not how I would rank among them. / By the autumn lake I gaze at the reflection of my emaciated body, / You shall take pity on me as I on you take pity" (1: 23).

Recalling Lijun's own narcissistic gaze, the poem stages an intriguing conversation between the poet and her reflection, to which Xiaoqing appeals for pity and understanding. Xiaoqing's self-reflexive gaze reveals her subjectivity as constructed through a series of images, which are transmitted from the portraits to the audience and back again. The last line of Xiaoqing's poem expands the visual structure by establishing an emotive bond between the text and the audience, from whom the poet invites a compassionate response. However, this emotive connection between the painted woman and the viewer is resolutely demarcated by the gendered positions of the audience. Extensively recycled by literati scholars, Xiaoqing's pathetic image may be only a construction of the male intellectuals of the time and of later generations, reflecting a male-oriented connoisseurship of feminine pathos and passive beauty. Ellen Widmer suggests that Xiaoqing's life "may be said to be a life waiting for legend to discover, or else the representation of a life that legend provided for people who needed to believe in her" ("Xiaoqing's Literary Legacy" 113). The image of the ailing Xiaoqing, beautiful as it is, lacks gendered agency and power. The "Xiaoqing lore" illustrates the complex and polemical relationship between the literate woman and her readers, whose points of view are profoundly conditioned by their own gendered positions (Ko, *Teachers* 93).

The fascinating scene of Lijun painting the self-portrait also recalls a similar scenario in the popular Ming dynasty drama 牡丹亭 (*Mudanting*, *The Peony Pavilion*; 1598), which serves as an important subtext for Chen's *tanci*. The protagonist Du Liniang (杜麗娘), the daughter of a high official, takes a walk in a spring garden. She falls asleep, and in a dream she encounters a young scholar named Liu Mengmei (柳夢梅). Afterward she dies of love-sickness, leaving a self-portrait in the garden where they first "met." Later Mengmei finds Liniang's portrait in the garden. Liniang's ghost visits Mengmei and comes back to life three years later with Mengmei's assistance, and marries him. This play has enjoyed enormous popularity among both male and female readers since the sixteenth century. For example, Wei Hua offers an analysis of an early Qing commentarial edition of Tang's play *Caizi Mudanting* (The Genius Peony Pavilion, first printed during the Yongzheng reign; 1723-1735) (see Hua, Wei, "On Feminine Consciousness"). The critic of the play, according to the preface of the text, is a female author called A Bang. This commentarial edition of *Mudanting* is exceptional because of "its encyclopedic content, its erotic commentary, and its selection by the female author of a female readership as the commentarial audience" (Hua, "How Dangerous" 741).

The popularity of Tang's play among women can be attributed to its illustration of "a young woman's love against the Neo-Confucian view of reason and of moral orthodoxy" (Hua, Wei, "How Dangerous" 749), When the love-sick Liniang finds the splendor of her looks fading due to illness, she hastens to make a self-portrait to preserve on paper her beauty at its zenith. Scrutinizing her own reflection in the mirror, she replicates that image in her self-portrait and urges her maid to compare her with it. This well-known episode in the play is seamlessly adapted into the scene of Lijun making her self-portrait in Chen's *tanci*. The theme of death and resurrection in *The Peony Pavilion* is also built into Destiny of Rebirth, explicitly resonating with the title, for instance. Similar motifs of karmic death and incarnation can also be found the seventeenth-century play 鴛鴦夢 (*Yuanyangmeng*, Dream of the Mandarin Ducks), by a woman playwright Ye Xiaowan (1613-1657). The play takes the form of a northern-style drama and is the only surviving text of a play written by a woman during the Ming period. Ye Xiaowan was the daughter of Ye Shaoyuan, who edited and published *Wumengtang ji* (Dream of the Meridian Hall), a collection of family women's poems and essays, containing writings by Ye's wife and daughters, as well as stories by genteel women authors who were related to the Ye family. Lijun's pathos at the sight of her portrait thus also reflects the woman's encounter with a life-and-death situation: her old home lost, her future abode undetermined. The rebirth or resurrection of Lijun's self, as a man, is inexorably connected to the viewing and transmission of her self-portrait, a surrogate for her person.

The ironic split between Lijun's self-portrait and her cross-dressed body is also associated with the coalescence and conflict of *The Peony Pavilion* and Destiny of Rebirth on the narrative level. As Wei Hua argues, *The Peony Pavilion* shows that "what cannot exist by virtue of reason or principle (*li*) can exist because of passion (*qing*)" (Hua, Wei, "How Dangerous" 749). The play is a vintage "woman-oriented" tale, with its narrative focus on the protagonist's discovery of love in a dream and her extraordinary experience crossing the boundary of life and death in search of love. Destiny of Rebirth sets the locus of the narrative on the protagonist's desire, while at once exposing a deviation, a kind of nonclosure, toward the end of the story. Unlike the resurrected Liniang, who is joyously reunited with Mengmei, the cross-dressed Lijun does not desire a consummated marriage, nor can she relinquish her prosperous official position for the role of a devoted wife and daughter possessed of filial piety. This disparity between the two texts reflects Chen's symptomatic anxiety concerning a woman's proper place in family and society (Zou, Ying, "Responding to *The Peony Pavilion*" 176-84). The author reconfigures the traditional theme of a woman in a painting coming to life in response to male desire, by rendering the cross-dresser Lijun an equivalent of a ghost, who leaves her body and "freely pursues its private, illicit desires" (Zeitlin, "Embodying the Disembodied"). Also, the classic episode of Liniang dreaming of her lover Mengmei in *The Peony Pavilion* was adopted in the depiction of a minor character Liang Suhua, who, originally named Su Yingxue, was Lijun's bosom sister and later becomes her "wife" in a mock marriage. At the beginning, Lijun's parents hold an archery contest for the many young men who hope to marry her. Huafu Shaohua ranks first among all the candidates. Su Yingxue, who was then a maid at Lijun's house, manages to get a glimpse of Shaohua by peeping through the curtains. That night Xingxue dreams of a romantic rendezvous with Shaohua (1: 3, 164). In her dream, Yingxue and Shaohua make a private marriage arrangement. The author draws a comparison between Yingxue and Liniang: "Apparently today's Su Yingxue bears a resemblance to the legendary Du Liniang" (1: 3, 164). This reference to *The Peony Pavilion* as a subtext foreshadows the possibility of Xingxue and Lijun both marrying Shaohua. However, Du Liniang's story is not completely transplanted in Destiny of Rebirth. The closure of a happy marriage in *The Peony Pavilion* is only projected as one of the possible choices for the cross-dressed Lijun, who later becomes reluctant to live her life as a woman again. The presence of Lijun invites spectators to gauge an aesthetic image of the woman from the portrait, and simultaneously unveils the dubious and constructed nature of the portrait itself.

When Lijun cross-dresses and flees from her home to escape an imposed marriage, her decision to dress as a man is made under the influence of two fictional characters, Liu Qingyun (柳卿雲) and Xie Xiang'e (謝湘娥), who impersonate men to escape from family crises and attain a grand fortune and long-lasting fame. Liu Qingyun and Xie Xiang'e were both women characters who cross-dressed and earned eminence after becoming top graduates in the civil service exam. Lijun ponders: "If I cross-dress and flee home, / I may follow the examples of Xie Xiang'e and Liu Qingyun. / If I become the Top Candidate in the Exam and meet the Emperor, / It will indeed display the outstanding talent of women in the inner chambers . . . / If I don't commit myself to this goal and become a heroic woman, / What's the use of having all these talents?" (3: 10, 274) (various versions of the Liu and Xie story appear in 小金錢 [*Xiaojinqian*, Little Gold Coins]; see also Tan and Tan, *Tanci xulu* 132-34).

After Lijun changes into the attire of a male scholar, she examines her new look in the mirror. This intriguing scene shows Lijun's self-reflective gaze directed to an image of herself disguised as a man, a visual act almost antithetical to the gaze toward her girl's appearance in the previous scene in which she ponders her self-portrait. When Lijun paints a self-portrait of herself as a girl before she flees home, the text depicts her painting and pondering her figure in front of the mirror and the portrait, which can be considered in two ways. It first recalls the scenario of the beauty portrait in late imperial literature, which is reflective of male intellectuals' connoisseurship of idealized women. In Chen's text, Lijun's examination of her self-portrait is antithetical to and sets off the later scene of her gazing at her disguised look after cross-dressing, foreshadowing the rebirth of Lijun's identity as a man's equal. The text stages an intense visual drama in which the woman's disguised body becomes emblematic of a gender trans/formation process. This process reflects the "deconstructive nature of the transvestite performance," which is "always undoing itself as part of its process of self-enactment" (Garber 149). In this self-confessing scene, the text displays a transition from a third-person narrator to a distinctive first-person voice. Lijun's feminine voice gradually dissolves in the following lines when she finishes her "transformation" and begins to imitate a man's manners. The text deftly returns to a third-person narrative voice, listing the details of "his" appearance, with minimum use of gendered pronouns.

> Afraid to be seen by someone else,
> Lijun lets down the curtain and sits by the back window.
> In the candlelight she hastens to open the mirror,
> And gently combs the hair into a man's coiffure.
> Then she removes the red candle and opens the golden trunk,
> Takes out a bundle of clothes and puts them on the bed.
> She ties on the headscarf and the sash,
> Binds her feet with thin white silk satin, and puts on boots.
> Fully dressed in an instant,
> She holds the mirror in hand to examine herself closely.
> Where are the cloud-like chignon and the beautiful feminine face?
> There is now only an admirably handsome young man.
> A hat embellished with jade and decked with soft wings, and a scholar's scarf;
> A white gauze robe and a small bag to hold poetry drafts.
> A pair of white ribbons set off refined looks;
> In those bachelor's boots, imitating the gait of a man.
> Complexion like a peach blossom, fair and rosy;
> Eyebrows shapely as willow leaves, long and dark.
> A straight sculptured nose and cherry-like mouth;
> Blush on the cheeks like rosy clouds, diffusing fragrance,
> Demeanor outstanding and absolutely unrivaled;
> A handsome appearance truly extraordinary.
> A gentle and graceful young lad,
> A man with porcelain skin and poetic sensibility.
> Such looks may overwhelm beautiful maidens,
> And break the hearts of goddesses.
> Lijun, after seeing this male look,
> Cannot help but admire the image. (3: 10, 287)

Lijun's scrutinizing gaze at herself as a "man" in the mirror reveals the creative involvement of the body in how the readers see what they see. Her cross-dressing passes as convincing, for her handsome appearance is completed with "unrivalled manners" and "poetic sensibility." By putting on the "scholarly scarf and the elegant robe," Lijun transforms herself into a "man" of refined manners. Gazing at her male look in the mirror, Lijun compares herself to other distinguished women cross-dressers. In the Lacanian mirror stage, what is seen is crucially constitutive of the subject's self-identification (Lacan, "The Mirror Stage" 1). The cross-dresser is not merely a spectator or a static participant, but displays a bodily responsiveness accompanying a womanly gaze into the mirror. Mimicking the walk and demeanor of a man, Lijun demonstrates an uncertain sexual identity and transforms her ambivalent self into a source of desire and anxiety for male and female audiences alike. Despite the physical appeal, her image is overridden with anxiety which comes mostly from her parents and her betrothed, who want her back, fitting into their domestic paradigm. Even Lijun herself is surprised by her flawless "male scholar" look.

> Ah, how curious!
> How is it that as soon as I change into the male outfit,
> I look completely different from my usual self.
> With this scholarly scarf and elegant robe I look even more genteel.
> Who upon seeing me could doubt that I resemble an immortal?
> Even the legendary cross-dressing ladies Liu Qingyun and Xie Xiang'e
> Might not have been as handsome as I.
> They were truly exceptional women;
> Both became immortals and lived in paradise.
> Liu Qingyun married a Miss Xiao, west of the Yangzi River,
> and had a happy family.
> She became a Top Candidate in the Civil Service Exam
> and earned eminence in her career;
> A marriage with several wives seemed only a game for her.
> Liu Qingyun and her "wives" are all remarried
> with Liu's husband Wang Jingxing.
> Liu's remarkable adventure was told from generation to generation.
> Another lady, Xie Xiang'e, disguised as her own brother,
> became a Top Candidate in the Exam
> And married a prime minister's daughter, Wang Shuxian.
> Since they were both women, in their marriage,
> They had true respect and sympathy for each other.
> When the truth was revealed, Wang Shuxian was
> remarried to Xiang'e's own brother.
> Xie and Liu were truly exceptional among all women.
> I myself am endowed with talent.
> If I am successful in future,
> I should follow the example of these ancient precursors.
> If I am married to a woman,
> I certainly have the most skill in drawing eyebrows for my wife.
> Ah, my dear Huangfu!
> If I follow the example of Liu Qingyun,
> Could you be Liu's husband Wang Jingxing? (3: 10, 287)

The expression "drawing eyebrows for my wife" is an allusion to a Han official, Zhang Chang (張敞, first century BC), who loved his wife very much and did eyebrow make-up for her every morning before leaving for work. The emperor heard of this anecdote and praised them as a couple who truly loved each other. Facing the mirror, Lijun orchestrates her own objectification and simultaneously seeks self-empowerment in spectating and speculating. The image of the protagonist is dramatized in the visual narrative underlying the text. The moment witnesses a fusion of viewing positions for Lijun, the narrator, and the targeted textual audience. Lijun's reflexive gaze on her "male" look in the mirror suggests her will to escape the boundaries of women in society. Embarking on an adventurous journey, Lijun is elated in spirit. "Letting out a breath and raising her chin, she takes on manly manners. / Her behavior is no longer feminine at all" (3: 10, 289). Following her precursors, Lijun performs a subjectivity that lies at the borders of life and legend, truth and fabrication.

Lijun's cross-dressing performance can further be considered with intertextual readings of historical and literary examples of cross-dressed women in late imperial China. These women, by taking on a masculine identity, consciously resisted the normalized understanding of gender and sexuality in the patriarchal society. I will discuss three prominent examples of women's cross-dressing, literary characters Huang Chonggu, Xie Xucai (謝絮才), and playwright Wu Zao (吳藻). After Lijun is appointed prime minister, local officials from a southern county send an opera troupe called 百花班 (*baihuaban*, Hundred-Flower Troupe) which consists of all women performers, hoping to please the minister with the beautiful opera singers. Lijun chooses a play staging the story of a woman who dresses as a man and becomes the top candidate in the civil service examination. The play alludes to a sixteenth-century popular play 女狀元 (*Nüzhuangyuan*, The Female Top Candidate) in which the cross-dressed character Huang Chonggu claims, "Who is responsible for good deeds in this world? It's not men; it's the women!" (Xu Wei, *Ci Mulan* 1766: 224-39). In the original story of the historical figure Huang Chonggu, Huang cross-dressed from childhood and impressed the minister with her talent in writing poetry. When the minister proposes to marry Huang to his daughter, Huang writes a poem to decline the marriage and confess her true sex, "If my lord wishes to have me as a son-in-law, I wish heaven could change me into a man instantly" (Peng Dingqiu 799: 8995). The allusion to this play in Destiny of Rebirth contributes to an intense scene in which Lijun watches a cross-dressed performer on stage. Lijun, together with the fictional audience, are all involved in the same sympathetic mood: "The scene pleases the viewers' minds with its subtlety; its implications are naturally and spontaneously accessible" (10: 43, 688). This play within a play demonstrates a sympathetic moment when Lijun and the woman performer face each other as actor and spectator. However, it ironically complicates Lijun's role as the spectator and subverted actor off the stage, revealing an engaged dialectic between life and theater, fact and representation, and the unstable, ever-changing space between these assumed polar opposites.

The above scene together with many other instances of theatrical performance in the text suggests the influence of a dramatic tradition dating to the Song (960-1279) and Yuan (1279-1368) dynasties. The intertextual references between *tanci* and theatrical works about women cross-dressers conditioned both the production and the reception of the text among the author's envisaged audience. In late imperial drama, cross-dressers' self-positioning necessarily remained indeterminate, conditioned by their unviable sociocultural status in the context of patriarchy (Hua, Wei, *Mingqing xiqu*). Lijun's story recalls a play 喬影 (*Qiaoying,* The Image in Disguise) by the woman poet and playwright Wu Zao (吳藻, 1799-1862). The play consists of a set of song suites in which the protagonist Xie Xucai (謝絮才) cross-dresses and paints a miniature of herself in official's robes. She describes herself as latter-day literati poet Qu Yuan (屈原, fourth to third century BCE), a loyal minister in the state of Chu, who, slandered, rejected, and exiled, wrote allegorical poems expressing his grievances. Xie expresses her frustration that the conflict between herself and her times prevents her from fully employing her talents. "Alas! Fettered by my physical form, I can only sigh all alone over my sadness. If one considers the matter carefully though, while miraculous transformations depend on Heaven, the initiative rests with oneself. That is why a few days ago I painted a small portrait of myself dressed in male attire" (Wu Zao 132). The protagonist's self-portrait, rather than being conceptualized as an aesthetic representation, is figured to be a shadow, lacking substance, as the title of the play illustrates. This scene of the cross-dressed Xie Xucai painting a portrait of herself as a man is another example that shows the appropriation and transformation of the beauty portrait convention. Xie, who herself is the painter, reinscribes her image as a man. (There are several translations of this play. One version is "Drinking Wine and Reading 'Encountering Sorrow': A Reflection in Disguise by Wu Zao (1799-1862)" by Sophie Volpp, in Mann and Cheng, *Under Confucian Eyes* 239-52; see also Idema and Grant, *Red Brush* 687-93). The play emphatically displays the complexity of transvestite identity, which appears multiplied and deceptive in cross-dressing performance.

Lijun's acts, as critics observe, are given justification by her apparent advocacy of filial piety and chastity, in order to protect her work from censorship and moralistic criticism from mainstream society (see Guo Moruo's comments in *Zaishengyuan* 14: 54, 546). However, despite this apparent authorial precaution, the progressive initiative in Destiny of Rebirth incurred disparagement from critics, with complaints about "demolishing cardinal human relationships" or "rebelling against primary principles." Lijun, as a "man," challenges the Confucian ethical principles in her relationship with the "ruler, father, and husband," which leads to the author's dilemma in closing the story. When Lijun's real identity is disclosed, the emperor presses her to revert to her feminine appearance and to become his concubine. Lijun claims that she "would rather take the punishment of death than follow this order" (*Zaishengyuan* 17: 68, 704). Chen's work breaks off at this point, showing Lijun, who has come down with a sudden illness after her identity is exposed, vomiting blood in front of the emperor. The text seems to suggest that death would be a better choice for the cross-dressed Lijun than reversion to a woman's identity. Hu Siao-chen has offered an intriguing analysis of war, violence, and blood in the voluminous *tanci* work *Liuhuameng* (Dream of the Pomegranate Flower, 1841), in which the metaphor of blood speaks of women's passion, anguish, or sisterly love (Hu, Siao-chen, "War" 249-83).

Lijun's unconventional actions are first demonstrated in her relationship with her fiancé Huangfu Shaohua. The author replaces the relationship between the couple with a hierarchical relation between teacher and student, with Lijun becoming Shaohua's mentor in his career. As an introductory poem to a chapter goes:

> With outstanding talent she rises from the inner chamber,
> Taking off her make-up, she passes as a fine scholar.
> A top candidate in the Imperial Exam,

> A dutiful and loyal Prime Minister in the palace.
> Fame and majesty widely admired by the world,
> Wisdom and ingenuity unrivalled among many.
> A beautiful countenance bewilders disciples like Shaohua,
> Who is uncertain whether the Minister is a woman or a man. (13: 49, 490)

The first two lines draw attention to the interchangeability of gender roles in the late imperial period. Like cross-dressing, applying and taking off make-up is already a gendered performance. Interestingly, before she transforms her appearance into that of a man, the protagonist plays up her identity as a woman by applying make-up. Taking off the make-up is an ironic process of "revealing" the feminine body beneath, which may appear indistinguishable from that of a refined young man. Beneath the robe, the cross-dresser's body presents the mobility of "his" gender identities. Lijun's body is in this way a dynamic text, captivating yet indecipherable to Shaohua, who cannot confirm that the minister is his lost fiancé. This opening poem reflects the author's vigorous struggle with socially prescribed gender categories and her efforts to innovate, to create new positions for women of the time.

Lijun's extraordinary character and achievement explain her rejection of marriage with Shaohua. The opening poem of *juan* 15 serves as another moment that foreshadows Lijun's ultimate unwillingness to revert to the role of the good wife.

> Heaven has it that a person with unique talent
>   will come from the embroidered chambers,
> Young and genteel as she is, she is appointed
>   the Prime Minister of the country.
> Without the least intention to be locked with her fiancé in marriage,
> She cross-dresses to express a desire to achieve, in whatever small way.
> She would never sacrifice her chastity to acquire fortune,
> Relying on her sagacity she stays away from
>   common people's suspicions.
> When her true identity is revealed in the future,
> The phoenix will ascend, hearing the melody of the *xiao*. (15: 57, 577)

The last line might suggest Lijun's reconciliation with Shaohua, and that both might become immortals in the end. The poem starts as a biography of the protagonist, who is destined to rise from the inner chambers and become the country's prime minister. The author's claim of Lijun's chastity, as the beginning of this section suggests, reflects the authorial concern for legitimizing her writing in the dominant patriarchal culture and may serve as a "cover" for the potentially subversive content in the text. A famous example is 肉蒲團 (*Rouputuan, The Carnal Prayer Mat*), an erotic novel written by Li Yü (李漁, 1610-1680). Although the sexual descriptions in the novel are extremely graphic, in the preface the author adopts a didactic tone and claims that his purpose is to warn his readers the danger of carnal pleasure by exposing the harmful outcome of deviant sexual behaviors. Chastity is strategically evoked and stressed to justify Lijun's cross-gender performances. This resonates with the ending lines of the poem, which allude to the legend of *chuixiao yinfeng* (吹簫引鳳), or "playing the instrument *xiao* to draw the phoenix," suggesting the possibility of Lijun marrying Shaohua when she reveals her true self. This expression regarding Lijun's possible reunion with Shaohua and her persistent rejection of marriage develops to a moment when Lijun's identity is exposed. Patricia Sieber suggests that *Zaishengyuan* "adumbrates the lure of modern forms of female self-determination—unfettered mobility, sexual choice, and professional power. Yet what this story also shows is that the girl had to renounce her female community once she began to pass for a man" (147). However, the gradual development of Lijun's autonomous character in the text contradicts this possibility of the couple's reunion. While the faithful Shaohua willingly risks being scolded by his parents and insists on waiting for Lijun's return, Lijun ridicules Shaohua's obstinacy. Unmoved by the faithful Shaohua, Lijun even scolds her own parents who collaborate with Shaohua to force her into confession. Yet contrary to the images of disobedient women which were often denounced as immoral in didactic books, Chen's Lijun is endowed with such psychological depth that the readers could only sympathize with the ambitious yet ill-fated heroine.

In comparison with the self-portrait scene, the text also depicts a scene of Lijun, now prime minister Li Xiangru, presiding over the civil service exam and reading the candidates' compositions.

> In a studio as warm as spring, a fire basin is placed, in which a fire is kept day and night.
> She is seated in the chair, a house servant waiting by the desk.
> Gallantly dressed in a fur coat, with elegance she wears a soft head covering.
> Two candles lit by the window, a scarlet brush held in hand.
> One moment, a smile and a circle of a few sentences.
> Another, fine eyebrows knit and a few sighs fall.
> Suddenly, a pause of the brush for more reading and chanting.
> Suddenly, turning of pages and writing corrections and comments.
> Writings in brush strokes and refined forms, filled the boxes and trunks, endlessly adding to the pile.
> Sometimes she reads out loud and sings a praise,
> Sometimes she nods and praises the clarity of writing. She is
> Annoyed by the maids' urges for dinner.
> Pleased to see good writings from the visiting disciples.
> . . . a really talented Minister.
> Truly young and wise, an honored and prominent official.
> Day by day she cannot spare a moment from reading the essays,
> And declines all meetings with relatives and students in the capital city.

In a similar setting of the domestic space is Lijun, who now is a married "man" and a prime minister who is fully devoted to "his" official duties. If the previous scenes of Lijun making a self-portrait and inspecting her cross-dressed self demonstrate her physical transformation, this scene of Lijun reading and ranking the exam candidates' essays displays her seamlessly performing a role as mentor of the selected male disciples and executing her intellectual power in evaluating their writing. The transformation of the heroine's inner chamber into a literati's studio demonstrates women's negotiation and reinvention of their identity in domestic and public spaces. The heroine, by taking on a masculine identity, successfully transforms her literary talent into a source of social power.

As Lijun's story reveals, women's cross-dressing is a form of gender mimicry, in that the subject actively takes part in constructing his or her own image by drawing on seemingly incongruent gender roles. Cross-dressing performance is represented by a transitive subjective position, with the cross-dresser strategically challenging and transforming dominant gender prescriptions. In another seventeenth-century *tanci* work, *Tianyuhua* (Heaven Rains Flowers), the heroine Zuo Yizhen, born in an upper-class family, has been educated as if she were a boy, and develops a fascination for her father's "coiling-dragon swords," which can expand and contract at will. She subsequently obtains these swords from her father and uses them first to kill an evil spirit that intrudes into the flower garden of her family, and later to execute the evil usurper Zheng Guotai (鄭國泰) (Idema and Grant, *Red Brush* 726; also see Epstein, "Patrimonial Bonds" 9). Although Yizhen's yearning for the father's sword may "symbolize her desire to take over the father's position and become a man herself," such a desire is ultimately frustrated. She subsequently marries a literati scholar Zuo Weiming (左維明) and lives a largely domestic life after marriage. In Destiny of Rebirth, however, Meng Lijun takes a more determined break from her feminine identity by cross-dressing. When the disguised Lijun is recognized by her parents, she rationalizes her unwillingness to marry her fiancé and go back to a woman's life. Lijun defends her choice in the name of filial piety, attempting to resist marriage and persuade her parents into keeping her sexual identity a secret. "Why don't you just let me go on and live the life of a man? / . . . Even though I was born a woman, / now I enter the royal palace and serve the Emperor. . . . / What is the need for me to be married? / Even the place of the Empress herself could not fit into my expectations!" (11: 44, 780).

This defiant statement in Destiny of Rebirth invited criticism from *tanci* authors of the time and in ensuing generations. Hou Zhi, for example, criticized Lijun for her political ambition and rebellious refusal to recognize her parents in public. Hu Siao-chen offers a reading of Hou Zhi's *Remaking Heaven*, which rewrote Destiny of Rebirth and depicted Lijun as a converted daughter and wife (*Cainü* 29). Perhaps because she was incapable of balancing the character's personal aspirations with the readers' desire to see Lijun's reunion with her fiancé, Chen Duansheng left the work unfinished. After Chen's death, a *tanci* writer Liang Desheng (1771-1847) added three volumes to the work. According to Chen Wenshu, Liang Desheng initially took on the writing with her husband and completed the sequel to Destiny of Rebirth together with him. However, authorial statements in the twentieth *juan* reveal that her husband died in the course of the project. Liang completed the writing alone (Sung 126-27). In the added ending, Lijun returns to the life of a wife in a polygamous family. As in the earlier *tanci* Jade Bracelets, the cross-dresser marries her betrothed fiancé, together with a sworn sister who had been her "wife" in the mock marriage.

Chen Duansheng's text exemplifies the liberating potential of cross-gender mimicry, a topic that many feminist scholars have theorized and explored. In women's *tanci* fiction, representations of women's same-sex desire frequently occur. These textual scenes either celebrate a spiritual harmony among the cross-dressed heroines and the feminine members in mock unions (some cross-dressers married more than once), or create a melodramatic irony by showing unsuspecting women's infatuation with the beautifully disguised cross-dressers. Women's homoeroticism in *tanci*, poignant or comical, constantly distorts gender boundaries and reveals cross-dressers as empowering characters who actively challenge patriarchal control of women's sexuality.

In Chen's work, when Lijun's bound feet are dramatically revealed, the multivalent identity of the cross-dresser causes a homoerotic tension between the cross-dresser and the unsuspecting women characters who have mistaken Lijun for a man. The theme of women's homoeroticism is crucially related to cross-dressing in many *tanci*, suggesting an alternative possibility of sexuality beyond the heterosexual norm. When the emperor suspects that Lijun (with the pseudonym of Li Mingtang [酈明堂]) is actually a cross-dresser, he schemes with the empress dowager to invite Li/Lijun to the palace and get him drunk. The empress dowager then orders two palace maids to take off Li/Lijun's shoes to see if "he" is a woman with bound feet. The text stages an intriguing scene in which the two maids are overawed by the sleeping minister's ravishing beauty while they muse on his or her sexual identity. The revelation of the bound feet is endlessly delayed. After the boots are taken off, the maids find both feet wrapped in satin socks. Driven by curiosity, they remove the socks and are surprised to see layer after layer of clothes binding the feet.

> Giggling in hushed tones,
> They take pleasure in looking, while pulling off the wrapping cloth.
> They see that the cloth on his feet seems endlessly long,
> Almost a *zhang* of white satin is scattered on the couch.
> After six or seven rounds, the shape of her refined shoes appears,
> pleasing as the newly sprung bamboo roots.
> Yet another layer removed, a pair of scarlet shoes is seen,
> red as dewy lotus flowers.
> After all the white satin is taken off,
> The two maidens are thrilled by the sight.
> When the satin foot binding cloth runs to the end,
> The scarlet embroidered shoes are revealed.
> The upper is sewn with interlocked golden threads and pale blue trimmings.
> The toes of the shoes are adorned with clusters of pearls secured with
> minute stitches.
> Free of stains and dust,
> These shoes are barely three inches long;
> The feet must be even smaller, because of the two shoes.
> The maids, upon seeing this,
> Cannot help beaming with joy. (16: 64, 1082)

The minister's feet are not fully revealed yet. The maids, surprised at the small size of Lijun's feet, remove the red shoes, and find another pair of sleeping shoes inside. In the cult of bound feet, the smallest ones are the more admirable. The narrator's jovial description of the scene stages the pleasure of the women spectators both in and out of the text. At the end, Lijun's feet are still wrapped in a pair of embroidered shoes, hidden from the sight of the audience. Possibly Chen makes such an arrangement so that Lijun will not lose face by having her body revealed in public. Although the bound feet are representative of traditional feminine beauty, they are always covered with embroidered shoes. The feet, deformed and mutilated, are considered unsightly and never revealed in public. Zeitlin notes that "bound feet, those man-made fetishes that had become the locus of the erotic imagination in late imperial China, are transformed into a natural and immutable proof of true femininity" (Zeitlin, *Historian of the Strange* 116). Lijun's bound feet trigger even more complex spectatorship as it is the women who are feasting on the sight of the lotus feet with desiring gazes. The text resists the exposure of its heroine's body, offering instead an opacity that blocks the gaze of both the reader and the palace maids. The "absence" of Lijun's feet figuratively suggests that there are no authentic original identities in transgender performances. The narrative creates a "scenographic space" of women's same-sex desire. Maaike Bleeker suggests that "scenographic space" refers to a theatrical space in which all that is seen is in a sense staged for a viewer (98). This quasi-theatrical episode is fraught with homoeroticism, with the women readers invited to share with the royal maids the pleasure of looking at Lijun's concealed feet. This unconventional visual structure of multiple women viewers gazing at a woman transforms the Freudian heterosexual model of fetishism, and submits the cross-dressed protagonist to an intensely homoerotic gaze from the audience. Intriguingly, in Destiny of Rebirth, Chen did not continue the narrative beyond the point at which Lijun is confronted with the emperor's proposal of marriage. Chen thus leaves the text and the protagonist Lijun in a tale of deferral, indicating the very impossibility of relegating the cross-dresser to a distinctively feminine subjectivity.

The maids' desirous gazes toward Lijun's bound feet also exhibit women's scopophilia. This desiring look possibly represents the maids' autoerotic appreciation of the ideal female body, which is then transferred toward the disguised ministers' perfectly shaped feet. The above scene constitutes another scenario of the mirror stage, in which the minister's fetishized feet represent a reflected body of the ideal ego for the maids, who are the bearers of the gaze. The feet constitute "the matrix of the imaginary, of recognition/misrecognition" (Mulvey, 836). Women's pleasure in looking at the bound feet, perverse as it may be, should be taken as a way for them to separate from their constrained life in the inner compound and play with their voyeuristic fantasy.

Chen Duansheng might have anticipated this crisis of Lijun's true identity being exposed as she wrote the first half of the book. Earlier in the book Chen depicts cross-dressed military leader Wei Yong'e, who was formerly the wife of a rebellious soldier in a troop that took shelter in the mountains. After her husband's death, Wei took the leadership of the group. When the Huangfu family was wrongly accused of treason and sent to the capital city in prisoners' cages, Wei led her troop and besieged the group, and subsequently saved Zhanghua and her mother. In the end Wei, following the suggestion of the Huangfus, surrendered to the emperor. When the emperor attempted to marry Wei to Zhanghua, Wei had to confess her true identity to the emperor and begged for his forgiveness. The emperor was deeply impressed by Wei's heroic deeds and her capability to maintain chastity while commanding a large military troop. He immediately pardoned Wei and praised her for keeping her chastity to her husband and for fulfilling her duty to the emperor by surrendering her military force to the government (8: 537-38). However, the text indicates, through Zhanghua's internal monologue, that the emperor might have the thought of taking Wei as one of his concubines. This episode foreshadows the conflict between Lijun's personal aspiration and the emperor's voracious domination when Lijun's true identity is found out. He insists on taking Lijun and Lijun's wife Liang Suhua both as his wives, trying to persuade Lijun that "as a woman, you should enjoy the prime prestige in taking such a husband" (17: 1127). As the emperor's preying character is gradually unraveled, Lijun is left with no choice of her own.

The narrative voice in Destiny of Rebirth is a distinctively feminine and semi-autobiographical voice. This autobiographical narrative impulse is not unique to the genre of *tanci* and can be found often in late imperial women's literature. In Ming and Qing women's poetry, the autobiographical poem is a subgenre which took its resources from folk poetry in feminine voices and from the poetry of the inner life. Since late Ming, women authors, through their self-representation in poetry prefaces, demonstrate evidences of their desire to become legitimate participants in literary culture (Robertson, "Changing the Subject" 182). The autobiographical insertions in Destiny of Rebirth resonate with these historical contexts, and demonstrate an authorial voice speaking to a community of women readers, drawing emotive support from them and evoking their sympathetic readings (Zhao 244-54). Grace S. Fong points out that by the Qing, educated gentry women had utilized poetry as a discursive field and a multifaceted process by means of which they were able to imagine themselves and one another as belonging to a group, defined by their ability to write, that transcended the normative limits of kinship and social systems (Fong, *Herself an Author* 144). Fong explores how this sense of belonging can be seen as expressed symbolically in the term "mingyuan" (notable women), used by women and men in the titles of anthologies of women's poetry (Berg, *Women Writers* 135).

At the beginning the narrator assumes an extradiegetic position,

> Looking through the lens of the marriage imperative:
> As an ancient saying goes,
> "Marriage is ordained five hundred years before the fact."
> I believe that
> Success and failure in love are both fated.
> Often a handsome horse is ridden by an uncouth villager;
> A clever wife commonly rests at the side of an imprudent husband.
> One should believe that such incidents are the doing of
> The karma of predestination, and are by no means accidental. (1: 1, 2)

The text displays a dialectic between a drive toward closure (a happy marriage) and the delay of that closure (the frustrated love relations in characters' past lives). The following lines, though, reveal a proleptic shift from the ancient tales to events that *will* take place in the characters' present lives.

> If once upon a time,
> A scholar marries a beautiful lady,
> It is mostly because of their destined bond in their last lives.
> If a couple has no luck to achieve a desired relationship
>   in their latest lives,
> They are connected through karmic bonds in this life.
> If they are not particular about their partners' looks,
> They will be able to resume their love bond with each other.
> . . .
> Why do I bring up the issue of predestination here?
> Because it is
> A vital matter in this story.
> Here I will tell
> An unusual tale of grief and joy, of separation and reunion,
> Titled Destiny of Rebirth;
> It is a quite unconventional story. (1: 1, 2)

The theme of predestination, which Chen brings up in her authorial assertions, is a narrative convention in the traditional *caizi jiaren* (才子佳人) fiction, or scholar and beauty novels, which became popular in the southern regions during the late Ming period (see Hu, Wanchuan 1994). This kind of fiction, which focuses on themes of marriage and love, also depicts women characters that are both beautiful and endowed with exceptional talents and independence. Chen Duansheng's tale, likewise, starts with an anticipation of the consummation of Lijun and Shaohua's love. This foreshadowing, nevertheless, does not lead to a corresponding closure, when the author would typically gradually unveil the discrepancy between Lijun's character and her predestined marriage. Lijun's destiny departs from the precursory tale of love and reunion. By disguising herself as a man, she already eludes the feminine body and resumes a new life after cross-dressing. The title word "rebirth" therefore indicates the cross-dresser's acquisition of a new life beyond gender boundaries or karmic circumstances. The concept "karma" in this context refers to the fact that star-dwelling immortals, for a reason, must live out a human life on earth.

The author's impulse for self-empowerment becomes most prominent in volume 17, where Chen contemplates the correlation between her life as a writer and possible endings for the story. After her family calamity, Chen lamented on the hardship of life and recalls her days before marriage:

> I scratch my head and call out to Heaven, wishing to ask,
> "Can the Way of Heaven be turned around?"
> Having tasted to the full all the bitter sufferings of the world,
> I recall the days of my earliest youth in the inner chambers:
> We sisters shared a couch as we listened to the night rain,
> And our parents assigned us rhymes and taught us poetry . . .

> In my ignorance I dared steal a glance at the affairs of the past.
> With brush in hand, I wrote Destiny of Rebirth. (17: 65, 1084)

The first line alludes to the poem "天問" ("Tianwen," "Questions to Heaven") in 楚辭 (*Chuci*, Songs of Chu), a monumental work representing the beginning of an ornate literary tradition in China. "Questions to Heaven" is a long questionnaire that begins with questions about the sky but soon progresses from cosmological, astronomical, and meteorological subjects to questions about the earth and about the affairs of men. Chen Duansheng's allusion to "Heavenly Questions" reflects a woman author's determination to break out of the snare of silence and to use the same format as a tool through which women can speak (Hawkes, *Songs of the South* 122-52). Qu Yuan (340 BC-278 BC) of *Songs of Chu* was a loyal minister to whom are attributed core texts of this anthology. During his life, he was banished and persecuted, and he consequently committed suicide by drowning. Chen Duansheng's strategic identification with the male poet enables her to articulate her own predicament in an affirmative and self-empowering voice. In the fictional space, Chen Duansheng is the reincarnated Qu Yuan in both her talent and banishment. The following lines recount the happiness of her marriage, which ended abruptly when Chen's husband was involved in the scandal of examination corruption and banished to a frontier province as a common soldier: "Then he was caught in the fetters of profit, the snares of fame. / Once a string on a zither has snapped, it is broken forever; / The half of a broken mirror can never be made round again: / Could it possibly have been an omen of our fate today, / That long ago I called this work Destiny of Rebirth? / During the day, my face in the mirror always provides the proof, / 'An orphaned star following daybreak' truly does apply to me" (17: 65, 1085).

Displaying a clear link between the circumstances of her life and the contents of her work, Chen evokes the image of the "broken mirror," which represents an irredeemable love relationship and inadvertently becomes prophetic of her own destiny. Like Lijun pondering her reflection in the mirror, Chen Duansheng casts a retrospective view on the text in search of her own face and own voice, suggesting that her audience engage in a double reading of her personal life and Lijun's story. In both cases the readers are engaged in the dialectic of rupture and return: like the author who waits for the return of her banished husband, the readers are held in suspense awaiting the fictional reunion of the cross-dressed Lijun and her fiancé Shaohua. Yet, as the symbol of the "broken mirror" implies, the relationship between the male and female is irrevocably shattered by reality. The text brings up irrevocable fissures between desire and destiny, between prescient visions and nostalgic longings. The "broken string on a zither" is an additional sign that this book, for all its plucking of rhymes, will be left without an ending. Chen speaks of the readers' prospect for closure:

> As it happens, my book has enjoyed a reputation for a time,
> And has found its way throughout the province of Zhejiang.
> My friends in the inner chambers have often voiced their admiration. . . .
> My elders in their screened halls have all let themselves be amused.
> They've buzzed about my ears, urging me to complete the book,
> as they all longed to see

The star-crossed lovers, that perfect couple, brought together at last.
"Huangfu Shaohua must be matched with his beautiful bride,
Minister Li must finally consummate her marriage!
As you have played the role of match maker on their behalf,
You should not play the Son of Heaven and keep them apart!"
The Creator should not blame me for this state of affairs;
I am only a woman with a broken heart grieving over her lonely life . . .
All the endless affairs of the last twelve years
Have passed in a tipsy dream of Li Mingtang! (17: 65, 1085)

This textual moment demonstrates the notable embeddedness of the protagonist, the author, and her envisaged readers in the inner chambers: that is, all three are at a vantage point to anticipate and recollect, becoming both the objects and the subjects of the narrative. Presenting a replica of the text within the text itself, Chen Duansheng concludes the *tanci* with a reflection of the past and the present, revealing the author's own unviable position as a textual subject and a woman author in real life (for Chen's feminine consciousness as an author, see Yue, Daiyun). Simultaneously, Chen's twelve years of writing is internally replicated in Lijun's dream, revealing a self-producing desire in the text that circulates between the author, the text, and her projected audience (see Zou, Ying, "Time Experience" 113-24). Chen's powerfully present authorial voice seeks to reclaim her self from silence, and articulates a woman author's conscious resistance of dominant modes of gender representation.

Cross-dressing, to conclude, brings out the heroine's power to negotiate and resist Confucian ethical codes, which prescribe women's subordinate relationship to men in the inner quarters and within the public sphere. The author's maneuver of these textual scenarios reveals a strategic negotiation between the social and cultural discourses on feminine chastity and filial piety on the one hand, and women's private desires to pursue autonomy and freedom beyond these regulations on the other. Destiny of Rebirth brings to the surface a feminine consciousness that challenges the dominant prescriptions of women's gender roles and reveals the author's emancipatory vision along with its unresolved problems. As Maureen Robertson suggests, in the study of late imperial women's extant writing as an art, it is important to give attention to the "writerly" character of this body of texts and its voices, which are specifically literary mediations of women's consciousness (Robertson, "Literary Authorship" 379). Chen's *Zaishengyuan* elucidates the author's conflicts and dilemmas about writing that were shared by other women authors in the Chinese patriarchal context. The most compelling textual evidence that reveals the narrative impasse is the sight of Lijun's bound feet, which proves her social identity as a woman and her internalization of such social prescriptions of her gendered identity. The author's predicament in her real life echoes the heroine's implied death in the end, as the ailing Lijun spits blood when pressed by the emperor's proposal, knowing that she would surely be executed if she rejected it. The open-endedness of the book suggests that Chen's vision of freedom, resembling Lijun's pursuit of freedom, could only find its fulfillment in the next life.

Chapter Two

Disguised Scholar, Fox Spirit, and Moralism in *Bishenghua* (Blossom from the Brush)

Chen Duansheng's *Zaishengyuan* (Destiny of Rebirth) leaves a lingering question: What would happen if the heroine were forced to return to the boudoir when her identity was disclosed? Among Chen's later peers, *tanci* author Liang Desheng (1771-1847) wrote an additional forty chapters of Chen's *tanci* in which Lijun compromises with the emperor and marries Shaohua. Later, Hou Zhi (1829-1764) refashioned Chen's *tanci* for readers by editing the text for reprint and composing a *tanci* work, 再造天 (*Zaizaotian*, Remaking Heaven), which is a sequel to *Zaishengyuan*. In *Zaizaotian*, Hou depicts the heroine Huangfu Feilong, the younger daughter of Meng Lijun. These ensuing narratives have revised Chen's work by recycling, modifying, and expanding its original narrative frame and plot elements. Whereas Liang and Hou both retold Chen's *tanci* by extending the original plot line, nineteenth-century author Qiu Xinru composed a new *tanci* about a cross-dressed heroine to remedy Lijun's moral imperfections (for a comparison of Qiu's and Hou's rewriting of *Zaishengyuan*, see Wu, Qingyun 9). In *Bishenghua* (Blossom from the Brush), the heroine Jiang Dehua is selected as one of the royal maidens to go to the palace. Formally engaged to a gallant young man, Wen Shaoxia (文少霞), she attempts suicide after being captured and sent to the capital. A benevolent fox spirit comes to her rescue, helping her to dress as a man in order to flee from the calamity. Later the disguised Dehua excels in the civil service exam and becomes a prime minister. When her identity is disclosed, she marries her fiancé Wen Shaoxia and retreats to the boudoir. Through conciliation with social pressure and changing back to her feminine identity, Dehua gains greater authority in the inner chambers, while continuing to enjoy the favor of the court. The text's portrayals of the fox spirit and women's aspirations for Daoist transcendentalism are an imaginative approach to obtaining spiritual agency. Qiu's authorial representation of her self-image creates an opportunity for enacting subjectivity from a gendered viewpoint and enables her to tell a personal history along with her extraordinary tale.

This chapter studies how *Bishenghua* emerges as an exceptional *tanci* after *Zaishengyuan*, by reworking the cross-dressing plot and rectifying the embedded moral values following the orthodox social and cultural values of the time. Whereas Qiu succeeds in reviving the tale of the cross-dressed heroine by imagining the life of Dehua after she reverts back to her feminine identity, the author's seemingly realistic depiction of the outcome exposes Qiu's own moral and ethical constraints in writing and her prescribed position as the moral instructress of her readers. As if to counterbalance this didactic tendency, Qiu resorts to supernatural narrative elements, including fox spirits and female immortals, to deliver imagined possibilities of women exerting new forms of subjectivity beyond the ethereal yokes. However, Qiu's narratives of the fantastic and the marvelous, like previous *tanci* tales, are also structured by Confucian moral ethics of filial piety and feminine virtue. The text's self-acclaimed feminine authorship, its dramatic representation of a diverse range of exceptional heroines, and the persistent quest for an alternatively conceived, morally upright feminine subjectivity all attest to Qiu's mastery of the aesthetical ramifications of *tanci* and to her reputable presence on a broader, ethical horizon of writing.

Bishenghua is set in the Ming Zhengde (正德) period (1506-21). The heroine Jiang Dehua is the daughter of a high-ranking official, Jiang Jinren. At her birth her mother, Mo Shi, dreams of a goddess who holds a colorful writing brush and a piece of brocade embroidered with palindromic poems. Because the goddess must make amends for improprieties she committed in heaven, she tells Mo Shi that she will be born as her mortal daughter. This textual detail foreshadows Dehua's exceptional talent. Later Dehua grows into a beautiful young woman who has learned literature and history through family education. She becomes engaged to Wen Shaoxia, a gallant and talented young man and the second son of an official, Wen Shanglin (文上林). However, Wen Shaoxia catches the eye of the despotic Chu Yuanfang (楚元方), whose daughter is the emperor's favorite concubine. Using his royal connection, Chu wants to force Shaoxia into marrying his daughter Chu Chunyi (楚春漪). The Wen family has a strong aversion to the tyrannous Chu and turns down his proposal. The conflict between the two families grows grave when Shaoxia's beautiful sister Wen Peilan (文佩蘭) also declines to marry Chu's son Chun Tinghui (楚廷輝) and is engaged to another scholar, Xie Chunrong (謝春溶). The revengeful Tinghui then abducts Peilan on her wedding day. Peilan attempts to drown herself but is rescued by a governor, Wang Shouren (王守仁), who adopts her as his daughter. Determined to destroy Shaoxia and Dehua's engagement, Chu Yuanfang recommends Dehua as a candidate when the emperor carries out a national selection of royal maidens. Dehua is captured and taken to the capital with other selected girls. When she attempts to hang herself in order to keep her chastity, a sympathetic fox spirit, Hu Yuexian (胡月仙), rescues her. The spirit, after helping her to cross-dress as a man and escape, goes to the palace in her place.

Later Dehua, using the name Jiang Junbi in her male identity, succeeds in the civil service exam and is appointed prime minister. Dedicated to her position, she gains distinction through achievements in defending the country and governing national affairs. She marries Xie Yunxian (謝韻仙), a minister's daughter who happens to be devoted to Daoist study and declines sexual intimacy. The disguised Junbi, intending to keep her cross-dressing secret, happily agrees to Yunxian's abstinence. Dehua's abandoned fiancé, Shaoxia, upset by the fact that Dehua has entered the palace, leaves the Jiang house where he has resided as a future son-in-law. On an excursion he passes by the house of his aunt, who loves Shaoxia's talent and marries her daughter Murong Chunniang (慕容純娘) to him. Shaoxia then leaves to attend the civil service exam. During his absence, the young bride Chunniang has the misfortune to be abducted and sold into Yunxia's house. Sympathetic to her adversity, the fox spirit Hu Yunxian persuades Jiang Junbi (姜峻璧, the disguised Dehua) into taking Chunniang as a concubine. It happens that Chunniang was pregnant with Shaoxia's child before she was abducted. She gives birth to a son, Xialang (霞郎), who is mistaken as Junbi's own child. Now with a son of "his" own, Junbi lives under the guise of a harmonious family with two "wives." The three decide to devote to Daoist pursuits after accomplishing their filial tasks of serving their parents.

After Shaoxia succeeds in the exam, he confesses to the emperor about his previous engagement. When he encounters the prime minister Jiang Junbi, he suspects Junbi of being his cross-dressed fiancée. After his tests of Junbi are frustrated, Shaoxia manages to make Dehua's father confirm Dehua's disguise. When the secret is revealed, the emperor is so amazed at Dehua's heroism that he awards her the title of the Marquis of Heroism and Chastity. He commands Shaoxia to live in Dehua's maternal household after their marriage and that their children will carry the maternal surname Jiang, inheriting their mother's title. When Dehua resigns from service to the emperor and withdraws to the boudoir, Shaoxia takes on the minister's position in her place. The second half of the *tanci* illustrates how Dehua deploys her ingenuity in restoring domestic harmony and pacifying family conflicts. She persuades her husband to take on three concubines to give birth to more children, helps her brother-in-law tame his ravenous wife, and even fasts for a year to fulfill a prayer that heaven will give her aged father a son to extend her family bloodline. After organizing donations for people who suffered in a flood in Shandong, the emperor grants her the title *Wulin zhongxiao duanhui gongzhu* (武林忠孝端惠公主), that is, Warring Affairs Princess of Loyalty, Filial Piety, Grace, and Benevolence, suggesting the transformation of her role into a daughter of the imperial court. This ingenuous reconfiguration of Dehua's relation to the emperor exempts her from falling prey to the emperor's domineering sexual desire, as did Lijun in *Zaishengyuan.* Dehua and Shaoxia give birth to a daughter and a son; both are well-educated and are happily married. After assisting Emperor Jiajing to put down a court rebellion and exterminate corrupting forces, the couple returns to the idyllic West Lake to practice Daoism and become immortals. The ending emphasizes earthly retribution, causal outcome, and the moral values of loyalty and filial love.

If Chen Duansheng's *Zaishengyuan* leaves Lijun's fate unsettled, Qiu's *Bishenghua* continues the tale of the cross-dressing woman after she takes off her disguise and makes tactical compromises with social reality, such as encouraging and even scheming to help her husband and her father take concubines to obtain more offspring, yielding political power to her husband, regulating the inner chambers by taming the shrews, resolving the disputes between the wives and the concubines and their respective broods, and securing the bloodline by arranging marriages. As a reward for these practical conciliations, Dehua enjoys social privilege and a degree of matriarchal power at home, with her husband making concessions regarding domestic affairs when she demands them. After she takes off her disguise, Dehua is endowed with a series of imperial noble titles that acknowledge her traditional virtues, which, like her physical disguise before, cloak her ambitions and personal pursuits in the name of loyalty and chastity.

The characters' names in Qiu's *tanci* are emblematic of moral implications or thematic associations, as scholar Chen Wenxuan suggests (175). The heroine's surname Jiang is one of the eight main prehistoric surnames in the matriarchal society. The author's surname Qiu originates from the ancient Jiang Taigong (姜太公), who was the prime minister of the Qi State. Because Jiang resided in the county of Yingqiu (營丘) in Shandong province, his descendants took the surname Qiu (丘) which evolved into the surname Qiu (邱) as in the author's surname. This association between the heroine and the author's surnames suggest the possibility of Qiu projecting her personal ideal onto the cross-dressed Jiang Dehua. Another character, Xie Xucai, takes her name from the cross-dressed poet Xie Xucai in the play *Qiaoying* (The Image in Disguise) by eighteenth-century female writer Wu Zao. Wen Peilan takes her given name from the famous Qing poet Xi Peilan (席佩蘭), renowned among the female disciples of Sui Garden under the mentorship of poet Yuan Mei. These allusions to the names of women scholars lend the characters an aura of distinguished learning. Likewise, Qiu gives her antiheroes and antiheroines satiric, ironic, or oxymoronic names. The name of Shaoxia's ravenous concubine Wo Lianggui (沃良規) puns on "without good discipline," indicating her immoral and rapacious personality.

Zaishengyuan serves as an important pretext for Qiu's conception of her tale. Toyoko Yoshida Chen, in her pioneering scholarship on Qiu's work, proposes that Qiu borrowed characters and plots from other *tanci* such as *Yuchuanyuan* (Jade Bracelets) and *Tianyuhua* (Heaven Rains Flowers), both of which have anonymous authorship, and prose fiction such as 紅樓夢 (*Hongloumeng*, The Dream of the Red Chamber) by Cao Xueqin (曹雪芹) and 萬花樓 (*Wanhualou*, Tower of Ten Thousand Flowers) by Li Yutang (李雨堂) (Chen, Toyoko Yoshida). The text of *Bishenghua* consists of four *juan* and thirty-two *hui*, in total nine hundred sixty thousand words. The author Qiu Xinru (about 1805-after 1873) was born in Shanyang (山陽), Jiangsu in the Qing Jiaqing period (1799-1820) (Tan, *Zhongguo nüxing* 438). Sheng Zhimei estimates that Qiu started writing her lengthy *tanci* in 1813 and finished the work roughly in 1843. A printed version was published as a woodblock edition in 1857, according to the preface by Chen Tongxun (陳同勛). The earliest retrieved text was a headscarf box edition published by Shanghai Shenbaoguan in 1879, which is currently held at Shanghai Normal University Library. Other editions include a lead-type print edition in 1884 at Nanjing City Library and a lithography edition by Shanjing Xiuhai Shanfang in 1894 (Sheng 285).

Since the early twentieth century, critics have probed into Qiu's family background, hoping to gather more information about the author and her family. Ding Zhi'An's research on Qiu's biographical information is particularly informative (Ding, "*Bishenghua*" 299-300). Based on an interview with Qiu's great grandson and including related studies, Ding's study confirms that Qiu's father was the scholar Qiu Guangye (邱廣業, 1771-1834), her mother Qin Shi (秦氏), and her maternal grandfather Qin Ao (秦鏊) (see Ropp 132). According to the gazetteer of Huai'An (淮安) County, Qiu Guangye earned a provincial academic degree of *juren* (舉人) in 1808. He was upright in conduct, loyal to his friends, and looked down upon monetary benefits. In 1827, he was appointed an official in Fengyang City and a 訓導 (*xundao*, instructor) in Linhuai (臨淮). Qiu Guangye composed a poetry collection 臨雲居詩草 (*Linyunju shicao*, Selected Poems of the Cloud Approaching Lodge). Qiu Xinru's two elder brothers both wrote poems as well (Gao vol. 38; Zhou and Duan vol. 13). Qiu's indebtedness to her illustrious family tradition may be traced in numerous passages of self-reflection in the text. Before her marriage she took to literature and poetry under the encouragement of her mother, when she composed the first five *hui* of *Bishenghua*. With the encouragement of her parents, she was able to pursue learning passionately. Qiu states in the introductory lines of a chapter: "Not aware of the ways of the world and the taste of hardship, / I only enjoy my born affinity with literature. / I loved to read my father's books and scan through ancient histories, / and followed my mother's instruction to take an interest in leisure writings. / Most books I read are writings by women on matters in the boudoir, / though I also have appreciated beautiful lines in poetry tradition" (1: 1, 1). The books that were accessible for her reading, as the above passage reveals, might have been carefully selected and contained literature, history, and didactic conduct books for women. Later she reflects on her parents' instructions, which emphasize virtue, caution, and self-restraint.

> My father taught me Domestic Regulations, literature, and classics;
> my mother urged me to commit to women's work and to be frugal and diligent.
> They instructed me that men should abstain from misusing a sharp tongue
> to overturn a country,
> that women should not resort to clever sayings to disrupt feminine virtue.
> Thus I was made to ponder my word choice all the time as if I could not speak,
> to mull over every matter time and again, afraid of committing a mistake.
> In ordinary days, I took to solitude, doing needlework and submitting
> myself to silence.
> Stealing a spare moment, I played with my writing brush and was rather
> contented. (2: 8, 327)

The above passage carries a melancholy tone when the author laments her fear of speaking and using writing as a way of articulating her inner thoughts. Li-Hsiang Lisa Rosenlee argues that female literacy and engagement with reading and writing implicitly challenged orthodox principles regarding gender roles and invited debates on the "compatibility of female literacy and female virtue" during the Ming and Qing periods (Rosenlee 108). The traditional view holds that the true calling of a virtuous woman rested primarily on her self-sacrifice and fidelity to patrilineage rather than on her personal needs to explore literary talent (Rosenlee 110). The above section of the text well presents Qiu's dilemma of self-positioning between developing female talent and upholding traditional virtue. Her extraordinary discretion about feminine virtue and her respect for her scholarly family lineage, in addition to the heavy duties of daily housework, possibly slowed her writing process. Qiu states that she took nearly three decades to write this *tanci*, including her first stage of writing before marriage covering the first five *hui*, the nineteen-year pause after her marriage, and the later years of composing the remaining twenty-seven *hui*. The preface for the *tanci* by her niece Chen Dongxun shows that the book was printed in 1857. Tracing her life trajectory, critic Tan Zhengbi proposes that Qiu might have started writing between 1821 and 1829, and finished the writing between 1851 and 1857. A later note dedicated to *Bishenghua* by a woman Tanghu yunyu nüshi (棠湖雲腴女士) reveals that by 1873 Qiu was still teaching disciples and struggling against poverty (Tan, *Zhongguo nüxing* 448-50).

The unusual gap between Qui's writing before and after marriage is attested to in her self-descriptions in the *tanci*. According to the authorial insertions, Qiu was married into a humble Zhang household and led a life of hardships. Although her mother-in-law and husband treated her well, her brothers-in-law and their wives remained distant and expressed jealousy and antipathy against her. Among her three children, the eldest daughter died of small pox; the younger daughter was married. Qiu was left with a son of her own with ordinary intelligence. Her life after marriage was overshadowed by a series of misfortunes including her father's death, her sister's widowhood, her elder brother's death, and the destitute condition of her widowed mother. Because of poverty, Qiu returned to her maternal family, opened a private school, and spent her time teaching, writing, and caring for her mother (Tan and Tan, *Tanci xulu* 252).

The textual reflections of her parents as a source of spiritual comfort and academic support mirror Qiu's journey from girlhood to marriage and her return to her mother's house. Ellen Widmer states that it was not unusual for talented women of the late imperial period to have strong emotional and intellectual support from their mothers, including the famous Ye sisters of Suzhou, whose mother was the poet Shen Yixiu, and the poet Wang Duan (汪端), who received continued support from *tanci* author Liang Desheng (Widmer, *Beauty* 114). Though no direct records of Qiu's mother are found outside the text, Qiu's writing illustrates a strong bond with her mother's family; she also was a very loving mother to her own daughters.

The book title *Bishenghua* comes from a historical anecdote about the medieval Chinese poet Li Bai (李白). In his youth Li dreamed that a flower blossomed from the tip of his writing brush. Later he composed numerous brilliant poems and was known under heaven for his exceptional talent (Wang, Renyu 38). This allusion is appropriated in Qiu's *tanci* to depict the heroine's birth, comparing the talented Dehua to the male poet Li Bai and foreshadowing Dehua's unusual achievement beyond the inner chambers. According to a preface dated 1857, composed by Chen Tongxun, a son of the author's maternal cousin, the earliest edition, Illustrated Blossom from the *tanci*, was published in 1857. Chen affirms the literary value and instructive function of Qiu's *tanci*: "The circulation of this work in the inner chambers will instruct others' sons and daughters . . . The book boasts an extraordinary talent equivalent to that of the ancient female historian Ban Jieyu and rivals the achievement of the classic text *Admonishment for Women*" (Chen, Tongxun, Preface, *Bishenghua* 1). Comparing *Bishenghua* to the didactic text of *Admonishment for Women*, Chen endows Qiu's *tanci* with a moral legitimacy and hopes her *tanci* will be viewed with a similar authority.

Chen continues his praise, saying that Qiu's work aspires to the lofty goal of "endorsing loyalty and upholding filial love, stimulating moral justice and advocating benevolence" (Qiu, *Bishenghua* 1). It succeeds in achieving fictional verisimilitude by creating the "life-like tones of the characters, and making their appearances and attitudes closely akin to real people" (Qiu, *Bishenghua* 1). To affirm Qiu's contribution to the *tanci* tradition, Chen comments that Qiu's achievements are comparable to famous *tanci* authors and editor Hou Zhi and her peers, and deserve shared ground in history. This comment shows that *tanci* had exerted an impact on women and some men, thanks to the development of the printing industry and women's contact with publishing firms. Chen continues to recount the heroine Dehua's accomplishments in eliminating the evil and rescuing the loyal, defending the nation and instructing the emperor. He praises her superb skills in mediating between the wives and concubines, reducing their rivalry and ensuring domestic harmony. Considering the virtuous and modest Dehua a mirror to Qiu herself, Chen notes, "My aunt's nature is one of the most filial. She relies on the brush and ink to please her parents, instead of taking pride in and boasting of her talent." Hence Chen reminds the readers "not to view this work as an ordinary *tanci*" (Qiu, *Bishenghua* 2).

If Chen's preface represents a male-oriented view of Qiu's work as continuing a tradition of women's *tanci*, a note dated 1872 in a later reprint of the *tanci* situates Qiu's work in the broader historical context of women's writing. The female author of the note, Tanghu Yunyu Nüshi, praises Qiu's achievement, writing that "her learning inherits that of the legendary Lady Wei Shuo" and that "her teaching follows the ways of the female master Xuanwen Jun" (Qiu, *Bishenghua* 1). She continues to praise Qiu's aesthetic achievements and experimental endeavors. "Following the precedent forms of old writings, her *tanci* produces new forms and structure. With an intention pure and innocent, her writing does not need to avoid depictions of intimate feelings; the events accounted are originally not from the classics, and thus are no more than anecdotes to be shared over wine or tea time" (Qiu, *Bishenghua* 1). As is often stated, the note classifies Qiu's writing as a product of leisure time and denies on Qiu's behalf any ambition to rival the classics. This ostensible paradox between the endorsement of Qiu's talent and underrepresentation of her authorial prestige suggests women's potent anxiety about self-positioning in a predominantly male cultural and intellectual environment.

The above discussions raise questions about the paratexts of Qiu's work, just as prefaces and author's inserted biographical reflections raise questions about Qiu's authorial intentions and the reception and criticism of her *tanci*. Does Qiu present a story that allows itself to be more meaningfully placed in a female historical context, or is the contexualization by later male and female critics and readers a necessary intervention? How do readers of today understand and access women authors' anxieties about learning and their self-fashioning in writing? In *tanci*, authorial self-fashioning is centrally reflected in authorial insertions about their lives, feelings, and writing practices at the beginning and ending of each *hui* (chapter). Qiu's authorial persona grapples with the textual space to articulate her emotions and sentiments in the inner chambers. Hu Siao-chen argues that prominent *tanci* including *Yuchuanyuan* (Jade Bracelets), *Zaishengyuan* (Destiny of Rebirth), *Zaizaotian* (Remaking Heaven), and *Bishenghua* (Blossom from the Brush) collectively mark the establishment of a feminine narrative tradition and characterize key features of talented women's reading and writing activities (Hu, *Cainü* 50). In *Bishenghua*, the authorial statements are exuberant, consisting of the following levels of self-representation: 1) Qiu Xinru's personal reflections on private feelings, family, and life events; 2) metanarrative reflections and examinations on the process and discourse of writing; and 3) authorial comment on characters' individual fates, often carrying an admonishing tone. Women authors' self-dramatization and verisimilitude projected in the biographical illustrations distinguish *tanci* from other late imperial vernacular genres as a personal and feminine narrative. The authorial insertions depict the poetic persona of a feminine subjectivity and assist the readers to imagine the author's presence with vivid details.

This dramatized authorial self constantly reflects on the ironic incompatibility of the fictional world and women's real lives. The beautiful tale that comes to full blossom under the writer's brush is nothing other than illusion, suggesting the author's irresolute position between realistic mimesis and self-generating meaning. Also, the didactic aspect of the authorial comments, usually at the end of a *hui* (chapter), depicts an authorial self who imparts moral messages to the readers or instructs the readers to follow moral principles, manifesting the impact of conduct literature on women's gender roles. The author, by adopting such a moralizing voice, obtains a form of ethical authority and claims an instructive intention far beyond the themes of private concerns and sentiments of loving couples, which are frequently found in less refined *tanci* romances. Aiming to establish a new *tanci* from the conventions, Qiu takes an ethical turn by substituting traditional formulas with a morally driven plot arrangement and characterization.

This self-admonishing authorial narrator, however, is far from a neutral presence without emotional involvement. In a tone of self-mockery and regret, she laments,

> Even though I have seen through the cause and outcome in my fate,
> I am after all not a wooden puppet without senses.
> Ill fated, I mock my birth into such a world,
> with an interest in literature it only burdens my heart.

> . . . I pity my daughter who is pleading for a livelihood from others
> and sigh for my brother who travels afar and has not returned.
> Half of my life I have worked diligently in vain,
> for the rest of my life I regret and feel ashamed for my mother's instruction.
> Though my nature inclines toward solitude, my sentiments are originally
> joyful,
> for daily expenses I have almost exhausted my means. (8: 29, 1328)

Reflecting the "events in her floating life" and "the sentiments and desires in the book," the author feels time-fastened by her writing process. She finds herself a distanced voyeur of changing nature, "Just witness the cuckoo bird chanting to death, spitting up blood; / suddenly perceive the migrating wild goose crossing the blue sky" (Qiu 1328). Reminiscent of Chen Duansheng's self-dramatizing narrator, *Bishenghua* (Blossom from the Brush) presents an embodied narrator "whose motivation for writing is existential," for writing is "directly connected with her practical experiences, with the joys and sorrows she has experienced, with her moods and needs" (Stanzel 93). The extensive self-portrayal of these embodied narrators in Destiny of Rebirth, Blossom from the Brush, and the later *Mengyingyuan* (Dream, Image, Destiny; preface dated 1843) by Zheng Danruo depicts a distinctive feminine authorial presence, and situates *tanci* fiction as a woman-oriented narrative form. That is to say, such autobiographical narrators, basing their reflections on women's writing experience, reach out to women readers in the inner chambers, and cultivate an author-reader relationship that is derived from women's experiences and reciprocally produces a form of feminine friendship between the author and her selected readers.

In Qiu's *tanci*, the authorial self-narrations engage the readers in a fictional universe in which the author's personal life experience, feelings, aspirations, and challenges in writing build on the text's narrative reliability and activate the readers' sympathetic understanding of human vice and worth. A representative passage that reflects Qiu's review of her life is at the beginning of the sixth *hui*. In comparison with the first five *hui*, which were composed before her marriage and carry a joyful tone, the following part of the novel was composed roughly nineteen years later when the author had suffered a series of misfortunes and was under economic strain. She laments,

> To this day, I have lived an immiserated life and struggled in vain.
> Only to find myself and my husband dressed in coarse coverings, weeping
> and sighing.
> All the diligence and frugality come to no avail,
> so is my ambition to pursue fame and fortune cut short.
> How could these days compare to my life before marriage,
> when I only cared to please my parents and relish life, worriless about
> adversities.
> I can only pause my needlework to pay off my poetry debt,
> or review episodes of writing to dispel my regret in heart. (2: 7, 279-80)

Such extensive, confessional portrayals of her life in Blossom from the Brush and many other *tanci* works, Hu Siao-chen suggests, reflect the porous and shifting division between the public and private. Whereas authors, with their opening lines in every section, invited readers for instruction and feedback, they garnered potential power relationships when their writings were handcopied or printed for circulation among women and some male readers. Hu Siao-chen argues that the author's self-references and insertions, though delivered in a confessional tone in the first-person voice, are voluminous and minute to the extent of self-exhibitionism. This narrative strategy showcases *tanci* authors' exploration of the writing medium between private and public worlds, using a private stance to share feelings and emotions with readers, ostensibly understating the public existence and the impact of their writings beyond the inner chambers (*Cainü*). Qiu's self-fashioning projects the authorial persona who strives to speak to the public in a feminine voice. This gendered voice grieves personal suffering and misfortune, aspiring to a fictional world of affluence, pleasure, and ethical justice.

Bishenghua reflects a semi-autobiographical approach to express personal feelings and desires. Qiu's appropriation of "private writing" or "secret writing" provides a prudent disguise of women's desire to obtain freedom and affirmation in the public space. However, the authorial reflections display Qiu's explorations of the rhetoric of inviting sympathy through characterization and the creation of narrative tropes. She states, "Do not say that writing is but a play with the brushes about fictional matters, / when the story comes to its crisis the author also agonizes for the characters" (1: 2, 46). She takes joy in creating events and making imaginary interventions to recreate the lives of the protagonists: "Overturning the clouds and raising the rain following my preferences, churning up the waves and stirring the tide I create them at my pleasure" (5: 18, 803). This creative freedom partly helps her "dispel worries" about her indigent life and enchants her with the allure and thrills of the fictional world: "Lamenting my situation, impoverished as I am, I am too ashamed to mention to others; borrowing the happiness [of the characters], what harm does it do to just boast affluence on paper?" (6: 23, 1033). Writing initiates her into intersubjective identification with her characters, yet brings up the ironic distance between her poetic ideal and the humble existence of human beings, as she expresses in the end of her book: "An allegory of man's earthly dream of fortune and eminence, this book on the glory of the world resembles the bubbles on the water" (7: 25, 1177). Meandering in and out of the story, Qiu's authorial narrator engages the audience of her tale on two levels, both as "the narrative audience that exists as on the same fictional plane as the narrator, and as the authorial audience that seeks to understand the whole communication from the author, as well as the function of the narrative audience" (Phelan 204). If the narrative strategy of Qiu's *tanci* is to questions the reader's position and his or her access to the truth, it supports an elusive authorial presence conditioned by orthodox gender propriety and frustrated by its uneasy speaking position.

Being a devoted reader of *Zaishengyuan* (Destiny of Rebirth), Qiu holds high regard for this *tanci*, but criticizes the unconventional character of the heroine Lijun and a few other characters whose deeds exceed the restraints of feminine virtue. Qiu's discontent with Destiny of Rebirth is not a unique case. Her predecessor, *tanci* author and editor Hou Zhi, criticized Chen's bold portrayal of the overtly adventurous Lijun and took to a form of corrective adaptation in *Zaizaotian* (Remaking Heaven, 1828) by editing and remolding the plot and characters on the basis of Chen's original *tanci*. Yet as Ellen Widmer points out, in probing beneath the surface of Hou's didactic *tanci*, "one discovers the ways in which the didacticism hides as well as conceals," and how "expressions of female talent might maneuver through taboos" (Widmer, *Beauty* 75). Qiu's work stages a likewise didactic author, who endeavors to redress the moral message of *Zaishengyuan* by telling another kind of cross-dressing story.

Qiu's authorial narrator comments:

> The newly printed Destiny of Rebirth,
> those who love *tanci* vied for circulating it.
> The style of the writing is refined and genteel, and not at all ordinary,
> the diction and knowledge of the author is truly exceptional and the work is well worth reading.
> Having evaluated all the *tanci*, I consider this one the best,
> except that the authorial intention bears minor imperfection.
> Liu Yanyu forges a secret engagement and fails to follow the "Three Obediences";
> how could she deserve to enjoy the prestigious name Lady of Chastity and Filial Piety?
> *Admonishment for Women* says, "Those who suffer lack in one act will bear corruption in every other act,"
> not to mention that Liu married without matchmaking, and could not be considered as virtuous.
> Li Baohe has competency in her talent, looks, chastity, and virtue;
> and is skillful in handling political affairs and composing literature.
> Yet she suffers the deficiency of failing at filial piety,
> even impulsively abandons her inborn indebtedness for her parents' meticulous nurturing.
> When I read the part of her declining to tell the truth to the Emperor in the Golden Palace,
> Her deeds of humiliating her father and deceiving the Emperor are far too erroneous.
> These are the real insufficiencies of this *tanci* despite its beauty,
> as the saying goes, out of the hundred virtues in the earthly realm, filial piety is of foremost importance.
> Thus I alter the previous *tanci*'s intention and renovate its tune,
> Privately ridicule my own ignorance, and venture to say some bold words.
> (1: 1, 1)

This extensive reflection on Destiny of Rebirth yields rich implications about Qiu's authorial stance, going beyond her self-effacement on the surface. Qiu's allusion to the Han didactic text, *Admonishment for Women*, authored by the female historian Ban Zhao, identifies her authorial position as that of a moral instructress. This ethically conscious self-positioning can be understood in the context of women's literature during the high Qing era. Brought up in a Confucian intellectual family background, Qiu was not alone among her predecessors and contemporaries, gentrified women authors whose writing positions were strongly conditioned by and perceived through Confucian social and ethical values. However, her evocation of the penultimate female mentor Ban Zhao and her writing plays a double role in the text. Rosenlee argues that, although conservative texts like *Nüjie* (Admonitions for Women) are a source for reinforcing orthodox values of gender propriety on women who are confined to the inner sphere, they are also a source of empowerment for erudite women authors (110). Adopting moral propriety as a source of empowerment within the orthodox discourses on feminine virtues, Qiu's representation of an ethically conscious authorial identity lays a moralist veneer over her intrinsic longing to tell a story of her own through adaptation and rewriting.

This ethical authorial stance finds strong articulation in Qiu's choice of having Dehua revert back to marriage and a domestic life when her cross-dressing is exposed. *Zaishengyuan* was a tale that left readers dangling in suspense when Lijun, pressed by the emperor to become his concubine, spits blood and nearly loses her life. Chen's dilemma in concluding the story is emblematic of a narrative contradiction in which "the desire to reach the end is the desire to see 'truth' unveiled" (Brooks, *Body Work* 19). Brooks, reflecting on Barthe's model of narrative as striptease, refers to the "classic" (or "readable") text that works toward a progressive solution of preliminary enigmas, toward a full predication of the narrative "sentence," toward a plenitude of meaning (*Body Work* 19). However, in *Zaishengyuan*, it is nearly unthinkable, as the text indicates, for the unyielding Lijun to concede to the truth, that is, her feminine identity, and revert to a domestic life. Chen's *tanci* visualizes Lijun's cross-dressed body as "a vehicle of narrative signification," and comes to a forced nonclosure with the implication of Lijun's death. In *Bishenghua*, Qiu circumvents this narrative dilemma by making Dehua convert to her feminine identity again, re-dressing Dehua with the moral raiment of virtue and heroism. Qiu's fictional brush strokes bestow her heroine with new forms of power and agency within the normative social and familial system. Dehua's conciliatory sacrifices paradoxically bring her a degree of autonomy in exchange, as her return to the inner chambers happens in a congenial situation.

Susan Mann insightfully argues that women's inner chambers can be considered "a haven" that protects elite women from "daily contact with material corruption (or the dusty world)" (*Precious Records* 49). The inner chambers also functioned as "a powerful trope in writings by men about women during the eighteenth century. For many men resisting the pressures of scholarly careers, women appeared as guardians of stability, order, and purity" (*Precious Records* 50). In *Bishenghua*, the heroine's return to the inner chambers reconfigures the domestic space as a site of feminine power and authority. Qiu's re-creation of the plot initiates the heroine into another life stage, in which she acts as an ideal daughter, prioritizes the prosperity of family, and strives to "fulfill her responsibility and make every person in the boudoir find her own place" (7: 26, 1208). She applies her ingenuity and military skills to governing her household, endorsing the filial and chaste, and taming the shrewish. Her glory is even passed onto her offspring, who share her surname and royal title. Her son is named Jiang Jisheng, or "continuing life," and her late-born younger brother is named Jiang Yousheng, or "born once again." These names suggest that Dehua has extended her life cycle and established continuous power and authority. The book ends with Dehua and her husband Shaoxia transforming into Daoist immortals. This ending projects an ideal of transcending death and achieving spiritual immortality and offers an imaginary alternative to Lijun's predicament of being forced to choose between death and returning to marriage. Dehua's compromise, in view of the plot development, appears to be both an ethical choice and a narrative necessity which ensures the survival of Dehua's tale after the exposure of her identity.

In refashioning the cross-dressing scenario, Qiu depicts Dehua's metamorphosis into a man as an outcome of supernatural intervention, rather than a self-made choice. After she is rescued from suicide by the fox spirit Yuexian, Dehua is given a man's attire and some magical pellets. "After taking the pellets, Dehua miraculously changes into a man's look, / It turns out that, after taking the magical pellets she has enhanced her courage, / and with elated spirit, she goes so far as to claim herself a man. / Not only is her intelligence superior to that of the old days, / she seems to also acquire more enhanced strength than before. / Hence she does not have any fear in her heart, / her mind is open and candid, with no vacillation" (2: 7, 306).

Dynastic Chinese literature and culture offer rich imaginative interpretations of the fox and its magical powers. In Qiu's refashioning of the cross-dressing plot, the supernatural intervention carries a deeper function than just enlivening the story. The preparation of Dehua's masculine makeover through the power of the fantastic eliminates the moral culpability of the heroine for boldly venturing into the exterior sphere. Qiu adds an intriguing scenario in which the cross-dressed heroine's bound feet are hidden. After changing her dress, Dehua is transformed into a young and handsome scholar. However, her three-inch bound feet are difficult to conceal in a pair of large men's boots. Yuexian offers assistance:

> With a smile the fairy lady tears up Dehua's feminine dress,
> saying that now this dress is useless.
> One strand after another, she tears the clothes into pieces and hands them to Dehua,
> who does not hesitate in wrapping her feet with the clothes.
> After finishing wrapping she stands up
> and takes a few steps slowly; her manner is quite proper and solemn.
> Yuexian claps her hands and praises, "Fanciful!"
> And mocks her as being indeed a genteel and beautiful young man. (2: 7, 305-06)

This process of binding the feet with Dehua's torn dress reflects Dehua's entrance into a new life. Unlike the solitary Lijun, who laments the risks of leaving home before cross-dressing, Dehua is blessed with Yuexian's assistance and instructions. Yuexian claims that she offers assistance to the chaste Dehua in order to mediate a heavenly mandate and to return the favor of being sheltered by Dehua's family for many years. Dehua's cross-dressing is doubly legitimized by the necessity of safeguarding her chastity and the rationale of moral compensation for the good. To protect Dehua, Yuexian ventures to substitute for her and to enjoy a playful journey to the palace. She says, "The king is laughably lascivious, / I shall tease him, and make him fruitlessly yearn for beauty" (2: 7, 306). This scenario illustrates the fox spirit as a supernatural agent who utilizes her powers to circumvent the emperor's evil tyranny.

Beautiful and talented, Dehua coalesces the strongest assets of the talented Lijun and several other characters in Chen's *Zaishengyuan*. One may find in Dehua mirror-images of Lijun's chaste Su Yingxue, who substitutes Lijun as the bride in the arranged marriage and attempts suicide to protect her chastity; the ingenious Huangfu Zhanghua, who boasts magical skills and swordsmanship; and the cross-dressed female general Lady Wei, who has exceptional valor and military strategies. Set in the historical context of the late Ming, when the palace was under the manipulation of eunuchs and rancorous royal relatives, Qiu portrays Dehua as a talented woman who is destined to rise in a polemical era to shield the court and defend the nation, indicating that the heroine is obliged to follow established moral principles in order to exert a personal effect on the country and the nation. When her identity is disclosed, the empress dowager praises her as "a goddess of literature who descends to the ordinary world" and even goes on to say, "How surprising, joyous, and admirable, / a woman assists the Emperor and ensures the peace of the country. / The land of the Ming palace is revived, / solely because of this lady" (6: 23, 1034). This passage attests to the moment when the heroine's achievement is not devalued by the disclosure of her cross-dressing, but rather reaches its most glorious moment because of her gender. The appreciative empress dowager endorses Dehua's meritorious triumph as a blessing for her country.

This fictional arrangement illustrates Qiu's possible aspiration to reassess the heroine's gendered identity and reconfigures the inner-outer continuum in broader social and national contexts. Susan Mann suggests that nineteenth-century women's writings show a keen interest in the state of the country and an astute cognizance of issues that belonged to the domain of men, "beyond the women's quarters" ("The Lady and the State" 283). Heroic women in *tanci* writings of this era portray numerous images of women warriors, leaders, and politicians who bespeak women as what Mann terms "a constituency of the polity" (286).

In Qiu's text, she might also have been drawn to illustrious images of heroic women warriors in the history of her hometown. Qiu's native Shanyang, or Huai'An county, was the hometown of the Song female warrior Liang Hongyu (梁紅玉, 1102-35), who was well known for her strategism and bravery while assisting her husband in warfare and presenting herself as epitomizing military morale (Dong, *Mulan's Legend* 21). Another historical figure is the celebrated late Ming female general Qin Liangyu (秦良玉, 1574-1648), who had triumphantly assisted Emperor Chongzhen in appeasing several local rebellions in the southwest regions (*Mulan's Legend* 26). Among several theories about Qin's birthplace, one school of thought holds that she was born in Huai'An County, Qiu's hometown. She was said to have dressed in men's clothing in the battlefield and taken on women's dress when going to the court. These two historical figures might have inspired Qiu in her characterization of the militant Dehua. Both female generals in history were awarded royal titles: Liang had the title Lady of Heroism and Chastity; Qin was honored as Marquise of Loyalty and Chastity. In the text, Dehua's title reflects those of both historical figures, suggesting a potent female military legacy.

As Lan Dong states in her study of the legacy of the legendary Mulan: "The image of the woman being a warrior on the battlefield or in martial confrontation violates the gender separation that requires women to stay inside the female living quarters. In this sense, a courageous heroine defies her assigned gender space by marching into a conventionally masculine territory where she either equals or frequently outwits and outperforms her male contemporaries" (*Mulan's Legend* 12). Such potentially transgressive acts on the part of fictional heroines or historical women are, however, carefully balanced with their "compliance with the simultaneously prevailing ethical codes" (12). Dehua's association with female military historical figures is illustrated through her dream encounter with the legendary Lady Sun, who herself is depicted as a personification of female virtue and heroism. One day Dehua dreams of the fox spirit Yuexian, who leads her to meet Lady Sun, the younger sister of the Wu general Sun Quan in the Three Kingdom period. A famous warrior, Lady Sun is married to Liu Bei (劉備), the King of the Shu Kingdom. After her parents' death, she is taken by grief and homesickness and commits suicide by drowning herself. The Jade Emperor in Heaven pities her and makes her an immortal who sees to it that chaste and filially devoted women are given blessings and fortune, and that the lascivious and shrewd are punished. Moved by Dehua's valiant deeds, Lady Sun makes Dehua an exemplar of the seminal virtues of loyalty, filial piety, chastity, and righteousness. She teaches Dehua military strategies, saying, "Now that the Holy Palace is suffering a misfortune, / how will it ever secure the country with writing brushes? / Today I shall instruct you in the art of war, / so that in the future you can assist the Emperor and accomplish remarkable achievements" (4: 16, 749). She offers Dehua a brocade book with a jade rod, which records the military heritage of the Wu Kingdom. Upon Dehua's request, Lady Sun puts on her armor, takes up her sword, and personally instructs Dehua in martial art skills. Lady Sun finally gives Dehua a precious sword as a gift and proves that her encounter in the dream is real. When Dehua wakes up, she finds by her side an authentic ancient sword which bears inscriptions made in the Han Dynasty and the era name of the Wu Kingdom.

The sword, as portrayed in the above scenario, is a frequently used metaphor in *tanci*, suggesting power, self-defense, and the possibility of action. Hu Siaochen incisively states, in *Tianyuhua* (Heaven Rains Flowers), when the heroine Zuo Yizhen requests that her father allow her to carry his sword for self-protection, that the presentation of the sword represents the transference of authority and power from the father to the daughter, a symbolic "borrowing" of the father's masculinity (Hu, Siao-chen, "The Daughter's Vision" 200-31; "War, Violence" 257; for women's poetic references of sword as a martial imagery, see Li, Wai-yee, "Late Ming Courtesan" 196-201). In Qiu's *tanci*, the reference of the sword is reworked to represent a matriarchal tradition of militancy, which substitutes the paternal authority that is often associated with the sword imagery. Dehua's dream encounter with Lady Sun signifies a ritual in which the heroine returns to the maternal ancestor for sustenance and empowerment. With the book and the sword, Dehua swiftly acquires excellent skills in swordsmanship and warfare, and puts her assets to use when she is summoned by the palace to put down political upheavals.

Unlike the ambitious Lijun, who would "exchange the feminine hairdo for an official coif," Dehua takes to the civil service exam rather passively, urged by her uncle Governor Xie who admires her talent in literature. The text illustrates her hesitation and fear of failure:

> When I change into men's clothing,
> I am only to escape from the turbulent conflicts with rapacious people in power.
> How could I go to the capital to attend the Exam?
> If my disguise is seen through by others,
> The disaster is nothing but small. . . .
> Yet judging by the situation, Uncle is determined to press me to attend the Exam.
> What should I do? Ay, all right! I will just go there once.
> Even though I am just a woman,
> I believe that my talent is competent to rank the first.
> Composing poems within seven steps, I am fearless.
> Finding the lines in the interval of crossing fingers eight times is nothing difficult for me.
> This time, if I am fortunate to rank high on the Golden Rolls,
> Then I can take my wife and return home with glory.
> This will save the parents from lamenting having no sons,
> By that time, my parents will enjoy prodigious honor themselves. (3: 9, 400)

The passage demonstrates that Dehua shares with Lijun the consciousness that a talented woman is frequently at odds with her fate. As Dehua's worries about the risk of attending the exam are replaced with concerns about family pressure, she takes on a more confident tone, comparing herself to two endowed male poets, including Cao Zhi (曹植, 192-232), who could compose a poem during the interval of taking seven steps, and Wen Tingjun (溫庭筠, 812-70), who could finish one rhyme in a short time while crossing his fingers, and the eight rhymes of a full poem after eight finger-crossings. Dehua's self-positioning vis-à-vis the male elites legitimizes her achievement as a learned woman. Reading Dehua's thoughts against the author's self-reflective statements about women's writing, readers may detect a subtle but visible linkage between the ambitious heroine and Qiu, and their shared concerns of enacting a feminine literati identity by actively inscribing women into the paternal literary lineage. The following lines, nonetheless, display her utilizing her success to bring her family and ancestors prestige, suggesting that Dehua, who by this time is cross-dressed and married to Yunxian, internalizes a masculine identity as defined and constructed by traditional Confucian family and moral values.

Dehua's internalization of an orthodox masculine subjectivity both liberates and constrains her life and actions after cross-dressing. While her disguise offers her autonomy and freedom to explore a man's life, she performs mostly as a substitute husband and later, with the birth of Xialang, as a substitute father when the real husband and father is absent. In Qiu's plot arrangement, Dehua's cross-dressing prepares for the establishment of her final marriage with Shaoxia, with Chunniang marrying Shaoxia as a concubine, and Xialang carrying on the name of his own father. This conventional arrangement is akin to that in Liang Desheng's sequel to *Zaishengyuan*, in which Liang makes the adventurous Lijun reconcile with the emperor and marry Shaohua, while her wife in mock marriage becomes Shaohua's concubine. Qiu's indoctrination of her characters with moral norms creates differences between Dehua and Lijun. Lijun passionately denies her cross-dressing when confronted by her own parents and cuts herself completely off from her relatives. This drastic denunciation of her female identity and the father-daughter relationship puts Lijun in an ethical dilemma for undermining the father-daughter hierarchical relation. In Qiu's *tanci*, Dehua confesses her secret to her parents before her cross-dressing is exposed. After she changes back to her feminine dress and marries Shaohua, she lives with her parents and even fasts a whole year to pray that heaven will endow her aged father with a son to carry on the maternal family name, Jiang. Qiu's conservative stance is also displayed in her depiction of male-female relationships. She changes the relationship between the heroine and her fiancée from that of the mentor-student relationship between Lijun and Shaohua in *Zaishengyuan* to a form of brotherhood between Dehua and Shaoxia. The disguised Dehua is therefore exempted from the moral hazard of drastically reverting to the husband-wife hierarchy.

Perhaps Qiu's depiction of the male-female relationship after Shaoxia and Dehua's marriage reveals a facet of gender relationships that Chen Duansheng did not choose or did not have a chance to depict. With Shaoxia residing with Dehua's maternal family, and Dehua preceding him in the prime minister's position, the wife Dehua holds more than the usual power in their marriage. This arrangement is an ingenious reconfiguration of the orthodox marriage. In traditional China, marriage was "a contract between two families that established a relationship in which the woman was unambiguously subordinate and in which husband and wife assumed legal standing and responsibility not only in regard to each other, but also in regard to each other's relatives" (Liu, Kwang-Ching 218). The relationships between husband and wife were "theoretically at once hierarchical and reciprocal." Although in practice, this was not always the case: "Reciprocity was generally neglected, and the husband's will and needs dominated. Still, unless a man could afford a concubine, he could not risk alienating his wife by oppressing her too severely, for it was through her 'uterine' family that he achieved immortality in the ritual sacrifices made to him by his descendants" (Liu, Kwang-Ching 223).

Bishenghua portrays an unusual reconfiguration of this traditional matrimonial system. After Dehua again dons her feminine dress, she returns to her maternal household and takes Shaoxia as her husband in her maternal family. She follows the emperor's command to use her surname Jiang as the family surname for her descendants. These measures strengthen the authority of the heroine's uterine family, ensuring her power in the boudoir, without breaking down the conventional marriage system. Rather, after her marriage, Dehua plays an active role in consolidating her husband's power and, by doing so, finds means of refurbishing her feminine virtue. When Shaoxia and Dehua are newly married, Dehua hopes to persuade Shaoxia into taking two serving maids as concubines, but the idea is rejected by Shaoxia, who alludes to the ancient affectionate couple Liang Hong and Meng Guang to express his determination to stay faithful to Dehua. Unwilling to upset Dehua, he pretends to accept her proposal of taking the concubines, while secretly plotting to upset Dehua's plan and have the two concubines married to two male study mates. The text presents a family melodrama in which husband and wife try to outwit each other. Afraid of upsetting Dehua and stirring up her grievances, Shaoxia ponders:

> Let me first give a vague response to Dehua and wait for another time to reason with her.
> Even ruling an army could not require too much deception,
> What is the harm in using a little scheming in governing a household?
> When the time comes, I shall take action and uphold the authority of the husband,
> and I shall definitely tame this brilliant and extraordinary troupe of women.
> When the meal is fully cooked,
> Dehua shall have no way to disagree with me.
> Thus my wife's heart can be appeased,
> the risk of family dissonance dissolved. (7: 26, 1199)

Despite his ingenuous plan, Dehua outwits Shaoxia when she sees through his scheme and arranges two other maidens to marry Shaoxia's study servants. She presses Shaoxia into accepting the concubines, who present themselves in wedding gowns and plead for the master to accept them. This subplot of Dehua appropriating Shaoxia's scheme to spoil his own plan recalls the melodramatic scenes in *Tianyuhua* (Heaven Rains Flowers), in which a male character Heng Yu, after marrying the genteel but stubborn lady Zuo Yizhen, sets up multiple contrivances in order to tame Yizhen, only making her more rebellious against his dominance in the house. Finally, she retreats to the garden and takes it as a personal space of autonomy. There is no textual evidence that proves Qiu read *Tianyuhua*. However, this seventeenth-century *tanci* was circulated through print and had achieved a prestigious reputation by Qiu's time. The subplot of Dehua coaxing her husband into taking concubines is also reminiscent of an episode in Heaven Rains Flowers in which the hero Weiming's mother, deceived by a housemaid, plots to make Weiming drunk and take the maid as his concubine. When Weiming wakes up, he instantly rejects the arrangement. Later in the story, the self-disciplined Weiming resists temptations laid out by a fox spirit, a palace maiden, and a lascivious nun. In Qiu's *tanci*, however, this moralistic impulse in the narrative is adapted to emphasize the values of feminine virtue. Dehua gains the upper hand by making her husband take the concubines as she desires, because her own children are commanded by the emperor to carry their maternal surname Jiang, instead of Shaoxia's surname Wen. Her seemingly disobedient arrangement against Shaohua's will is made precisely in order to endorse the husband's authority.

Having transcended earthly yearnings, Dehua assists Shaoxia to obtain more offspring and solidifies her own sovereignty.

Qiu also modelled her text upon previous *tanci* works in order to highlight the heroine's moral agency. *Xiaojinqian* (Little Gold Coins), for instance, tells the tale of a childless heroine Chen Yuechan (陳月嬋), who offers incense to the heavenly emperor and pleads with him to give her a child. She succeeds in moving heaven with her sincere wishes and later gives birth to two children. This scenario is alluded to in *Bishenghua* (4: 15, 695). One day, when Dehua is still cross-dressed as Jiang Junbi, her mother-in-law summons a female *tanci* storyteller to the inner chambers to perform this episode in *Xiaojinqian*. Later in Qiu's *tanci*, a similar scenario is portrayed. Dehua has been given the emperor's verdict that her son shall carry the maternal surname Jiang. One day, her son Jiang Wencai (姜文彩) tells her that a relative of the family mocks Wencai for not being the direct descendant of the Jiangs, saying that he should use his father's surname Wen. To extinguish such talk, Dehua decides to help her aged parents give birth to a brother who carries on the family surname. She vows to live an abstinent life for a whole year, and every night offers fragrance to the moon, praying for heaven to give her parents a son. Her filial deeds eventually move heaven; her father's concubine gives birth to a son. Qiu's adaptation accentuates the heroine's feminine virtue and love for her parents, which distinguishes Dehua from the rebellious Lijun and elevates the original plot from one about conjugal love in *Xiaojinqian* (Little Gold Coins) to a morally instructive tale about filial devotion.

Qiu's propagation of orthodox moral values and gender propriety reproduces her *tanci* as an alternate cross-dressing story to Chen Duansheng's *Zaishengyuan*. Qiu's strong ethical awareness underlies her choice of rewriting the story and making Dehua revert back to her feminine identity to become one of Shaoxia's wives in a polygamous family. Whereas Dehua's return to her female identity opens up new narrative possibilities, Qiu's text cannot avoid the narrative conventions of previous *tanci* tales in undercutting Dehua's mobility with the constraints of feminine virtue. The text empowers the heroine by adding elements of supernatural intervention and evoking the legacy of female military agency. Conversely, these measures are cautiously made to legitimize the orthodox rationales of filial piety and feminine chastity. Although Dehua's unusual achievement reflects women's extraordinary potential to achieve success as men's peers, Dehua's personal identity has rarely been more than that of a substitute son, husband, or father. The text's lively depiction of Dehua's domestic life after marrying Shaoxia, though showing her continued authority and power, cannot conceal her considerable reconciliation and sacrifice. Whether such an arrangement reflects a conciliatory and realistic vision or Qiu's internalization of Confucian moral values, the readers cannot ignore the painful conflicts between personal ideal and societal pressure, between individual pursuits and familial obligations. In a nutshell, Qiu's choice of making Dehua a Daoist immortal is an ultimate, if imaginary, device used to resolve the author's reconfiguration of the plot and the impossibility of finding correspondent external cultural and social references.

As in *Zaishengyuan*, motifs of supernatural forces play a crucial role in the development of plot in *Bishenghua*. The fox spirit Yuexian rescues Dehua from drowning herself, transforms into Dehua's form, and takes her place in the palace. Ming and Qing fictional works often depict stories of a beautiful fox lady who assists young and impoverished scholars to study and obtain success. In Qiu's text, the fox serves as a supernatural device who substitutes for the heroine and helps her protect her virginity and pursue her personal desire beyond gender boundaries. Qiu's reconfiguration of the fox image illustrates the blurred boundaries between *nüxian* (女仙), or female immortals or celestials, and *nüyao* (女妖), the female spirit transformed from female demons or spirits in traditional narratives.

The difference between a demonic and celestial being lies in the figure's origin and the point of view of the person referring to it. In Chinese folk imagination, demons and spirits derive from animals or from inanimate objects such as statues, as portrayed in the Qing classic story collection 聊齋誌異 (*Liaozhai zhiyi*, *Strange Tales from a Chinese Studio*). Through self-cultivation or absorbing the essence of nature, often for thousands of years, these animals and objects are able to attain supernatural powers and transform into human forms. The celestials or immortals were either humans who had attained their elevated status and powers through being taught the secrets by other celestials, or beings who had an affinity with the heavenly realm or reincarnated spirits. Yunxian "had a celestial root in her previous life, and thus, could easily become an immortal" with practice (8: 30, 1438). Thanks to her virtuous deeds, the fox spirit is elevated to a higher rank equal to that of an immortal such as Lady Sun, the heroic woman who was transformed into an immortal because of her filial piety. Yunxian, a self-cultivated immortal, is honored together with the fox spirit in the Sanctuary of Three Immortals. The fluid boundaries between demons, humans, immortals, and celestials are redefined by the moral principles of chastity and filial piety (Chen, Fan Pen Li, *Chinese Shadow Theater*).

Qiu's rendering of the fox spirit can be understood in light of dynastic imaginings related to fox spirits. According to the sixteenth-century folk fiction 封神演義 (*Fengshen yanyi*, The Investiture of the Gods), in the ancient dynasty of Shang, a concubine, Su Daji (蘇妲己), was killed by a fox spirit who transformed into her beautiful form in order to seduce King Zhou with carnal pleasure and to bewitch him into abandoning his governance of the country. The fox spirit Daji is portrayed in later historical novels as representing licentious women who were often created "to present a contrast between virtuous heroes who resist them and the virtueless villains who yield to them . . . representing the lusts of the flesh, these women bring forward an illustration that lust (for women) is disaster-prone and must be curbed" (Chang, Shelley Hsueh-lun 149-50). Daji is also portrayed in the form of a femme fatale who preys on men in the Ming text *Fengshen yanyi*. During the High Qing era, the popularity of the fox in novels, popular stories, and folk religion reached a climax. The image of the fox borders between the monster and the transcendent, the human and nonhuman. In romance and love tales, the fox is often a symbol of sexual passion and desire, stirred up by human beings' own moral weaknesses or misbehavior

(Huntington, *Alien Kind* 6). As Huntington argues, in Ming and Qing, there were folk practices of fox worship conducted to establish a connection with the supernatural. Fox spirits in popular religious practices were elevated to the level of "divine beings, particularly beautiful women, who have acquired immortality through Daoist self-cultivation. To call a fox spirit a *xian* is to make it become morally acceptable" (Huntington, *Alien Kind* 134).

In *Bishenghua*, this blending of fox spirit and immorality is characterized by the mischievous yet sympathetic Hu Yuexian, whose surname puns on the sound of "fox" and whose given name literally means "moon goddess." When, on her way to the capital, Dehua attempts to hang herself to die chaste for her fiancé, the fox spirit Yuexian raises a gust of wind to carry the heroine into a small lodging and uses magic powers to breathe life into her body. When Dehua wakes up, she is astonished to see a lady who seems to be the fairy lady she had previously met in a garden at her own house. The lady introduces herself:

> Don't say that I belong to the alien kind,
> After many years I have attained the Dao and possess the ingenuous perception.
> I have wanted to leave this body and ascend to heaven,
> However, I was bound by destiny to you and have not reached my time.
> In your respectful garden, I have borrowed a place to reside.
> With your family I am also sheltered safely,
> Thanks to your lady who has treated me with courtesy and never beguiled me.
> Thus I have carried a wish to return your favor,
> And come to save your life, and exempt you from calamities.
> Now you shall follow the good scheme of "shedding your cover like the golden cicada."
> I also bring a set of scholarly attire as a gift for you.
> From now on you should put on the disguise,
> And go to the governor of Shandong whose wife is your maternal aunt. (2: 7, 305)

The text represents the fox spirit Hu Yuexian as a divine agent whose magic rescues the heroine from suicide. The scene in which Yuexian binds Dehua's feet with her torn dress reflects Dehua's entrance into a completely new life. Yuexian is a trickster-like character who has the ability to summon magical powers, transform into other's appearances, or vanish into thin air. She ventures to take the place of Dehua to "enjoy a playful journey to the palace," using her powers to circumvent the emperor's tyranny.

The text later portrays Yunxian as a disciple of the fox spirit, who, after assisting Dehua and her family to survive many calamities, is honored with the rank of female immortal. After Dehua changes back to feminine dress, her "wife" Yunxian, who is devoted to Daoist practice, strongly opposes marrying Shaohua as his concubine. Instead, having heard of the fox spirit's heroic deeds, she decides to take to private Daoist practice in a secluded garden in the Jiang house, where the fox spirit had previously resided and where she returned after she vanished from the wedding with Shaohua. Hu Siao-chen proposes that Yunxian's identification with the transcendent fox spirit, her denunciation of familial linkages, and her rejection of a marriage prospect indicate women's self-exile from orthodox social relationships. The garden where she resides in seclusion becomes a private space of agency, locating her beyond the restrictions of womanly virtue and family relationships ("Mimi huayuan" 299; on Ming garden culture, see Clunas 63-103). This arrangement presents Yunxian and Dehua as doubles choosing divergent paths: one fleeing from the secular, the other continuing her worldly journey after reverting back to her feminine identity. Hu holds that such an arrangement reveals "an authorial desire for a secret garden of self-exile, seclusion, and spiritual transcendence" ("Mimi huayuan" 299; also see Che 97-101).

Qiu's reconfiguration of the fox trope in the novel is constituent of her overall idealization of Daoist immortality. The subplot of Yunxian becoming a female immortal through Daoist practice reflects a trend of women seeking to substitute marriage with the pursuit of immortality. The representation of female immortals in Chinese culture may be found in the ancient book 搜神記 (*Soushen ji*, *In Search of the Supernatural*) by Gan Bao (干寶, 217-419 CE), where the Daoist search for immortality was widely recorded in stories and popular narratives. In several stories in Gan's text, the female immortals are devoted to comforting men and bringing them extraordinary children and gifts. These immortals always cater to men's needs, whether supporting them materially or bearing their children (Wang, Robin 197). In *Bishenghua*, however, Yunxian's Daoist practice is justified by her intention to keep her virginity and her spiritual pursuit beyond the constraint of the marriage paradigm. Her image is reminiscent of female Daoist immortals in Qing dynasty popular literature who are characterized by their refusal to marry in order to live lives of celibacy, or, in some more subversive texts, to transcend socially inscribed gender roles (Grant, "Patterns" 9-13; see also Cleary, *Immortal Sisters*). In the text, Yunxian's Daoist practice is shielded and supported by the cross-dressed Dehua, who plays the role of Yunxian's husband to the elders and the outsiders and hides her secret of spiritual alchemy. After Dehua converts back to her female identity, Yunxian's devotion to Daoism protects her from being married to Shaohua in a polygamous family. When she is pressed by her parents to marry Shaoxia as his concubine, Yunxian instantly protests against such a fate and suggests suicide:

> Grabbing her jade hairpin, she thrusts it on the floor.
> With a piercing sound, the hairpin breaks in halves.
> Turning back, she calls on her father:
> My father, your child would rather be beheaded than change her intention.
> When time comes up for me to remarry, I shall be the same as this broken hairpin.
> If my parents still have pity for their daughter,
> Please allow her to linger in the world for some more time.
> Refining my true nature, comprehending the real principles,
> I shall certainly complete my practice one day and ascend to the Nine Heavens.
> It has been said that a child who ascends to heaven shall take his relatives

with him;
By that time, isn't it true that my parents shall become immortals as well?
Why am I obliged to fulfill the marriage engagement?
In this situation, what esteem will I have when I put back on a girl's dress
and hairpins?
After saying this, the young lady turns pale,
Minister Xie feels at once angry, incredulous, and compassionate. (6: 22, 1022)

After persuading her parents, Yunxian puts on a Daoist robe. Her astonished relatives "see that she is dressed in an extraordinary way all over, / her long dress with long sleeves is replaced with a Daoist robe. / With no make-up or flower decorations, she wears instead a nun's crown and a robe" (6: 22, 1023). Her self-transformation through religious pursuit represents a cultural trend in Ming Qing women's religious practice which is considered harmless to the patriarchal hierarchy and allows women to transcend social reality and aspire to spiritual freedom (see Zhou, Yiqun 109-55). It should also be noted that there was a strong social trend of Daoist pursuit for immortality during the Ming Jiajing period, which is the era chosen by Qiu as the context for the second half of her *tanci*. Maggie C. K. Wan offers a study of Ming emperor Jiajing's retreat to *Xiyuan* (西苑), the West Park in 1542 which she holds is closely related to his lifelong belief in Daoism and his pursuit of physical immorality (Wan 65-99). Late imperial household instructions and values "placed enormous stress on female propriety as a primary symbol of domestic virtue, not by expecting women to be active guardians of a 'feminized' realm of culture, but simply by making women objects of paternalistic molding. On the other hand, wives were seen as the main source of religious heterodoxy within the family" (Liu, Kwang-Ching 202). Liu further suggests that "there is reason to believe that some forms of popular worship, both inside and outside the home, were a female sphere in late traditional China. Women presided over the religious mediation of fertility, childbirth, and many illnesses, requiring the services of specialists devoted to a variety of popular spirits. Many visited temples on holidays" (202). Likewise, Beata Grant states that literati women viewed visiting convents and monasteries as a means of emotional release, and they enjoyed exchanging conversations with women monastics (Grant, *Eminent Nuns* 97). Female forms of religious practice, whether driven by piety or a preoccupation with otherworldly salvation, were largely carried on within the framework of the patriarchal home and offered the system little to fear. In the medieval Song era (960-1279), for example, women's ascetic self-cultivation—including fasting, seclusion, and vegetarianism—as gendered practices were customary and endorsed by literati as fitting in the "paradigm of feminine virtue" (Lu, Huitzu 73-108). Female religious practice, in other words, suits the pattern of "religious pluralism" coexisting with "moral orthodoxy" (Liu, Kwang-Ching 202). Popular religious texts of the late imperial period, in addition to illustrating celibate women Daoists, portrayed heroines who were not capable of avoiding marriage or childbearing, some of whom persisted in Daoist practice in search of spiritual life and salvation (Grant, "Patterns" 16).

In the text, the ideal of becoming a female immortal is centrally represented by Yunxian's experience. In the more advanced stage of her practice, she is able to vanish into thin air, and even predict the fate of others, by reading astrology. When her sister-in-law Peilan's life is at risk during childbirth, Yunxian draws a magic talisman and has it delivered to Peilan. After Peilan drinks a cup of water mixed with the ashes of the burned talisman, she miraculously recovers and gives birth to a daughter. Later, Yunxian accomplishes her study and ascends to heaven. To commemorate her love for Yunxian, Dehua draws a portrait of her and offers incense to it. Later in the story, Yunxian is a mediator between the earth and the heavenly realm. She enters Dehua's dream and gives her a bottle of magical wine. After she drinks the wine, the elders of the Wen and Jiang families enjoy health and longevity. Dehua and her husband Shaoxia, both being immortal in their previous lives, obtain ageless beauty from the wine, and become immortals themselves. Another concubine of Shaoxia's, the stubborn and vengeful Chu Chunyi, takes to religious meditation for comfort and goes to the Sanctuary of Three Immortals by the West Lake to continue her study. The sanctuary was originally built by the emperor to commemorate the fox spirit who rescued Dehua from losing her life. Later Dehua and Shaoxia also return to the temple to study alchemy.

Reminiscent of the scene in which Lijun composes a poem before leaving her parents, Yunxian leaves two poems before she becomes an immortal, one for her parents, the other for Dehua. The poems go as follows:

> First:
> Borrowing your eminent lodging, I lived twenty years;
> This heart of mine is not tainted by even a speckle of dust.
> Only that I know the transcendent pleasures of the clouds, water, fog, and dawn light,
> Without pursuing the romantic affinity with the wind, flower, snow, and moon.
> Without being involved in trivial matters, one cannot have a life in the world;
> Those who can explore and decipher their own destinies can ascend to the immortal world.
> Now that I ride the crane and return to the mountains,
> Hope my parents treasure their own wellbeing and do not suffer from the loss.
>
> At the back of the poem is written, "The unfilial daughter Xucai, with a hundred bows, composes with caution for her parents' gracious viewing."
>
> Second:
> For three years we lived in harmony and had our wishes fulfilled,
> I believe you understand my intentions.
> Meticulously and diligently, I pursue Dao like the female immortal Wang Miaoxiang,
> Out of the ordinary, I do not imitate the acts of the reincarnated goddess Du Lanxiang.
> With respect I follow the demand of heaven and leave from now on,

and send my words to women in the Golden Chambers to forsake grieving.
In another day I shall come to fetch you, holding a sacred flag,
In the depths of white clouds, we shall fly together with full freedom.

At the back of the poem is written, "Your humble elder sister Xie, leaving this poem to commemorate her departure; please immediately show it to my kind younger sister Dehua. Hope the viewer gives me gracious understanding by not disclosing this poem to others." (8: 30, 1437)

The above represents a scenario comparable to the scene in which Lijun composes a poem on her self-portrait before leaving her parents and cross-dressing to flee from home. In Qiu's adaptation, Yunxian pursues an ideal of transcendental subjectivity through Daoism, and is an alternate self to the heroine Dehua. The first poem, addressed to the parents, shows Yunxian's determination to pursue Daoist study instead of romance and marriage. In the first two lines, Yunxian describes herself as one born with a celestial root, bound to return to the immortal world after borrowing shelter with her parents in her short ethereal journey. Her practice of spiritual alchemy also justifies her moral integrity and filial intentions, although she could not serve her parents personally until the end of their lives. The second poem, addressed to Dehua, evokes the legendary immortals as precursory examples for her pursuit. Wang Miaoxiang (王妙想) is a lengendary figure who practices the art of *pigu* (辟穀), or spontaneous fasting, in the Huangting Monastery by Mount Hengshan in Hunan and later ascends to the immortal world (Li, Fang, *Taiping guangji, juan* 61, *hui* 6). Du Lanxiang (杜蘭香) is a legendary fairy lady who is punished for misdeeds by having to descend to earth, who later returns to heaven (see Li Fang, *Taiping yulan*). Both allusions in Yunxian's second poem suggest that Yunxian will function as a mediator between heaven and earth, and assist Dehua's ultimate return to the immortal realm in the future. The instructive note after the poem indicates a gentry woman's exceptional caution that the poem is a private message to a designated viewer only, and that the heavenly mandate shall not be viewed in public.

These two poems offer a perception of Yunxian's practice beyond that of asceticism, portraying her as a transcendent subject beyond the male/female gender categories, in-between the ethereal and the sanctified. The ending lines carry an embedded narrative prolepsis, "a narrative maneuver that consists in narrating or evoking in advance an event that will take place" (Genette, *Narrative* 40), and suggest Daoist transcendence as the final ending of the *tanci*. It is also worth scrutiny that Qiu revises the scene in which Lijun makes a self-portrait of her female self before cross-dressing. However, in *Bishenghua*, after Yunxian ascends to heaven, Dehua takes up her painting brush to make a portrait of her so that a statue of Yunxian can be made and honored at the Sanctuary of Three Immortals. Whereas Lijun's portrait in *Zaishengyuan* is possessed by the lovesick Shaohua and becomes an object of male desire, Yunxian's portrait is made to commemorate her moral purity, suggesting the author's rectification of the plot to emphasize the propriety in repurposing the beauty portrait.

Parallel to these examples of immortal spirits, the story also depicts several examples of vicious women who are reincarnated from animal spirits or reborn to pay the price for their misconduct in previous lives. An example is the Shaoxia's ferocious concubine Wo Lianggui, the daughter of a middle-ranking official. In her previous life, Wo Lianggui was a female wolf who attacked Shaoxia. The two are destined to re-encounter each other in this life as husband and wife. A ravenous wife, Wo assaults Shaoxia when he is in adversity, ridiculing his poverty and frail appearance. When the cross-dressed Dehua visits their household, Wo is immediately attracted to the prime minister's handsome appearance and eminent position and even attempts to seduce Dehua. Because of her erroneous behavior and persistent assault on Shaoxia and even Shaoxia's sister, Wo is locked up in private in the Wen household and finally suffers death in childbirth. Before her death, she dreams of her deceased father, who, himself a wandering ghost repenting from his sinful deeds in life, reveals to Wo her misconduct and her doomed fate.

Qiu's portrayal of the fox spirit and female immortals represents Daoist self-cultivation as a means of self-elevation for both the alien kind in nature and human beings who were born with a celestial bond. Qiu illustrates the heroine's cross-dressing as initiated and facilitated by the compassionate fox spirit, and relies on the power of the fantastic to exempt the heroine from possible moral culpability due to her cross-dressing. This plot arrangement, in addition to adding a supernatural flair to the story to enchant the readers, reflects a late imperial trend of women's fascination with and practice of popular religions that were considered allowable by orthodox society and harmless to feminine virtue. By depicting the fox spirit as a Daoist immortal and mentor, the author breaks down the boundaries between human, beast, and immortal and opens up new spaces for imaginary subjective positions for women in the inner chambers. Also, by employing Yunxian as a double of Dehua and portraying her pursuit of spiritual alchemy, the author foreshadows the heroine's eventual transcendence of earthly bonds through Daoist pursuits, and thus envisions the heroine's final achievement of autonomy without bearing the reproach of breaking the orthodox moral values of filial piety and gender propriety. If narrative motifs such as fox spirits and female immortals are symptomatic of the marvelous and fantastic, such narratives work in Qiu's *tanci* mostly repeat and reinforce the moral of the story: that a filially devoted women will always be rewarded with a good fate, and that the good and just shall triumph over the evil and shrewd.

Qiu's *tanci*, in conclusion, could be considered a didactic adaptation of *Zaishengyuan*, recounted by an ethically self-reflexive feminine author. Qiu's authorial insertions orchestrate a dramatized storyteller who endeavors to tell a morally sound tale and guide the readers' reception of the story. This authorial persona is distinctively gendered as feminine and situated in the context of the history of women's writing, a context which both empowers Qiu with a feminine legacy of writing in dynastic eras and displays the constraint on women's speech in the orthodox and male-centered social environment. Though the plot and characters of *Bishenghua* are much indebted to *Zaishengyuan*, Qiu's *tanci* is far more intricate than an actual sequel. Rather, by arranging the cross-dressed heroine's return to the inner chambers, Qiu demonstrates how the adventurous Dehua transforms and reclaims the domestic sphere as a space of feminine agency and authority. Eager to exempt her protagonist from the accusation of being overtly ambitious, Qiu creates a fox spirit Hu Yuexian, who represents the force of supernatural intervention and assists Dehua in taking a male disguise. Here, the fantastic impulse in the story, though ostensibly transgressive, serves as a moralistic rationale for the heroine's cross-dressing and thus offers an ethical shield for the virtuous heroine. Dissimilar to *Zaishengyuan,* which ends with Lijun's impending death under the emperor's tyrannous pressure, *Bishenghua* offers an alternative closure in which the heroine becomes immortal through Daoist practice and hence achieves true transcendence. This imaginary ending, echoing the title of the book Blossom from the Brush, suggests the novel's own verisimilitude (that is, its fictional kernel), and ironizes the author's realistic compromises in plot development and characterization.

Chapter Three

Ethics, Filial Piety, and Narrative Sympathy in *Mengyingyuan* (Dream, Image, Destiny)

If storytelling frequently involves putting forth a narrative that rewards the virtuous and punishes the villainous, such a convention of poetic justice certainly becomes reconfigured when an author inserts a powerfully gender-conscious voice in the narrative. This is compellingly represented in the seminal *tanci* work, *Mengyingyuan* (Dream, Image, Destiny; preface dated 1843), by Zheng Danruo (鄭澹若, 1811-1860). Zheng states in her insertion in the text, "My writing brush is accustomed to articulate anger against injustice, / The *Jingwei* bird who fills the sea with pebbles has a most resolute heart. / Voicing agony and regret for my precursors, / I shall eliminate vice and malevolence, and widely execute regulation" (2: 20, 104). This passage foregrounds an authorial narrator who executes her writing in comportment with moral principles and displays her determination through an empathetic identification with the legendary bird *Jingwei* (精衛), an ancient symbol of feminine heroism. In *Mengyingyuan*, this authorial narrative voice conjures up empathetic identifications with the fictional characters by articulating their feelings through her own voice. Narrative empathy is central to this work and to its social and political interventions in the predominant discourse of the time. Authorial statements in this *tanci* explicate Zheng's profound anxiety about the social and cultural turmoil of the late Qing dynasty and her persistent struggle to create a space for self-expression. Zheng's epic undertaking in *tanci* gives prominence to women's self-inscription through writing and projects women authors' possibility of participating in social, cultural, and historical-structural transformations.

Zheng's *tanci* commences with a predestined relationship between two heavenly spirits, Kuifang Xianzi (魁芳仙子, Premium Flower Goddess) and Mengyin Zhenren (夢隱真人, Dream-Concealed Deity). The two heavenly spirits are summoned by the heavenly emperor to descend to earth to lead the scholar Zhuang of the Song Dynasty (960-1279) in his ascension to the immortal world. The emperor demands that Dream-Concealed Deity enter the world and be reincarnated as Mengyu, the son of the Zhuang family. When Mengyu grows up, he will take the place of his father and serve his country and emperor. Together with the twelve flower goddesses, Premium Flower Goddess and the Dream-Concealed Deity descend to present the principles through personal practices in order to instruct people in the world (1: 1, 3). The main plot line then follows the family of the reincarnated immortal Zhuang Yuan (莊淵), who descends to the world during the Song dynasty. After serving the emperor with dedication for many years, Zhuang resigns from his position, to avoid conflict with a treacherous high official. He retreats to his home in the countryside with his wife, Mrs. Zhuang, a highly talented woman who also happens to be the reincarnated Premium Flower Goddess and the leader of the twelve flower goddesses. Zhuang's son Zhuang Mengyu (莊夢玉), who is originally the Dream-Concealed Deity, comes down to the world to redress social customs. The Plum Goddess, who shares a predestined bond with Mengyu and follows him to earth, is born into Lin's family, carrying the name of Lin Xianyu. When Xianyu's father General Lin Wu (林武) meets Zhuang Yuan and becomes his friend, he arranges a union of the two reincarnated deities. The tales of the other flower goddesses overlap with Lin and Zhuang's romance. Each of these goddesses possesses an exceptional talent or has an outstanding virtue. The major plotline develops around Zhuang Mengyu and two other flower goddesses, Lin Xianyu (林纖玉) and Song Renfang (宋紉芳), both of whom marry Mengyu to fulfill a preordained relationship.

Zheng's exhilarating endeavor to startle and transform readers through her story suggests that upper class women in mid Qing enjoyed the aspiration of expressing themselves and reaching to readers outside the inner chambers. Like the prior *tanci* author Chen Duansheng, Zheng was a member of the gentry class. Her father was a vice censor-in-chief in the government (Hu, Wenkai 740). She was born in Wucheng county of Zhejiang province in the early nineteenth century. In Zheng's early years, she established her fame as a poet under the name of Zheng Zhenhua (鄭貞華), meaning "flower of chastity." Before composing her *tanci*, she completed a poetry collection, 綠飲樓詩遺 (*Lüyinlou shiyi*, Remained Poems of the Green Water Pavilion), which was published around 1833 (Hu, Wenkai 740). Later, she became known as a master of *tanci*. A literary critic of Zheng's time commented on her outstanding *tanci* and her augmentation of women's writing: "Zheng Danruo wrote the renowned *Mengyingyuan*, which stood out with its erudition, splendid style, and refined diction, and consequently brought about a transformation of the genre of *tanci*" (Bao 269).

Zheng's literary achievement is attested to by her extensive poetry exchanges with other women of the time. These poems provide some of the little biographical information that remains about her. For example, Wang Yaofen (王瑤芬), who was a close female friend and a family relative of Zheng, had several poems referring to Zheng in 寫韻樓詩鈔 (*Xieyunlou shichao*, Poetry Collections of the Rhyme Composition Pavilion). Zheng's daughter Zhou Yingfang married Wang Yaofen's son (Bao 269). Some of the poems dedicated to her by her women friends also shed some light on her literary reputation and style of writing. In a poem composed for the celebration of Zheng's birthday, the poet Yan Yonghua (嚴永華), who was a close friend of

Zheng's, comments that she had long known that Zheng's "magic brush was born with an immortal spirit" (Yan 1.10a). Yan honored Zheng as *nüzongshi* (女宗師), the woman master in poetry, and in comparison called herself a *shidizi* (詩弟子), a poetry disciple. These references attest to the author's poetic talent, which is consequently displayed in the large amount of poetry and verse games in *Mengyingyuan*. Regarding Zheng's poetry collection *Green Water Pavilion,* a poem dedicated to Zheng from a later woman poet notes, "Her chaste spirit, together with her poetry collection Green Water Pavilion, left no traces" (Chen Yun 23b). The poem, punning on Zheng's formal name Zhenhua (貞華), that is, chaste flower, suggests that the poet did not leave many poems after her tragic suicide in 1860.

This suicide, which is probably the most important piece of extant biographical information, can be contextualized with the mass suicide of women that occurred during the Taiping Rebellion, a social upheaval that nearly overthrew the late Qing government. When the rebels occupied the southern cities, local residents were forced to leave their families and live in separate camps for men and women. As their domestic lives were shattered, many women of the gentry class committed suicide to defend their chastity. Zheng's husband was the head official of Hangzhou when the rebels broke into the city in 1860. Probably to preserve her chastity, Zheng committed suicide by taking poison. For late imperial women, "once the boundaries of the chaste body, the virtuous reputation, the proper interaction, or the inner quarters had been violated, only a publicly known and violent vindication of the chastity that was destroyed could restore the moral integrity that was integral to so many women's sense of self" (Theiss 134). Zheng's death might be understood as an attempt to express her selfhood in a shattered society by the spectacle of suicide.

As Susan Mann suggests, scholars of Qing women's literature in the late nineteenth century should "draw a line between the writings of women who lived through the Taiping Rebellion, and those who never experienced it" ("The Lady and the State" 313). Whereas some women authors who survived the tragic incident were able to write reflective poems on their traumatic experiences, Zheng's death in the Taiping attack situates her and her *tanci* in a crucial historical time which precedes a profound change of women's literary production caused by traumatic historical transformation. Tobie Meyer-Fong, in her 2013 book, points out that during the Taiping Rebellion, the massive number of suicides committed by women who drowned themselves at the fall of Hangzhou was testified to by records of foreign missionaries who witnessed the tragedy and to whom such a phenomenon possibly represented a form of moral violence. However "for a nineteenth-century Chinese observer," such event "is meant to be read as the expression of collective virtue, the fulfillment of an obligation entailed by fundamental human relationships and thus an act worthy of commemoration and official honors" (Meyer-Fong 119-20).

The cult of female chastity in the late imperial period has caught the attention of many critics. Wenjing Lu offers valuable research on Ming and Qing faithful maidens, that is, betrothed women whose fiancés died before marriage, but who maintained lifelong chastity or committed suicide to join their "husbands" in death.

Lu proposes that these faithful maidens, rather than becoming passive victims of oppression, were active agents who appropriated the Confucian ethical codes to assert their sense of identity (Lu, Wenjing, *True to Her Word* 247; Mann, "Widows" 37-56). Corresponding with the author's personal demonstration of moral integrity, Zheng's *tanci* manifests the widespread moral concern with chastity and filial piety which formed the basis of feminine heroism (see Hinsch 169-204). Feminine virtue is evoked and reinforced by her authorial insertions and comments at the beginning of the chapters, which is a stylistic feature of many *tanci*. Zheng's women characters manifest acts of chastity as a form of resistance. While they are faithful unmarried maidens who commit suicide in the name of reuniting with their deceased fiancés, they also reject marriage in the name of preserving their filially pious service to their parents. When the heroines are forced to marry under the pressure of their natal families, they commit suicide to preserve their sexual and moral purity. The heroines assert their own moral value by actively appropriating the Confucian cult of chastity, revealing the profound social, cultural, and psychological meaning of women's suicide in this era.

One of the earliest remaining versions of the text was an illustrated lithographed edition in 1895 by publisher Zhujianzhai in Hangzhou, with the author's self-preface dated 1843 (Hu, Wenkai 740). The text threads together the individual stories of the goddesses through intricate plot manipulation. The author stresses four basic virtues for human beings, including 孝 (*xiao*, filial devotion), 忠 (*zhong,* loyalty), 節 (*jie,* chastity), and 烈 (*lie*, uncorrupted purity), which are presented through the unusual deeds of the twelve reincarnated goddesses. Almost all the women characters resist marriage and express the wish to stay unmarried to enact their filial duties to their own parents. Unlike in the cult of widow suicide or faithful maiden suicide, many reincarnated women characters pass away in illness or regret before they are arranged to be married by force. This kind of death before marriage or even engagement reveals the author's modification of the notion of chastity in the Confucian moral system. Women's moral integrity is presented as a spiritual agency which is of higher importance than her obligation to her parents, her husband, or her in-laws.

In accounting tales of extraordinary heroines, Zheng frequently intervenes in the narrative, affirming the heroic deeds of fictional characters and even speaking on their behalf in internal monologues. The tension and reciprocal influence between character depiction and authorial self-representation can be traced to the title of the work, *Mengyingyuan* (Dream, Image, Destiny). In this *tanci*, characters often dream of others or their previous lives. The "dream" is a narrative strategy frequently used to embed and tell stories from the characters' perspectives. Also, dream is a metaphor in motion and is analogous to the narration process in which the authorial narrator connects the "fragmented snapshots" of the characters' tales, imposes structure to the text, or expresses her "waking thoughts" by speaking directly to the audience (Kilroe 2000). The word "image," by contrast, represents characters depicted in the text. David Rolston observes that a narrative strategy in late imperial fiction is *shexing quying* (舍形取影), that is, "letting go of the outward body in favor of its images." This is often the intention of the author, who, when depicting characters in the book, begins from their mirrored images rather than from their speaking selves (Rolston, *How to Read* 329). Zheng, regarding this intriguing relation between "form" and "image," suggests that "the form is not much different from its image, sending out fragrance before my sense comes to it" (Zheng, Preface). If the "form" represents the authorial power over fictional characters, Zheng's interpretation implies an identifiable relation between the form and the image, between the authorial speaking self and the fictional characters. A close reading of *Mengyingyuan*, in this sense, moves the reader deeper into the empathetic relationships between the authorial voice, the character's viewpoint, and the reader's engaged gaze that beholds the characters.

In Zheng's *Mengyingyuan*, the narrative voice shifts between the first-person narrative voice and the third-person narrative voice. As a result, the distance between the narrator and the story world becomes dynamic and changeable. Zheng's authorial narrator asserts a voice of "I" at the beginning and ending of each chapter, dexterously mediating between the multiple embedded narratives. The positions of the authorial narrator in the multifarious narrative lead the reader to question the shifting boundaries between the authorial narrator, the fictional character, and the actual author. The first-person authorial insertions demonstrate the relation between *tanci* works and some subgenres in China's vernacular fiction. The beginning lines by the narrator in each chapter are reminiscent of the so-called *meipi* (眉批) or "eyebrow note" in Ming and Qing printed fiction, which is inserted in a margin above the text and consists of simulated handwritten comments to deliver a personal message related to the text (Brokaw and Chow 284). However, in *tanci*, women authors' comments are written as part of the texts and often provide rich self-reflections and autobiographical information. The unique narrative authority given to the feminine authorial narrator in such a stylistic arrangement is discussed in current scholarship on the narrative points of view in late imperial fiction. Liang Xiaoping states that there are three major narrative perspectives in Ming and Qing domestic fiction, including "omniscient hetero-diegetic narrative perspective," "limited narrative perspective attached to a fictional character," and "pure objective narrative perspective" (Liang, Xiaoping 170). In Zheng's text, the first-person voice reveals the connection between *tanci* and vernacular storyteller fiction in which the authorial voice appears in the prologue, opening, and ending sessions with criticism and direct address to the readers. Zheng's narrator may occupy a position akin to what Liang calls "omniscient hetero-diegetic narrative perspective," but by itself also signifies an ongoing paratext to the main body of the *tanci*. The inserted lines by the author in fiction is not unique to *tanci*. David Rolston suggests that in Qing, "it became standard for longer works of vernacular fiction in the literati mode to contain opening and closing sections in which the author (or implied author) spoke more directly to the reader than in the bulk of the text. Under the influence of *Honglou meng*, the prologue sections of many nineteenth-century and late Qing novels are written in the first person" (Rolston, "Points of View"123).

Rolston's observation recalls writer Li Yü's story collection 無聲戲 (*Wusheng xi*, Silent Operas) in late Ming, in which Li speaks explicitly to the readers in the opening and closing sessions. The application of first-person narration in the opening and closing sessions is not rare in Ming and Qing vernacular literature. A prominent example is *Rouputuan* (*The Carnal Prayer Mat*) by Li. The author robes his vivid descriptions about sexuality with didactic moralization, claiming in the prologue that his purpose in writing a book about the hero's sexual adventures is to intrigue the readers with outrageous incidents and then to insert moralistic criticism to startle them. A compelling example is Wu Jianren's novel 二十年目睹之怪現狀 (*Ershinian mudu zhi guai xianzhuang*, Strange Things Observed over the Past Twenty Years; 1905). Hanan states that the earliest use of the first-person pronoun was in 悔罪之大略 (*Huizui zhi dalue*, A Treatise on Repentance, 1839), a tract by the missionary Karl Gützlaff that takes the form of a Chinese novel told by an "I" narrator ("The Missionary Novels" 165). Zheng's *Mengyingyuan*, however, precedes *A Treatise on Repentance* by over half a century in making use of a first-person narrative frame.

Aside from these tradition-breaking examples of the first-person narrative voice in fiction, Ming and Qing memoirs might have influenced Zheng's writing in other ways. In these memoirs, the narrator is often a main character or the witness of an event and accounts the events from a personal point of view. Examples include the Ming novel 癡婆子傳 (*Chipozi zhuan*, Memoir of a Crazy Old Woman) by Furong Zhuren (芙蓉主人), the Qing novel 影梅庵憶語 (*Yingmei'an yiyü*, Memoir of the Shadow Plum Pavilion) by Mao Xiang (冒襄, 1611-1693), and 浮生六記 (*Fusheng liuji*, Six Records of a Floating Life, 1809) by Shen Fu (沈復, 1763-1825), which is a blend of autobiography, love story, and social document (Liang, Xiaoping 170). Likewise, personal narrative perspective is prominent in many *tanci*, when the authors insert their speaking voices into the beginning and end of each *juan* (scroll or volume) and *hui* (chapter), describing their lives in the inner chambers and commenting on characters and events. In such situations, the narrator's voice is personal and occasionally dramatized, as in a memoir. The authorial narrator is heterodiegetic; rather than participating in the plot, the narrator recounts the development of the plot from a distance.

This narrating "I" in *tanci* at the beginning and closing lines of each chapter offers a rare case that has not been sufficiently examined in narratological studies of the first-person voice, since written *tanci* borders on fiction, drama, and oral narratives, and more often than not foregrounds a distinctively feminine authorial narrator. Zheng's *Mengyingyuan* revives "the situation of live communication between the storyteller and the audience," and thereby creates spaces of sharing and exchanges characteristics of live communication (Brooks, *Reading* 99). This simulation of orality in writing offers a compelling case for the study of women's narrative enunciation, when the female author self-consciously plays with narrative tactics. One may suggest that Zheng is confronted with the slippage between "woman" as a signifier defined by male discourses in history and "women" as individual subjects devoted to the transformation of social and historical discourses through writing and reading. The narrating "I," constructed as a female authorial presence, represents a form of self-empowerment through speaking. In *Mengyingyuan* and many *tanci* works, it is a woman, rather than a man, who plays the role of the authoritative enunciator.

In depicting her female characters, the author relies on creating ideals of filial virtue and chastity as moral paradigms. The authorial narrator claims, "My sole concern is to sweep away the abominable thoughts in people's minds, and wash out a copious space of pure sentiment in their minds. Filial piety, justice, loyalty, and chastity are all most honest qualities; even sentimental writings should appeal to pure feelings" (1: 1, 1). Zheng's endorsement of filial devotion finds expression through the male characters Zhuang Yuan and his son, Zhuang Mengyu, both of whom aspire to flee to the heavenly realm to enjoy reunion with their immortal ancestors. The quality of loyalty is highlighted in the male protagonists' faithful service to the emperor and in the servants' loyal caring for the Zhuang family. Bret Hinsch proposes that the emergence of female chastity was closely tied to the honor culture of early Chinese masculinity (169-204). Zheng also creates new varieties of chastity by depicting women who would lose their lives in order to keep their virginal innocence rather than submit to forceful marriage arrangements. Chastity becomes both a moral register and a new model for feminine subjectivity.

A reverberating example of filial passion appears in the *tanci* as well. The reincarnated immortal Zhuang Mengyu, in order to cure his ailing father, resorts to his innate magical powers to transfer the father's illness to himself. In her comments on Mengyu's filial act, the author evokes the concern with 情 (*qing,* emotions) in contemporary vernacular fiction, but offers an innovative interpretation of *qing* in light of loyalty and filial piety. She comments on Mengyu's sacrificial action to save his father: "The most profound human emotions are loyalty and filial piety. Only in being devoted children and faithful officials can human beings have these feelings. Who then is the leading figure in the field of sentiments? The most devoted one is a person of faithful and filial passions" (1: 7, 95). In contrast to the sensualized interpretation of *qing* as romantic love or even sexual passion in some Ming and Qing popular novels, Zheng holds that only those who implement filially devoted and loyal actions have the "purest *qing*." Subsequently Zheng asserts her own moral integrity and self-cultivation. Richard Davis states that the appropriation of *qing* by disenfranchised literati might be a means to assert their status as *shi* (scholars) (206). This is an indication of the interest in *qing* in the literati culture of late Ming and early Qing, 100 years before *Mengyingyuan* was written. Answering to this existing tradition, the authorial narrator offers an inventive interpretation of *qing* as an emotive expression of sincerity and moral purity. "The song of 'The Calling Ospreys' initiates the rituals and customs [in the matter of marriage], / only chaste emotions can be expressed through words. / A beautiful lady should marry a gentleman, / even though he is sleepless because of longing for her; it is understandable. / [In some cases,] one may have a friend with the same heart, / and should not carelessly search for another lover" (1: 11, 157).

The song "關雎" ("guanjü," "The Calling Ospreys") alludes to a song of the same name which is placed first in *The Book of Odes* (1046-771 BCE) because of its influence to transform and normalize human relations and feelings in the institution and rituals of marriage (Deng Xiang 1: 1). *Qing* or "chaste emotions" is in *Mengyingyuan* explicitly interpreted as an emotive bond between the companions, based on sincerity and chaste feelings for each other. Chastity, rather than desire, is emphasized as a determining component of *qing*. The narrator's moralistic concerns are presented in her female characters, who are virtuous women. When the reincarnated goddess Lin Xianyu sees that her aging mother-in-law, Mrs. Zhuang, loses her beauty, Lin prays in private to be able to compromise her own beauty and lifespan to redeem Mrs. Zhuang's good looks. The narrator, in her comments on Xianyu's filial act, evokes 勸孝歌 *(Quanxiao ge*, A Song to Persuade People to Be Filially Pious), a popular pedagogical text for children in Weixin county in the southern Yun'nan province. It was composed by a Qing scholar Xu Xin in the mid-nineteenth century. In the text the author states, "The most moving text is *A Song for Filial Piety*; / how on earth could people understand the meaning of it? / When the wife is as beautiful as jade, the mother's looks have declined to that of dust. / Who could have taken up this filial intention again?" (4: 43,125). Only the most thoughtful children can sympathize with the parents. In describing Xianyu, the narrator notes that using her magical power to decrease her own beauty and to redeem Mrs. Zhuang's looks is "an imaginary and exceptional incident; / I would allow others to laugh at my speculative description" (4: 43, 125). Zheng's depiction of the heroine can be understood in light of chaste women depicted in Chinese history and literary writings. These writings belong to "an elite discourse on chastity" and are male presentations of idealized women (Mann, "Widows" 40). In the writings about "notable women," these chaste and filially devoted women are often "stripped of their personal traits," and their lives are reduced to simplistic moral categories of good or evil in ways that were almost ahistorical (Davis 206). In comparison with the dispassionate, and almost "stoically virtuous" women in some didactic texts (Davis 206), Zheng's depiction of Xianyu suggests her personal affections and may elicit an emotional response from readers.

In Zheng's text, some women also make claims of filial piety to justify their persistence in virginity and the renunciation of marriage, because not marrying allows daughters to stay home and serve their parents. Virginity is an exceptional case of women's virtue, surpassing chastity by its complete rejection of sexual desire. In her preface, Zheng criticizes the writings of her time which lose their uniqueness by pursuing popular themes of love and romance and fame and fortune. She claims that her purpose is to counterbalance some morally corrupting "scholar and beauty" romances with tales of women who preserve their virginity and moral virtue. She notes, "[in my work] the unrivaled scholar with poetic sensibilities shall follow the example of the unaffected Liu Xiahui [who avoids sexual craving]. A couple who hold a true understanding of each other would still emulate the virtuous Liu Xiahui, who guards their wills against sexual temptations, and maintains their virginity as the Children of the North Palace" (author's preface). The quote refers to Liu Xiahui

(柳下惠, 720 BCE-621 BCE), a model of moral integrity. Once Liu was traveling in a remote area and met a woman who asked to stay at his place on a cold day. Liu, concerned that the woman might not be able to resist the cold weather, held her in his arms and covered her body with his clothes. Throughout the night he did not make any offensive move toward her (Hu, Bingwen 190). Another reference is to the *beigong ying* (北宮嬰), or Infant of the North Palace, which refers to women who take vows of lifelong virginity. *Beigong*, the North Palace, or the queen's palace, is an allusion to parents. *Beigong ying* or "infant of the North Palace" indicates devoted daughters, according to a story about 嬰兒子 (*Ying'er zi,* Infant Girl), a daughter in the State of Qi (齊, 1046 BCE-221 BCE), who never married in order to serve her parents (Liu Xiang, *Zhan'guoce* 11: 6-8). Most women in *Mengyingyuan* never enter into marriage and instead express their wish to live a consecrated life in the name of serving their natal parents. When they are forced to marry, some protest by suicide or illness. As the text goes, "all the chaste wives and filially pious daughters have sacrificed their lives to preserving their integrity; such a family custom of loyalty and filial piety could hardly find a match in any household" (4: 46, 197). Although the main couple, Mengyu and Xianyu, ties the knot in the end, the wife has been solemnly dedicated to lifetime virginity and avoids sexual intimacy with her husband. As the preface portrays, Zheng's insistence on women's virginity is potentially transformative and emancipatory. The Confucian notion of women's chastity emphasizes the married widows' abstinence from sexual desire. Nonetheless, women's vows of lifetime virginity openly renounce marriage, which enmeshes women's social identity in the family system, placing upon them an obligation to produce the next generation of their husbands' lineage.

The question of chastity and fidelity in Zheng's text points to the conundrum of authorial ethics, which is reflected in the narrator's extensive observations on the challenges of being a writer. Zheng laments, "Allowing bad writing to circulate is as harmful as commiting a murder without leaving a trace." She stresses a writer's responsibility to articulate truth and improve society: "I put all my heart into composing [this] work. Those exceptionally perceptive will see the purpose of my writing" (author's preface). The author claims her right to a cultural voice, yet she remains uncertain of the influence of her work when transmitted, edited, and circulated through the publication business. Authorial ethics displays a charged dilemma between the private and public worlds of the woman *tanci* writer. Such ethical concern is manifested in the author's awareness of her moral responsibility to awaken and inspire her readers. Zheng explains in the preface, "I wish to strike the morning bell and the night drum, and with every beat stir lost souls; in the bright and aromatic hues [of language)], every word must be filled with bitter tears." This passionate self-expression is in tune with the opening of the novel, *The Dream of the Red Chamber*, by Cao Xueqin: "Pages full of idle words, / penned with hot and bitter tears. / All men call the author fool. / None his secret message hears" (3). Pervaded by irony, the authorial lament in Cao's text exposes the incommensurable distance between the author and his imagined readers. Zheng's preface presents similar emotional expressions of the authorial narrator, but it also carries a distinctive ethical appeal, establishing the credibility of the author and calling on the reader's moral judgment. Dorothy Ko observes that late imperial women authors were extremely creative in crafting a space from within the prevailing gender system that gave them meaning, solace, and dignity (Ko, *Teachers* 9). This authorial tactic of creating a space for self-expression perhaps provides the ground for Zheng's explicit claim of rewriting history through her personal literary practice. In Zheng's *tanci*, the amplified opening and closing passages articulate the reinforced narrative voice of a feminine subject who vigorously brings together the collected voices of talented women in her words. The author notes,

> As a woman I am filled with anger against injustice;
> my heart does not take change over time.
> While writing history I review the story three times
> and would not carelessly write false facts.
> Don't say that wine can wash away this regret in my heart.
> To dissolve the sorrows one has to put them into words.
> I will avenge for the upright and the honest in ancient times,
> retrace their cases and obliterate the evil ones.
> How amusing that such a task cannot be accomplished by a substitute,
> only those involved in such situations have the power to exercise
> transformation. (3: 30, 49)

The text brings forth an explicitly female narrator who tells the audience that justice awaits the villains. The narrator's technique of proclaiming history to the audience makes apparent women authors' anxiety about writing in a literary tradition that is largely created by men. The author stresses the moral responsibility of each individual, or 個中人 (*gezhong ren,* those who are involved) for achieving these demanding tasks. Here, the narrator's voice goes further into a form of emotional self-dramatization: "If people in the world scold me for ridiculous sayings, / why should I argue and explain my true purpose? / Everyone has his own mindset; / it is difficult to reach common understanding with others. / I can only turn toward myself for reassurance" (4: 45, 160). The anguished narrating self of the first-person narrator mirrors the focus of the author's consciousness, offering an illuminating portrayal of the author's struggle against social constraints on her speech.

Zheng's ethical concerns are associated with her intellect, energy, and sense of frustration in the quest for self-articulation. Her lament brings forth a feminine voice which beseeches freedom from socially prescribed gender roles. This voice aspires to leave the secular world and search for a space of freedom and agency:

> I have also contemplated leaving behind worldly concerns and escaping
> into the secluded mountains,
> concealing my name and hiding my tracks.
> Only that I was shackled by my life as a woman;
> despite my ideals, I could not take this journey and can only sigh in regret.
> Though aware of my situation, I cannot escape fate; never can I flee the
> material limits.

> The chains of karmic bonds cannot be easily shaken off.
> Even though my mind and heart are as pure as ice and snow, I cannot but pity myself. (1: 1, 1)

The author's lament over her shackled life as a woman shows an impulse to retreat from worldly affairs reminiscent of late imperial women authors' aspiration for Buddhist beliefs in spiritual transcendence. Critic Lijian Wang states that many talented women poets in the Qing period attributed their miserable lives to the karmic fate of predestination. Wang cites from the poets Wu Zao and Jiang Zhu (江珠), who both displayed their regret for their lives in a patriarchal society and turned to Buddhism to strengthen their purity through meditation. Wang quotes from the female poet Jiang Jixiu (蔣機秀): "If women take to religious meditation and admire Daoist meditation, they are most likely caught in a desperate situation, and do so because of external pressure" (Wang, Lijian 35). Women's despair was often caused by failure in marriage. In many cases, however, women authors expressed discontent with society and their desire for a life of reclusion. Zheng's narration demonstrates the author's dilemma between entering or renouncing the world. The text displays an ironic contrast between the authorial narrator's performative efficacy and Zheng's unviable existence in real life.

The possible influence of religious beliefs in predestination and reincarnation on these women authors can be situated in the late imperial historical and social contexts. In a study of women in eighteenth-century China, Susan Mann argues, "Buddhism and Daoism . . . repositioned Confucian family values for women, enriching the spiritual and emotional existence of motherhood, widowhood, old age and even creating a tiny space where filially pious daughters could refuse marriage entirely" (Mann, *Precious Records* 200). Mann's comment sheds light on Zheng's filially pious and chaste heroines, who protect their virginity by becoming devotees of established poems of spiritual self-cultivation. Also, the authorial narrator recurrently evokes a religious philosophy of redemption. She laments human mortality and the difficulty of completing her ambitious task. She asks, "Where is the path for regeneration, once my bones disintegrate into powdery dust? / Therefore, I shall make use of this body while it still bears breath, and seek to redeem my mistakes" (1: 1, 1). In the preface the author expresses herself in the present moment, searches for spiritual freedom through writing, and thus enacts a moral position to which she is deeply committed.

Zheng's profound concern over moral propriety opens up considerable space for a study of nineteenth-century female public readership. Literary works of the time allowed scholars to posit a group of women readers that included but was larger than the elite literary circles of the Jiangnan regions. This community of readers might have affected the shape of literary work with protofeminist potentials, such as 鏡花緣 (*Jinghuayuan*, Flower in the Mirror; 1828) by Li Ruzhen (李汝珍) and *Zaizaotian* (Remaking Heaven, 1826) by Hou Zhi. Zheng's *Mengyingyuan* was published in 1843, shortly after these two texts. It is possible that Zheng's moral concerns shore up a tactful authorial choice in meeting the need of her women readers.

This concern with the historical readership of her work might explain some apparent incongruities in the authorial voice in *Mengyingyuan*. In the authorial insertions, the narrator's expressions of personal ambitions and literary aspirations are often cloaked in modest and self-effacing statements. The author's disposition seems to be cautiously reconciled with moral instructions concerning virtue and filial devotion. She says, for example, that "virtuous deeds are foremost in importance, literary talent secondary" (1: 5, 69), and that "one should by no means boast of unusual literary talent, but should rely on his filial deeds to move heaven" (1: 5, 69). These remarks indicate reconciliation with, if not a submission to, the prevailing norms, with a possible purpose of meeting the demands of women readers. This authorial prudence also influences her choice of narrative style.

> The matter at hand seems fantastic but not a fantasy.
> However, when did I ever imitate *Strange Tales from a Chinese Studio* and tell eccentric stories?
> I talk leisurely about feelings which surface spontaneously in writing;
> subtly I imply an intention that comes across to my readers without misapprehension.
> Nonetheless, right and wrong might not have been properly distinguished in my writing;
> and I worry that I cannot completely remove ornamented expressions.
> Thus I claim that this is a tale about a filially devoted child and disciple,
> hoping to sweep away shallow and commonplace sentimental writings.
> (1: 1, 5)

In the above passage, *Strange Tales from a Chinese Studio* is a collection of nearly five hundred mostly supernatural tales about fox spirits and ghosts, written by Pu Songling in classical Chinese during the early eighteenth century. Zheng's evocation of this text represents her fear of limited efficacy in writing and an invincible sense of social responsibility. The recounted tales of the characters are fantastic stories; by contrast, the author insists that the basis of her work is filial piety and loyalty. The fantastic motif in the narrative, she suggests, is adopted to illustrate the moral rightness of the characters. Unlike the romance stories about fox spirits and ghosts in *Strange Tales from a Chinese Studio*, Zheng's text, as she claims, intends to present emotions with simplicity and propriety, without resorting to "ornamented language." The "shallow and commonplace sentimental writing" here might refer to the popular fiction of love and romance in the early nineteenth century. Some of these writings were condemned as *xiaxie xiaoshuo* (狹邪小說), or licentious fiction, because of their direct depictions of sexuality and their crude diction. Despite the government's open censorship, these writings enjoyed great popularity among less-educated people and even influenced women and children. The moralizing tone in the narration insinuates Zheng's effort to establish moral and personal integrity through writing and thereby instruct her selected readers.

Zheng's ethical dilemma about writing, furthermore, is specifically manifested in her understanding of the controversies about the *tanci* genre, as well as her choice of breaking away from the "scholar and beauty" convention in vernacular literature.

She states in her own preface that to restore moral integrity to people's minds, she will distinguish her writing from the conventions of romantic love in popular fiction and take an innovative approach in plot arrangement. Zheng compares the genres of drama, fiction, and *tanci*, and concludes that *tanci* is a particularly accessible genre for her. This passage draws attention to the correlation between Zheng's choice of *tanci* and her literary aspirations, as well as to the mutual fitness of the two. Zheng holds a critical view of the genre of *tanci*. She bewails the deterioration of readers who were under the influence of some *tanci* writings of the time.

> I am regretful that casual gift exchange between men and women
> has caused people's habits to degenerate; *tanci* have fallen into clichéd writing.
> How could these stories match the tales of those children who dress in colorful clothing, to dance and to entertain their parents?
> The true feelings of sons and daughters shall prove their filial piety.
> I regret that these degraded writings are circulated in the inner chambers,
> making it difficult to distinguish chastity from licentiousness.
> Hence I will do without the conventions of previous authors,
> and depict the genuine chastity and pure virtue of women. (2: 15, 37)

Filial piety and chastity are presented as the fundamental standards for good *tanci* fiction, distinguishing Zheng's work from other *tanci* writings on love and romance. Zheng articulates a determination to dispel morally degraded writing and instead to circulate morally instructive writing in the inner quarters. This statement supports the image of a virtuous woman and asserts this author's distinctive literary voice. Also, the passage reveals women authors' ambivalent attitudes toward these fictional genres. As a genre, *tanci* had been considered acceptable to write, although unsuitable for women to publish, until the nineteenth century. In *Mengyingyuan*, Zheng's moralizing tone possibly demonstrates her concern to speak in the right manner to her targeted audience. It seems that only through telling the stories of filially pious and chaste characters could the author truly celebrate her identity as a woman writer.

The narrative *tanci* written by women demonstrate the tension between the social discourse of gender roles and women's desire for a habitable social space. In *Mengyingyuan*, the author's refusal or inability to resolve the tension between these poles produces a narrative intensified by the narrator, whose voice brings forth an explicit appeal for the reader's emotive response. This narrative voice destabilizes the distance between the authorial narrator, the character, and the reader, and draws attention to the ironic aperture between these subjective positions. Zheng's *tanci* foregrounds the explicit narrative voice of a woman, a speaking self who adopts a panoramic view of the fictional world, accessing the thoughts and minds of the talented women characters from an external and elevated perspective. Yet the author's own immediate writing situation drives her to intervene in the story and assert a recurring narrative voice in the text, which partially constitutes the emotive bonds between the readers and the characters as well as the authorial identification with the characters. While the narrator and the readers are both story-sharing creatures, emotional contagion between these subjective positions becomes crucial in the transmission and development of the text. Sympathy functions as an empowering experience for both the author and the readers. Authorial laments about the difficulty of writing invite the readers' sympathetic understanding of the fictional characters, creating an emotional bond between the readers and the characters. In *Mengyingyuan*, the author's lament and strong empathetic identification with the character is reinforced by the distinctive first-person narrative voice "wo" (I) and numerous references to intense emotional expressions such as 嘆 (*tan,* lament), 傷逝感 (*shangshi gan,* desolate feelings), 可憐 (*kanlian,* deserving pity), and 恨 (*hen,* regret). This form of passionate emotional expression is especially compelling in the following example.

One of the reincarnated flower goddesses, Liu Lingjuan (劉令娟), becomes a victim to her cousin's scheme and is forced to marry him by her parents. Enraged by this injustice, Lingjuan spits blood and dies instantly. Her death is proclaimed as that of a chaste woman by the narrator, who, seeing the character's calamity, turns to comment on her personal misfortune. "I sigh that in this life all people have suffered death and loss. / Pitiable are those of great beauty who pass away at an early age. / I regret there is no magic brush to capture their images, / and that instead there are ten thousand thoughts and powerless desires. / Like her I could not forget my own sisters, and suffered misfortunes, / although our fates are different. / I try to resolve the dilemma with this cup of wine, only to be filled with more regret" (3: 36, 219).

The dramatized lament on the grief of losing a companion is rendered with ambiguity in the text, for the lack of a distinctive pronoun in these lines opens up the space for multiple interpretations. One may ask whose regret is presented here. In a comparative study of focalization in Western and Chinese narrative theories, Chinese narratologist Dan Shen argues that in certain cases, although a character's perception in the narrative belongs to the level of the story, it might also be "adopted by the narrator at this moment as a means of transmitting the story" (Dan 232). Additionally, "in its role as temporary 'angle of vision,' it also takes on a discourse function. . . . When a character's 'diegetic consciousness' is adopted by the narrator in rendering the story, it will unavoidably take on a dual nature, constituting at once part of what is narrated and a means of presentation" (Dan 232). In the above example, the root for this sentiment of regret is ambivalent. As the narrative lens gradually zooms in on the authorial narrator's interior world, the text brings out the resonance between the narrator's lament on the misfortunate woman character and her own personal lament on the loss of friends in the inner quarters. The text, in this example, suggests the multiple scales in which narrative sympathy takes place.

The narrator's grievance on separation and loss also illustrates her split sense of self, which underlies her overt appeal to an implied readership. Specifically, the text demonstrates an intimate, personal connection between the authorial narrator and readers in the boudoir, who are repetitively invoked and deeply inscribed in the text. The function of the reader/narratee is meaningful because it exists on the same diegetic level as the authorial narrator. This dialectical relationship between the authorial narrator and her targeted audience is presented in the following passage.

Please do not complain about the many exclamations in the story;
it is truly because of the difficulty to convert people's hearts.
If I were to use my tongue carelessly, I would certainly suffer false accusations,
for I am not good at words myself.
Yet if there are some friends in the boudoir who will appreciate my story,
they will confirm that my words are not far-fetched and imaginary. Since
ancient times, the legend of Zhong Ziqi and Bo Ya's friendship has been
widely applauded;
to imitate them, I started composing this book. . . .
Exposing my amateurish writing to experts in literature,
I might only make them have a good laugh.
If writing is uninspired, how can it be passed down?
I don't mind being considered an unabashed imitator,
for the word sincerity is not necessarily outdated. (1: 13, 204)

The authorial narrator addresses the narratee and pleads for sympathy. She expresses concern over her right to write, talking to her readers, the intrafictional addressee of her discourse. The authorial narrator tells the story in a humbled, confessional tone but also maintains that she is well educated and is a competent writer. She is actively engaged with the projected audience, her "friends in the boudoir"; their relationship is an intimate, personal one, and is frequently invoked to support the authorial narrator. She later states, "If my clumsy brush composes a witty work, / it depends on the outstanding talents of my friends who themselves are experts in writing poetry. / I will rely on you my readers to revise my rough lines into refined texts, / so that they can be circulated widely in the inner chambers" (2: 16, 53). Here Zheng might be referring to the womanly practice of hand copying *tanci* and circulating them in the inner chambers. This group of friends in the inner chambers is akin to a fictional character who listens to the narrator's story, even though the narrator is not active on the plot level and exists only "offstage." The authorial insertions, in these situations, elicit ample interplay between authorial and readerly sympathy.

While the narrator starts the tale by presenting a panoramic perspective of society and history, the narrative always comes to a point where the narrator is engaged in a sympathetic relationship with the characters in the story. When the male protagonist Zhuang Yuan, a descendent of the immortals, decides to leave the world and return to the heavenly realm, Zhuang's close friend Lin Wu (林武) is overwhelmed with sorrow over his departure. In the closing lines of this chapter, the author is so profoundly moved by the plot that she laments on her own separation from friends: "At this instant I could not continue writing, / dismayed by the fact that the few friends I have are scattered to other parts of the world. / Even though there are a few really intimate friends, / we cannot see each other anymore because of death or distance" (2: 16, 53). From this lament on the loss of her friends in life, the author continues to address an imaginary group of readers, who might be sympathetic to her personal experience.

When emotions are harnessed, regret grows;
one becomes impulsive, laughing, talking, singing, or weeping.

> To overpraise a person is no less than to degrade him;
> shall I meet my female friends again, it is difficult to find appropriate words.
> With this cup of wine I hope to dispel my regrets,
> my untainted heart finds articulation at the tip of the writing brush.
> When my story is compiled by dear friends,
> it will have the luck to attract their perceptive eyes and make them
> understand my mind. (2: 16, 53)

In these lines, the correspondence between "my pure heart" and "perceptive eyes" demonstrates the mutual dependence of the writer and the reader. The text presents a dialectic relationship between the author and audience; in the reader's reciprocation the text takes it fullest shape. This moment demonstrates the imaginary relationship between reader and writer when a reader interprets a text. In the cited passage, the narrator's lament on the loss of personal friends is gradually replaced with a longing for a sympathetic readership. By fostering an imagined community of sympathetic readers, the author empowers the articulation of her literary identity.

The theme of narrative sympathy in traditional Chinese fiction and drama is addressed as 設身處地 (*sheshen chudi*, putting oneself in another's case). David Rolston notes that this practice of imaginary identification with characters (historical or not) different from oneself is a facility very important to creative work in fiction or drama (Rolston, *How to Read* 25). "Imagining oneself in the situation of the other" produces an important situation of sympathy. Min Tian, in a study of traditional theatrical performances, notes that *sheshen chudi* means for the performing artist "to forget that he is acting and merge himself into the part. Only then can he depict these feelings profoundly and meticulously" (Tian, Min 54). The Qing playwright Li Yü uses the famous novel 水滸傳 (*Shuihuzhuan, The Water Margin*) to explain how a writer should "put himself in another's case" to achieve vibrancy and similitude in characterization.

> One's words voice his heart. If the author hopes to articulate a character's words, he should articulate the character's heart on his behalf; if the author has not dreamed of or traveled in spirit to the character's circumstances, how can he claim to have "put himself in the character's case"? For those characters who have erected upright thoughts, I shall put myself in that situation, and ruminate rightful thoughts on their behalf; if I meet those characters who have generated evil and inequitable ideas, I should also discard the principles and follow their powers, and temporarily speak their evil and unjust thoughts. The author should, in the depiction of internal thoughts and delicate feelings, make the characters speak out naturally and spontaneously; in speaking as a character, sound like him, instead of making him identical to others or become ordinary and indistinguishable. (Li Yü, *Xianqing ouji* 25)

For Li Yü, *sheshen chudi* encompasses three levels of sympathetic identification, including authorial identification with characters in literary texts, authorial identification with actors who play theatrical roles, and authorial identification with the theatrical audience. In Zheng's *tanci*, the first level of sympathetic identification (between the author and the characters) is particularly striking, and is also often blended with the third level of identification, that is, between the author and the reader/audience.

In the text, "putting oneself in another's case" is prominently presented as the identification of the authorial narrator with the characters at moments of pathetic or emotional appeals. When the reincarnated immortal Zhuang Yuan retreats to the sacred mountains to search for his parents, his friend Lin Wu suffers from his absence. The author states, "Very often I allow the character to suffer emotional turmoil. / As an author, one has to make adjustments as the story demands." She then comments on her relationship with the characters, that "it is not easy to imagine myself in the character's case. / Such an endeavor does not just successfully happen overnight" (4: 40, 82). For the author, "putting oneself in the other's situation" implies sincere and heartfelt depiction of the characters' emotions. In imitating the characters' emotions, the authorial voice interpolates with the diegesis and speaks in the manner of the character.

Reverberating with Li Yü's idea that the author should articulate the character's heart, Zheng's *Mengyingyuan* effectively presents the empathetic identification between the author and the character in the following example. When the male protagonist Zhuang Yuan leaves his family and goes in search of his ancestors in the immortal world, Mrs. Zhuang then asks their adopted daughter Renfang to compose a biography for Zhuang Yuan. Renfang finds it an extremely challenging task, for "to depict his deeds is nothing outstanding; / as an author she must meticulously portray his heart and emotions" (2: 25, 201). Associating her own filial affection for her father Zhuang Yuan, Renfang finds it a tremendous challenge to write about her father's own filially devoted deeds. "Before even writing down a word she sheds tears; / her heart, drenched in sorrow, is unusually downcast" (2: 25, 201). When the biography is finished it elicits the same pathos from the family relatives who "shed tears when reading, unable to hold back their sadness" (2: 25, 201). This fictional example of authorial identification with character mirrors Zheng's understanding of the empathetic author, whose writing depends on her sincere emotive associations with the fictional character.

This authorial identification with fictional characters is sometimes manifested explicitly as a case of narrative mimicry, that is, when the heterodiegetic narrator's voice intervenes and mimics the voice of the character in the story. In the following example, when Zhuang Yuan leaves the earth in order to search for his immortal ancestors in the mountains, the narrator takes on the perspective of his friend Lin Wu and contemplates Lin's melancholy from his point of view. "How does one cross a city of a thousand miles of sorrow? The most affectionate person is none other than he who, in melancholy, encounters another who is also burdened with grief, changing his mind to dissolve his feelings, only to find more burdens in his mind" (3: 28, 1). The lack of identifiable pronouns, characteristic of pre-twentieth-century Chinese poetic narratives, allows the narrative voice a certain mobility to shift between the extradiegesis and the character's consciousness, and further, reduces the traces of the narrator's subjectivity. The narrator relates what the male character thinks and sees from his perspective. By "putting herself in the case" of the sentimental Lin Wu, the authorial narrator transcribes the character's conjectures. This example indicates that *sheshen chudi* implies a fusion of subjective positions between the authorial narrator and the character, regardless of the differences between their genders and backgrounds. It is not within the scope of this chapter to examine whether sympathetic identification between the narrator and the character always implies a case of narrative mimicry. Nonetheless, one may notice the irony in textual moments like this, when a character's consciousness is filtered through the narrator's presentation no matter how well the narrator's presence is concealed.

The narrator's direct sympathetic identification with the fictional characters is ubiquitous in *Mengyingyuan*. The narrator comments on Han Ziying, the daughter of a rich family, who was committed to changing her mother's lavish life style. "She ventured to use her personal power to transform degraded social customs; / I agonize for her that she could not carry this out in practice, even though she was ambitious. / Before writing about her, I first let out a sigh, / for this woman was very exceptional. / Like a multihued phoenix perching in the thorny bushes, / she must have found it hard to withhold sorrow when looking at her own forlorn shadow" (3: 34, 151). The narrator's presence is explicitly asserted through the use of the first-person pronoun. The narrator's compassionate lament, or *tan*, is thus interwoven in the emotive commentary on the woman character. In this case, the word "lament" is both an affirmation of the woman's usual achievements and a lament on the vicissitudes of her fate. The narrative lens shifts from the external narrator to the psychological realm of the character, projected through the narrator's sympathetic identification. The last line, "she must have found it hard to withhold regret when looking at her own forlorn shadow," suggests a readerly sympathy for the character's situation that mirrors the fate of the authorial narrator herself. Accordingly, the last word, 悲 (*bei*, sorrow), calls forth feelings generated by a fusion of the narrator and the character, the self and the other. The text thus demonstrates an involved author who dedicates herself to the task of transforming social customs through the personal practice of writing. Sorrow is seen as moral emotion by the narrator, who discloses an awareness of herself as capable of inhabiting the feelings of others. The following example conveys a similar situation in which the authorial voice makes an explicit emotional appeal to the readers.

> Simple are my words, far-reaching their meaning.
> Three times I let out sighs; nine times affection and rage penetrate my body.
> My heart's devotion is that of the *Jingwei* bird;
> like the *Jingwei* who sought in vain to fill up the sea with small pebbles, I
> mourn the frustration that comes in advance.
> My simple life has been ridden with divine retribution.
> Who would trust that my words are true?
> I hope you do not disbelieve my words.
> Please meditate on this piece three times, and trust my good intention.
> (3: 33, 144)

The first-person narrator here lays out a communicative frame from which the story continues. She interrupts and delays the storytelling process by inserting sighs and exclamations. The usage of the imperative "please meditate on this piece three times" further reveals the narrator's desire to engage the listener/reader in a dialogic situation. To create a narrative relay by affecting emotive interventions, the narrator takes deliberate pauses to achieve an aesthetic distance from the events being recounted, heightening the readers' awareness of the gripping story. An example of this comes when the princess falls in love with the male protagonist Zhuang Mengyu, who is already married to Lin Xianyu. The emperor disguises himself and exits the palace in order to look for help in persuading Mengyu to accept the marriage proposal. The narrator builds suspense by commenting, "My readers, you should close the book and ponder the story; / the writer (*zuoshuren*) shall steal a moment of leisure and recede" (4: 42, 101). These personal remarks of the authorial narrator shift the readers' attention from the accounted events to the concrete communicative situation between the narrator and reader. This conclusive move also resonates with formulaic narrative expressions in many late imperial Chinese fiction works, when the omnipresent authorial narrator, claiming himself as 作書人 (*zuoshuren*, the one who composes the book) or 說書人 (*shuoshuren,* the one who tells the story), dwells in a vacillating position between the writer and the narrator (for a discussion of *zuoshuren* and *shuoshuren* in the evolution of Chinese fiction, see Chen, Pingyuan, *Zhongguo xiaoshuo* 62). This more distanced, omnipotent narrative stance is particularly conspicuous in the opening and closing lines of each chapter, revealing some disparity and restraint when compared with the more sympathetic depiction of the characters in the narration process.

The theme of sympathy in *Mengyingyuan* also invites a study of *qing,* or emotion/affection, a key theme in late imperial literature. The author evokes *qing* with an emphasis on filial piety and chastity, and suggests that Zheng rewrites the cult of *qing* in vernacular fiction to assert the importance of moral rectitude. The multifaceted meaning of *qing* gains momentum when contextualized in late imperial philosophy, culture, and literature. *Qing* amplifies the concept of narrative sympathy in a Western context, opening up space for an innovative understanding of the emotive connection between the authorial narrator in *tanci* and her targeted readers. Zheng's appropriation of *qing* exemplifies a personal author-reader relationship that reinforces the sympathetic bond among women in the domestic compound. As a modulating register, *qing* is recharged with different energy in this *tanci* and serves as an overarching sentiment presiding over and facilitating human relationships.

The idea of *qing* was endowed with varying implications in late imperial Chinese literature and philosophy. Before the Ming dynasty, *qing* was used to refer to the individual's emotions and feelings; it has been traditionally considered an opposite to the concept of *zhi* (誌), which indicated ideas and aspirations, representing Confucian social and political philosophy. The expression of *qing*, or individual ruminations and feelings, was guided and regulated by *zhi*. However, beginning with the Wei and Jin dynasties (220 CE-589 CE), scholars gradually replenished the concept of *qing* and celebrated it as an important aesthetic value. Several important aesthetic and philosophical works contributed to this transformation of thought, including 童心說 (*Tongxinshuo,* Theory on Child's Heart) by philosopher Li Zhi (李贄, 1527-1602), and 唯情說 (*Weiqingshuo,* Theory on Genuine Emotions) by playwright Tang Xianzu (1550-1616). Li Zhi holds that *tongxin* (童心) or "child's heart," is the pure "heart that generates man's thinking from the beginning," and is the root of men and women's natural desire (Li Zhi, *Fenshu* 273). Tang Xianzu, the author of *The Peony Pavilion*, holds that *qing* is a powerful sentiment that transcends the boundary between the physical and the spiritual, and can "take the life of the living and resurrect the deceased" (Tang, *Mudanting* 1093; see also Lou, 152-73; Zou, Zizhen). The interpretations of *qing* in Li's and Tang's theories challenged Confucian orthodox thinking (Liu, Guo 17; for discussion of *qing* as human desire, see Huang, "Sentiments"). The Ming philosopher Wang Yangming (王陽明, 1472-1528) furthered earlier scholars' theories and proposed that "the heart is the master of both *xing* [性human nature] and *qing* [human emotion]. *Xing* [is one's] heart and body; *qing* [is the] execution of the heart" (Wang Yangming 88). Wang Yangming's aesthetic theory marks an important transitional period in late imperial philosophy, leaving an impact on the literary works of the time and later generations.

One prominent literary example that gives evidence to the influence of the late Ming intellectuals' endorsement of *qing* is 情史 (*Qingshi*, A History of *Qing*), a fiction work by the late Ming author Feng Menglong (馮夢龍). For Feng, *qing* regulates and moderates the Confucian concept of *li* (principle). "Since ancient times, one's actions concerning loyalty, filial devotion, chastity, and purity, when executed following *li*, inevitably look forced and unnatural. When these acts are implemented in the name of *qing*, however, they will be more real and sincere . . . The scholars in the world only know that *li* is the model for *qing*. Who could know that *qing* would be the power of preservation for *li*?" (Feng, *Qingshi* 21). Feng Menglong's theory reconciles the seemingly disparate notions of *qing* (human emotions) and *li* (Confucian principles), and reinvests the cultural register of *qing* with innovative meanings. The collected stories in Feng's *Qingshi* (A History of *Qing*) display various implications for *qing*, ranging from a shared universal sentiment of human beings, heterosexual or same-sex love, desire, regret, or sorrow. Feng's reinterpretation of *qing* recalls critic Anthony Yu's suggestion that *qing* implies a kind of universal disposition of human beings. He notes, "The pervasive . . . and universal characteristic of *qing* is precisely based on the perception of it as the essential endowment of the human that cuts across social and cultural stratifications; it unifies the noble and the humble, the foolish and the wise, the worthy and the unworthy" (Yu 60). This understanding of *qing* as a universal human disposition also resonates in some late imperial women authors' writings and commentaries on literature. For example, in 吳吳山三婦合評牡丹亭 (*Wuwushan sanfu heping Mudanting*, Three Wives' Commentary on *The Peony Pavilion*; 1694), three female critics commenting on *The Peony Pavilion* consider *qing*, including romantic and sexual love, as "a noble sentiment that gives meaning to human life" (Ko, *Teachers* 84). *Three Wives' Commentary on* The Peony Pavilion is a work of commentary on Tang's play by three female scholars: Qian Yi (錢宜), Chen Tong (陳同), and Tan Ze (談則). This work received much critical attention among scholars of later generations because it offers a feminine perspective on the characters in Tang's well-known work. Dorothy Ko, regarding these women authors, states that, "similar to Feng Menglong's reduction of loyalty and filial piety to sincerity of heart, these women affirmed that *qing* is an overarching principle governing all human relationships . . . and is not the prerogative of either sex alone" (*Teachers* 84). For the three women critics, *qing* is a universal sentiment which strikes a sympathetic bond between the readers and the text. The *Three Wives' Commentary* itself provides evidence for the outcome of this emotive connection between the women readers and the text of *The Peony Pavilion* (see Ye, Chang-Hai 105-36; Yang Fuji 165).

In *Mengyingyuan*, Zheng claims that her goal in writing is "to portray truly delightful situations in the heavenly realm of *qing*" (4: 48, 247). The sentiment of *qing* is first rendered as an imaginative ability to identify with the other, to feel along with the passions of the other. Simultaneously, in *Mengyingyuan*, *qing* embraces both emotional affinity and moral rectitude. Zheng insists that "to talk about *qing*, one must first put right his heart" (2: 15, 37). She takes pains distinguishing her *tanci* from the popular *yanqing xiaoshuo* (言情小說), or delinquent love stories (1: 10, 141). Zheng recurrently states her aspiration to "wash away the dirty parts in the field of *qing*, / so that the real *qing* can be revealed and grow more powerful" (4: 39, 43). *Qing* transcends the constricted concept of love, encompassing feelings of friendship, filial devotion, and empathetic understanding with others. As an ability to empathize with the other, *qing* is also endowed with a moral agency and bears the potential to carry out spiritual transformations. The twelve female characters, who could be considered the agents of real *qing*, devote themselves to "transforming social customs and advocating sacred beliefs, so that women under heaven can abandon depravity and return to the right path" (1: 10, 141).

In the narrative, *qing* operates in the relationship between the readers and the fictional characters with whom they identify, as well as in the relationship between the readers and the authorial narrator who, in her inserted episodes, explicitly appeals for the readers' emotional understanding. The following passage from Zheng's work expresses such a notion of *qing*. It takes place when the narrator grieves over two reborn flower goddesses, Tao Xianbi and Liu Lingjuan (劉令娟), both of whom die in anguish when their families force them to marry.

> Life and death are always related to one's *qing*.
> When *qing* reaches those who understand with sincerity, these are real feelings.
> Even a thousand miles of distance can be reduced to inches;
> when the spirit is startled, she will return to the sacred island with chastity preserved.
> What a pity that those who treasure the spring hold their sentiments in vain;
> the blossom and the falling of flowers cannot not be predicted by human beings.
> Profound or simple, one's affinity with others is predestined.
> Long-lasting or brief in time, one's dream can always be traced to a previous cause.

Only those who can distance themselves from the world may have good
fortune in their turn.
At this moment I myself cannot distinguish my *qing* of happiness from
that of grief. (4: 41, 83)

Qing is depicted as a sympathetic bond between the deceased and the living, the fictional and the real. Zheng appropriates the word *qing* to address the readers' sympathetic identification with the characters. Haiyan Lee argues that *qing* figured prominently in the late Qing *xieqing xiaoshuo* (寫情小說), or novels of sentiment (4). The story is no longer a unidirectional projection to the reader. The narrator is not merely puncturing the illusion of reality. Instead, the text engages the readers in direct communication with the narrator, building mutual trust between them. The first two lines indicate that *qing* or emotions can only be testified to by a sympathetic understanding between two subjects. This emotional affiliation between the characters reduces the spatial distance between them. The fifth and sixth lines, however, address the changeable nature of human beings' lives, bringing up the Buddhist theme of predestination. At the end of the passage, the intrusion of the first-person "I" reveals a moment of narrative irony, when the personalized narrator acknowledges the distance between herself and the characters with respect to knowledge. In Zheng's *tanci*, *qing* might imply sincerity, benevolence, compassion, filial piety, or propriety, depending on the context. The author describes *qing* as an innate sentiment of human beings harbored in *chizi zhixin*, or the "hearts of the sincere children," a sentiment that incites man's moral actions (preface to *Mengyingyuan*). Hu Siao-chen, in a study of *Mengyingyuan*, offers a discussion of *qing* as filial devotion, and explores the interconnection between this *tanci* and the possible influence of late Ming *Qingjiao* or the "School of *Qing*" (*Cainü* 265-315). To conclude, the authorial narrator rewrites the cult of *qing* by including sympathetic identification as a form of emotive affinity between the narrator and the narratee and between the raconteur and the fictional character. In the dialectic relationship between the author, readers, and fictional characters, the authorial narrator voices her "self" and gives voice to the others. One may, again, relate the multifarious nature of the authorial narrator to the oral tradition, the origin of *tanci*. The narrator, like the storyteller, establishes a sympathetic connection between the audience and the characters as a certain mode of persuasion.

Mirroring the author's self-dramatization, many women characters have also addressed the issue of writing and authorship directly. These fictional characters' experience of writing parallels that of the authorial narrator. It is not that the narrator takes on a "double" in the text, but rather that the narrator finds partial identification with multiple heroines presented therein. In some parts of the text, the characters comment on choices of genres in writing and the lack of appreciative audiences, which indicates the involvement of the *tanci* author in the text. These textual moments are notable cases of self-reference, although the word *tanci* is not directly used, but only vaguely referred to as "half drama, and half novel," revealing the author's caution in utilizing this controversial narrative form (4: 35, 175).

In Zheng's *Mengyingyuan*, there are numerous depictions of women's poetry contests and games, and their ruminations about literary philosophy and stylistic choices. The text emplots twelve reincarnated flower goddesses who are well read in literary and historical masterworks. A main character, Lin Wenwan, is an outstanding poet herself and even drafts a memorial to the emperor on behalf of her father. Another prominent woman author is Tao Xianbi, who learns all the classes by heart at the age of three and later also becomes a women's doctor, offering medical service for women. At an early age, her parents pass away. She is then adopted by her aunt and uncle, and she learns writing and medicine. In her spare time she composes prose in the hybrid genres of drama and fiction; however, she dares not risk having these private writings published in public under her name, deeply concerned that her writings might be distorted by her capricious relatives. She talks over this dilemma with another character, Xianyu, who is herself a poet: "In the past I was adopted by my uncle, who constantly let me read popular plays. / Then he asked me to sing those lines to him. / In vain I tried to avoid such performances. / Then he used to change my words carelessly when he would read the text out. / I have thought of burning all my writing. / Regretfully I don't have the power to do so, even should I try very hard" (4: 35, 175).

Tao's confession indicates her worries that her ethical rights as an author may be violated. Her concern over having her writings made public indicates women authors' dilemmas with publication and the printing business of nineteenth-century China. Talented women of the late imperial period were discouraged from publishing before their marriage, or they refrained from doing so themselves because of social taboos. Some authors, forced to conceal their literary activities, would burn most of their work and leave little trace of it for others. Writing by women was published posthumously, and although some managed to publish their works, often with family assistance, these frequently suffered from extensive abridgement and even distortion. Because of these concerns, women relied on networking with other women writers and assistance from mentors to have their works published in a proper manner. As Dorothy Ko states, in the Qing some women who suffered the death of husbands or lost financial support became "teachers of the inner chambers," namely, private tutors of young 閨秀 (*guixiu*, talented women) (Ko, *Teachers* 118). The scenario of twelve flower spirits learning poetry from Mrs. Zhuang in Zheng's text is based on the phenomenon of women's learning of poetry and literature from literati scholars of the time, as exemplified by the famous scholar Yuan Mei, who was master to many female students, and poet Chen Wenshu (陳文述) who taught many women disciples (see Yu, Dan, "Huashen"). Among the talented female characters, Tao Xianbi (陶纖碧) grows up in a lower-class household and is forced to hide her writings from her prying uncle and aunt. Lin Xianyu, by contrast, is an upper-class woman whose works are composed with a moralistic purpose, including stories of pious children and loyal officials. These characters' anxiety about authorship and publication is also related to the genre that they have chosen for writing. Xianbi asks Xianyu,

"How many pieces have you written today?
You should have them published, so that your original purpose is accomplished."
Xianyu replied, "I have only thirty pieces.
Once I obtain approval from my parents, I will submit them for publication.
My writings are half drama and half fiction,
retelling the deeds of loyal officials and filially pious sons and daughters.
We should make known the outstanding deeds of women in the boudoir,
and gradually gather their stories together as a collection.
We shall conform people's mind to the ancient ways of thinking,
bring about a swift cleansing of their hearts, and enlighten them.
Yet this is not an easy process, and we might very likely be frustrated,
because some people of this time are blind,
even if they have eyes, and cannot understand our intentions."
Xianbi let out a sigh.
"Even so, there might be someone who could immediately understand us by reading our writings." (4: 35, 175)

In this passage, Xianyu speaks of herself as a *tanci* author, indicating that her writing borders between the genres of drama and fiction. The character is endowed with the thoughts and concerns of the *tanci* author who interpolates her own voice into the fictional character's voice and addresses the issue of women's writing with noticeable self-referentiality. The text illuminates the skewed relation between women and commercial publishing in the late imperial period. The appearance of women as both author and audience was in itself "one of the most remarkable elements of the urban culture taking shape in Jiangnan market towns from the mid-sixteenth century onward" (Ko, *Teachers* 30). The quickening pace of commercial publishing and the circulation of books "created a fertile ground for cross-pollination between the ideas of men and women, local and cosmopolitan cultures, and written and oral traditions" (Ko, *Teachers* 30). Nonetheless, the publication of women's writing in the late Ming and early Qing was largely paid for and controlled by their families (Widmer and Chang, *Writing Women* 147-70). In *Mengyingyuan*, Xianbi's writings are under the control of her crude uncle, who modifies her writings for public singing performances with liberty, and forces her to perform these works for him. Later with the help of her mentor General Lin Wu, Tao Xianbi has her writings preserved properly during preparation for publication as a literary work.

In these ways, Xianbi and Xianyu's conversation offers a look into women's literary activities of the nineteenth century. The female characters' discussion above is a direct statement of the necessity to endorse women writers' learning and achievement, in order to prevent violations of their ethical rights as writers and countervail the largely masculine decorum of the public print sphere. The text also displays these women authors' creative approach to popularizing tales of exceptional women by appropriating dominant discourses of filial piety and chastity. This authorial stance shields women authors from censorship by male editors and energizes women authors' voices in the public sphere.

The author's self-projection in the *tanci* is profoundly mirrored by women characters who themselves write and are confronted with similar ethical concerns about authorship and writing. The text contains extensive discussions of the genre of *tanci*, criticizes the narrative conventions of romance and marriage, and emphasizes the author's educational and moralistic concerns. When the Zhuang family eventually reunites with the twelve flower goddesses in the immortal world, Mrs. Zhuang proposes that a book should be written to record the experiences of the deities who have descended to the earth to redeem people's innocence and virtue. The characters' conversation about the choice of genre resonates with the authorial narrator's comment on her preference of *tanci* in writing at the beginning of the work. Mrs. Zhuang suggests, "Our story should not be composed into lyrics for stringed music, / lest it be contaminated by common singing girls. / It is better to let the *tanci* performers sing our tales, / so that even the most uneducated people will be enlightened" (4: 48, 241). Zhuang Yuan replies, "Although *tanci* is a minor genre, / its value depends on whether the author has set high goals or not. / If the author has an unconventional mind, / he or she would be able to adapt this genre to suit his or her purpose" (4: 48, 241). The characters' words draw attention to the authorial motive or purpose, which defines the literary positioning of *tanci* among diverse trends and genres. Remarkably, the characters answer the question of how their own stories should be told, suggesting that this *tanci* is to be completed. The ending lays bare a cyclical narrative structure that weaves back into the tale. Upon his parent's request, Mengyu composes a melody to commemorate the family reunion in heaven, accompanied by the musical performance of the flower goddesses. In regard to the authorial purpose in *tanci*, Zhuang Yuan comments that an author's goals in writing will determine the value of the work, regardless of the narrative form that one uses. Here, the fictional characters ponder and affirm the authorial choice of *tanci*, signaling a mutually empowering alignment between author and characters. The character is endowed by the author with a certain degree of autonomy in the narrative. The author opens herself to the character's critical scrutiny, and allows her characters to celebrate the use of *tanci* in narrating "their" stories. Perhaps Zheng wishes to stress the validity of her choice of genre and uses this scene within the diegesis to support her own decision.

Zheng establishes her moralizing voice by adapting discourses of filial piety and chastity to depict talented and virtuous women. The authorial voice empowers the readers by inviting the readers' sympathetic identification with the idealized women characters. This notion of empowerment takes place when the author endows the characters with the autonomy to assess the narrative form of the work. The characters' affirmative comments on the value of *tanci* give support to the stylistic choice of the author and affirm her presence in the literary text. In many passages, the text presents the authorial narrator as a cultured woman who articulates her grievances with the hardships of life and claims the right to her own "voice." This voice finds its power from retelling moral stories from the past. "Cleaning my ears, I will be as untainted as upright scholars; / contemplating in my heart, I approve only the words of ancient people. / Saddened by the fact that the field of *qing* has been corrupted in the world, / I shall recount the upright deeds of the worthy and refined in times gone by (1: 1, 3).

In recounting tales of previous scholars of moral worth, the authorial voice finds its moral empowerment. The narrative is developed with an explicit focus on reinstating the moral order in society through the instruction of readers. This is possibly the reason the author locates the story in the Song dynasty of the tenth century and depicts the fictional characters as historical figures. On a related note, this authorial emphasis on moral obligation foregrounds a general view concerning the goal of women's writing in pre-twentieth-century China. Whether Zheng intended to create the work as an imagined history of unusual women is probably not within the scope of the current discussion to judge. It is clear, however, that the authorial narrator in *Mengyingyuan* plays a role analogous to a historiographer or a chronicler. This narrator recounts the individual characters' stories as historical narratives that are relevant to lives in the present.

The authorial narrator's acts of self-empowerment are conducted through mimicking and rewriting the literary traditions of the time. For instance, the narrator notes that her depiction of Zhuang Yuan and Lin Wu's friendship in the story is modeled on an ancient legend of friendship.

> Since ancient times, the legend of Zhong Ziqi and Bo Ya's friendship has been widely applauded;
> to imitate them, I started composing this book.
> Exposing my amateurish writing to experts in literature,
> I might only make them have a good laugh.
> If my writing is without true feelings, it will not circulate.
> Alluding three times to the images of fragrant grass and the beautiful being in *An Elegy on Encountering Sorrows* (*Li Sao*),
> I have pondered the nuances of the poem.
> I do not mind being perceived as an unabashed imitator,
> for the word sincerity is not really out of date. (1: 13, 204)

The author, in the passage above, frames her own story within extant narratives, and develops her fictional authority by so doing. The authorial narrator states that Zhuang Yuan and Lin Wu's friendship is a reincarnated tale of the vowed friendship of Bo Ya (伯牙) and Zhong Ziqi (鐘子期). The story of Bo Ya and Zhong Ziqi takes place in spring and autumn. When Bo Ya plays music, suggesting the images of high mountains and flowing spring, Zhong Ziqi can detect his thoughts. When Zhong Ziqi passes away, Bo Ya destroys his instrument, cutting the strings, believing that no one else in the world can understand his music (Liu An 1029). Also, the evocation of the classical poem *Li Sao* (*An Elegy on Encountering Sorrows*), written by Qu Yuan (340 BCE-278 BCE), represents a mimetic impulse at work in the narrative. The images of 香草 (*xiangcao,* fragrant grass) and 美人 (*meiren,* beautiful being) in Qu Yuan's poem are allegorical references to the poet and the king. The term *meiren* usually means a beautiful woman. In early Chinese literature, however, it can refer to a man or to a virtuous person (see the annotated version of the poem in Wei Yuzhang 3, and the translation of the text in Hawkes, *Songs of the South*). The author might have conjured these images to denote Zhuang Yuan's relationship with the emperor. The loyal Qu Yuan is clearly the model for Zhuang, who is depicted as a faithful but unrecognized official of the emperor. By implying these intertextual connections between Qu Yuan's poem and her own work, Zheng asserts her status as a competent writer. These references indicate a case of narrative cross-dressing, in which the author takes on the position of a male poet and performs.

To return to Zheng's identification with the Jingwei bird cited at the beginning of this chapter, readers may trace a shared thematic tradition of feminine action, agency, and resilience between Zheng's *tanci* and that of the later female revolutionary martyr Qiu Jin, 精衛石 (*Jingweishi,* Pebbles of the Jingwei Bird; 1905; a substantial analysis of Qiu Jin and her work is in Wang, Lingzhen 1-27). Zheng's work, in retrospect, may carry women-oriented incentives for feminine self-articulation and self-reification against social pressure and turmoil, and anticipate ensuing narratives by progressive women authors in late Qing and turn of the twentieth century periods, including Qiu Jin's *tanci* and another protofeminist fiction, 女獄花 (*Nüyuhua*, Flowers of the Women's Prison; 1904), by Wang Miaoru (王妙如). The authorial insertions in Zheng's *tanci* offer a glimpse into the communicational structure of *tanci* and lead the readers to imagine the narrator and characters as speakers with whom they could share empathetic visions of life. Such empathetic associations between the narrator, the fictional characters, and the readers are channeled through and reinforced by the narrative model of *sheshen chudi*, or putting oneself in the situation of the other. Zheng's narrator is at once confessional and instructive, and often overtly comments on the lesson, purpose, and messages of her story. Presenting the moral qualities of filial piety and chastity as the most important human sentiments, or *qing*, the text replaces typical narratives of chaste widows with tales of young women who renounce marriage entirely in order to preserve their virginity during their lifetimes. Zheng's moral concern, to sum up, lends credence to her right to self-expression, to reify her self-empowerment, and to provide evidence that *tanci* works were morally and aesthetically empowering narratives for women.

Chapter Four

Gender, Spectatorship, and Literary Portraiture in *Mengyingyuan*

In *Mengyingyuan*, the reader's sympathetic identification with specific characters is activated by Zheng Danruo's use of the motif of portraiture. The portrait scenario as used in her work calls into question traditional gender constructions in the late imperial context. While Zheng modifies extant literary representations of the "painted beauty," she transforms these scenes by rewriting them. In *Mengyingyuan*, literary texts fuse diverse spatio-temporal viewing positions. However, the imperative for the reader is to identify with certain fictional characters and find her place within the story's space. In this process, the reader's sympathetic identification with the characters takes place. Particularly, the painted image of the woman transforms conventional codes of verisimilitude and dismantles the male-oriented visual structure by gazing out at the male voyeur/artist. Viewing an image is, in Zheng's *tanci*, a process in which the author transforms the reader into a spectator of certain cultural images or scenarios that are themselves connected to the gendered codes of the late imperial period. Also, the process of viewing the portraits invites the spectator's sympathy for the painted image and, through sympathetic identification, provisionally modifies the viewer's sense of identity.

The opening of *Mengyingyuan* accentuates the visual nature of the narrative. At the very beginning, the text is already habituating the readers to frames and focusing on visual spectacles. Locating the story at the beginning of the world, the storyteller introduces the readers to a field of vision in which the real is represented as a series of images.

> When the world first comes into being, the light and clear *qi* floats above and forms the sky, wherein a fog drifts with wind and transforms into an insect. With fluttering jade-colored wings, the insect absorbs the essence of sunlight and morning dew, and draws the quintessence of the sun and the moon. After a thousand years' of preparation, it transforms into a human being, and names himself "Mengyin Zhenren." One time he collects and makes medicines in the Luofu Mountain in eastern Yue province. When

> the medicine is made, it widely benefits the ordinary people. The Heavenly Emperor thus awards him with the honor of Luofu Xianjun, making him the Lord of this mountain. He leads five hundred deities and inhabits a blessed dwelling in endless pleasure. When the human world goes through the East Zhou dynasty and the period of the Warring States, by accident he thinks of going to the common world, and descends to earth to play. However, he eventually risks degeneration. Fortunately, the Plum Goddess from the Mountain transforms into a human being and comes to awaken him. Thus, he is able to return to the immortal realm and live his previous life. With no further intention of descending to the earth, he hides his form and obscures his tracks. The Plum Goddess is then honored as Kuifang Xianzi, with the alternate name of Bihua xianshi; her origin, however, is unknown. (1: 1, 1)

This opening, written in fictional narrative, presents an attenuated perception of the world, in which the real is inexorably filtered through multifarious manifestations. The world is but an image, thereby engulfing the readers and inviting them to seek themselves in it. The invisible 氣 (*qi,* or air), harboring the holy spirit that was incarnated in the protagonist, acquires its human figure from a thousand years' metaphysical practice, naming himself Dream-Concealed Deity (*Mengying zhenren*). His title *zhenren* (真人), or "real person," is a Daoist title referring to a god or a deified mortal, representing an ideal immortal being who transcends earthly desires and dangers. The word *yin* (隱), meaning "concealed," bears significance in late imperial literature, and implies the ironic rupture between objects and their allegorical meanings. The deity's self-chosen title, 夢隱 (*Mengyin,* dream-concealed), possibly carries an allusion to the famous Qing novel *Hongloumeng* (*The Dream of the Red Chamber*), indicating the tension and interrelation between human and heavenly dimensions of existence that are mimetically credible. The opening of the text bears much resemblance to that of *The Dream of the Red Chamber,* in that the narrative revolves around the journey of an incarnated male protagonist who seeks self-perfection through his worldly adventures. The diegesis of the narrative situates the relation between the main characters in medias res as a great part of the story, that is, Kuifang's help for Mengyin's redemption has already taken place.

Zheng's text carries a comparable narrative frame, as in *The Dream of the Red Chamber*, but with a subtle subversion of the male and female protagonists' affiliation at the beginning. The characters' names, Zhuang Yuan and Lin Xianyu, suggest possible association with the protagonists Jia Baoyu (賈寶玉) and Lin Daiyu (林黛玉) in Cao's text. Cao's hero Baoyu is originally a sacred stone and divine attendant named *Shenying shizhe* (神瑛侍者), or Luminescent Stone-in-Waiting; he waters a heavenly plant, Crimson Pearl Flower (*Jiangzhu xiancao,* 絳珠仙草), which eventually transforms into a goddess. To return his favor, the goddess descends to the world with the stone and is preordained to show gratitude to him by *huanlei* (還淚), or "returning the tears." The stone in this novel, as Andrew Plaks observes, serves as "an eyewitness of its own history and informs us that what we read is based on its memoir" (207). The stone not only transforms the flower fairy into a human being, but also endows her with emotions and gratitude. In *Mengyingyuan*, however, when the divine spirit falls into the human world by fault and risks being bereft of his divine rank, it is the Plum Goddess who transforms into a human being and descends to earth to enlighten him. The moral redemption of Mengyin is accomplished through the assistance of the Plum Goddess, who later is awarded the title of Premium Flower Goddess (Kuifang Xianzi) for her exceptional deeds. The above opening passage attests to Zheng's claim in the preface that her story was composed to record women's unusual deeds in the inner chambers. The passage ends in suspense, without revealing the identity and whereabouts of the mythical goddess: "as to the Plum Goddess, her origin however is unknown" (1: 1, 1). The text thus builds up the readers' anticipation of re-encountering this character in the tale. This preliminary storyline foreshadows the heroine as an active agent, whose talent and virtue will find endorsement through the plot development.

In contrast with the stone which serves as a proponent of verisimilitude in *The Dream of the Red Chamber,* which is also called 石頭記 (*Shitouji*, *Story of the Stone*), the portrait functions as the mimetic surface in *Mengyingyuan* onto which meaning is projected. The painting, when treated as a visual text, showcases a situation of narrative prolepsis. Prolepsis in narrative, as outlined by Genette in *Narrative Discourse,* can be conceived as "telling before time" (1). Genette holds that the essence of prolepsis lies in the mismatch between the order of the narrative and a notional chronological story. Prolepsis occurs when an event is told earlier in the order of the narrative than it would be if the strict chronological order of events of the story were followed. Zheng's *tanci* commences with a portrait of the Zhuang family that represents domestic bliss and foreshadows Zhuang Yuan and his wife's predestined return to the heavenly realm. The narrator describes the portrait through the eyes of the wife of Zhuang Yuan's nephew, who was invited to visit the couple after Zhuang Yuan resigned from the position of prime minister and returned to his hometown (1: 1, 35).

> In the middle of the hall there hangs a dark board,
> on which is inscribed, "Hall of Everlasting Admiration."
> The arrangement in the room inside is simple and elegant.
> In the center of the wall hangs a portrait,
> which seems to depict a scene of a backyard,
> with ancient trees and meandering corridors between buildings.
> On a pavilion by the water, a person rests by the rail,
> in flowing headwear and light-colored robe, dressed as if he is a deity.
> Another person sits on a stone by the pond;
> her hair looks like wind, her clothes like cloud.
> A maid waits on her by her side, her refined hands holding a flower bucket.
> . . .
> The wife of Zhuang Yuan's nephew ponders on the portrait.
> The person who sits alone watching the fish bears an elegance that
> resembles Uncle Zhuang. His whole stature closely resembles Uncle.
> At most, the painted image has three strands of beard.
> Otherwise, he looks not at all different from the real person.
> Could it be that the painting was intentionally made older than he was?

What is more suspicious is the person who smiles, holding the flower,
looks very like Aunt.
Even the young maid looks exactly like Sister E; they are almost perfectly
the same.
This is indeed a picture of a common family enjoying a good time together.
Why then was the picture hung in the central hall? . . .
At first, I mistook it as a portrait of deities,
a portrait of the mythical deities, such as Lu Dongbin and He Xian'gu. . . .
The other day when I scrutinized the painting again,
I found the resemblance of the painted figures to Uncle and Aunt.
As for the kind Sister Cai E,
even she is a person in that painting! (1: 2, 35-36)

The position of looking is crucial to the visual structure established in the actual viewing process (Mao, *Wu, Xingbie* 34). When the story begins, the Zhuang family's portrait, hanging on the north wall of the central hall, raises many questions and theories about its origin and implications. Yet both Zhuang Yuan and his wife are extremely reluctant to speak of the origin of the painting. The portrait is claimed to be one of the deceased parents of Zhuang Yuan, their maid, and Yuan himself when he was a child. However, in the picture, not only does Zhuang Yuan's father resemble Zhuang Yuan, but also his mother resembles the later Mrs. Zhuang, who married Zhuang Yuan many years after the portrait was made. Additionally, the maid in the portrait resembles the later Mrs. Zhuang's maid, which convinces the viewer that the picture is a complete depiction of the real Zhuang's family. Through the eyes of the female character, the readers are challenged to view the painting frequently. Such recurrent viewing is comparable to a process of reading, in that paintings are analogous to narrative frames that constantly open up new realms of interpretation. Intriguingly, this family painting is produced by an anonymous artist whose identity is never revealed throughout the *tanci*. The absence of the "author" of the painting further suggests the anachronistic nature of the narrative, the origin of which is inadvertently lost.

Visualization in the late imperial period can be considered in relation to the production, circulation, function, and reception of portraits. The significant development of printing technology since the mid Ming has enabled authors to insert figures, images, and miniatures in their writings to draw customers' attention. Distinguished fiction and drama works, such as *Mudanting* (*The Peony Pavilion*) and 西廂記 (*Xixiangji*, The West Chamber) by Wang Shifu (王實甫, 1260-1336), were published with many editions that contained large numbers of drawings as complementary parts of the texts. Robert Hegel, in *Reading Illustrated Fiction*, provides a contextualized analysis of novel illustrations. Hegel suggests that the art of printing in medieval Buddhist sutras demonstrated the interrelation between illustration and narrative (178). In the Ming and Qing, popular narratives such as *pinghua* (chantefables) and *chuanqi* (plays) were illustrated to facilitate reading and circulation. Whereas publishing fiction became commercialized during the Yuan period, Hegel suggests that the use of block-printed book illustrations were conditioned by the publishers' economic concerns (179). In the tradition of *tanci* fiction, published texts like *Zaishengyuan* (Destiny of Rebirth, late eighteenth century), *Jinguijie* (Heroes in the Golden Chambers, prefaced dated 1824), *Bishenghua* (Blossom from the Brush, nineteenth century), and *Mengyingyuan* (Dream, Image and Destiny, author's self-preface dated 1843) were frequently published in illustrated editions and contain abundant portraits and miniatures. Some illustrations in *tanci* also carry poetic inscriptions or rhymed lines addressing the character or theme in each painting, as in the 1840 edition of 繡像十美圖 (*Xiuxiang shimeitu*, Illustrated Portraits of the Ten Beauties) (Sheng, *Qingdai* 377). Making and appreciating portraiture constitute a crucial textual theme in late imperial literature. In this context, Zheng's *tanci*, which depicts characters making, viewing, exchanging, and interacting with portraits, modifies extant narratives associated with portraits of and by women, and display the transformative potential of women's presence in portrait scenarios.

A close reading shows that the text contains an intertextual reference to *The Peony Pavilion* by Tang Xianzu (1550-1616). In Tang's play, the heroine Du Liniang's ghost is startled in the underworld by her lover Liu Mengmei's call to her painted image, and visits Liu in order to fulfill their relationship projected in a prior dream. Likewise, in *Mengyingyuan*, the metaphysical dream trope is brought into a dialectical relation with the "image," for, as the title indicates, the destined affinity between the characters is produced through the interplay of "dream" and "image." The male protagonist's name, Mengyu (literally, "dream stone"), is an intertextual reference to the earlier novel, *The Dream of the Red Chamber*, in which the male protagonist bears a similar name: Baoyu ("precious stone"). If the dream represents a fusion of past with present and forshadows the characters' reunion in marriage at the end, it is the painted "image" that recurrently unravels multilayered possibilities of reading that complicate and potentially disrupt the development of the plot toward a consummate narrative closure.

Verisimilitude, in *Mengyingyuan*, is evoked to generate sympathetic relationships between the viewers and the portraits. The painted images of Zhuang Yuan's parents, who become immortals, bear an exact likeness to Zhuang Yuan, his wife, and their maid.. This refined likeness of the immortals' portrait to the private life of the Zhuangs possibly reflects the authorial ideal of putting the immortals into reincarnation in order to execute worldly transformation. The text presents the overlap between narrative pictures and portraits. The portrait of Zhuang Yuan's parents and maid can be interpreted as having important narrative elements. As a portrait of the immortals, it reinforces the message of ethereal happiness and transient pleasures, and foreshadows Zhuang Yuan's later decision to search for his immortal parents in the mountains. Perusing the portrait, for the characters in the story, strikes a chord of their preordained interrelations with each other (2: 16, 40). In Dream, Image, Destiny the author rewrites this scenario of *wanzhen* 玩真 (playing with the portrait) in two different episodes, one of which features Zhuang Yuan's son Mengyu's painting of Lin Xianyu, and the other of which concerns Xianyu painting her would-be father-in-law, Zhuang Yuan. In each case, the act of viewing prompts the viewer's sympathy for the painted image, and in return modifies the viewer's self through sympathetic identification.

Representations of women in literature by literati scholars are frequently conditioned and constructed by the elite, male-dominated literary discourse about women's social roles. Do these texts represent the controlling of women's desire through narrative framing? How does Zheng's text modify these narratives and project an innovative interpretation of the portrait scenario? How does *Mengyingyuan* explore the possibility of reconfiguring this tradition of "beauty portraits" by presenting spaces of reversal and transgression? Zheng says at the beginning of the first chapter that she has borrowed from extant narrative conventions regarding the appearance of portraits in writing, with an eye to transforming these conventions and endowing them with new meanings. "Twice in this book I have rewritten the 'playing with the portrait' scenario, / for one must agree that a fledgling phoenix has a more refreshing voice than a mature one" (1: 11, 173). The allusion to *wanzhen* (appreciating the portrait of a person) can be traced to the ninth-century story "Huagong" (The Portrait Maker) from *Songchuang zaji* (Pine Window Miscellany) by Du Xunhe (see Zhang, Jing'er 486). In the story, a painting of a beautiful woman comes alive when a male scholar calls the subject's name, Zhenzhen (真真). The woman then steps down from the painting and marries the scholar. The name of the painted woman—Zhenzhen, literally meaning "real" or "genuine"—ironically shows the woman's imagined existence, for she only becomes real when her name is spoken by the man.

The scene in which Zhuang Mengyu makes a portrait of Lin Xianyu, his predestined bride, provides a compelling example of the visual dynamics between the male artist and the painted women, who occupy different gendered viewpoints. In this scene, Xianyu's resistance against being captured in the painting reveals her wish to counteract the male protagonist's subordination of her body by calling and naming her painted body. In the story, Mengyu has long had excellent painting skills and is praised by his mother, Mrs. Zhuang, for having magic hands that could capture the spirit and fragrance of the image. When he reached the age of twelve, Mrs. Zhuang intended to marry him to Song Renfang, a daughter of Zhuang's friend. However, Mengyu has feelings for the Plum Goddess, who is reborn as Xianyu and shares a predestined bond with him. Mengyu is thus unwilling to marry another woman. However, as a devoted son, he cannot reject his mother's suggestion. In response to his mother's request, he paints an image of his ideal wife, based on his inborn memory of the goddess.

> Mrs. Zhuang stands behind Mengyu and looks frequently at the painted image.
> She sees the facial features and is very startled that the image looks so real.
> Then she sees him painting the refined shoulders, hands, and waist.
> The painted girl, dressed like a goddess, is naturally beautiful . . .
> Fully smiling, the image seems about to talk;
> her eloquent eyes appear to be looking at the audience, enhancing her beauty all the more.
> Anguished with admiration in facing the image,
> the kind-hearted mother cannot help feeling compassion and pity.
> After a long interval, she calls upon Mengyu joyfully,
> "It is truly a different person!

She and Miss Song both have endless grace;
one could not tell which one is more beautiful.
Yet Miss Song's body often bears so much fragrance,
and no less than you who bear so much fragrance like the legendary Xun
    Ling, whose fragrance lingers in places where he has sat.
The painted image is indeed very beautiful,
yet it is most difficult to pass through the fragrance of it.
She is, after all, not comparable to Miss Song;
even though she is predestined to marry you,
she should let Miss Song be the first one."
Mengyu then replies to his mother, smiling,
"Please observe the painting carefully."
Mrs. Zhuang then approaches to smell the image,
which exudes whiffs of subtle fragrance from the beautiful woman's sleeves.
(1: 11, 163)

Xun Yu (荀彧, 163-212), who is mentioned in the above passage, is known for the intense fragrance that he was born with. This allusion to Xun Yu's fragrance is later extended to refer to the elegance of a literary scholar (Li Fang, *Taiping yulan* 703: 3113). With Mrs. Zhuang's close inspection of the painted beauty, the text invites a close observation of the image and controls the reader's sensory experience. Like Mrs. Zhuang, the reader is engaged in a process of looking, feeling, identifying, and empathizing with the painted goddess. The text situates the reader in a dynamic visual space in which he or she is constantly constructed as a sympathetic subject. The painted beauty is desirable, but inaccessible. Mengyu's hands, which "capture the fragrance and soul" of the image, inch by inch, inscribe the imagined desire of the male subject toward the woman. The visual structure represented in this scene highlights what Laura Mulvey calls the "to-be-looked-at-ness" of what is represented. However, the painted beauty transforms this desire by "looking back," controlling and reverting the gaze of the male artist/viewer. In fact, her image is so breathtaking that it even "daunts" the viewer (1: 11, 163).

The reader, along with Mrs. Zhuang, is invited by the painter to look at the portrait repeatedly. Upon first glance, Mrs. Zhuang takes the painted image as her selected daughter-in-law Song. Gradually, the image gains life under the viewers' scrutiny, and even emits a subtle fragrance to the viewers. The grace of the painted image is displayed through her bodily actions: with a smiling face, she looks at the viewer with eloquent eyes. The "gaze" from the painted beauty undermines the male-dominated visual structure and supplements the one-way viewing gaze into an associative one. The goddess exchanges gazes with the viewer and prompts the viewer's sympathetic identification. This scene stages a shifted power relation between the mother Mrs. Zhuang and Mengyu. Mengyu, a child of six, insists on his autonomy in choosing his own spouse by painting the woman that he wants to marry. His filial devotion to his mother allows room for his autonomous choice. He pleases his mother with the beautiful painting and expresses his wish to have a choice in marriage. The author's dramatization of the power dynamics among the painted woman, the male viewer, and his mother expresses an innovative understanding of the underlying familial relationship among the characters. Both Mrs. Zhuang's son and her future daughter-in-law display individual autonomy in addition to their filial devotion.

The viewer's sympathetic response in the above scene also affirms the image's representational potential, its power to reverberate within the viewer's mind and body. The painted goddess responds to the viewer's desire, emanating a delicate scent from the sleeves, implying the imperceptible motion of the woman's hands. The scene exposes a narrative embedded in the identity of the painted woman, whose illusory presence supplements the male artist/viewer's own loss of self. The painted beauty is a consolation for Mengyu's loss of Xianyu, and evokes his desire to restore his celestial self to his physical being in this life. The text depicts the subtle movements of the image as follows:

> Mrs. Zhuang turned back. She saw that
> the painted beauty, her jade ornaments stirred by her movements, was about to approach them.
> Mrs. Zhuang smiled and called Mengyu to see the painting.
> "Your magic brush can truly capture the body and soul of the woman.
> If you can call the beauty to life,
> you might as well name her."
> Upon these words, Lanjun thought privately,
> "If I call upon her name, I am afraid that I will imprison her spirit.
> I am afraid that I would take the life away from her fragile body;
> even though she is skillful in maintaining her heavenly spirit,
> she is but a physical being." (1: 11, 171)

The scenario wherein a painted beauty comes to life when called upon by a male viewer, as discussed above, alludes to a legendary painted beauty who is revived from the paper and marries a male scholar. The story, widely circulated, elicited the emulation of later writers. A similar example is in *Mudanting* (*The Peony Pavilion*, author's preface dated 1598), when the love-enchanted Du Liniang takes up her paint brush and makes a self-portrait. She laments, "How futile is it to make this self-portrait? / Who would weep over it? / Were I the legendary painted beauty Zhenzhen, / still no one would call my name" (Tang, *Mudanting* 36). Liniang's melancholy is provoked by the absence of the male viewer Liu Mengmei, while she projects herself into the imaginary subject position of the legendary Zhenzhen. The textual moment is an example of melodramatic pathos, wherein the subject's grief is caused by the deferral of narrative closure. Liu does not discover her self-portrait until after her death. This pathetic scenario of Liniang's narcissistic gaze at her own portrait has been replicated extensively in later literary texts.

The above passage of Mengyu painting a portrait of his predestined companion possibly alludes to the seventeenth-century play 畫中人 (*Huazhongren*, The Painted Beauty) by Wu Bing (吳炳, 1595-1648). The play depicts a love story between the scholar Yu Qi and the painted beauty Zheng Qiongzhi (鄭瓊芝), who is resurrected from the portrait scroll and marries Yu Qi. The plot of the play bears a similarity to that of the earlier *The Peony Pavilion*. Wu closes *Huazhongren* with the comment, "What can be as effectual as [the power of] *qing*? / It could even make the image in scattered painting powders come to life" (Wu Bing 5). In Wu's play, the portrait becomes a vehicle of *qing* (desire) and makes possible both the rebirth of the deceased and the reunion of the separated. The resurrection of the painted woman depends on the mechanism of human emotions, a topic which has been extensively discussed in the study of late imperial literature. Kathryn Lowry, in a study of the genre of 情書 (*qingshu,* love letters) in late imperial China, argues that love letters enlist popular reading materials to conjure *qing*, "feeling" or "desire." The language of desire is the result of a discursive process of reading (Zeitlin, Liu, and Widmer 239-69). Wu's play depicts a visual space that draws the readers' attention to the dialectic between the observed beauty and the male observer. In *Mengyingyuan*, this dialectic between the fetishizing male spectator and the woman's image is amplified; she is not simply an object submitted for the male viewer's contemplation—she also carries a notably unsettling power to stimulate desire, reverse the viewer's gaze, or even dismantle the voyeuristic visual scenario.

Women themselves, in *Mengyingyuan*, also paint portraits of men. Their artistic practice breathes life into their painted images and constracts a gendered perspective on chastity and filial devotion. The author compares her heroine Xianyu with the famous Liniang: "Liniang's much acclaimed story of a departed soul searching for love / has been passed down for hundreds of years and won much praise. / In comparison with Bihua Xianshi, / one can perceive the difference in the significance of the matter. / I admire Xianyu's heart, which is as pure as water, / and far surpasses those sentimental writings that speak of overt emotions" (1: 12, 46). Zheng's allusion expresses admiration for the legend of Liniang's resurrection by the power of love. However, unlike Liniang, who internalized the man's desire and awaited his call to come back to life, Zheng's heroine Xianyu resisted the summoning of Mengyu and the entrancement of his desire for her in the portrait. Zheng's mockery of Liniang's pathos rewrites conventional narrative representations of women. In *Mudanting*, Liniang's subjectivity is inscribed for an imaginary male viewer and awaits affirmation from the male spectator. Xianyu's character, however, is more praiseworthy for her resistance to the male gaze, and her refusal of the narrative closure of predestined marriage. By rewriting the portrait scenario, Zheng reveals the woman's resistance to becoming an object of male connoisseurship. Mengyu's calling on Xianyu signifies the subordination of the woman's body by naming. When Mengyu and his mother observe the painted image, the reincarnated Plum Goddess Xianyu falls mortally ill because of her emotional connection with Mengyu. She blames Mengyu for taking the liberty to summon her spirit, and decides to keep her virginity during her lifetime, despite their predestined relationship. A comparison of Xianyu and Liniang highlights Zheng's endorsement of Xianyu's virginity and her disagreement with stereotypical representations of pathetic women in literati literature. Zheng thus distinguishes her writing from the negative stereotypes of sentimental women, and indicates that women in her work are dedicated to a higher standard of moral integrity.

Stereotypes of women in nineteenth-century court art, Wu Hung writes, suggest "thematic, stylistic and iconographic generalization in art and literature" (306).

Such stereotypes should be contextualized in the "complex historical process in which a uniform pattern of imagination and representation gradually prevails to control not only the fictional characters, but also the self-imaging of the author, reader, and viewer" (307). Zheng's text, in this light, reprocesses the beauty portrait motif in a women-oriented narrative, doing away with the stereotypes of passivity attached to women. The portrait carries symbolic associations with death and resurrection, as is the case in *The Peony Pavilion*. Liniang paints her portrait when lovesickness has begun to take its toll on her looks, as a response to her knowledge of her mortality. After she passes away, Liu Mengmei finds the portrait, which she has buried in the garden. He calls on the painted image and startles Liniang's spirit. The portrait has a life-giving power, activated by the male viewer's gaze upon the painted woman. Likewise, in *Mengyingyuan*, Mengyu's gaze upon the painted Xianyu is so powerful that it almost takes away the spirit of the heroine. "One night when the mother and son are both viewing the painting, / they see the image of the beauty frequently casting affectionate glances. / Turning her shoulder, she seems to come out of the painting, or go into the depth of the picture. / Seized by the sight, Mengyu cannot hold back his tears (1: 11, 172).

The return of the painted goddess to life reveals a reversed visual structure, with the painted woman repeatedly flashing a gleam back at the viewers. Her unsettling gazes lead to continual raptures in the textual presentation and anticipate Xianyu's resistance against her prescribed role. The painted beauty is located in a place from which the male protagonist and the reader observe her. When she turns a gaze back, Mengyu is startled by her dismantling gaze. He weeps, hoping to call her name, yet refrains from doing so, for fear of taking her spirit away from her body. The physical being of the woman, the ideal of beauty, appears in sublimated form, as the physiognomic expression of the spiritual. The physical incarnation of the heroine in the portrait bespeaks the yearnings of the viewers. Yet the woman casts brooding glances towards and behind the viewer into the distance, disrupting the unilateral visual structure and transforming the direction of the look. In a melancholy mood, she tosses her shoulders, as if to escape into the deep end of the painting, or to flee from it. The motion of the painted woman suggests a sorrowful beauty who suffers from loneliness and estrangement, her celestial purity perpetually out of place in the surrounding human world. While the story highlights the suture between authenticity and imitation, the portrait is an ironic reference to a male desire to frame and control the woman through a subordinating visual structure. This visual structure consists of the male artist who himself is an observer, the painted woman, and the subject of the painting, Xianyu, who is summoned by the male artist's imagination. The mother's observation of the portrait also displays a deep level of gender socialization, as she ponders and assesses her as a future daughter-in-law.

This scenario of resurrecting the painted beauty through the spectator's gaze recurs later in the tale. After Zhuang Yuan becomes a good friend with Lin's father Lin Wu and arranges Mengyu to marry Xianyu, Mrs. Zhuang visits the Lin family to meet with Xianyu. Upon her first sight of the beautiful girl, Mrs. Zhuang is instantly struck by the resemblance of the portrait to Xianyu's appearance. "Mrs. Zhuang was overjoyed to find that the painted beauty Zhenzhen was her real daughter-in-law!" (1: 11, 172). The text reifies the heroine's image with the illusion of verisimilitude. Yet what Mrs. Zhuang perceives as "real" in the portrait has already dissipated. The painted woman is given the embellished name of Zhenzhen, the painted beauty who came alive when called upon by a scholar. The affirmation of Xianyu as the legendary Zhenzhen represents the woman's body as an idealized medium, which stimulates the spectator's desire and makes the woman a culturally inscribed object.

In the former scene in which Mengyu makes a portrait of Xianyu, the painted woman's image is idealized and subjected to sexual objectification, mirroring an objectification of women at the social and cultural level. Mengyu acquires a "misrecognition" of an imaginary relationship with the painted image. In this particular scene, the imagery of the woman implies possible modes of resistance in the visual structure. Xianyu's image is activated and gains life under the gaze of Mengyu and her future mother-in-law. For the viewers of the portrait, and the readers as well, her body seems to make involuntary movements by casting meaningful gazes back. These bodily movements, however, cannot change the fact that her image is a silenced one. Xianyu's painted woman lacks a voice to counteract the subordination of her body, and consequently she cannot speak back to resist her destined matrimonial bond (for a similar story on the romance between a scholar and a painted beauty, see Zhang, Jing'er 493-98).

When Xianyu's soul is summoned by Mengyu's portrait and departs from her body, it is her reincarnated celestial sister, the doctor Tao Xianbi, who awakens her from a fatal spell by calling Xianyu's childhood name. Seeing the seriously ill Xianyu, Xianbi thinks to herself, "From what I can see, the reason for Miss Lin's illness is none other than that someone has seized her soul by making a portrait of her. / Yet where can I find the person who made the portrait, / so that the painting can be destroyed, and she can recover? / Even though my medicine has some effect, it cannot counter the skills of the painter. / She is not simply suffering a temporary illness. / When looked at closely, it seems her facial features are not real" (1: 12, 188). Intriguingly, as Xianyu's disease worsens, her body increasingly loses its substance and becomes indistinguishable from the painted image. As Mengyu exerts his influence, Xianyu is gradually displaced from her physical being and becomes merely a sign for the painter's own desires. The tension between Lin's body and the portrait is dramatized to such a degree that the portrait even threatens to take away her life. Her presence is reduced to a void space in his imaginary screen. This crisis, however, is resolved by Xianbi, who perceives the effect of the portrait and counteracts its magic by calling Xianyu's childhood name. Contrary to the story of Zhenzhen, in which the scholar gives life to the painted woman by calling her name, Xianyu retains her life by denying the naming act of the male spectator. This act against Mengyu's control is legitimated afterwards: by taking back her natal family's name, she fulfills the obligation of filial piety, a moral obligation more important than her duty to her future husband.

The portraits in *Mengyingyuan* possess such immediacy that the boundaries between the real and the representational are dismantled. The painted image at first appears to be the product of the male protagonist's imagination. Xianyu is a reflective image; her presence is only a figurative one. Later, with a burdened conscience, Mengyu burns the painting to finally exempt Xianyu from the painting's spell: "the image in the painting dissipated in a mere moment; / only a faint fragrance of the plum flower was detectable in the air" (1: 11, 172). The burning of the portrait shows the author's intention to divert from the prospect of marriage and demonstrates resistance against such narrative impulses. Liniang's self-portrait, in *Mudanting*, is preserved after her death as proof of her resurrection and marriage with Mengmei. In *Mengyingyuan*, however, Mengyu's portrait of Xianyu is destroyed. This dissimilarity between the two texts suggests Zheng's search for an alternative closure, in which the heroine's fate is no longer constrained by the pledge of love.

An example in Zheng's *tanci* that addresses women's ironized bond with their painted images involves the beauty Wang Zhaojun (王昭君), who falls victim to the portrait maker's manipulation. The reincarnated goddess Xianyu, with her exceptional painting skills, crafts a portrait of Wang to applaud her "purity, constancy, loyalty, and chastity" (2: 2, 135). She asks her father General Lin to compose a poem on this portrait. The poem, reminiscent of the famous female poet Xi Peilan's satirical poem on Wang's life, goes as follows: "The melancholy tune of the *pipa* penetrated the Yanmen Gate [at the frontier], / Across ten thousand miles her chained soul returns to her home country. / Her tomb is imperishable, so is the Fragrance Creek; / Never did the portrait bring joy to the beautiful maiden" (2: 21, 136). The 香溪 (*Xiangxi,* Fragrance Creek) is a branch of the Yangzi River in South China. Legend has it that Wang was born in a small county by the river and was selected to be a royal consort during the reign of Emperor Yuan of the Han Dynasty (74 BC-33 BC). Resonant with Xi Peilan's poem, the passage illustrates Wang's tragic fate caused by the misrepresenting portrait, indicating the painting could not actually speak for the woman herself. In Zheng's *Mengyingyuan*, this episode appears before Xianyu's illness caused by the portrait, indicating Xianyu's reluctance to submit to the hero's voyeuristic control.

Such revisions of the portrait scenario can be found in many late imperial *tanci* works. In *Zaishengyuan*, Meng Lijun leaves her parents a self-portrait as a surrogate for her person and flees her home, exploring new possibilities of life by disguising herself as a man. Likewise, Zheng's modification of the portrait scenario depicts a woman in search of her own desire, discarding imposed social and cultural frames as encoded in the portraits of women. The narrator criticizes Mengyu for making the portrait of his beloved carelessly: "I blame him for often using the portrait without caution; / overwhelmed with love, he neglects Xianyu's parents. / Addicted with desire, his mind is demeaned and impish. / His behavior really diminishes the name of scholar and beauty" (1: 11, 173). Xianyu's words indicate that the image scenario is oftentimes employed without enough caution, and consequently denigrates the reputation of women. The reluctance to offer her own image as a passive visual object is possibly the reason Xianyu refuses to become one of the painted beauties in the shadow, lacking substance. When Xianyu is asked by her father to create a portrait of the "hundred beauties," that is, one hundred women noted in history, she declines to paint her own image among them, even though her parents encourage her to do so.

The question of gendered, as the above textual scenario displays, is of prominent importance when it comes to portraits of women. Imperial literati intellectuals approached portraits of women from the stance of connoisseurs of feminine beauty. However, women themselves had a tradition of making their own portraits, as well as making statements about their ideals through these painted images. Talented women, many of whom were skilled in painting, composed poems for their friends' paintings. References to women making self-portraits can be found in many historical records since ancient times. Some scholars hold that painting was initially an artistic practice of women. One of the earliest painters is a woman, Lei (嫘), who was a younger sister of the ancient Emperor Shun (23-2 century BCE). Lei was the first person who took to painting, and thus was named the Painter Lei (Liao, "Guige hua" 31). Lei had the power of creating the world and deserved the name of the "Progenitor of Painting" (Mingmo Shilong 147). These earlier records found resonance in similar stories of women making portraits in later generations. In the eighth century, a talented woman, Xue Yuan, to call back her husband who was traveling, made a self-portrait on which she composed a poem to show her longing for him. The poem was entitled, "A Self-Portrait for the Traveler."

> Before making the first stroke with the painting brush,
> I took up the precious mirror and had a look at myself.
> Already shocked by my withered look,
> Now the hair around my temples is even thinner.
> Easy to sketch these eyes filled with tears,
> Difficult to compose lines that speak of my melancholy heart.
> [I] hope you my lord do not forget about me,
> And will open this scroll at times to have a look. (Ji, *Tangshi* 1122)

As the title of the poem suggests, the woman's self-portrait invites a compassionate gaze from the male viewer and suggests the wife's subordinate relation to the husband. The poem internalizes a male-oriented perspective, presenting the woman as a passive object under the masculine gaze. Unlike Yuan's poem, Zheng's text enables the reader to imagine a feminine perspective that undermines and even reverses this male-oriented visual scenario so common in literary and historical narratives about painted women.

Ming and Qing literary and historical records provide evidence that women played multifarious roles in the making and circulation of portraits. Some women's activities were recorded by literati authors. Yuan Mei's work *Suiyuan shihua* (Sui Garden Remarks on Poetry, 1790), for example, include a record of anecdotes about poets, and some entries reflect women poets' relationships with paintings. He notes, "In ancient times there were no miniatures. [The tradition of portraiture] may be traced to the paintings of the ancient worthy and chaste women in the Wuliang Temple of the Han Dynasty" (Yuan, *Suiyuan shihua* 231). Yuan's comment suggests that the ancient portraits of women might have been initially created to advocate women's chastity and filial devotion, topics presented in mainstream social discourses about women's virtue.

In Yuan Mei's story, "紅袖添香圖" ("Hongxiu tianxiang tu," "Portrait of the Added Fragrance of Scarlet Sleeves," eighteenth century), a scholar, Feng, paints a portrait of an imaginary woman, having no particular person in mind. Later, Qiu, a friend of Feng, sees the painting and is struck by the resemblance of the image to his own maid, Hua. Qiu then invites Feng to his house and gives the maid to Feng as his wife. In this tale, the scholar's portrait of the imagined woman becomes a pledge for an unanticipated marriage with a maid the painter had never met (Yuan, *Suiyuan shihua* 206). This anecdote suggests that portraits of women, idealized or realistic, were important parts of the literati culture. A similar example in the pre-twentieth-century English literary tradition is Robert Browning's well-known poem "My Last Duchess," in which the Duke Ferra presents to his guests a portrait of his former wife, while negotiating a second marriage with a daughter from a rich family. While the poem carries signs that the Duke had murdered this former wife himself, the portrait of the woman survives and displaces the woman's actual presence. The poem represents the Duke's appreciation of art as well as his controlling and manipulative nature.

Many women in late imperial China were themselves accomplished painters. In the late nineteenth century, scholar Tang Suyu edited a collection entitled 玉臺畫史 (*Yutai huashi*, A History of Paintings of the Jade Terrace; 1871), in which she listed four kinds of women painters, including palace maids, noted women of the gentry, women servants, and famous courtesans. Painting, like poetry, was one of the areas of artistry in which a talented woman might excel. For example, in the eighteenth century, Sun Biwu (孫碧梧), a student of Yuan Mei, once invited Yuan and thirteen talented women to a banquet in Hangzhou city. At the gathering, the women poets exchanged poems and paintings with one another as gifts (Yuan, *Suiyuan shihua* 553). An attending female scholar, Xu Yuxin (徐裕馨), made a portrait of this gathering titled "隨園湖樓請業圖" ("Suiyuan hulou qingye tu," "A Gathering of the *Suiyuan* Poets at Hulou"; see Yuan, *Suiyuan shihua* 553). Some well-known late imperial women poets and painters were Liu Shi (柳是, 1618-1664), Li Yin (李因, 1610-1685), Fang Wanyi (方婉儀, 1732-1779), Yang Guxue (楊古雪, late eighteenth and early nineteenth century) and Liao Yunjing (廖雲錦, nineteenth century). Liu Shi published a collection of paintings, 月堤煙柳小卷 (*Yuedi yanliu xiaojuan*, A Small Scroll of the Moonlit Dam and Shadowy Willow). There were also a few women who earned a living by selling their paintings; the early nineteenth-century poet Shen Shanbao, who was born in a humble family and lost her father in childhood, sold her poetry and paintings to support her widowed mother (Chen Yun 8b).

Some portraits depicted women as cross-dressers. Late eighteenth-century woman poet Shen Xiang (沈纕) described a portrait of the courtesan Liu Shi, in which Liu cross-dressed as a young scholar to pay a personal visit to a male scholar. In Shen Xiang's poem about this painting, she notes, "Who could tell the truth from the appearance of a person after all? Beauty or scholar, now both are seen as one" (Shen Xiang 15a). This unique example depicts Liu Shi's cross-dressed image, which recalls other similar examples of portraits of women in men's garb. In Wu Zao's play, 飲酒讀騷 (*Yinjiu dusao*, Drinking Wine and Reading *Li Sao*; nineteenth century), similarly, the protagonist cross-dresses and makes a portrait of herself in a man's robe. She laments her fate in being born a woman under social constraints, mimicking the ancient poet Qu Yuan. Images of cross-dressed women such as these suggest late imperial women authors' conceptions of alternative gender representations in literary works.

Readers may find many poems composed about Ming and Qing women's portraits or as inscriptions on paintings in poetry collections. A particularly important genre of poetry is the set of poems dedicated to paintings. Mao Wenfang proposes that these poems composed on paintings reflect "a dialogic relation" between the painted image and the observer who composed the poem on the painting (Mao, "Yige qingdai" 56). While poems composed about or inscribed upon paintings can be used by readers to reconstruct some of the details of paintings that have been lost (Mao, "Yige qingdai" 56), originally these poems were likely to have served to enrich the viewer's experience of interacting with the painted image. Mao's study focuses on the famous poet Gu Taiqing (顧太清, 1798-1877). Gu and her husband Yu Hui both had their portraits made, and then each composed poems on the other's portrait. Gu also composed poems for the portraits of her friends in the inner quarters, including Li Renlan (李紉蘭), Xu Yunlin (許雲林), and Shen Xiangpei (沈湘佩). Xi Peilan also commented on paintings by women and had her own portraits commented upon by others (Yuan, *Suiyuan nudizi shixuan* 1: 213). Poems by women about portraits show that the women depicted were not merely passive objects of male artistic connoisseurship. In women's own literary communities, portraits of and by women may even have counteracted the male-oriented voyeuristic visual structure, by foregrounding a woman's perspective.

A good example of the ironized relation between portraits and the painted woman is a poem by Xi Peilan, from her work 題美人冊子: 王嬙 (*Ti meiren cezi: Wang Qiang*, A Collection of Poems on Beautiful Women: Wang Qiang) (Xi 2.7b). The poem alludes to a historical woman named Wang Qiang, more often called Wang Zhaojun (王昭君), a woman in the harem of Emperor Wu of the Han Dynasty (156 BCE-87 BCE). The emperor selected his concubines according to the women's painted appearances. To win an emperor's favor, many women bribed the painter in the palace into making beautiful portraits of them. Wang Zhaojun, an honest and beautiful maiden, refused to do the same and consequently failed to attract Emperor Hanwu's attention. In 33 BC, the Huns of the north wanted to establish friendly relations with the Han through marriage with a Han princess. Unwilling to marry off either his own daughter or a real beauty to the nomadic Huns, the emperor ordered the plainest maid to be chosen as the candidate. Wang, whose portrait was among the least attractive, was selected. As she departs for the Huns, the emperor sees her in person and regrets his choice instantly but cannot reverse his decision. Instead, he grants Wang a generous dowry, and she travels north, playing the *pipa* on her solitary journey to the remote country. After she joins the Huns, Wang devotes her life to the spreading of Han culture and civilization. Back at the palace, the emperor, enraged by the portrait maker's deception, puts him to death. Xi alludes to this incident in a poem: "Falling out of the regal favor due to a portrait, she fled to a foreign land. / In the cold snow and frontier wind, the radiance of her looks declined. / The melody of *pipa* beyond the frontier, the dances in the royal palace, / All the same, they took pains to offer the emperor pleasure" (Xi 2.7b). The poet's reference to the portrait in the first line presents the ironic situation of the portrait, a determinant of women's fate, failing to do its subject justice and making her a misfit. The last two lines deepen the irony, suggesting that both the favored women and the one in exile are no more than objects of pleasure for the male ruler. The poet's comments suggest the pathos in the women's situation and the absence of a woman's perspective from these portraits.

If portrait is a product embodying the artist's person and his or her inner mind, in what ways are the female artist's portraits revelatory of women's autonomy? In *Mengyingyuan*, Xianyu's portrait is made by Mengyu to celebrate his own subjectivity and virility; the text, however, presents the visual objectification of the female image as morally problematic and as having potentially emancipating power. The painted images are not just the erotic or sexual objects under the artist's brushes; instead, portraits resist this and other forms of objectification. Zheng's inventive use of the portrait scenario exemplifies women's creative appropriation of portraits to endorse chastity and filial devotion. In Zheng's *tanci*, women's determination to preserve virginity in the name of serving their natal parents is also seen in the character of Liu Lingjuan, who paints a self-portrait to show her determination to stay unmarried for her lifetime. In these two stories, chastity is an exemplifying form of gendered filial devotion. Along with these stories about chastity, Zheng also converses the theme of filial devotion through the portrait of Zhuang Yuan. This portrait, named "Portrait of a Filial Heart," was painted by the talented heroine Xianyu to commemorate Zhuang Yuan's good deeds toward his parents and his loyal service to the emperor. Zheng portrays women's artistic authorship as having prodigious value in advocating the moral principle of filial devotion, echoing Zheng's proposition that the transformation of social customs shall begin from the inner quarters.

Paintings in the text display the author's moral interpretation of gender relationships in marriage. Zhuang Yuan and Mrs. Zhang have respectively made marriage arrangements for Mengyu, with two talented women, Lin and Song. Both of them, as the narrator reveals, are reincarnated flower goddesses in a predestined bond with Mengyu (2: 22, 148). The father Zhuang Yuan has fittingly made a painting of 歲寒三友 (*suihan sanyou,* Three Friends of the Winter), referring to the three images of friendship, including the pine tree, bamboo, and plum tree. He then inscribed on the painting the birth dates of the male protagonist Mengyu and his two future spouses, indicating an idealized matrimonial structure (2: 16, 40). The portrait here serves as a vehicle for forging matrimonial bonds between Mengyu, Lin, and Song. The allegorical reference to the "Three Friends of the Winter" is ridden with implications of chastity and moral integrity. As the fourteenth-century scholar Hu

Han stated, "The gentleman respects the pine tree for its chastity, the bamboo for its straightness, and the plum blossom for its purity" (Brinker 39). The author appropriates this scenario to underwrite an idealized matrimonial structure based on men's and women's spiritual companionship, which alters the traditional belief of women's subordinate relationship with men.

Moral obligation, especially women's chastity, becomes one of the most prominent messages that is delivered by the paintings in the text. Liu Lingjuan, a disciple of Mrs. Zhuang, paints a self-portrait to express her determination to remain unmarried. She tells Mrs. Zhuang, "My teacher, if you want to perceive my ice-pure wish of staying free from marriage, / please behold this embroidered self-portrait" (3: 36, 199). The author describes Lingjuan's resistance to marriage as revealing the "heart of a sincere child." Unlike the portrait in *The Peony Pavilion*, which symbolizes the love knot that leads to a consummated marriage, Lingjuan's self-portrait pictures an imagined self who strives to escape the social control of women through marriage. Such social emphasis on women's chastity surfaced in Song Neo-Confucian culture in the eleventh and twelfth centuries, and became much more intense after the Manchu conquest in the mid seventeenth century. In the Yuan, Ming, and Qing dynasties, governmental policies rewarding and encouraging widows' chastity partially contributed to the cult of marital fidelity. Due to the impact of the chastity cult, many Chinese women in the eighteenth century committed suicide after they were sexually compromised, molested, or raped (Theiss 68). This concern about maintaining chastity is reflected in Lingjuan's self-portrait, which, as it is embroidered on white silk, reveals her wish to preserve her virginity. Lingjuan's image of an integrated self, however, is shattered when she falls victim to her cousin's malicious scheme. In the story, Lingjuan's cousin Jingsheng falls in love with her and bribes her maid into stealing her jade swallow-shaped hairpin for him. Jingsheng then reveals her hairpin to her mother, claiming that Lingjuan has asked the maid to give him the hairpin as a pledge of her affection for him. Persuaded by Jingsheng, Lingjuan's parents decide to marry her to him. Lingjuan discovers her cousin's scheme with the maid, which has contaminated her chaste name, and, enraged by the injustice, vomits blood excessively and dies instantly. Lingjuan's portrayal of *beigong ying* (Infant of the North Palace) projects a form of imagined feminine autonomy (for discussion of this allusion see the previous chapter). The image of the woman as an eternal infant suggests that for women, preservation of their virginity is a means of rejecting socialization through marriage.

Feminine virginity in the context of late imperial literature also assumes various contextual meanings, reflecting specific social, historical, and cultural conditions. For example, women's "religious virginity," symbolized by goddesses and religious nuns, "was concerned less with physiological integrity than sexual renunciation and rejection of the married condition" (Menegon 313). *Mengyingyuan* manifests such influences of Buddhism and Daoism, depicting twelve immortals who descend to earth to redeem the moral trend of the ethereal world. The idealized virgin goddesses might have appealed to women readers of the time who were victims of imposed marriages. Virginity, in this context, is a form of "celibate chastity" (Menegon 313) that deserves more appreciation. In dynastic China, however, feminine virginity was assessed from the male-oriented viewpoint as a guarantee of the purity of the ancestral line in the husband's family. When a girl was disgraced with a promiscuous name before marriage, such as in Lingjuan's case, she had no other choice but to die or commit suicide. Such situations of women's suicide are related to Neo-Confucian codes about female chastity. By the time of Ming, however, arguments against women's suicides on account of chastity were increasing (for a discussion of the Confucian regulation of feminine virtue, see Harvey, *Sex*; Carlitz, "Desire" 101-25). Lingjuan's death underscores the poignant fact that she was already possessed as a piece of property before marriage and had no other space to claim as her own.

The text praises Lingjuan as a martyr, an example of those "chaste women who excel in both talent and virtue" (3: 36, 218). However, her almost defiant devotion to chastity against her parents' desire shows that she is by no means a passive character. Her death by spitting blood indicates a kind of self-inflicted violence caused by rage against injustice and suggests that only in death could she speak on her own behalf. The portrait is then an object of self-warning for the heroine to guard her chastity and it suggests her power to defy her socially prescribed identity. The author's interpretation of the cult of chastity focuses on the woman's devotion to moral integrity for her own sake, her potential to renounce marriage and resist social control, and her power of defending herself through death. Feminine virtue, in Zheng's text, can be used to speak for women's own interest and choices. Filial devotion to one's parents can justify one's wish to stay unmarried. The heroine Lin Xianyu, for example, resists a marriage with Mengyu, blaming him for carelessly capturing her image with the portrait. In order to please his parents, he has both put her life in danger and upset her parents. She contemplates, "With all the means to entertain your family, / why do you have to make a portrait of me to please your parents? / For our predestined bond, I am willing to sacrifice my life. / I am disappointed because you took advantage of my passion to please your parents. / I am regretful that without true honesty and generosity you could not be truly filially devoted; / and that you do not know how to put yourself in my situation and sympathize with me" (1: 11, 193).

Xianyu's rejection of physical manipulation also foreshadows her insistence on her virginity after her marriage with Mengyu. In her choice of filial devotion over respect for her husband, the readers may perceive a counterbalance of power and resistance. The text, by employing and rewriting the discourse of feminine virtue, suggests that in women's lives there are times "when disobedience is filial and resistance is loyal" (Stone 261). By exploring the conflicts between moral obligations for women, and by presenting filial devotion as a higher obligation than submission to the husband, Zheng indicates a space for women's resistance against the orthodox social and cultural systems of her time.

In *Mengyingyuan*, women characters make portraits to show their wish to preserve their virginity. Their self-portraits retain a transformative power by replacing the fetishizing viewpoint of literati intellectuals with women's own point of view. In the aforementioned case, the portrait bespeaks Xianyu's wish to retain her virginity and to live an autonomous life outside the marriage system. In Xianyu's situation, the woman's body becomes a dramatized site of resistance. Lin's painted image disrupts the male-dominated visual structure by looking back at the viewers. In both heroines' circumstances, women appropriate the discourses of women's virtue to speak for their own interests. Zheng's view of virginity reflects her indignation at the social victimization of women. The twelve protagonists all remain virgins, and many pass away in illness before marriage. The text's depiction of women's celibacy and death suggests the exclusion of women from their social and cultural surroundings. The goddesses' return to the heavenly realm is only an imaginary alternative to most women's tragic outcomes in reality. This is perhaps the reason why, at the end of the work, none of the reincarnated goddesses wishes to be reborn as a woman.

Painting, like poetry, marks women's accomplishments in the late imperial period. The heroine Lin, for instance, is asked by her father to paint a portrait of Zhuang Yuan, entitled 心孝子圖 ("Xin xiaozi tu," "Portrait of a Filial Heart"). The painted Zhuang Yuan, of the "filial heart" to which the name of the painting refers, is applauded as an exemplar of loyalty to the emperor and filial devotion to his parents. By creating the painting, Lin not only pleases her own father Lin Wu, but also fulfills her filial duty to the Zhuang family, for she is soon to be married to Zhuang Yuan's son, Mengyu. Making this portrait is thus her personal endeavor, and it reflectively endorses her commitment to moral principles. The portrait is completed with a biography titled *Biography of a Filial Child*, composed by Song Renfang, another reincarnated flower goddess, who later also marries Mengyu and becomes Zhuang's daughter-in-law. The purpose of this painting, as Lin Wu suggests, is to advocate Zhuang's good deeds and educate the people of the world. In making the portrait, Lin, who has never seen Zhuang Yuan in person, encounters her celestial vision in a dream: "Suddenly she recalls that one day she dreamed of Zhuang Yuan and his son Mengyu, / who closely resemble each other. / Since she has met Mengyu in the Luofu Mountain in the dream, and still remembers some of his appearance, / maybe she can make a portrait of Zhuang Yuan based on the dream, and meet her father's desire" (2: 25, 206).

Xianyu's celestial vision, parallel to Mengyu's portrait of her, vividly depicts the image of Zhuang Yuan. When she finishes the painting, the image of Zhuang Yuan is so lifelike and exuberant that it instantly fills Xianyu's chamber with fragrance. Her father, who is a close friend of Zhuang Yuan himself, becomes enchanted with the portrait and often gazes at it, praying for the happiness of Zhuang, as if the image were alive. In that she produces an extremely lifelike image of Zhuang Yuan, the heroine displays a fantastic power. When she finishes the painting, the painted figure is so lifelike that it takes the observing maid by surprise:

> Lifting the lamp, seated by the window,
> Xianyu contemplates Mr. Zhuang's image from recollection,
> "It is impossible to depict this deity under worldly circumstances.
> I will first try to depict his facial features."
> Her skills are truly distinguished.
> The painted image gazes with glaring eyes, his spirit coming alive on paper.

> The clever and appreciative maid is frightened;
> she hurries to Xianyu and calls her, clinging to her dress,
> "Although your father's order cannot be disobeyed,
> how can you use your skillful hand to prey on his spirit?
> If his soul departs from his body, you will be blamed for the consequences."
> (2: 25, 209)

This scene evokes the custom of *dianjing* (點睛), or dotting the eyes, in the traditional Chinese painting; having finished sketching the image of a painted being, the artist dots the eyes and makes the image lively on the page. Her skill in painting, as the maid suggests, is so overpowering that it can take the life of the painted subject. The above example exposes a fissure between the the portrait itself and the woman's act of making the painting. Although Xianyu creates the painting to show her filial devotion to her own father, her act of painting the image suggests a captivating power over the painted image of Zhuang Yuan, her yet-to-be "father." The scene is also reminiscent of a scene in *Zaishengyuan*, when Lijun creates a portrait of herself and asks the maid whether the portrait resembles her likeness. In both scenes, the attending maid represents a bystander's perspective, confirming the heroine's power and skill. In the latter case, the maid enlightens the protagonist about the fantastic power of the portrait to summon the painted person's soul. The maid's tone is didactic, warning the talented mistress of the disrupting moral implication of the painting. This refined scene is embedded with several visual frames, showing the artist viewing the portrait, the portrait reverting the gaze, and the observing maid, who perceives and articulates the moral implication of the portrait for the readers.

In the text, both the portrait and Zhuang Yuan's biography are copied and circulated for the moral education of the public. This particular incident shows that the "transformation of social customs shall take its beginning in the inner chambers. Such practices will gradually expand their influence to the outside" (1: 1, 3). The inner chamber is a space in which women acquire a certain authority by exercising their moral agency; and the portrait gives the woman artist this power. Xianyu's talent in painting is displayed in her ability to make portraits of loyal officials and distinguished scholars in history. As a preliminary practice for making the "Portrait of a Filial Heart" she paints a picture of the famous Zhuge Kongming (諸葛孔明, 181 AD-234 AD), a loyal minister and outstanding military strategist of the Three Kingdoms Period (57 BC-668 AD). The text depicts the artist's aesthetic control over the man's painted image, reversing the hierarchical relationship between the male artist and his objectified feminine subject. The woman becomes the maker and the spectator of the man's image; she enlivens his likeness, but she also has the power to seize his spirit with her magic brush. The story presents the notable tension between these seemingly incongruous representations of gender relationships that underlie the theme of moral virtue. Whether didactic in purpose or not, the portraits allow the spectator to interpret them from a moral standpoint.

Zheng's maneuver of portrait viewing and gendered spectatorship calls for a close reading of the changeable relationship between the portrait and its sympathetic audience. Zheng presents several instances in which the spectators sympathize with and make emotive responses to a painted image. When Mengyu realizes that his portrait of Xianyu may put her life at risk, he destroys the painting out of sympathy for her. In another episode, Xianyu's painting of Zhuang Yuan draws emotional responses from the Zhuang family. When the portrait becomes a stand-in for the subject, it elicits feelings from the viewers, amplifying the viewers' emotional experience. The text encompasses multifarious depictions of both men and women observing portraits from diverse angles. Zheng's refined illustration of the spectator's experience is instructive, augmenting the readers' own awareness of their relations to the painted image and the observing characters.

Although many examples from authorial insertions carry signs that the author is addressing women readers, the actual community of historical readers of *Mengyingyuan* might have included men as well. A study of the text invites an elucidation of the connections between the general audience of the *tanci* and the particular women-oriented perspective that the author brought forth with portrait scenarios. This women-oriented perspective does not necessarily imply a community that only includes women readers or viewers. The sympathetic perspective in the text is a gendered viewpoint but does not exclude men as possible sympathetic viewers.

Mengyu's sympathy for the heroine occurs when he realizes that the portrait has caused Xianyu a grave illness and nearly taken her life. Stricken by grief, "he becomes conscientious and burns the painting" (1: 11, 193). Xianyu's illness recalls a similar scenario where the enchanted Liniang dies of lovesickness after an imaginary encounter with the scholar Mengmei. Liniang later returns to life when called upon by a male viewer, whom she once addressed as the "cure" for her ailment (2: 20, 116). In *Mengyingyuan*, several women avoid arranged marriage by committing suicide or otherwise dying. In contrast with the spare narrative style of *zhiguai* (tales of anomalies), which allows less room for exploring human inner tendencies, *Mengyingyuan* contains detailed psychological accounts and depicts the internal consciousness of these women characters (for a study of female suicide in the dynastic narrative genre *zhiguai*, which are supernatural stories about ghosts, fox spirits, and other strange phenomena, see Huntington, *Alien Kind*; "Ghosts Seeking Substitutes"). Death, in Zheng's text, becomes another means of feminine expression, which challenges representations of the female body as a silent and nondiscursive space upon which the male artist/voyeur exercises his power. The narrative convention of the erotic fused with magic and disease is changed greatly in *Mengyingyuan*. Love and desire are secondary to true sympathy for one's companion. Thanks to Mengyu's conscientiousness and his concomitant act of burning the painting, Xianyu is cured of her disease. The *tanci* conjures up a scenario of narrative sympathy in which the painting facilitates a sense of identification between the male artist/viewer and the heroine, whose image has been seized and who suffers a consequent illness. Mengyu is deeply immersed in the image of the woman, but finally sees beyond the painting and acquires an extended perception. Rae Grenier defines this idealized relationship as "extra-sensory intersubjectivity" (309). Mengyu's vision is amplified when he adopts the viewpoint of the feminine protagonist. It is no coincidence that Mengyu cross-dresses several times as a girl to dance and entertain his parents, demonstrating his remarkable mobility in inhabiting male and female gender roles.

The male viewer in this case evolves into an "impartial spectator" characterized by "not a feeling-into, but a feeling-along-with the state of mind and emotions of another" (Greiner 307). The idealized male spectator is part of the larger social and cultural context that influenced the women writers of the late imperial period. Here the literary scenario of the portrait explores the subjectivity of reading and interpretation, inviting the readers to immerse themselves in the worlds of the characters. As the portrait teaches its viewers to perceive what is beyond the painting, the author instructs her readers to engage themselves in the text with critical attention. In this way, Zheng resembles Western fiction authors such as Samuel Richardson, Henry Fielding, and Jane Austen, who "appropriate, interrogate, and transform the spectator-as-reader trope . . . as they jockey for critical authority in their novels" (Gardiner 11). Zheng's imaginative creation of an idealized male spectator represents the author's desire for a more sympathetic audience, including men who are capable of empathizing with a woman-oriented point of view. At the end, when Mengyu and the goddesses ascend to heaven and unite with his parents, he volunteers to return to the world again, incarnated as a woman, in order to write the stories of the goddesses into a *tanci* (4: 48, 240). This ending suggests potential gender reversal, when the sympathetic hero can be reborn as a woman in his next life and write the story from a woman's perspective.

In *Mengyingyuan*, portraiture inspires a sense of spirituality in the viewers. Zhuang Yuan and his family members often worship and meditate on the portraiture of their ancestors, in order to understand the hidden truth of life (4: 40, 66). Viewing the portraiture is a remedial process in which predestined causes dawn on the viewers and help them overcome the loss of a family member or a sworn friend. The reincarnated goddesses, when viewing the portraiture, are reminded of their predetermined bonds and foresee their awaiting destinies. Portraits are marked with an arresting responsive efficacy: the painted images, when viewed by their sympathetic viewers, respond to them with subtle gestures, expressions, and even whispering voices.

The emotional efficacy of the portraits could be manipulated for various purposes by the artist. For Lingjuan, her embroidered self-portrait expresses a determination to practice female asceticism and an endorsement of virginal chastity. For Xianyu, portraiture could be appropriated as a way of telling a visual story of Mengyu's and her own filial piety. After Mengyu ranks high in the imperial exam and becomes a favorite official of the emperor, he finds it difficult to extricate himself from the court and return to his hometown to take care of his mother. After the emperor rejects his request to resign many times, Mengyu's wife Xianyu makes a painting titled 慈鳥望哺圖 ("*Ciniao wangbu tu*," "The Mother Bird Longing for Feeding") which, making an analogy of the mother bird and Mengyu's aged mother, moves the emperor to tears; Mengyu is eventually allowed to resign and return to his hometown (4: 40, 66). This portrait like the previous "Portrait of a Filial Heart" exemplifies Xianyu's capacity to exercise a form of moral agency through visual images. Through these affecting portraits, a female artist could transform social and ethical relationships, reshaping and augmenting the beholders' feelings of parental, filial, and conjugal love.

The following scene portrays several male characters engaged in a sympathetic relationship with the image in the painting. After Zhuang Yuan leaves, his family longs for his presence and finds comfort in looking at his portrait. One day, Zhuang Yuan's aged uncle pays a visit and sees the portrait, and, unable to withhold his passion, calls Zhuang Yuan's name.

> Driven by sorrow and anger, Mr. Zhuang loses control of himself, and cries at the portrait, "My nephew! You are born outstanding and unrivalled in this world, and do not belong here. You should have followed the example of Liu Gang, who took his wife when becoming an immortal, instead of becoming another Mei Fu who completely deserted his family. Even though you have ascended to the realm of bliss and reunited with your own father, you will suffer from loneliness, with no companion except your own shadow. Isn't it regretful when two love birds can no longer fly together?" (3: 2, 198)

In this passage, Liu Gang is a legendary Daoist alchemist, who ascends to heaven with his wife Fan Yunqiao. According to 神仙傳 (*Shenxian zhuan*, Biographies of the Immortal Beings, fourth century), a work by Daoist Ge Hong (284-364), Fan used to outrival her husband Liu Gang with her expertise in alchemy. Lady Fan, a distinguished poet herself, composed a number of poems on Daoist practices (Ge 129). Another legendary figure alluded to, Mei Fu, was a loyal official of the Han dynasty, and was famous for offering honest advice for the emperor Cheng (51 BCE-7 BCE). Later, to escape from the Wang Mang Rebellion, which threw down the Han Empire, Mei Fu fled to the mountains and became a Daoist recluse to avoid political persecution. Legend has it that he became an immortal at last (Ban Gu 2917). Occupying the central portion of the painting, Zhuang Yuan's image successfully elicits the old uncle's passion; without anticipating this, the uncle exclaims his thoughts to the portrait. The viewer's involuntary physical response shows the portrait's function of moving observers to action. Hu Siao-chen argues that Zheng's infatuation with the portrait is related to the theory of 感應 (*ganying,* stimulus and response), which undergirds much of ancient Chinese thought. According to this theory, a portrait's power of disconcerting and capturing the spirit of human beings was evidence of the artist's superb skill (*Cainü* 288; Yu, Anthony, *Rereading the Stone* 68). The scene of the uncle calling to the image attests to the fantastic power of the heroine, whose skills have resurrected the deceased on paper. The old uncle's regret is provoked by a comparison of the portrait of Zhuang Yuan with the family portrait of Zhuang Yuan's parents, which the uncle has seen before. Zhuang has followed his father's path in searching for the immortal world. However, within the viewer's associative gaze, the portrait implies that in the immortal world, he is still suffering from the ethereal afflictions of solitude and separation from his wife and children.

The portrait constitutes itself as a sympathetic text, with its variable surface reflecting its ability to embody the reader's desire. This desire sometimes displays the reader's attentive reading of the progressive potentials in the painted image. In some places, the text presents women looking at the portraits and making adventurous interpretations (for Ming and Qing paintings that possibly were done for women, see Cahill 1-54). When Xianyu finishes the painting of Zhuang Yuan, her mother, Mrs. Lin, is greatly offended by the strength of the resemblance to the man who will be her father-in-law. In comparison, her friend Su Yunxian, who is also a reincarnated goddess, interprets the painting from a much more sympathetic point of view. "Seeing the portrait, Yunxian is completely enthralled, / thinking that she must have seen this person some place before. / Then she recalls (having seen him in the immortal world) the deity who resides on the holy Luofu Mountain. / It turns out that Zhuang Yuan looks very much like this deity, who is his father. / Yet how could Xianyu know of them both?" (2: 25, 210).

The portrait itself represents manifold narratives, portraying the painted person's face as a screen upon which the reader's imagination is projected. For Yunxian, Xianyu's sister and one of the reincarnated flower goddesses, the portrait evokes a connection between the feminine subject and the image. Misrecognizing the image as someone whom she had seen before, Yunxian gradually recognizes that the painted Zhuang Yuan very much resembles his deceased father, whom she had encountered during her past "life" in the heavenly realm. As Yunxian approaches the painting, the focus of her view moves from 性 (*xing,* form or body) of the painted image to its face, both of which resemble those of Zhuang Yuan's father. In Yunxian's viewpoint, the painting of Zhuang Yuan revives his father's image, folding the immortal realm into the ethereal world, suggesting the permeable boundary between these spaces. The same painted image, however, elicits a significantly different response from Xianyu's mother, who is offended by it. When Mrs. Lin comes to see the painting, she is astonished as soon as she enters the room. She asks her daughter if she owns a portrait of Mr. Zhuang. Xianyu replies that the portrait should look exactly like the real person. When Mrs. Lin hears this answer, she cannot suppress her anger, and throws the painting into the stove.

> Scornfully, she laughs and turns to Xianyu:
> "Why is it that you were born with such a cold heart?
> How could you take so much liberty and stir his spirit by inscribing a real person?
> . . .
> In the past, when Xianyu fell seriously ill,
> the doctor said that it was because someone painted her image.
> Even though such sayings were only half-true,
> one should be wary of the magic powers of the portraits.
> When have you ever seen a depicted image painted the same as a real person?
> You might as well imitate the portraits of the deceased.
> How dare you paint a person who is still alive!"

> The mother thinks to herself, "How detestable it is that she does not want to
> become a daughter-in-law of the Zhuang family,
> and dares to treat her father-in-law as a stranger.
> This is all because the General has been too lenient toward her.
> The father and daughter are both careless in action." (2: 25, 209)

In her eyes, the painting threatens the life of Zhuang Yuan, who has been away from home for years, and whose family does not know whether he is alive or dead. At this time, Xianyu has already declined the first marriage proposal of the Zhuang family and expressed her wish to stay unmarried all her life in order to attend to her parents. The portrait once again reveals Xianyu's disobedience to her parents' wish for her marriage, as she treats Mengyu's father, Mr. Zhuang, as an unrelated person instead of a father-in-law. Xianyu's mother scorns her daughter for her recklessness, saying, "Don't you know that with persistent persuasion, / you could have changed your father's mind in having the portrait made? / This should be the appropriate way of being a filially devoted child. / Now you have behaved recklessly to please your father; / I am afraid that you have been noted for the shame of unfiliality in heaven" (2: 25, 211). Underneath the mother's reproach is her disapproval of Lin's intention to display through the painting her determination to preserve her virginity. Lin confesses to her father, "I will wait on your side for the rest of my life. / Even if the whole world changes, I shall not alter my mind" (2: 25, 213). The text vividly delivers the family dispute over the portrait, underlying which is the conflict between a woman's moral obligations and her free choice about marriage.

The chapter ends with the father's approval of Xianyu's plea to stay unmarried, for he perceives from his daughter's exceptional artistic skill that she was not born a common woman. Xianyu then asks her father to remove her name from the portrait of "three friends in winter," which is a pledge for the matrimonial bond between her, Mengyu, and Renfang. She asks that her name be replaced by that of Su Yunxian, who is her father's adopted daughter, and an ideal surrogate bride for Mengyu. The trope of replacement shows the woman's rejection of marriage and is frequently used in *tanci*. In *Mengyingyuan*, a flower goddess, Song Renfang, considers herself as a substitute for Xianyu in marriage (2: 22,153). Likewise, in *Zaishengyuan*, Lijun asks her sworn sister to stand in for her in an imperial marriage before dressing herself in men's clothing and fleeing her home. Praising Xianyu's ingenuous plan, Zheng states, "A most outstanding person has a unique mind; / in comparison with Xianyu, those women who gaze into the mirror and lament their loss of youth are quite derisible" (2: 25, 213). The author's mockery of sentimental women is reminiscent of the narcissistic Liniang, who laments the absence of her compassionate male companion and weans herself from grief. Nevertheless, the association between Xianyu and her painting possibly implies the artist's interest in exploring a moral identity that transcends social definitions of gender norms. The woman painter's alliance with the painted image is self-reflexive but not narcissistic; the painting of Zhuang Yuan manifests a surrogate identity of the heroine, who strives to explore a social identity outside regulated spaces.

Perceptive observers of these portraits may explore the painted images and discover disruptive potentials within them. The idealized portrayal of the male protagonist as a sympathetic viewer may be a projection of the author's desire for an expanded, appreciative audience. "Portrait of a Filial Heart" displays the artist's capability of establishing a moral authority, as well as her craving to find a surrogate social identity that can move beyond the social constraints on women and the norms of femininity. In *Mengyingyuan*, portraits are vehicles for the communication and representation of a feminine consciousness that finds expression through intersubjective encounters with viewers/readers. These portraits of women or by women manifest an innovative form of sympathetic spectatorship that constitutes and reinforces a gendered viewpoint, which can sometimes be adopted by a sympathetic male viewer/reader. This gendered perspective reflects that in the late imperial context, women's painted images are ridden with irony and mis/representation. Such mis/representations can be made by male painters who construct stereotypical images of women from a male-centered point of view. In earlier times, as in the story of Liniang, the woman internalizes the male other's viewpoint and mis/recognizes the self-portrait as her real self. Her "self" no longer exists for her, and is only brought to life through the male viewer's appreciative gaze. In either of these situations, the woman's image/self-image is misconstrued. In *Zaishenguan*, Lijun's self-portrait before the scene of her cross-dressing represents a pre-image, before she is "reborn" as a man, bespeaking her dilemma and lack of identity as a woman. *Mengyingyuan* modifies these scenarios about portraits/self-portraits, and implies that the portraits of women or by women can inscribe their authority and autonomous power. *Mengyingyuan* makes important contributions to the tradition of portrait narratives in *tanci* as well as in the larger context of late imperial literature. Zheng's text projects the possibility for portraits to be considered from a doubly gendered point of view, inviting sympathetic gazes from both men and women readers/viewers. The inner chambers, for the author, presents a space in which paintings of women or by women could be viewed and appreciated privately by their own eyes. Perhaps for contemporary readers, reading the work is not unlike General Li's experience of reading Xianyu's poems on legendary beauties. Their emotional bonds with the depicted characters outweigh their concern with the actual portrayal of the images of these outstanding women with unique minds, who lived in another place or another time. As General Li comments on Xianyu's poems, "Who would have expected to meet a person of the same understanding from another dynasty? / Not to mention that the brilliance of her diction and style is as such. / Transmitting a beauty's ice-pure heart and delicate appearance, / Are [indeed] more eloquent than a painting of her face [in reality]" (1: 13, 199).

Chapter Five

Cross-Dressing as a Collective Act in *Xianü qunying shi* (A History of Women Warriors)

"Because of my pity for the imperiled and the weak in the world, / I depict the hearts of heroic and valiant women in the inner chambers. / Even though I cannot dispel the conventions of filial piety, faith, loyalty, and chastity, / these events of sadness and joy, departure and reunion, still have extraordinary meanings" (*Xianü* 5: 18, 23). These passionate lines are authorial insertions in a fin-de-siècle *tanci*, *Xianü qunying shi* (A History of Women Warriors, 1905, henceforth *Xianü*), which, according to the text's prefaces, was written jointly by three sisters, Yonglan, Youmei, and Shuzhu. This *tanci* depicts cross-dressed women as erudite scholars and heroic warriors who uphold the good, punish the evil, and save the country fearlessly at moments of national crisis. The cross-dressers' stories reveal the important theme of gender and the nation, providing a counterdiscursive interpretation vis-à-vis the male-centered nation-state discourses of Confucian society. *Xianü*, specifically, stands out in the way that it addresses and foretells issues about women's collective agency and empowerment, two profoundly significant themes to contemporary audiences. The text's depiction of a group of cross-dressed female characters represents a case of legacy writing in *tanci* fiction tradition and provides a source of empowerment and liberation. Simultaneously, the subversion of the gender hierarchy in *Xianü* presents a relatively optimistic vision when it comes to imagining possibilities for women's sexual, social, and political freedom.

Cross-dressing, as a narrative element, has come to be the carrier for these acts of progressive imagination since the late imperial period. Before the twentieth century, numerous works portrayed a male protagonist embarking on a journey towards happiness and fulfillment. Women *tanci* authors took up this narrative type, appropriating it and recasting the protagonists as women who leave the inner quarters and travel while dressed as men. These unconventional heroines generally cross-dress to escape from imposed marriage and to explore an alternative social identity outside the domestic sphere. In the fictional space, *tanci* authors depicted women's cross-dressing as a progressive practice verging on a challenge to the ideal of women's submissiveness as described in the classics and ritual texts, as well as in the Confucian social philosophy of stable gender roles. Writing *tanci*, therefore, was itself an adventurous act for late imperial women authors, whose literary practices were under strict social regulation. They sallied forth with their heroic protagonists, as it were, and in so doing invited readers to envision a life of autonomy and freedom outside the domestic space.

Progressive impulses toward freedom and agency are well portrayed in *Xianü*. The text includes successive chapters composed by the three sisters in turn, telling the story of a group of erudite women in Zhejiang province who dress as men and explore adventurous lives outside the inner quarters. Little evidence is available about the historical audience of *Xianü*. The only remaining biographical information about the authors' lives comes from their brother's preface to the work and from a preface written by the husband of one of the authors. However, since the writers have all used pseudonyms, the authorship of the work cannot be verified in historical records or local chronicles. Unlike some cross-dressed heroines in earlier *tanci*, most cross-dressers in *Xianü* do not revert to their feminine identity, but continue to conduct their lives as men's social equals. In their private lives, cross-dressed women manage to marry other women and are sometimes married to more than one wife. Their former male fiancés are depicted as "male widows" who wait for the cross-dressers' return in vain. The authors' unconventional rendering of gender roles suggests that cross-dressed women of the time might have enjoyed more social tolerance and a certain freedom to exercise their social and political power.

Tolerance and freedom are not without their complications, however. Throughout the text, many scenes demonstrate cross-dressers' strategic renegotiation, circumvention, and transformation of conventional conceptions of femininity. One of the protagonists, Qing Shunxin (慶順馨), is abducted as a child on the evening of the Lantern Festival and is saved and adopted by a high-ranking official. She then changes her name to Qin Ling and becomes the first on the list of those passing the highest level of the imperial examinations. When, still dressed as a man, she again encounters her fiancé, Lin Mengyun (林夢雲), she refuses to reveal her true identity. Another female protagonist, Pang Yulong (龐玉龍), begins cross-dressing at birth with her mother's assistance to gain the right to her patrimony. Eventually she is married to a female friend who consents to her scheme of mock marriage. Likewise, another female protagonist, Su Zixiu (蘇子秀), has enjoyed dressing herself in male attire since childhood. After a family crisis, she is separated from her parents and adopted by a well-off family. To conceal her identity, Su Zixiu disguises herself as a man and, when she meets her fiancé again, denies her femininity. An exceptional case is the cross-dresser Mu Hualong (沐化龍), who is wedded to a female relative. Mu's fiancé Zheng Hua (鄭華), yearning to disclose Mu's identity, cross-dresses himself as a woman and marries Mu as "his" concubine. On the wedding night, Zheng Hua confronts Mu and succeeds in disclosing her true identity. The other female cross-dressers in the story, however, do not suffer the exposure of their identity, but marry one or even two wives, and become national heroes who rescue the country from subversion and rebellion. Like the earlier *tanci* work *Zaishengyuan*,

Xianü qunyingshi is open-ended. In the last extant chapter, the author Youmei, after describing a major military victory of the cross-dressed General Su Zixiu, suggests that she cannot pass along the work to her eldest sister Yonglan, who is departing on a long journey to celebrate the birthday of their great-aunt. The story breaks off at this moment, and no further chapters of the work have been discovered.

The text embeds the story of Qin Ling in a conversation between two Daoist hermits in the beginning. From the conversation between the hermits, the reader learns that one of them once had a vision of the heavenly palace where rows of heavenly maids were paying tribute to Xi Wangmu, the Queen Mother of the West. Then the hermit saw the Queen Mother of the West giving out a command, and soon all the female deities had changed into male attire and were bowing to the Queen to thank her for her bounteousness. Several of these cross-dressed deities descended to earth alongside rows of children holding gilded tablets. Lines on the tablets state: "Three times [she] will rank high in the Imperial Exam, / and then she will exterminate the bandits at the frontier. / Rescuing people from danger and poverty, she frequently practices good deeds. / A female hero shall take the task of saving the nation. / Exceptional men and valiant women are bonded with faith and chastity" (1: 1, 4).

These inscriptions on the tablets are written in *jie* (gatha, a Buddhist verse), and they carry clues about the stories of the heroic women soon to be depicted, such as their passing the civil service exam, exterminating invading bandits, saving people from danger and poverty, and fulfilling certain missions for the country. The Queen Mother of the West, in Chinese mythology, is one of the most important goddesses of the Daoist pantheon, a supreme matriarch who governs the other female deities and resides on the sacred Kunlun Mountain. Told through the hermit's point of view, the story presents the female deities who cross-dress and descend to the Red Dust to affirm the good and rescue people from peril and poverty.

The text of *Xianü* is composed of 10 *juan* (volumes) for a total of 40 *hui* (chapters), 802 pages. Written in the late nineteenth century and later published in 1905, *Xianü* perhaps is addressed to a historical audience receptive to protofeminist writings. It was in the year 1905 that the feminist writer and social activist Qiu Jin returned to Beijing after receiving education in Japan and devoted herself to revolutionary activities against the late Qing government. Numerous literary works of this time display a distinctive progressive tendency, urging women to step out of the inner compounds and take an active role in social affairs. For example, in 1905, the famous writer Liu Yazi (柳亞子, 1887-1958) published an essay, "Lun nüjie zhi qiantu" ("On the Future of the Women's Realm"), in which he proposes, "We should not just imagine a women's world of virtuous mothers and gentle wives, but should rather envision a women's world of heroes and leaders. We should welcome and applaud the women's world, rather than denouncing and forsaking it" (57). The publication of this essay was the prelude to a series of progressive activities among women in early twentieth-century China. At the same time, male intellectuals, editors, and book publishers played an important role in editing and distributing protofeminist writings (see Jin Tianhe, *The Women's Bell*).

The title page of *Xianü* states that it was written by three anonymous sisters who identified themselves as 湘州女史 (*Xiangzhou nüshi*), which refers to female scholars from Xiangzhou. The mention of Xiangzhou suggests that these authors were from the Changsha area. One of the prefaces to the book was composed by a man with the literary name of Xin'An (心庵), the husband of Yonglan. The second preface was composed by the three women's youngest brother, whose pen name is Mengjü. Mengjü was also the editor of this work. The two prefaces reveal to contemporary readers that the four siblings were named after 梅 (*mei,* plum), 蘭 (*lan*, orchid), 竹 (*zhu*, bamboo), and 菊 (*jü*, chrysanthemum), four images in nature frequently evoked in traditional Chinese poetry, and in general representing moral qualities of fortitude, grace, uprightness, and purity.

Importantly, although some progressive male authors at this period also took to *tanci* to write tales, their stories were often much shorter in length, and purportedly were geared toward a male-oriented political ideal of China's nationalist rejuvenation and oftentimes represented women, including Chinese and Western heroines, playing orthodox gender roles or representing Confucian virtues of loyalty and chastity. A prominent example is the male writer and editor Zhou Shoujuan (1895-1968), who published a short *tanci* tale, *Yanzhi xue* (Rouge Blood), under the feminine pen name Qi Hong, which literally means "weeping blood." Strikingly dissimilar to these fin-de-siècle male authors' short *tanci* tales, *Xianü* manifests a distinctive inheritance of the stylistic features of women's traditional long *tanci* fiction, containing ample descriptions of the three sisters' domestic life, their exchange of and comments on one another's writings, and their individual reflections on the process of writing. Neither the authors nor the preface authors revealed real names and leave little biographical information beyond what is indicated in the two prefaces. However, the textual features of the entire *tanci*, its exuberant self-reflections by the three sisters, and its female-oriented descriptions of women's domestic life indicate a profound identification with feminine authorship and a distinctive inheritance of precursory women's *tanci* fiction conventions.

In his preface, Xin'An, the husband of Yonglan, offers a political reading of the *tanci*, emphasizing the association between *tanci* and women's self-empowerment in the early twentieth century. He suggests, "A woman in the boudoir might have wished to travel throughout the five continents and achieve fame that lasts for generations! Such desire would be a specificity of women's rights. This book is born with a similar ambition" (1: 1, 1). Xin'An further claims that the purpose of the book is "to stir and to rouse a new social inspiration" among both male and female readers (1: 1, 1). However, his choice of what to emphasize and what to play down are authorial decisions with significant ramifications. The "woman" represented in the editor's vision changes from "my" (the editor's) gendered, hierarchized "other" into "my" equal, or a political mirror image of the male narrator. The relation between the progressive male intellectual and the three anonymous women authors is an example of the cultural phenomenon that took place in turn-of-the-century China, in which male writers began to project gendered imaginations onto women. Xin'An's reading of the *tanci*, on the other hand, seems anachronistic. In contrast to other protofeminist *tanci* of the early twentieth century, such as *Jingwei shi* (Stones of the Jingwei Bird, 1905) and *Faguo nüyingxiong tanci* (Tale of a French Woman Hero, 1905), *Xianü qunying shi* displays strong continuity with antecedent *tanci* works in that it emphasizes gender masquerade and cross-dressing performance (on *tanci* and women's cultural sentiment at the turn of the century, see Hu, Siao-chen, "Zhixu zhuiqiu" 89-128). For contemporary readers, the discrepancy between the progressive husband's preface and the women's text indicates that this *tanci* was published as an embedded narrative, for the main story is presented second-hand via an enclosing frame, the husband's preface. Although the book was published in 1905, just as China was on the threshold of modernity, the texts must have been composed much earlier, considering the remarkable length of the project and the assiduous process of writing as revealed by the authorial comments in the opening and closing sections.

The incongruity between the preface by Xin'An and the content of the work perhaps indicates that the publication of *Xianü* was targeted at progressive audiences of the time, although this cannot be proven, due to the scarcity of contextual information about this *tanci*. Importantly, during this time in China, many progressive feminist journals were also being published and circulated, such as 女報 (*Nübao,* Women's Journal; 1907), edited by the feminist revolutionist Qiu Jin (1875-1907) and 女蘇報 (*Nü subao*, Women's Jiangsu Journal; 1899), edited by Chen Xiefen (陳擷芬, 1883-1923) (Hu, Wenkai 955). In comparison with Xin'An's work, another preface to the *tanci* written by the authors' brother Mengjü (夢菊) provides more detailed biographical information about the authors and claims that the *tanci* would find its value when popularized among women in all corners of the world. He comments, "The writing was originally made to be enjoyed by women at home in their rooms, or offered as entertainment for parents. Yet a gentleman now submits the writing for publication, so that all the sisters under heaven can share the pleasure in reading it. All the parents on earth can share this work and be entertained. Evoking sympathy, admiration, fellow-feeling, or appreciation in readers, this work will bring reward to my three sisters" (1: 1, 1). The value of this *tanci*, as Xin'An puts it, lies in its capacity to evoke compassion and familial human emotions among its readers.

The narrative form of *tanci* is at once aesthetically appealing and morally instructive to women. Xin'An says, "When the writing is disseminated widely in the world and reaches every alley and every corner, women in the refined chambers will have new songs to chant. As for the events in ancient records and bamboo scrolls, one may still learn about them in official histories—but cannot directly experience them. So long, then, as the writing at hand has been endowed with color and sound, why does one need to prove with evidence whether it is true or false? If readers absorb its advocacy of the good and its condemnations of the evil, what need is there to question whether it is official history or *tanci*?" (1: 1, 2). This quotation emphasizes literary quality ("color and sound") and didacticism ("good and evil") as a means to legitimize *tanci*. Simultaneously, Xin'An's comparison of "official histories" with *tanci* that recount historical events is reminiscent of similar discussions in Murasaki Shikibu's *Genji Monogatari*, or *The Tale of Genji*, a famous eleventh-century Japanese fiction work that explores the domestic lives of the governing class, as well as themes of love, filial loyalty, and family bonds. The male protagonist Genji, when discussing the difference between the fictional genre *monogatari* (tale) and "historical writings," comments that authors of *monogatari* use this literary form to portray historical incidents, with the didactic purpose of endorsing virtue as well as condemning vice and folly. Both the genres of *tanci* and *monogatari* demonstrate a blending of history and fiction: as in *monogatari*, the events portrayed by *tanci* are not pure fictional inventions, but are literary depictions based on historical incidents which are garnered in the text and reconfigured for various authorial purposes (Shikibu 501-02).

The phenomenon of women sharing common interests in *tanci* also underlies the authors' process of composing *Xianü*. One of the authors reflects on the scene of the three sisters writing and editing their works together, vividly depicting writing as part of their everyday activities.

> In the inner chambers the sisters have no other distractions;
> in talking about composing books we have increased interest.
> Dividing the lines and locating the insufficiencies,
> when it comes to the middle session the story is as confused as entangled hemp.
> Always contemplating polished lines and getting closer to perfection,
> we take pains to sift through the words.
> Debating and raising laughter,
> we compete in composing new lines and boast of our own writings.
> (10: 40, 56)

The responses among the three sisters are abundant in many of the chapters' opening and closing lines, demonstrating the multivocal nature of *Xianü*. In one chapter, the eldest sister discloses a nostalgic feeling for the years before her marriage. Her affective bond with her sisters as both siblings and fellow authors can be traced in the following lines: "My intelligent and talented sisters have finished their works, / I am ashamed of my shallow knowledge, and my difficulties in finding good lines" (1: 1, 19). The literary exchange among the three sisters, as the authorial insertions reveal, develops a form of dialogic relation between authorial positions, which can be traced to the tradition of late imperial women's poetry exchanges. For women writers, poetic dialogues and literary exchanges offer an opportunity to experiment with alternative notions of selfhood and "refute the gender system to which they were subordinate" (Yang, Haihong 192).

In *Xianü,* specifically, the autobiographical narrative segments present details about how the authors produced, edited, and described their work. Each individual chapter is claimed to have been written by one of the three women and gestures toward the topic of the next chapter or volume. In comparison with previous *tanci* written by a single author with either a real or assumed name, *Xianü* reveals the process of women writing privately together, revising versions for publication. Hu

Ying points out that the role of the *tanci* narrator replicates the role of a historian in "explaining her [the woman character] to the world"; accordingly, resonance between the female community within the text and the one outside the text is achieved through the latter's reading of or listening to the *tanci* (Hu, Ying, *Tales of Translation* 153-97). *Xianü* likewise displays this meaningful exchange of support and encouragement among the three authors as well as between the writers and the readers. The text questions the proprietary figure of the modern author, as it includes work by the three anonymous women as well as readerly intervention by their female friends in the inner chambers. In the closing passage of one chapter, the narrator confesses, "Those who are hearing the story are eager to hear what happens afterward. / The author herself was even more enchanted than the audience. / Her heart entranced, she seemed to become a book worm. / Hurriedly she took to a work as difficult as catching the fireflies" (9: 36, 89). While the text resists established modes or conventions of reading by opening itself to plural interpretations, it also engages readers as producers of meaning. In a collaborative text, narratives and memories are threaded together, leaving gaps and openings for the other authors, the readers, and the editors to continue the narrative. The text can be read as a compendium of women's utopian desire for a communal identity, and its progressive potential rests in this ongoing process of collaborative writing.

The progressive potential of this *tanci* is centrally demonstrated in its vivacious depiction of cross-dressed women of outstanding literary and military gifts. Whereas these cross-dressers refuse to revert back to their feminine identity, their male companions spend years waiting for them in vain. The text's dramatic presentation of female scholars and "male widows" challenges the Confucian moral codes of chastity and feminine virtue and displays a dynamic understanding of gender relations in the late imperial social and cultural context. When the cross-dresser Su Zixiu is appointed prime minister and marries two women, her fiancé Wu Musu (吳穆蘇) waits for her return in futility. In the preface, the editor includes a poem that depicts a scene of Wu Musu offering a sacrifice for his lost fiancée by the Dongting Lake: "The male phoenix rests while the female travels afar, generating a thousand casks of regret. / Leaving his official position behind, he comes to commemorate his wife by the Dongting Lake. / In vain he composes lines of laments, / for the beloved one already accomplished such achievements and was appointed an eminent official" (*Xianü* 7).

"A thousand casks of regret" suggests a melodramatic expressive code, emphasizing the overflow of emotions. The cross-dresser's refusal to resume her feminine identity provokes an excessive emotional response from her fiancé (Thomas Elsaesser describes an "excess" in the "melos" or music of melodrama—a "melos" supplemented by extraordinary and often startling effects. In film, melodrama's "expressive code" of sound and light is sustained through the "exaggerated rise-and-fall pattern in human actions and emotional responses" [3]). This scene is reminiscent of *Zaishengyuan*, in which the cross-dressed Meng Lijun repeatedly denies her feminine identity to postpone the marriage event. Her lovesick fiancé Shaohua laments the loss of his missing fiancée day and night, going through the daily routine of grief rituals like an ordinary woman who suffers the loss of her husband. By making Shaohua play the role of a constant "spouse," the text mocks the Confucian code of women's chastity with a representation of male "widowhood." (In the text Shaohua has rejected remarriage for three years after Lijun's disappearance to keep his faithfulness to his fiancée. There are numerous examples of Shaohua's passionate confessions of his loyalty to Lijun, particularly in a number of comical scenes wherein he confronts the prime minister, that is, the cross-dressed Lijun, and tests "his" real identity.)

In these examples, the emotional expression of the male protagonist is endowed with a melodramatic quality, showing parody, derision or even the inversion of conventional gender roles. These quasi-theatrical scenes in *tanci* stage comical encounters between the cross-dresser and her husband and their inverted relationship (Hua and Wang, *Mingqing xiqu* 622). In *Xianü*, another riveting case of this kind takes place when a cross-dresser's fiancé, in order to reveal her identity, disguises himself as a woman and takes her as a concubine. The narrator comments, "The situation is reversed in comparison with their former engagement. / To prove their relationship, he comes up with a more refined plan. / In the flickering candlelight, their shadows sway; both of them are bashful. / Holding up nuptial wine cups, the two seem equally pensive. / Another day in the wedding chamber, they shall blame each other, / for the groom has married another groom" (7: 26, 38).

The representation of gender roles in this passage reveals a melodramatic confrontation between the cross-dressed "husband" and the disguised "wife" (7: 26, 36). On their wedding night, the fiancé Zheng Hua confesses to the cross-dresser Mu Hualong: "I see that you are in high spirits for taking a concubine. / How regretful! You have mistaken me for a woman. / Have you heard of the ancient story of Mulan? / Today I have inverted the situation and disguised myself as a woman" (7: 26, 38). The audience is confronted with a striking case of theatricality, and the challenge of deconstructing the opposition between presence and gendered representation. The cross-dresser Mu Hualong is capable of achieving a companionate marriage only through women's friendship: "It is only because the sisters have deep friendship, / that the disguised couple can joyfully celebrate a nuptial union" (7: 26, 39). The contrast between the disguised husband and the disguised wife shows yet another transformation of the "mock marriage." The irony is returned to the cross-dresser herself, who receives a shock when confronted with a male cross-dresser. The text reveals two distinctive cases of crossgender performance. Mu Hualong represents the idealized androgynous subject, who in turn represents a union of the handsome scholar and the talented beauty. The male cross-dresser Zheng Hua, who exaggerates the performance with his "glaring glances" and "eight-inch embroidered shoes," might be a parody of the effeminate male characters in Ming Qing fiction who adopt feminine personae (7: 26, 38).

This example of a man cross-dressing as a woman is reminiscent of many examples of temporary transgression and even inversion of gender codes in late imperial literature. For instance, a comic scene in the famous novel, *Flowers in the*

Mirror by Li Ruzhen (1763-1830), depicts a utopian 女兒國 (*Nü'er guo,* Women's Country) where men dress as women and are in charge of the household, while women dress as men and manage affairs outside the inner quarters. The cross-dressed male protagonist Lin Zhiyang (林之洋) travels through this country and is captured as a concubine for the empress. He, viewed as a beautiful woman, is then forced to dress in women's clothing and undergo foot-binding, ear-piercing, and many of the mutilating bodily practices that ordinary women suffered. The text is a vicarious satire of orthodox gender representation. The author claims that should his tale appear absurd, it is only because he hopes to bring the audience amusement. All the same, in the author's burlesque depiction of the Women's Country, gendered roles are still carefully preserved, even when genders of the characters assuming such roles have been subverted. Li Ruzhen's depiction of this place, where gender and dress codes are inverted, mediated through the perspective of the male protagonist, is a scathing satire of social reality through fictional representation.

If male cross-dressing in *Flowers in the Mirror* was largely depicted for a satirical purpose, a similar scenario in the Ming play 男王後 (*Nan wanghou,* The Male Queen; sixteenth century) carries stronger implications for gender transgression. Authored by Wang Jide (王驥德, 1540-1623), the play tells the love story of Emperor Chen Qian and a man, Han Zigao (韓子高), who dresses as a woman and becomes Emperor Chen's queen. The princess Yuhua (玉華) is enchanted by the new queen's beautiful appearance, and finds out that the queen is a disguised man. Determined to marry a handsome man like Han Zigao, the princess threatens to hang herself if Han does not agree to have an intimate relationship with her. When the emperor discovers the princess's relationship with his queen, he is moved by their love and encourages Han Zigao to marry Princess Yuhua. Zigao, who is viewed as more beautiful in women's dress, is wedded to the princess wearing embroidered clothes. The cross-dressed Zigao claims, "When I was the queen I would not reveal my lotus feet; now as the princess's husband, I am still wearing the embroidered dress. How difficult it is to distinguish the disguised from the original, the false from the real" (Wang Jide 28). As a transvestite, Zigao engages in feminine masquerade, playing the role of the emperor's submissive wife. Princess Yuhua, in contrast with Zigao's performance of femininity, shows a dramatically masculine trait, urging the cross-dressed Zigao to secretly marry her. Zigao's transvestite performance ridicules stereotypes of domesticated women conceived from a male perspective. Princess Yuhua, however, plays the role of the man in proposing marriage to Zigao and even threatens to commit suicide in front of him. The author, through the role of the king, comments that this event is an unusual tale for the entertainment of later readers. In sum, Zigao's case presents both male homoeroticism (between Zigao and the emperor) and "a subplot of female homoeroticism" (Volpp 11). The princess falls in love with Zigao while he is dressed in feminine attire, and she marries him while he is still in disguise (on male homosexual love, see Ng 76-89).

This fascination with male cross-dressing in drama recalls the representation of male homoeroticism in the *tanci* work 鳳雙飛 (*Fengshuangfei*, Flying Phoenixes;

1899), written by nineteenth-century author Cheng Huiying 程惠英 (Hu, Wenkai, 647). This important *tanci* depicts numerous scenes of male homoeroticism and female same-sex desire. Wenjia Liu offers a valuable study of Feng Huiying's rewriting of male same-sex eroticism and the author's use of allegories as metaphorical social and political criticism (see Liu, Wenjia; Wu, Cuncun 3-7). In the text, one of the protagonists, Bai Ruyu, is depicted as an effeminate man whose toxic sexual appeal attracts the emperor and high officials and nearly topples the nation. In comparison with Zigao, Bai's crossgender performance does not involve disguising himself in women's clothing, but represents a man's social cross-dressing by openly taking up a position of the opposite gender. Like the "male queen" Zigao, the dashing Bai Ruyu changes gender roles and plays out the identity of femme fatale, to the extent of jeopardizing principle gender and social relationships. Cheng Huiying's extraordinary depiction of male transvestite performance is a meaningful intervention in the cross-dressing convention, showing the author's relative mobility in reflecting on gender issues through imaginary characters.

What distinguishes women's cross-dressing in *tanci* from these examples of male cross-dressing is that women's deployment of cross-dressing is an important means of social self-empowerment and demonstrates a remarkable spirit of heroism. In *Xianü*, one female character comments about the cross-dresser Zixiu, "Delicate yet capable of heroic deeds, / the refined lady could act in the position of a high official" (5: 19, 56). Such performances were widely presented in Ming and Qing women's writings and had their predecessors in fiction and in Chinese history. Zixiu's bride in the mock marriage, who had been a childhood friend of hers, exclaims when Zixiu reveals her cross-dressing: "Who would expect that you follow the example of the extraordinary woman of the Tang times? / Who would expect such multiple talents in literature and military affairs? / Who would expect that you were given such an eminent position in the royal palace and married a refined companion? / Who would expect that in selecting my companion, I am engaged to you, a woman?" (5: 19, 56).

For cross-dressers, the ideal of marriage is replaced by mock marriages forged of trust and friendship between women. The cross-dressed Zixiu, for instance, talks with her bride about the future of their marriage, saying,

> Since, younger sister, I am only an impersonated man,
> you will not suffer damage and lose your pure integrity.
> Even if the titles are forged for the moment, how could this damage your chastity after all?
> If you follow a disguised scholar for the rest of your life,
> you will fulfill the wishes of your beloved parents,
> and avoid being talked about by petty people everywhere.
> I, your humble sister, have obtained eminence today
> and will never change this male clothing. . . .
> After serving our parents until the end of their lives,
> we may go to the mountains and look for Buddhist mentors.
> On that heavenly terrain, we will find an idyllic cave,
> where we shall take joy in learning the art of alchemy.

> This is much superior to those women who depend on men for fortune,
> and spend their entire lives in the silk and brocade chambers. (5: 19, 57)

Here Zixiu's suggestion to her bride about leaving the world and pursuing immortal happiness through alchemy is reminiscent of women's *youxian shi*, or poetry on roaming as a transcendent, a poetic subgenre which demonstrates some women's impulses to search for a kind of immortality "defined and poeticized by women themselves" (Wang, Yanning 102). Scholar Yanning Wang offers a study of *youxian* (遊仙) poems by Qing women authors, specifically those poems on the theme of *nü youxian* (女遊仙), or women roaming as transcendents. Wang argues that *youxian* poems provided a unique literary space for women's poetic and autobiographical voices in the late imperial period, reflecting women writers' increasing consciousness of self. In *Xianü*, women's aspiration to transcend their earthly yokes and achieve spiritual freedom strikes a chord with the female cross-dresser's desire to explore a pleasurable and rewarding life outside the domestic sphere. Like legendary female transcendents, the cross-dresser demonstrates a kind of embodied agency in late imperial women. In *Xianü*, this trend of women aspiring toward immortality even replaces the conventional plot ending in marriage. As the cross-dressed Zixiu envisions it, the two women in mock marriages can cultivate themselves through exercises to pursue the pleasure of immortality, instead of being yoked to their domestic duties.

These same-sex unions or mock marriages have a long tradition that can be traced to previous *tanci* works such as *Zaishengyuan* (Destiny of Rebirth) and *Fengshuangfei* (Flying Phoenixes). Zixiu, by reconfiguring herself as a husband and mate, empowers herself within the structure of marriage and subverts many constraints on her freedom. Zixiu's bride Xuejuan, whose former fiancé passed away before their marriage, determines to keep her chastity but is forced by her parents to marry Zixiu as "his" concubine. There is also a comic scene in which Zixiu, before revealing her identity, teasingly approaches Xuejuan, asking for sexual intimacy. Mimicking the tone of a libertine, Zixiu says to Xuejuan,

> Even if you want to keep your chastity,
> what fame and fortune can you gain from it?
> Although I myself have no good looks and outstanding talents,
> at least I am a good match for you.
> Since we have completed the nuptial ceremony,
> we should be a well-matched couple,
> like two lotus flowers born from the same root.
> In the Tiantai Mountains the legendary meal of *huma* seeds is ready for us
> [to taste];
> we will not be like the self-deluded Liu Chen who just happened to
> encounter the [female] immortals by himself.
> I bid you take advantage of this marriage and become my mate.
> If you return home, both Mr. Zhang and our mother will be disgraced.
> (5: 19, 58)

The "meal of *huma* seeds" in the above passage alludes to a legend in the East Han period (206 BCE-220 CE). Two men, Liu Chen (劉晨) and Ruan Zhao

(阮肇), enter the Tiantai (天臺) Mountains to collect medicinal herbs. They meet two female immortals, who invite them to their lodgings and offer them a bountiful feast, including rice with the seeds of *huma* (胡麻), dried goat meat, beef, and fresh peaches. After what had seemed like half a year's time, Liu and Ruan return home, only to discover that seven generations have passed by and that they are left alone in the world (Li, Fang, *Taiping yulan* 61: 383). Zixiu mockingly pleads for sexual intercourse and rationalizes "his" position by arguing against the social custom of women's chastity. Zixiu's impersonation of the male libertine is so convincing that Xuejuan becomes enraged and attempts to commit suicide to preserve her chastity. This episode is a mockery of the practice of women's chastity-related suicide. And as luck would have it, the women characters' virtue is preserved and left indisputable, as Xuejuan marries a woman, and both of them are able to keep their virginity.

In a conversation, male characters Lin Mengyun and Zheng Hua reveal their suspicions that Mu Hualong might be the cross-dressed fiancée of Zheng Hua. Lin Mengyun cautions Zheng that since Miss Mu has already married Mu Hualong, "the two ladies must now enjoy each other's company all the more, / just like the legendary empresses Mo and Huang living in the same household" (7: 26, 30). Tradition holds that Empress Mo was the wife of the ancient Yellow Emperor, who reigned from 2697 to 2597 BCE. Empress Huang was said to be the wife of Emperor Shun, who reigned from 2255 to 2195 BCE. In the text, Lin Mengyun, who had long thought that Qin Ling was his cross-dressed fiancée Qing Shunxin, helps Zheng disclose Mu Hualong's identity as an example to Qin Lin. He thinks to himself, "Today women are really deviant, / and all think of becoming officials at the court. / What could I do to disclose Miss Shui's identity / so that the others will be alarmed while watching from a distance?" (7: 26, 30).

Cross-dressing for Qin Ling and Mu Hualong is a marker of a newly acquired identity. Qin Ling is physically strong and well-versed in literature. "Unlike the other delicate women, / she was born with a pair of strong arms and has greater strength over others. / An exceptional woman who could remember writings with a glance, / she even surpasses the talented poet Xie Daoyun" (1: 1, 2). These cross-dressed heroines are not only talented scholars and courageous military leaders, but are also endowed with multiple talents. Su Zixiu knows the art of divination and can anticipate the outcomes of battles. The text depicts her as a female counterpart to the famous military leader and scholar Zhuge Kongming (181-234 CE) (6: 22, 26). In the following scene, for example, Su Zixiu and Pang Yulong, the two runner-up candidates in the civil service examination, admire Qin Ling's handsome looks and accomplishments in martial arts, not knowing that Qin is also a cross-dressed woman.

The Second and Third Candidates in the Exam are also pondering in private.

> "Who would recognize me as a woman now?
> At last I am able to raise my chin, release a breath, and act as an exceptional hero.
> How detestable are those common people who ridicule women as not
>   human beings.
> In my view, the wise and the foolish are not equivalent;

even among men themselves, not everyone can be the same.
Some men are bandits and thieves, some men are upright and prominent officials.
Among women, there are exemplary women like Mulan and Huang Chonggu;
some are ignorant and vulgar shrews.
Men and women can be both virtuous and ignorant;
how could one use a single standard in assessing them?
One exceptional case is my honorable brother Qin Ling,
whose good looks ranks first among all the officials and is even hard to find among women.
Moreover, his expertise in martial arts and heroism has made him a true pillar of the nation.
Yet even he does not know about my secret,
that a woman could also stride in the lofty sphere of eminence. (6: 23, 34)

The above passage in *Xianü* is written in the first-person, simulating the combined voices of the two cross-dressed women. Remarkably, the passage contains protofeminist reflections on gender equality, referring to the famous heroines Mulan and Huang Chonggu. The narrator foregrounds a woman's perspective on gender difference, denouncing prejudice against women's capabilities. The cross-dresser Qin Ling is considered an exception among men, who surpasses others in good looks and expertise in martial arts. Qin Ling's name and character suggests that she might be based on the heroic Ming female general Qin Liangyu (1574-1648), who surpassed her male peers in skills of horse archery and martial combat, and who also had outstanding talent for poetry. In her lifetime Qin succeeded in several battles against local warlords in southwest China and later led battles against the invading Manchurians. Unaware of the others' real gender, each of the three cross-dressed women are awed by the others' looks and achievements. At the moment of the cross-dresser's misrecognition of Qin Ling, one can detect the theatrical impulse of irony in the characterization of the cross-dresser and the text's exaltation of the androgynous personality. The text shows a comic paradox in which the cross-dresser Qin Ling plays the role of a nonmale for the other two cross-dressers, who perceive "him" as such. On the surface, Qin is an exception among men; underlying the text's ironic representation, "his" appraisal of the masculine role makes Qin neither female nor male. "His" feminine appearance passes flawlessly as the effeminate countenance of a refined scholar, suggesting an androgynous subjectivity that eludes the orthodox definition of gendered subjectivity.

Current scholarship on late imperial women's cross-dressing focuses on the liberatory potentials of fictional women to women readers who aspire toward alternative lives outside the domestic sphere. Dorothy Ko, in her study of seventeenth-century women authors, points out that "instead of challenging the ideology of separate spheres by mixing and redefining gender roles, these heroines encouraged their female readers to aspire to be more like men." Ko points out that the proliferate depictions of male-looking heroines in dramas and stories show no more than women's temporary transgressions. Ko notes, "Male concerns in public domains are still considered as superior." Tales of gender inversions "perpetuate the prevailing gender ideology" without fundamentally challenging the ideology of separate spheres of the inner and the outer or the domestic and the social (Ko, *Teachers* 140). An important result of these visionary women authors' interventions is that their stories of cross-dressers break down "the century-old divisions between inner and outer and between male and female spheres" (Ko, *Teachers* 142). Likewise, Siu Leung Li, in a study of cross-dressing in Chinese opera of the Yuan period (1279-1368), makes the proposition that women's cross-dressing in performance texts reveals an "interactive negotiation between subversion and containment" and the vexing desire circulated between stage enactment and the audience (Li, Siu Leung 22). Ko and Li both raise the question of women's desire to question and disrupt the ideological distinction between spaces of the inner and the outer. At the same time, uch progressive endeavors are still conditioned and constrained by the authors' historical and social conditions in the patriarchal society. The proposition of "masculine" women characters from late imperial literary works by and large reinforces the division between the male and female worlds, instead of completely redefining the relations between these gendered spheres (Ko, *Teachers* 140).

The above considerations raise further questions about how issues of androgynous gender identity should be understood in the late imperial social and historical context. Androgyny, characteristic of cross-dressed men and women, is significantly depicted in late imperial literature as a gender subjectivity alternative to the male and female binary gender system (see Zhou, Zuyan). Depictions of androgynous heroines are profuse in *tanci* by women. The renowned *Zaishengyuan* depicts Meng Lijun, who cross-dresses to escape from marriage. *Xianü*, in comparison, represents a group of women who disguise themselves as men and surpass their peers on the imperial exam. In *tanci*, cross-dressing was often invoked by late imperial women authors to depict characters who actively take part in constructing their own image by drawing on disparate gender roles. Cross-dressing is a strategy for women in literary works, as it was in real life, to renounce marriage (often supplemented by "mock marriages" between women privately agreeing to play the role of an ideal couple), and a way for women to renounce their sexuality.

All the women cross-dressers refuse to resume wearing their feminine attire in the text. For example, when Qin Ling is confronted by her fiancé Lin Mengyun, who, to test Qin Ling's true identity, claims that he will abide by their engagement for the rest of his life, Qin Ling senses Mengyun's intention and replies, "I will give you my advice. In the world there are monumental plates that are erected for chaste widows, but I have not seen any temple built in honor of a loyal husband" (5: 18, 29). This passage contains an explicit mockery of the Confucian doctrine of women's chastity, as it replaces the traditionally passive woman with a husband who awaits her return with chaste piety. The woman flees from her socially prescribed role through cross-dressing and cleverly rejects her fiancé's consent to marry. The frustrated Lin Mengyun thinks, "How regretful; she is now neither alive nor dead, leaving no trace in the world. / How ashamed I am of my own reputation for talent; she is really more intelligent than I" (5: 18, 32). The cross-dresser transcends social and sexual norms, yet paradoxically triggers complicated patterns of desire. Moving across social and economic boundaries, she comes to life through the text's dramatic representation.

Like Qin Ling, another character, Su Zixiu, who also cross-dresses, refuses to admit her true identity to her fiancé. During childhood Zixiu is separated from her family in an accident and is later rescued by a high official. She then dresses as a man and passes the civil service exam. Years later, Zixiu meets her fiancé Wu Musu, who immediately suspects Zixiu's real identity. However, Zixiu refuses to admit her true identity in front of Wu Musu. On the other hand, when Zixiu's mother finds out that the young official is her long lost daughter, Zixiu pleads with her not to disclose the secret, asking her to pretend that she is still suffering from her daughter's disappearance. Then, Zixiu pleads with her mother to persuade her fiancé (who is now her male peer in the palace) to look for another wife and stop interrogating her. Exasperated, she even threatens to commit suicide: "If someone dares to reveal your daughter's secret of cross-dressing, / I will immediately take up the sword and slit my own throat" (5: 19, 59). The text demonstrates a resonance with the motif of women's suicide in late imperial literature. Many late imperial literary works reflect the social custom of chastity-related suicide, such as widows committing suicide after their husbands' deaths, sometimes at the prompting of the deceased husbands' families (for a detailed discussion of this topic, see Mann, "Widows" 37-56; Judge, *Precious Raft* 34-59). Yet, here, this convention is evoked in a different situation: the woman threatens to kill herself not in defense of her chastity, but to resist the confinement of marriage, insisting that she would prefer death to losing the freedom she has when she is disguised as a man. When challenged by her fiancé's inquisitive questions about her real identity, Zixiu ponders her situation. She thinks to herself, "If you want me to change into feminine attire, / that will only take place when heaven topples down and the earth overturns. / Those people are most despicable who say that women should follow the doctrines and not venture to make a career like men out in the world. / I would rather rely on my talents and enjoy fortune, / and entirely dismiss the fact that I was born a woman. / I have learned all kinds of arts and have fortunately had my name among the first few in the Exam. / I take a vow that I will not change my attire again. What can you do about me then?" (9: 34, 24).

These audacious statements strongly resonate with the famous Lijun in *Zaishengyuan*, who, when recognized by her parents, rationalizes her unwillingness to go back to a woman's life. She defends her choice in the name of filial piety, attempting to persuade her parents to keep her sexual identity a secret.

> Even though you would like me to return to your side,
> I can only end up marrying into another household and serving the parents-in-law.
> What is the benefit of this for my own parents?
> Why don't you just let me go on and live the life of a man? . . .
> Even though I was born a woman,
> now I enter the royal palace and serve the Emperor. . . .

> What is the need for me to be married?
> Even the place of the Empress herself could not fit into my expectations!
> (11: 44, 761)

These defiant statements in *Zaishengyuan* invited criticism from *tanci* authors of the time and in later generations. Perhaps because Chen Duansheng was incapable of balancing the character's personal aspirations with the readers' desire to see Lijun's reunion with her fiancé, she left the work unfinished; it ends after Lijun's sexual identity is accidentally disclosed. Modern adaptations of *Zaishengyuan* in local operas and film and television dramas have presented multiple interpretations of Lijun's fate. For both Meng Lijun and Su Zixiu, cross-dressing represents the rebirth of a new life. These stories show that in the late imperial social context, cross-dressing was an imaginary means for women to escape prearranged marriage and explore freedom outside the domestic sphere. However, under the pervasive influence of Confucian ideology, ordinary women's desire to have an independent life was by and large frustrated by social reality. In *Bishenghua* (Blossom from the Brush, preface dated 1857), the heroine, Jiang Dehua, is nearly compelled to commit suicide when she is forced to enter the palace as a royal maid. She is saved by a fox spirit and then cross-dresses as a man to explore a new life. However, a comparison between Meng Lijun and Jiang Dehua shows that women cross-dressers' presence is still constrained by the pervasive Confucian ideology. Lijun is nearly sentenced to death when the emperor discovers her cross-dressing. The open ending of the work shows that the cross-dresser, once disclosed, has no space of her own outside the inner quarters. Jiang Dehua, even though she is disguised as a man, has internalized the moral codes of virtue and chastity and is transformed into an exemplary *nü daoxue,* that is, a female Confucian intellectual. Even in her male disguise, she adheres to feminine virtue and will not be touched by men, nor will she eat at the same table with men. In Jiang's case, cross-dressing is not radically transgressive, but rather shows the reinforcement of traditional gender ideologies. When Jiang's cross-dressing is discovered, the emperor orders her to marry her former fiancé Lin Wenbing. Jiang then is transformed into a virtuous woman who devotes her talent to governing the household and settling disputes between the concubines (a biography of Qiu is in Ye, Dejun 743-44; see also Hu, Wenkai 402-03).

As indicated by the title 俠女群英史 (*Xianü qunying shi*, A History of Women Warriors), women's cross-dressing is often related to heroism in the text. In chapter 32, volume 8, when a rebellion against the emperor bursts out, the protagonist Wen Xiaxian disguises herself as a golden-faced deity, sneaks into the palace, and rescues the infant prince from the rebellious armies. The textual depiction is imbued with fantastic color. While the besieged palace falls into chaos, "Suddenly a deity descends from the roof dressed in a scarlet short jacket and pants; / he has three strands of beard on a face of golden color. / In a thunderous voice, he says, 'Don't be afraid. / I am a deity who comes to rescue the prince.' / Upon saying this, he hurries to approach the Queen, / and hastens to carry the Prince in his hands. / As if flying, he steps outside; / in a light jump he vanishes like a cloud" (8: 32, 85).

The passage depicts the protagonist as a 俠女忠臣 (*xianü zhongchen,* female knight and loyal official) who saves the prince in a moment of national crisis and secures the future of the country. The text might have been influenced by stories about the female knight-errant in traditional Chinese narratives, and is reminiscent of the swordswomen tales in the late imperial vernacular tradition. In late imperial fiction, a famous example of swordswoman is Nie Yinniang in *Strange Tales in a Chinese Studio*. In the text, the authors possibly adopted the tradition of female swordsmen in depicting the cross-dressers to emphasize the heroism of the women (for a study of female knights in traditional Chinese literature, see Altenburger 2009). Wen Xiaxian, the heroine in the above passage, also cross-dresses as a swordsman to rescue an honest scholar who is persecuted by a scheming high official. In these two examples, the cross-dresser displays a spirit of heroism, loyalty, and moral uprightness. The subject of the book, as one of the authors, Yonglan, states, is "the loyal and chaste noble heroes, / the heroic women who support the poor and rescue the endangered" (4: 13, 1). In male attire, the woman explores the variations of gender roles and demonstrates an emancipating power to rescue the weak and redress injustice.

Women's cross-dressing is not unique to *tanci*, but has been demonstrated in many analogous depictions in late imperial history and literature. An example in fiction is a *huaben* story entitled "The Maid Li Xiuqing Becomes the Swear-Sister of the Chaste Maid Miss Huang," which appears in the short story collection 喻世明言 (*Yushi mingyan*, Illustrious Words to Instruct the World; 1620) (For a translation of this text, see Feng Menglong, *Stories Old and New*). The author Feng Menglong (1574-1647) depicts a cross-dressed heroine named Huang Shancong (黃善聰). A merchant's daughter, Shancong cross-dresses to travel with her father. On their journey, her father falls ill and passes away, yet Shancong keeps up her disguise to preserve her virginity. After seven years, Shancong is reunited with her family. Her relatives think that she must have become the secret wife of her traveling companion, Li Xiuqing (李秀卿). To prove her purity, Shancong consents to a private test, the result of which shows that she is still a virgin. The story ends with Shancong's marriage to Li Xiuqing, to which the family has given their blessing. The narrator's stress on female chastity outweighs the text's acclamation of female heroism: "For seven years," the narrator explains, "she cross-dressed as a man, without showing any tiny trace; upon her return [to the family] she held her cool and unstirred heart in solitude. I compiled this tale to educate those in the inner chambers, and cleanse the tales of romance and love" (Feng Menglong, *Yüshi mingyan* 541). Shancong is compared to heroic cross-dressers such as Hua Mulan and Huang Chonggu (early tenth century), who according to the narrator are "disguised men without manliness, real women who wear males' hairdress" (530).

Huang Chonggu in Feng's story is a well-known woman who disguises herself as a literati scholar and impresses the minister with her talent in writing poetry. When the minister proposes a marriage between Huang and his own daughter, Huang writes a poem, "辭蜀相妻女詩" ("Ci shuxiang qinü shi," "Declining the Proposal of the Minister of the Shu Kingdom That I Marry His Daughter"). In the poem she confesses her true sex: "If my lord wishes to have me as a son-in-law, I wish heaven could change me into a man instantly" (Peng 799: 8995). Huang's legacy can be traced in numerous examples of female cross-dressing in late imperial women's poetry, playwriting, and fiction. For instance, a late eighteenth-century woman poet named Shen Xiang describes a portrait of the courtesan poet Liu Shi, in which Liu cross-dresses as a young scholar to pay a personal visit to a male scholar. In Shen Xiang's poem about this painting, she says, "Who can tell the truth from the appearance of a person after all? Beauty or scholar, both are now seen as one" (Shen Xiang 15a). This unique example shows Liu Shi's cross-dressed image, which recalls other similar portraits of cross-dressed women. In the Ming play *Qiaoying* (The Image in Disguise) by the woman poet and playwright Wu Zao, the protagonist Xie Xucai cross-dresses and paints a miniature of herself in official's robes. Describing herself as a latter-day Qu Yuan, Xie expresses her frustration that the disjunction between herself and her times prevents her from fully employing her talents. "Alas! Fettered by my physical form, I can only sigh all alone over my sadness. If one considers the matter carefully, though, while miraculous transformations depend on Heaven, the initiative rests with oneself. That is why a few days ago I painted a small portrait of myself dressed in male attire" (132). Wai-Yee Li suggests that the author's purpose for writing this play is "explained by her frustrations with the limitations imposed by her gender role and her wish to transcend them" (Li, "Heroic Transformations" 367). This sense of frustration is similarly shared by the heroine Du Lanxian in the play 梨花夢 (*Lihuameng*, Dream of the Pear Flower; 1840) by He Peizhu. In the play Du makes a self-portrait of her female image before cross-dressing as a man. Taiwanese scholar Lijian Wang suggests that in both plays the self-portrait reflects women's sexual displacement and self-estrangement in Confucian society (Wang, Lijian 82-89). It should be noted that such examples of women performing men's roles are not rare in late imperial women's drama. An important example is *Yuanyangmeng* (Dream of the Mandarin Ducks) by Ye Xiaowan, which portrays three female immortals who, following men's ways, secretly become sworn brothers and offend the West Palace Empress (*Wumengtang ji* 1: 1-16). As a punishment for their offense, they are incarnated as male scholars and sent to the earth to experience the hardship of men's mortal life. The author, through the incarnated male scholars, voices women's grievances against social constraints, and their aspiration for an imaginary realm of immortality and freedom. These earlier examples of women's cross-dressing set the groundwork for later *tanci* narratives that encompass a rich exploration of women's capacity to perform as the equals of men.

The legacy of female heroism, demonstrated by these cross-dressed women in fiction and history, presages women's activism in real life in turn-of-the-century China. An important example is the protofeminist writer and revolutionist, Qiu Jin. Qiu Jin was a prolific writer in many genres and composed an unfinished *tanci* entitled精衛石 (*Jingwei shi*, Stones of the Jingwei Bird; 1905), which was published in the same year as *Xianü*. The temporal setting and plot of these two works, however, are vastly different. *Jingwei shi* depicts a group of young women who escape from their domestic bonds and travelabroad to Japan to study modern culture. These heroines, like the author herself, dedicate themselves to advancing the cause of women's liberation on a national scale. In her lifetime, Qiu frequently disguised herself as a man and actively participated in social and political events. In 1907, when she became the principal of the Datong Normal School in Hangzhou, she trained female students in military gymnastics and was known as an infamous woman who rode through the town dressed in men's clothing (Judge, *Precious Raft* 219). Qiu Jin's activism, as Joan Judge argues, is reflective of her self-positioning as one of the "heroic educators of Chinese women" and her effort to inscribe a new identity in national history that transcends the identity of "woman." In her life time, Qiu Jin posed for photos while dressed in Chinese men's dress and Western men's suits, and successfully "adopted masculine skills, from riding astride on horseback to powerful oratory" (Judge, *Precious Raft* 219). Compared with her predecessors in *tanci*, Qiu's cross-dressing takes on multiple forms, fashioning her identity as a "new-style heroine" whose aspirations are channeled through the cause of nationalism (Judge, *Precious Raft* 218-20). Qiu's personal undertaking brought out the progressive potential of the Mulan legend with vigor. Such tales of cross-dressing, legendary or historical, question and destabilize conventional social gender roles and suggest new possibilities for women's social and political empowerment.

How do the readings of cross-dressing in *tanci* amplify contemporary readers' understanding of subjectivity and gendered spectatorship in and beyond late imperial and early modern China? How do the performances of cross-dressers expose ways in which gender roles can be negotiated and reconstructed? As the text demonstrates, the female-to-male cross-dresser in particular becomes an eroticized character and has to adopt vigorous, spirited, and even exaggerated actions. Mu Hualong, who becomes one of the top three candidates in the civil service examination, "always felt abashed, and behaved with a certain gentleness. / She was afraid that people might see her femininity through her demeanor, / so she could only pretend to imitate the liberal behavior of men" (4: 14, 25). The woman's disguised body reveals the ironic relation between seeing and acting. "He" observes and imitates men, learns from this observation, and responds to the gaze of others. "His" performance, consequently, is constructed and modified in an interactive relationship with the observing audience.

This dynamic interaction between cross-dressed women and the observing audience in the text sometimes exhibits great dramatic irony. When Qin Ling ranks first in the civil service exam and becomes the top candidate, the emperor's brother Lord Zhongjing proposes to marry his daughter to Qin Ling, knowing that Qin already has a fiancée (who is actually Qin's own cousin, but who does not know about Qin's real identity). Finally, Qin Ling is persuaded to take both women as "his" wives in a joint wedding ceremony. On Qin's way home, the people in the streets vie with each other to see the handsome top candidate, praising him as "outstanding both in appearance and talent, and carrying true loyalty; / in the Hall of the Golden Throne, he dared to reject the Emperor's marriage arrangement for him" (4: 14, 24). Despite the admiring gaze of the crowd, Qin's mind is peppered with worries. "He" thinks, "The wedding night is in just a few days. / Who knows how I should make arrangements for two wives?" (4: 14, 24). This scenario is a satirical take on the polygamous marriage system in which the husband is married to several wives. Even though the marriage is one between "phony phoenixes," the cross-dresser manages to establish a harmonious relationship with his two "wives." On the first family gathering the morning after the wedding, the two wives, gazing at the handsome Qin, "could not help but become overjoyed, pondering, 'No wonder he has been regarded as the most affable and ideal potential husband'" (4: 15, 39). In comparison with the mock marriage between Meng Lijun and Liang Suhua in *Zaishengyuan*, the cross-dressers' marriages in *Xianü* may or may not involve women's mutual understanding or knowledge of the "husband's" disguise. In this example, the cross-dresser's performance is so powerful that even the wives are convinced and believe "him." The polygamous marriage system is even exploited to the cross-dresser's advantage. Not only does Qin Ling enjoy the highest authority in the house, but "his" social identity as a married "man" further prevents the suspicious fiancé Lin Mengyun from probing into "his" sexual identity. Qin's cross-dressing performance is carried out with almost full approval from the people around him.

This interaction between cross-dressed women and their fiancés who recurrently evaluate and attempt to identify their sexuality creates many moments of tension and melodrama. After Mu Hualong's cross-dressing is disclosed, she is exempted from punishment by the emperor, but has to marry her former fiancé. The name Hualong (化龍) means "transforming into dragon," suggesting a woman changing into a man, since the symbol of the dragon represents masculinity (just as the phoenix represents femininity). Seeing Mu's reversion to a feminine identity, Lin Mengyun becomes all the more anxious to prove that Qin Ling is his former betrothed companion. He ponders, "Even though I tested him several times, / his responses were always as sharp as sword blades" (8: 32, 86). Nor does his behavior resemble that of a woman in close examination. (A related fact is that Pang Yulong's wife is Wu Musu's sister. It happens that Wu's sister is devoted to Daoist practice and rejects sexual intimacy with men. This proves to be convenient for Pang Yulong, who does not have to sleep in the same room at night with "his" wife. While the couple lives in harmony, Wu, driven by anxiety, suspects that his own sister has become a conspirator with Pang and intentionally has kept him from knowing Pang's true sexuality.) After all, how could a cross-dresser live in a house with two wives so effortlessly? Likewise, Wu Musu, who is the fiancé of the cross-dresser Pang Yulong, suspects Pang is his betrothed bride, but can not imagine "how a woman dared to complete the matrimonial ceremony with another woman" (4: 16, 68). The moment is reminiscent of Xu Wei's play adapted from the *Ballad of Mulan*, in which the androgynous protagonist confesses, "For seventeen years I was a girl, for twelve years I have been a man. Under the gaze of tens and thousands of people, who could really tell whether I am a man or a woman? Now it is evident that man or woman cannot be distinguished with eyes" (Xu Wei, *Ci Mulan* 224). In *Xianü*, the literary figure of Mulan has found rebirth in the group of women cross-dressers who blend characteristics of male and female genders, striving to explore the social space as men's equals.

To sum up, in late imperial China, *tanci* authors wielded their brushes to enact new forms of identities by positioning the personal within the fictional realm and reconfiguring moral commitments and desires through memorable storylines. The author becomes a speaking subject and conceptualizes the self by exploring multiple possibilities of subjectivity. For women, writing in this textual form is an audacious choice, showing their desire to represent a space in which traditional definitions of womanhood can be displaced and unconventional gender identities can be imagined. The text of *Xianü* demonstrates the tension between the cross-dressers and the public, who probe into and repeatedly test the masquerading women. However, other than Mu Hualong, none of the women cross-dressers are exposed. Su Zixiu and Qin Ling become high military officials and play a fundamental role in putting down several regional rebellions. Pang Yulong is married to a princess and becomes the emperor's son-in-law. In comparison with Meng Lijun, who is left with no choice but to revert back to a woman's life, the women cross-dressers in *Xianü* are depicted as having more freedom and independence to pursue their lives unconfined. If earlier *tanci* before the twentieth century, such as *Zaishengyuan,* display an imagining of women's alternate lives in male disguise outside the inner chambers, *Xianü* impresses the readers with its insistence that cross-dressed women can find their place in the social sphere, and that marriage may not be an obstacle to women exercising their intellectual powers. Conversely, the authors clearly invite comparison of these cross-dressers by having one woman found out and the others not. This comparison gives readers a critical indication that not all women can fully embrace such ambitious lives in an unyielding social world which still awaits transformations in the generations to come.

Chapter Six

Illustrating a New Woman in *Fengliu zuiren* (The Valiant and The Culprit)

Continuing the exploration of women's *tanci* fiction in the modern period, this last chapter studies the Shanghainese writer Jiang Yingqing, whose portrayal of the modern woman in 1920s and 1930s Shanghai attests to the continuing development of the tradition of women's written *tanci* in the late imperial period. During the interwar years (1920-1937), Shanghai witnessed a polemical historical period in which competing discourses on China's national identity shaped the public image of modern Chinese women and their societal roles. From the contentious social-cultural discourses of this period, the ideal of female citizenship emerged as a nascent model of feminine social and political identity (see Liu, Huiying 156-80). Jiang's *Fengliu zuiren* (The Valiant and the Culprit) employs the traditional *tanci* as a narrative vessel to disseminate modern ideals of female citizenship and, subsequently, innovative visions of women's social and political agency. In the early twentieth century, women's public participation in the anti-Qing rebellion and the founding of the New Republic carved out a public space in which a collective political identity of women could be envisioned and developed. Responding to contemporary feminist discourses, Jiang's text suggests that a woman's emancipation should be achieved through constructive relationships with her personal identity, her community, and the nation. The heroine Jia Tuanhua travels to the West and comes back to work as a doctor. Ambitious to contribute to the benefit of her people, she rejects the male protagonist's marriage proposal; he, contrary to the independent heroine, is yoked by a conventional marriage arranged by his family and eventually abandons his personal ambition. The narrative's forward looking portrayal of a self-determined heroine represents the social and cultural discourses about women and work in 1920s China, highlighting women's self-empowerment through intellectual undertakings and the pursuit of social freedom.

Published first as a newspaper series from 1924-1925, Jiang's *tanci,* 社會之花 (*Shehui zhi hua*, Flower of the Society), brings to light the author's conscious exploration of a larger audience community for traditional *tanci*. Herself a teacher at a women's school in Shanghai, Jiang uses familial tales to suggest women's new social agency, and adapts traditional *tanci* conventions to the modern era. In traditional *tanci*, authors oftentimes portray women achieving imaginative freedom by cross-dressing and taking on men's social roles. However, women's social mobility in these traditional *tanci* is constrained by the resolution of the plot, which frequently involves the heroine's return to her feminine identity in the domestic sphere. In contrast with these earlier *tanci*, Jiang's work appraises the vexed relationship between gender and modernization and projects a vision of women's identity that takes into account the innovative societal roles open to women during the interwar period.

The story begins with a scene at the beautiful West Lake in the southern city of Hangzhou. A libertine, Gu Tan (古檀), taking a leisurely stroll, meets the beautiful Jia Tanhua, falls in love with her, and subsequently schemes with matchmaker Wang Sansao (汪三嫂) to seduce her. Tanhua is a young woman born into a wealthy family, whose parents are already deceased. Like many elite women of her time, Tanhua receives a modern education and aspires to devote herself to women's education and freedom. In her exchanges and meetings with progressive intellectuals, she is attracted to Zhen Chaoying (甄超英), a young scholar who recently returned to China after his education at Hong Kong Queen's College and six years of study in London. Enamored by Tanhua's talent, beauty, and wisdom, Chaoying proposes to her. However, Tanhua, knowing that Chaoying's mother has arranged for him to marry a prosperous Shanghai businessman's daughter, Hong Qingjiao (洪青椒), declines Chaoying's proposal. Later, Tanhua travels to the United States to study medicine, then returns to Shanghai as the director of a hospital, devoting herself to the ill and impoverished. In the hospital, Tanhua re-encounters Gu Tan, who dies of syphilis due to his corrupted lifestyle. His pregnant girlfriend, who elopes with Gu Tan and stays in the hospital to wait for the birth of their child, is so heartbroken by Gu Tan's death that she dies with the unborn baby. Meanwhile, disheartened by Tanhua's rejection, the male protagonist Chaoying follows his mother's orders and marries Hong Qingjiao. Because Qingjiao loves the glamorous Shanghai, Chaoying moves there with her, hoping to find a job in a bank with his father-in-law's help. However, the couple falls into a series of family disputes due to Qingjiao's behavior, including her conflicts with Chaoying's conservative mother. Chaoying's unhappy marriage leads to the deterioration of his health. Near the end of the story, Chaoying meets Tanhua by accident while staying in her hospital as a patient. He has divorced his wife and now again proposes marriage to Tanhua. The heroine, determined to remain single and devote herself to her career, leaves Chaoying a long letter and departs for a journey overseas.

Tanhua is portrayed as an image of the modern woman through the unconventional gender and power relationships between her and Chaoying. The names of the male and female characters Jia Tanhua and Zhen Chaoying (28: 9) resonate with characters in Cao Xueqin's novel *The Dream of the Red Chamber*. The antithesis of their personal destinies is underlined by their surnames, Jia, which puns on illusion or falsehood, and Zhen, which puns on truth or reality. This double entendre in names is frequently employed in Cao's novel to indicate characters of paradoxical destinations, such as the ill-fated scholar Zhen Shiyin (甄士隱, literally, truth concealed), and the ambitious and later prospering character Jia Yucun (賈雨村, falsehood contained). Later in Cao's text, a minor character Zhen Baoyu (甄寶玉, which puns on real stone) steps on the stage and evokes a convoluted relation with the hero Jia Baoyu (false stone) (Gu 159). This contrast between truth and fiction, as Anthony C. Yu suggests, implies "the emptiness of fiction": "Just as the real world is considered empty and unreal in the Buddhist vision, so the invented world of story is 'baseless' (*huangtang*), 'absurd' (*dahuang*), 'unverifiable' (*wuji*), and 'undatable' (*wu chaodai nianji*)" (168). Jiang's *tanci* inherits this narrative antithesis of truth and fiction, but modifies the male and female characters' personal destinies considerably. In Cao's novel, Jia Baoyu flees the world and takes to Daoism at the collapse of his family, but then decides to pursue knowledge abroad and re-enter the world with an activist attitude. Zhen Chaoying, however, is an effeminate and passive hero who is unfulfilled in marriage and career and then falls seriously ill, akin to the sentimental and delicate heroine Lin Daiyu in Cao's novel. Tanhua, unlike the frail Daiyu, is a sagacious and self-educated modern woman who enjoys more social mobility and personal power. If Chaoying's illness is symbolic of China's ill society, Tanhua's hospital is a symbol of hope and regeneration, a personal effort to heal the nation and the people. The ending of the text, which might otherwise herald Tanhua's newfound power as a professional woman, the head of the hospital, is weighed down by the cultural pressures of a traditional society that is pitted against progressive women. This ending is foreshadowed in the name of Tanhua, which, punning on the popular saying "tanhua yixian" (as fleeting as the blossom of the epiphyllum flower), suggests the ephemerality of Tanhua's personal ideal.

The tensions between the personal and the social, the traditional and the modern are prominent in Jiang's personal life. Born in 1884, Jiang was educated at the Shanghai Women's School, one of the earliest educational institutions for women, and later taught at the Songjiang Women's School in Shanghai. Because of her talents in composing traditional poems and her expertise in *tanci*, she gained great popularity among the readers of the time. Jiang's husband Chen Zuotong (陳佐彤), poet and editor of her book 彈詞開篇集 (*Tanci kaipian ji,* Collected *Tanci* Introductory Songs), was a personal acquaintance of Wang Dungen (王鈍根), the chief editor of the prominent newspaper 申報 (*Shenbao,* Shanghai Journal). Through the connection with Wang, Jiang's writings were in dialogue with the literary societies to which ordinary women writers did not have easy access. A contemporary reader, when tracing Jiang's life trajectory, may find himself or herself unraveling multiple spaces of reality: accounts of Jiang's life by her male peers and her son, her husband's edited works of her texts, and her *tanci* published serially in *Shehui zhi hua* (Flower of the Society, 1924-1925). The newspaper, representing the voice of bourgeois intellectuals of the time, aimed at reforming social customs through education of the masses, although the editors declined to align with the leftist writers who became prominent after the May Fourth Movement. Some of its contributors, such as Zhou Shoujuan, identified themselves more with the so-called 鴛鴦蝴蝶派 (*Yuanyang hudie pai*, Mandarin Ducks and Butterflies School), and claimed an interconnection with traditional literature.

In her *tanci* composed for oral performance, Jiang's depiction of the modern woman suggests disjuncture and inconsistency. Traditional tales of love and marriage are appropriated and rewritten, reflecting a negotiation between the public and personal. In the *tanci* song, "摩登女郎嘆" ("*Modeng nülang tan*," "Lament of A Modern Woman"), the narrator recounts in the first person the fall of a modern woman, a follower of "freedom in love" who regrets her choice when she suffers a broken marriage. The theme of 自由戀愛 (*ziyou lian'ai*, free love) was considered a feasible solution to the women's problem according to some contributors to 婦女雜誌 (*Funü zazhi*, Lady's Journal) in 1922. Jiang's *tanci*, however, departs from the ideal of free love and sexual emancipation promoted by progressive intellectuals, addressing the women's problem in a self-reflexive voice.

In the early years of Jiang's career, before she composed The Valiant and the Culprit, she published a voluminous work 玉鏡臺 (*Yujingtai*, Jade Terrace) in the format of traditional *tanci* fiction, which, despite its aesthetic achievement, did not meet with much commercial success. Jiang's later profound involvement with print media, however, assisted her in transforming the *tanci* genre into a medium through which diverse discourses on woman and selfhood could be facilitated, and thus prepared for the broad impact of The Valiant and the Culprit on readers. As Rebecca Karl argues, after 1895, China's journalism came to be appropriated as a mode of "political, intellectual, and social activism and advocacy" (Karl 540). Jiang's marriage with the newspaper publisher Chen Zuotong and her connections with progressive journalists such as Wang Dungen positioned her writings in a broad public forum and drew attention to them from a wide range of audiences. The Valiant and the Culprit was published under the subtitle of *shishi tanci*, or *tanci* of current events, suggesting the editor's effort to distinguish this *tanci* work from other traditional *tanci* and an editorial intent to tie the work to the journal's overall goal of social reform. In comparison with Hou Zhi, the Qing *tanci* author who was likewise engaged in the publishing field to advocate for women's writing, Jiang's involvement with print media could possibly have endowed her with more autonomy because of the evolved and more open social environment. The symbiotic relationship between the journal Flowers of the Society and Jiang's serial *tanci*, published under her own name, suggests that women authors were enjoying an unprecedented autonomy in the public sphere.

Some of Jiang's *tanci* songs are autobiographical, such as "十年前之我" ("*Shinian qian zhi wo*," "I Myself Ten Years' Ago"), "自笑" ("*Zixiao*," "Self-mockery"), "私語" ("*Siyu*," "Words in Private"), and "病榻的回顧" ("*Bingta de huigu*," "Reflections in Time of Illness"). These songs reveal Jiang's evolving notions of self and her need to find a space of self-expression. Her adaptation of traditional *tanci* exposes fissures in China's own protofeminist projects. In Jiang's *tanci* songs, one can find abundant examples of her urging women to transpose the Confucian model of women's familial service into the new realm of national service. She emphasizes women's inborn duty as mother, openly opposes divorce, and endorses a daughter's love to her parents. The primary question for Jiang, as her writings reveal, is when the Chinese woman is given the choice of adapting Western ways or joining the new global order, how definitively women should break with their own past.

The discrepancies in Jiang's representation of the modern woman reflect an anxiety characteristic of the new Chinese woman, whose identity oscillates between the fantasy of a nascent subjectivity and an internal resistance against homogenized identity. The above photo of Jiang dressed as an ancient beauty possibly implies an ambivalent stance toward modernity. The dress, hairstyle, and painted decorative strands around her arms are signifiers of tradition, yet her ambiguous image is even more enlarged by these details created by the photo. She becomes a "media-created" woman (Van Zoonen 66). Jiang Yingjiang's case reflects the "doubling-up" of the woman both as the object and subject of attention in feminist studies. The author is the subject and enunciator of feminist issues, and the receiver of the impact of feminist thinking, revealing the diverse meanings and contents ascribed to the term "modern woman."

In Jiang's *tanci*, the author's multivalent representations of republican women are centered around the heroine Jia Tanhua, who declines the male protagonist's marriage proposal, prioritizing her duty as a national citizen over becoming a good wife and mother. In the last years of the nineteenth century, Chinese reformers became convinced of the need to mobilize the energies of women to serve the nation and to nationalize women's education by borrowing from the educational initiatives of foreigners. Consequently, the government began to open its own private women's schools in the late nineteenth and early twentieth centuries. Custom, however, prohibited male instruction of female students. In many cases, men depended on women employees to conduct teaching and administrative duties.

The conceptions of Chinese female citizenship were formulated by cultural and political elites and framed by national and Social Darwinist concerns (Judge, "Citizens" 43). The rise of female citizenship was often mediated through examples of Western heroines in fin-de-siècle literature. However, women's political rights were construed as rights to act in the national rather than the personal interest. Late Qing reformists who advocated for women's rights were more concerned with providing women with the knowledge necessary to assume their national duties, rather than with promoting the right to education per se (Judge, "Citizens" 43).

In this historical context, how does the text refract women's citizenship through the representations of Tanhua, as well as diverse women characters? Does Tanhua's image represent continuity with classical feminine virtues in a mediated modern form, or does Tanhua, who aspires toward New Literature and who studied abroad, represent a continuation of the May Fourth tradition? What textual adaptations does Jiang make to change the traditional form of *tanci* into an effective medium to represent women's historical experiences and reveal social reality? The above questions provoke a recontextualization of the *tanci* genre and its relation to public media and women's political activism in the republican period. In this period, the new urban media played a pivotal role in the awakening of women who came to be prominent reformers and who were devoted to save fellow oppressed women. Many feminist journals were being published and circulated, including Women's Journal

(1902), edited by Chen Xiefen (1883-1923), and 中華女報 (*Zhonghua nübao*, Chinese Women's Periodical; 1907), edited by the feminist revolutionist Qiu Jin (1875-1907). These women's magazines conveyed new representations of womanhood through their pictorial covers and progressive content, defining women's newfound social roles as teachers, students, athletes, and social activists. Many progressive *tanci* were published in newspapers and journals. In giving voice to oppressed women, *tanci* writers critiqued the orthodox ideological forces that were perpetuating women's subordination, and they enacted in print the moral imperatives for social and self-transformation. Women's appropriation of the literary form of *tanci* created a new space for women writers, constructing a new social life for themselves as well as their largely female audience.

During this period, biographies of heroic women in both China and the West represent new ideals of womanhood channeled through sociopolitical discourses of the nation-state. These texts project the hybrid images of the new Chinese woman—and of the new Chinese nation—which were products of mutual transformations, paragons of possibilities, and contradictions which existed both within the local and between the local and global contexts (Judge, "Blended Wish Images" 105). "Late Qing authors claimed that the function of the Chinese and Western exemplars in turn-of-the-century texts corresponded to the dual objectives of modern Chinese nationalism: to preserve (or construct) an authentic Chinese cultural essence while securing China's place in the new international order of the nation-states" (Judge, "Blended Wish Images" 105). Particularly, early twentieth-century Chinese history witnesses the rise of "a new feminine-heroic subject" whose existence was "an effect of the early twentieth-century national crisis, and a mark of archeomodern and presentist responses to that crisis. Many of the new heroines considered their personal aspirations inseparable from broader national aspirations. This new ethos was, however, ridden with gender paradoxes. Heroines claimed their new historical role both as representative females and as surrogate males, simultaneously embracing and rejecting the identity of 'women'" (Judge, *Precious Raft* 198). This nascent female citizenship is well exemplified by the revolutionary martyr Qiu Jin, who writes in her poem "Mian nüquan" (Song for Women's Rights), "Ours is a generation that loves freedom, / we strive for freedom on one single cup of wine. / Equal rights for men and women are endowed by nature; / how then is it that you willingly live in subordination? / Outstanding women citizens must not fail to shoulder national responsibilities" (48). Qiu Jin's appeal toward women's responsibilities as national citizens can be contextualized in the history of late Qing and early Republic women's political revolution and social activism.

Thanks to women's public participation in the anti-Qing rebellion and the founding of the New Republic, the 1920s and 1930s witnessed women's successful campaigns for political equality and the development of a "space in which a sense of a legitimate women's political collective identity could develop" (Edwards, *Gender* 66). Women's suffrage movements made substantial progress and became an important constituent of the New Culture Movement (新文化運動)

from 1919 to 1923. The earliest branch of the progressive United Women's Association was founded in Shanghai in 1919, and later became supported by the newly formed Chinese Communist Party in 1921, renamed as 上海中華女界聯合會 (*Shanghai zhonghua nüjie lianhe hui*, Shanghai China Union of Women's Association, or Shanghai China UWA). Through the leftist journal 女聲 (*Nüsheng*, Women's Voice), Shanghai UWA exerted significant impact on the women's suffrage movements in the 1920s.

In The Valiant and The Culprit, the vexed relationship between female heroism and national crisis and women's political consciousness is centrally reflected in the scene in which Tanhua declines Chaoying's proposal by expressing her first ideal of saving the country and fulfilling her individual duties to the nation. For Tanhua, such a personal choice is an important political gesture and expresses her ideal of contributing to China's national reform. She says to Chaoying, "A great misfortune of our people is that we live in such an era of chaos and ten thousand evils. Men or women, we should all summon our individual learning and knowledge, participate in reforming the society, diligently fulfill our natural duties as national citizens. We shall not let the splendid nation of China disintegrate, fall apart and become enslaved by other nations, and finally fall into utterly irredeemable circumstances. This is the proper way of it" (13: 4).

In this dialogue, Tanhua's epochal sentiment elevates love and manifests its moral aspect. In the tumultuous historical era, she says, those who are addicted to emotion "may seem amorous to the ignorant; yet the sagacious ones view them as egocentric" (13: 4). She continues to lament the decline of the country,

> I regret that such a great nation is in a periled situation as if holding on by a thin hair.
> Anxieties at home and dangers outside have made people's bitterness endless.
> The atmosphere in the government is exceedingly degenerated;
> the officials sitting in high positions put on grand appearances but only love money.
> Those who are educated are not acquainted with worldly ways;
> when their talents are not put into use, they lament the uselessness of their learning.
> The businessmen are sly, peasants and workers slothful,
> the government exhausts the use of natural resources and increases people's taxes.
> The warlords are rampant and hold towering powers.
> They each rule a region and fight against each other. . . .
> The ancient saying goes that there are four borders of our nation, which are all lost today.
> I am afraid that in a short instant great calamity will follow.
> Every time I compare our nation with Japan, our neighbor in the east,
> I feel truly ashamed by their strength and our weakness.
> Hence we should, like the ancient Emperor Yue Goujian, sleep on brushwood and taste gall every day to wash off the previous dishonor.
> Ten thousand people, one heart, we shoulder the responsibility together.
> At the loss of our benefits and rights, we plan on recovery,

and gradually work toward the prosperity of the nation and the peacefulness of our people.
Today, China is a swallow's nest in a dangerous situation.
In vain we wait for the clarification of the situation; it is really difficult for people to live a long life.
In such a circumstance, one should cease his desire for love and hold onto his power;
a man should not forfeit his duties to his beautiful motherlands.
I myself, though one of the powerless women,
will devote myself to the career of highest importance and challenge, and regard death as a mere return to my fate.
Suppose that I fall in love with fame and fortune and change my morale,
even if I steal a life in the world I would always have regrets and shame.
(13: 5)

The heroine's voice takes this textual moment, expressing women's strong social awareness and desire to act as a social agents, which is no longer restricted to the usual boundaries of gender, age, and family background. A nascent sense of identity as a national citizen amplifies Tanhua's sense of self and distinguishes her from the preceding *tanci* heroines, whose transgression of social boundaries is often imaginative and temporary. The author imagines the woman's true emancipation as part of the national course of emancipation and self-empowerment, the individual's agency as part of the nation's journey toward agency and sovereignty. Tanhua appeals to Chaoying for comradeship between men and women that will ultimately contribute to the course of national rejuvenation. Such a new relationship is made possible by displacing her gender role as a wife. Tanhua's rejection of Chaoying has shown a remarkable degree of women's autonomy and agency, for Tanhua, now unyoked by marriage, enjoys the freedom to travel across national boundaries. In Jiang's *tanci*, a fraternal, nonhierarchical relationship between men and women is evoked to displace love. Benedict Anderson discusses the nation imagined this way as a community based on a deep, horizontal comradeship (57).

In Jiang's text, women's social agency and empowerment is achieved through evocative relationships with one's self, the social community, and the nation. Chinese reformers simultaneously took on the themes of national rejuvenation and female liberation and considered women's liberation in the larger contexts of social and national reform (for male discourse on women in the May Fourth era, see Chan 13-32). Jiang Yingqing's *tanci*, resounding with these prevalent sociohistorical discourses, takes on the relationship between women and nation as a pivotal position from which to reimagine modern women's gender agency and self-empowerment. Joan Wallach Scott suggests that the definition of gender can be considered with two propositions: "gender is a constitutive element of social relationships based on perceived differences between the sexes, and gender is a primary way of signifying relationships of power" (42). In *Fengliu zuiren*, Tanhua is portrayed as a social agent who possesses the knowledge, wisdom, and power to lead women's collective self-empowerment. Tanhua's political enthusiasm and nationalistic passion show that her role is not simply symbolic. Devoting herself to the course of national agency,

Tanhua has been endowed with individual agency to pursue knowledge and power. When the gravely ill Chaoying meets Tanhua, who now has returned from abroad and has become the head of a hospital in Shanghai, he recalls Tanhua's lofty aspiration that accounts for her current success. He ponders, "In the past she confided to me her thoughts, and deeply regretted / the corruption among the officials and the lack of management in the government. / She said that for women to be impotent is certainly a shame. / For men, if they are uneducated they should feel the shame all the more. / She is indeed not interested in excelling with her peers in feminine arts such as knitting her eyebrows or contriving her smiles. / In the women's world, her aspiration and knowledge should be deemed as the best" (32: 7).

In this passage, the male protagonist's perspective reveals that Tanhua's spirit of leadership among progressive women separates her from the self-centered modern girls represented by Gu Xuefen (古雪芬) and Hong Qingjiao (洪青椒). Tanhua's selflessness in serving society is clearly demonstrated by a female schoolmate's comments about her: "In the Women's World you are really devoted to public affairs, / sacrificing yourself and becoming famous for your work for the benefit of others; / the ill and impoverished local people have bathed in your grace and generosity. / Men can not compare to you in achievement; / despite being a woman you are sophisticated and worldly" (32: 11). Tanhua's devotion to curing the ill and supporting the poor conveys that she is no longer merely restrained by the elite class to which she was born, but finds a new social role by immersing herself with the working-class and the socially disadvantaged. Jiang's text, as the above passage shows, illustrates the moral importance of obtaining modern knowledge and Tanhua's exercise of personal knowledge for empowerment of others.

Jiang's depiction of Tanhua's character could be a form of self-reflection on the social activism of educated women during the New Culture Movement in the 1910s and 1920s, women who play a leadership role as agents of social change among the masses. The New Culture Movement was promoted by Chinese intellectuals who were disillusioned by the 1911 Revolution's failure to establish a strong modern nation-state. Preceding the May Fourth Movement in 1919, the New Culture Movement was launched with the publication of Chen Duxiu's essay, "Appeal to Youth," in 新青年 (*Xin qingnian*, New Youth) in 1915. In the essay, Chen states that Chinese civilization represents decay and conservatism. China fell behind the West because of the West's dynamism, science, and high ethical principles of democracy and socialism. Chen promotes Western values in the names of 德先生 (*De xiansheng,* Mr. Democracy) and 賽先生 (*Sai xiansheng,* Mr. Science) which represent two core values of the New Culture Movement. The movement was considered to be a reaction of a relatively small number of influential intellectuals to circumstances surrounding the presidency of the military lord Yuan Shikai. The May Fourth Movement, which took place a few years later, was a more activist political movement involving younger students and sought to appeal to different social groups (Zarrow 128-45). In this historical context, Tanhua represents a group of intellectuals who hope to rejuvenate Chinese culture by replacing some of China's "traditional" customs with "modern" Western literature and culture. Her experience of studying in the United States is reflective of certain progressive youth groups of the time who studied and returned to China and devoted themselves to the course of national reform.

The heroine's life trajectory refracts contemporary views of modernization and social progress. Judge states that in the early twentieth century, progressive male intellectuals "encouraged their female compatriots to follow Western women into linear, national, masculine time" (Judge, *Precious Raft* 14). Women's trajectory of leaving the backward China and studying in the West reflects such a linear model of historical progress. For a woman to travel overseas and devote herself to advocating for women's rights further represents a lofty sociopolitical ideal of the reformers. Particularly, feminism in republican China "was considered part of the universal truth and an indicator of a higher stage of civilization" because its adoption was seen as a "crucial strategy for China to accelerate the speed of evolution in its race against the West" (Wang, Zheng 358). Jiang's *tanci* demonstrates these progressive traits as well as the irruptions of the traditional into the progressive, showing the uneven temporalities of past and present characteristics of the era. Her career as a female doctor and her choice to save the masses from ailment and pain is reminiscent of Western-trained women doctors, including the famous female doctor Kang Aide (康愛德, 1873-1931), whom the late Qing reformist Liang Qichao (梁啟超, 1873-1929) highly praised (Liang, Qichao, "Ji Jiangxi kangnüshi"). An ensuing example is Yang Buwei (楊步偉, 1889-1981), the wife of the famous modern Chinese linguist Zhao Yuanren (趙元任, 1892-1982). Yang was the first modern Chinese woman who received a doctoral degree in medicine in the United States and had been a school principal and physician running her own clinic after studying in Japan before marrying Zhao (see Yang, Buwei).

In comparison with Tanhua, who develops a successful career after returning from overseas, Chaoying suffers the frustration of his personal ideals and gives in to his parents' marriage arrangement, since his ravenous wife and her dominant family determine whether or not he can secure a job in Shanghai. These characters' lives in cosmopolitan Shanghai reveal the modern individuals' frustrations, relapses, and feelings of alienation. The gender dynamics between the two main characters is palpably portrayed in Tanhua's two rejections of Chaoying's marriage proposals. When Chaoying first proposes marriage to Tanhua, she declines by stating her personal aspiration to further the cause of women's rights. She proclaims,

> Today women's rights are developing at the initial stage;
> faithfulness and generosity are the same principles everywhere in the globe.
> I heard that you have been formally engaged to the daughter of the Hong family in Moli;
> how could you, then, change your love and desert her?
> An ordinary woman like me has little education and could not be a good match for you.
> Let us then go our own ways and never force each other to change.
> It may show a high level of affection if you remain my teacher and friend.
> Keeping this pure intention all my life,
> I take an oath to stay single to return your affection for me. (13: 3)

The protofeminist initiative does not stand in contradiction to the conventions of chastity and loyalty, but endorses the rights of both modern and traditional women. Employing traditional moral principles and vowing to keep her virginity, Tanhua acquires both moral agency and the freedom to pursue knowledge and independence. The author mediates feminist initiative with traditional notions of chastity and faithfulness, arguing that, for Chaoying, to marry his fiancée will bring a familial happiness and please his mother, a way of fulfilling his duties as a son and a faithful husband. She herself would rather be a virgin for the rest of her life to return his favor toward her. When the amorous Chaoying vows to live a single life like Tanhua to keep their friendship, Tanhua, concerned about his lingering affections for her, uses the traditional notion of filial piety to persuade Chaoying to marry his fiancée Qingjiao to fulfill his parents' expectation of having a grandchild (13: 6).

The modern educated heroine, as this example suggests, displays much empathy toward traditional women. Putting herself in the place of Chaoying's fiancée, she ponders the risky situation into which she might put the fiancée, and she is aware that her personal freedom may endanger Chaoying's family solidarity. Had she given Chaoying her hand, "Using force to deprive her of the marriage would be truly base. / The two families will suffer from ocean-wide and irresolvable grievance. / If I could persuade Chaoying into changing his thoughts, / which will make the Zhen family full of happiness" (13: 8). Tanhua's character discloses a blending of traditional feminine virtues of chastity and filial piety with feminist thought. Jiang Yingqing's *tanci* passes along feminist potential through traditional moral principles of loyalty and empathy, showing that both the modern Chinese female citizen and China as a nation are products of mutual transformations of the local and the translocal. As a textbook author explains, the historical Chinese women served as "the past leaders of the new Chinese female citizen," while the "modern" Western heroines were a reflection of her "future image" (Judge, "Blended Wish Images" 105). Jiang Yingqing's presentation of the modern woman illustrates the tradition/modern binary, that is, "proponents of different agendas for the present and programs for the future found authority in different historical locations often in ways that defied ideological logic" (Judge, "Blended Wish Images" 132). Jiang's *tanci*, one may say, facilitates a re-imagination of femininity through epochal encounters between the historical and the present, between revolutionary love and customary responsibilities. Tanhua's refusal of Chaoying's first proposal might also be caused by her reluctance to be involved in a lawsuit over her romance with Chaoying, which could cause her to lose her innocent name (13: 9). At this period there were more divorce lawsuits in Shanghai, and in such cases the woman who was divorced was generally in a morally disadvantageous position. A *tanci* song by Jiang, "爱河波" ("*Aihe bo*," "Torrents in the River of Love") talks about a case in which a divorced woman regrets her choice (*Tanci kaipian ji* 48). Similar portrayals of divorced women's regrets can also be found in a silent film 情海重吻 (*Qinghai chongwen*, Oceans of Passion, Re-Kissing; 1928), in which a woman, after divorcing her husband, regrets her choice and remarries her ex-husband.

At the end of the story, when Chaoying finds out that he cannot live a harmonious life with Hong Qingjiao and divorces her, he meets Tanhua again after she has returned from abroad and is working as a principal of a local hospital in Shanghai. When Chaoying, his affection revived for Tanhua, proposes to her again, Tanhua chooses to decline by writing him a letter, stating her choice of a professional woman's life over marriage. She suggests his failed proposal is a sign that they shall not be married by fate. The letter describes an interface between past and present, between the way it could have been and the impossibility of a complicit reunion between them. Tanhua understands that Chaoying's proposal was made in the name of love, but it actually pushes her into fleeing this grimy and muddled world as soon as possible (32: 32). The text portrays the heroine's alienated and short-lived existence in a degenerated social circumstance, although she is morally intact and uncontaminated by the corrupted ways of modern life. She can not continue to work at the hospital, and finally leaves Shanghai for a life abroad. In the letter, she uses an archaic prosaic style to elevate her and Chaoying's emotions to a more universal level.

> When I recall those times when you could seize the chance and take action, heaven did not allow the unfitted union between us. This must make our intimate relationship become estranged, who have been close but separate from each other. Until now, when time and tide change, you say that we must be predestined on the "Stone of Three Lives"; I do not think that this is doable. Those who are blind to the current times are not wise, those who countervail heavenly ways are not blessed. As a gentleman, why should you make such a choice of the unwise and the unblessed? Alas, I am not the legendary beauty Bao Si whose charm fells a city, but you do have an avaricious heart as Han Emperor Guangwu who covets the land of the *Shu* after capturing the land of *Long*. Beware that one's beauty and talent both are tender flowers which may wither overnight. The romance between the talented scholar Han Zhong and the beautiful maid Ziyu, for example, ends with Ziyu's death of illness and dissipation of her spirit upon Han Zhong's return from a journey overseas. Looking into each other's face, we can not anticipate the day of reunion. Please do not be heart-broken and fall ill again. (32: 36)

The text is embedded with a proverb, "delong wangshu" (Coveting Shu After Conquering Long), alluding to Emperor Liu Xiu of the East Han (CE 25-220). During a conquest in AD 32, the emperor was said to give orders to his general upon conquest of the land of Long, "Now that we have conquered Long, go and acquire the land of Shu." The expression illustrates "having insatiable desires" (Fan 47: 17). The passage alludes to the legendary romance between Ziyu and Han Zhong. Ziyu is the daughter of the Wu emperor Fuchai who falls in love with a servant, Han Zhong. The emperor is enraged with their love affair and forbids her marriage with Han. The disheartened Ziyu dies of lovesickness. Years later, when Han Zhong returns from traveling overseas, Ziyu's spirit reappears and gives Han a pearl as gift. She passes along her greetings to the emperor by entering his dream. The empress hears about Ziyu's return and hurries out to embrace her, only to find her daughter's body evaporates like light smoke into the air. The allusion thus refers to young women who pass away at any early age (Gan 554-58). This letter displays a prominent degree of narrative agency ascribed to the female character by the author, telling the story from Tanhua's point of view. Through this letter Tanhua expresses her desire for freedom and social mobility, which will be impossible if she agrees to marry him. In contrast, Chaoying's inability to take effective action and break away from the yokes of his family is the ultimate reason for their separation. His proposal goes against the tides of life and the world.

The reference to 三生石 (*sanshengshi*, Stone of Three Lives) evokes archaic feelings of friendship and destiny, rather than love and desire. The "Stone of Three Lives" alludes to the Tang dynasty monk Yuanguan (圓觀). While taking a walk near Yangzi River with his friend Li Yuan, they see a pregnant woman who is carrying water from the river along with other women. Yuanguan weeps at the sight and tells Li that he will pass away soon and be reborn as the son of this pregnant woman, and that twelve years later, he will become a shepherd, and reunite with Li in the Tianzhu Temple in Hangzhou. That night, Yuanguan passes away. Three days later, Li visits the pregnant woman and sees that the baby is born as predicted; the baby smiles at Li as if recognizing his face. Twelve years later, Li visits the temple in Hangzhou and meets with the reincarnated Yuanguan as foretold. To commemorate Yuanguan, who predicts his three lives after death, people name a stone near the Tianzhu Temple as the Stone of Three Lives. Legend has it that Li Yuan and Yuanguan meet each other near this stone (Yuan Jiao 831). The text unveils Tanhua's determination to defy the circle of destiny and to imagine a new life in a new era and a new worldly order. The ensuing lines are stylistically akin to poetic responses between traditional courtesan poets and their literati friends, indicating that she does not desire love from him. The passage emphasizes the ironic distance between the two, indicating that the parted paths of the two make the reunion unattainable. The language, form, and content of the letter insinuate Tanhua's propriety and determination, articulating adroitly her determination to pursue autonomy through the fictional personae of a traditional talented woman.

Tanhua's final journey abroad implies she may live an independent life outside familial and social boundaries, a vanguard life outside marriage. In comparison to traditional women characters in earlier *tanci*, who resort to cross-dressing and even death to flee from imposed marriage arrangements, Tanhua's decision is open and public. In the context of early twentieth-century women's social activism, Tanhua's choice also reflects a form of self-sacrifice for the course of women's emancipation. A 1919 essay asserts that "to be in the vanguard of women's emancipation requires self-sacrifice." The author appeals for recruiting the vanguard comrades and those who are determined to remain single (Zhang Ruoming 197-206). To live a single life, for Zhang, opens up a space for women's individual and social agency.

Such forms of social understanding and advocacy, though provoking and controversial, were manifested widely in numerous debates about women's right to stay single and is strongly endorsed by the author in Jiang's *tanci.* The narrator applauds Tanhua's choice of a single life. "Her single life breaks the diurnal dream of love; / her unrivalled beauty refuses to be tainted. / Even when the rocks collapse and the sea dries up, / her admirable story will be passed along in people's words / and shall reverberate on the strings of *pipa* for a thousand years" (32: 37). As this ending shows, women's celibacy in Jiang's *tanci* is presented as a suitable alternative to marriage and vows of love. Hence, Tanhua berates those who force upon her a life not based on her profession and social aspirations.

The question of modern women's celibacy was extensively discussed in newspapers and media in 1920s Shanghai. Modern critics carried out a series of journalistic debates on women's celibacy and its relation to modern society, the traditional family system, and civilization. Jiang's contemporary, social critic Zhou Jianren (周建人), reviewed three kinds of social discourses about women's celibacy (Zhou Jianren 7-15). The first school is 善種學者 (*Shanzhong xuezhe,* the Eugenics School), which upholds women's inborn responsibility to give birth and cultivate excellent descendants. The second is 禁欲主義 (*Jinyu zhuyi,* the Asceticism School), which respects women's virginity and regards sexual desire as impure and undesirable. The third category is 自發的獨身 (*zifa de dushen,* self-chosen celibacy), in which the woman makes a self-conscious choice to be single, due to lack of time, strong devotion to study or work, lack of an ideal match, or failure in a former relationship. Zhou empathizes with women's disadvantaged social and economic status and argues that, because women have always been regarded as a form of commodity, a woman's value must be attached to a husband and manifested through her marriage. Consequently, a woman rarely has the opportunity to choose a single life. Zhou agrees that women of the elite social class, who have received education and can live outside marriage, display both the progression of the society and resistance to the old constrictive family system ("Zhongguo nüzi" 7-15). Another critic, Kong Xiangwo (孔襄我), held that absolute celibacy, in the case of those who resist marriage from the beginning, reduces the pleasure of life, causes a lack of moral restrictions on sexual behaviors, and ultimately results in the regression of the society (Kong 10-11).

Many critics were strongly supportive of women living a single life. In 1922, Youtong (友彤) translated an essay by a Japanese scholar who discussed why the famous Swedish educator and activist Madame Ellen Key advocated celibacy through her own personal example (Youtong 12-15). The Japanese scholar proposes that Ellen Key possibly did not marry due to her religious devotion to Christianity. Rather, she finally becomes not just a mother to a few children, but "the mother of the tens and thousands of people in the world" (Youtong 15). The author suggests that women who live by their will and their beliefs like Ellen Key should all live with passion as she did. Wei Ruzhi (魏如芝) alludes to the ancient story of the "Infant of Northern Palace" who would decline marriage and devote her whole life to taking care of her parents. Wei, in his discussion of women's celibacy and its relation with family and society, by including real examples from women and their friends, provides a powerful argument that living a single life is largely beneficial to the welfare of society and the nation, and hence should be endorsed and strongly encouraged (Wei Ruzhi 25-28). These debates on women's celibacy during Jiang's time provide a historically situated perspective for the current discussion of the celibate heroine in Jiang's *tanci*. Tanhua's rejection of marriage is imbued with nascent meanings in the historical context of women's awakening and is increasingly supported by public activism in the 1920s. A real historical example of single women in Jiang's time is Lü Bicheng (吕碧城, 1883-1943). Lü was a poet, the first female journalist in China, and the principal of Beiyang Women's Public School. Her achievement in literature, business, and political activism was so outstanding that her husband-to-be broke his engagement with her because her excellence had exceeded the rank of her fiancé's family. Having lived a single woman's life, Lü traveled to Europe. During World War I, she returned to China and took to Buddhism for spiritual self-comfort. Lü's life reveals that an intellectually accomplished woman in the republican period still suffered extensive constraints from social reality (Fong, Qian, and Zurndorfer, *Beyond Traditions* 12-60). Even the male protagonist Chaoying, after being turned down by Tanhua, admires her political aspiration and thinks of emulating her deeds.

Tanhua's role as a single and professional woman also provokes further study of journalistic debates about Chinese women's return home in the 1930s. In 1934, Liu Meijun published an essay in the leftist journal *Nüsheng* (Women's Voice), in which she counters the position that women should return home to increase the percentage of sound marriages and the healthy birth of a new population, and that professional women should be completely rescinded so that men who are out of work can be given better employment opportunities (Liu Meijun 6). Liu criticizes such opinions as objectifying women and limiting their social value to their ability of giving birth at a time of war and national turmoil. Similar debates have appeared in other journals such as 玲瓏 (*Linglong,* 1936) and 新世界 (*Xinshijie*, Today's World, 1937), and 女青年 (*Nü qingnian*, Female Youth 1937), offering multivalent perspectives on professional women's personal choices between marriage and work, and how such choices were influenced by the national discourses on reform and modernization.

Tanhua's choice of devotion to social activism over marriage displays women's self-conscious exploration of new societal roles in a historical era of social and political activism. Although Tanhua has chosen to live a single life, she has devoted her knowledge and wisdom to the education of fellow women schoolmates and the benefit of disempowered women of lower social classes. A persuasive example in the text demonstrates how Tanhua helps her classmate Lin Daoyu (林道腴) solve a family dispute. Lin Daoyu's sister, Lin Daoxuan (林道瑄), is seduced by a libertine Gu Tan due to the corrupting influence of a female friend, Zhang Ouling (張藕玲), in the women's school. Daoyu and Daoxuan's father, ashamed by Daoxuan's deeds, suddenly leaves home. Their disheartened mother then attempts to commit suicide due to this family scandal. The desperate Daoyu hopes that Tanhua, her educated classmate, can mediate between her parents. The text offers a critical reflection of women's schools and suggests that, because the administrative system of such schools is not complete and mature, some women who merely attend the school to pursue fashion are not really well educated and can impose a negative influence on other female students. Through this example, the author offers a scathing criticism of those who have acted wrongly in the name of advocating 新女界 (*xin nüjie,* new woman's world) (14: 12). Upon Daoyu's request, the benevolent Tanhua immediately visits Shanghai, helping Daoyu to comfort her aged parents and restore their confidence in Daoxuan's innocent nature, acting as a teacher, mentor, and adviser for other women. This chapter illustrates the amplification of Tanhua's character through the intimate conversation between Tanhua and Daoxuan. Tanhua's noble nature is set in sharp contrast with Daoxuan's misfortune and carelessness. Daoxuan's mother comments that the individual's moral achievement is dependent on her individual choice, and does not have a direct relationship with attending the women's school, a comment reminiscent of contemporary controversies about the negative influence of women's schools on social morality (15: 6). Chen Weike suggests that in late imperial Beijing, women used the girls' schools as stepping stones for "going public." When the education of women increasingly became a public concern in the early twentieth century, there were widespread debates about the value, means, and methods adopted in these women's schools (Chen Weike 107-44).

Tanhua's intelligence and feminine consciousness are also reflected in a scene in which she reads the Qing novel *The Dream of the Red Chamber* with Daoyu. Reading an early chapter in which the protagonist Jia Baoyu takes an oath to become a monk, Tanhua ponders that if no one had hindered Baoyu and he had been allowed to leave the secular world, the heroine Daiyu may not have had to suffer death from loss of love at the end of the story. Tanhua's interpretation of the novel creates a feminine perspective on reading traditional literature and exposes her consciousness of looking for an alternative outcome for the ill-fated heroine Daiyu, whose death is also a tragedy caused by her powerless social circumstances, which may be changed in a modern epoch.

Tanhua's endorsement of new women's social commitment is evidenced by her frequent contact with progressive male intellectuals. She openly meets male intellectuals at her house, showing a degree of openness for women's social activities. In one of their early meetings, Tanhua and Chaoying have a conversation about 新文學 (*xin wenxue,* New Literature). Chaoying, fluent in offering replies and criticism, impresses Tanhua with his knowledge and wisdom. Their mutual friend asks them to maintain communication to talk about questions related to literature and arts. The textual depiction of Chaoying, Tanhua, and their friends indicate that they are open-minded intellectuals who possibly have been influenced by the May Fourth Movement and the vernacular literature which had replaced the traditional 文言 (*wenyan,* classical Chinese text) since 1920 and led to a profound reform in literature and art. Chen Duxiu, a leading figure advocating New Literature, suggests that literature plays an instrumental role in transmitting ideas (Chen Duxiu, "Wenxue geming lun"). Likewise Hu Shi states that vernacular literature can be used as "a vehicle for new ideas and new mentalities" (Hu Shi 174; Cai).

In comparison with the hero's journey back from abroad, a return to the traditional and the local, Tanhua's itinerary from Hangzhou to the West represents a future-oriented journey toward the outside world in search of a society beyond the traditional and the local. While Tanhua represents the few educated women who could support themselves with work, many other women of lesser education or family wealth could not or would not follow the heroine's path toward living an independent life. While the text illustrates Tanhua's social and political ideals, it also implies clearly that in such a historical context, a modern woman's social roles and freedoms are inevitably contingent on her economic status. Tanhua's resistance to being objectified distinguishes her from many others and reflects her conscious search for an autonomous life beyond marriage. Jiang's *tanci* also portrays an antiheroine. Hong Qingjiao, Chaoying's wife, is a modern girl in Shanghai whose character reflects the commoditization of modern women and their lack of self-consciousness. As the antiheroine, Qingjiao is described with a moralistic tone of voice by the narrator, representing the negative, alienating effect of modernization on women.

Tanhua's character as a modern woman committed to social activism evokes questions about the socioeconomic conditions that underpin women's choices concerning love, marriage, and work in the republican era. In his essay, "What Happens After Nora Leaves Home?" Lu Xun, commenting on Ibsen's famous play, argues that the core question for women who seek to live outside marriage is economic rights, which are central to their true social freedom. "There must be a fair sharing out between men and women in the family; second, men and women must have equal rights in society" (Lu 151). A discussion of women's economic status and the marriage system can be found in a 1930 article "New and Old Merchandise vs. New and Old Women," in which the author proposes that women who have been liberated from the dangers of abduction, seduction, and male manipulation must devote themselves to the reform of the commercial society for true self-liberation (Tao Xisheng 2-5). In Jiang's text, Chaoying's wife Qingjiao is such an example. In contrast with Tanhua's other-oriented character, Hong Qingjiao is a conceited, material-driven modern girl in Shanghai. Mrs. Hong's daughter is an illicit child whose father is the son of a fallen Qing official, a unique component of the dominant social class, many of whom were bankers and stockbrokers who dominated social economy. To the Hong family, Chaoying was erudite, handsome, and also genteel, a perfect match for their Qingjiao. Hong Qingjiao's character, reminiscent of the archetype of the modern girl, portrays a kind of modern woman who enjoys the comfort of modern life but cannot truly do away with old-fashioned habits. Before marriage, Qingjiao likes to go to the dancing halls, wear heavy make-up, and flirt with men of rich families. In the evening, she finds excuses to go out and lies to her parents, saying that she needs to take English classes. She loves the city life so much that she rejects the expectation to live with Chaoying's parents in Hangzhou (8: 6).

The difference between Hangzhou and Shanghai is one between a traditional city of pastoral beauty and a metropolis of modern expediency and glamour. This contrast also lays the ground for the social difference between the affluent Hong family and the traditional, middle-class family of Chaoying. Chaoying's father-in-law is concerned only with earning money and working at the trade union. The narrator describes the self-content of a bourgeois family that enjoys the conveniences of obtaining food and clothing in the urban city. Not only does Qingjiao demonstrate a condescending attitude to Chaoying, who comes from Hangzhou, but the pragmatic

Mrs. Hong also looks down on Chaoying's bookishness. Economically dependent on Qingjiao's family in Shanghai, Chaoying becomes conciliatory to his wife, since her family provides the house and the opportunity of a job in a bank in Shanghai.

The inevitable collision of the two different families takes place immediately when Chaoying and his mother arrive in Shanghai to meet Qingjiao at the railway station. Qingjiao is embarrassed by a fashionable young male playmate of hers, who, not knowing that she is now married, comes by and greets her in a teasing manner in front of her old-fashioned, foot-bound mother-in-law. Chaoying's mother is greatly offended by the sight of the flirtation and suspects that the matchmaker has lied to them, and that the daughter-in-law is not virtuous and has received little education. Afraid that her mother-in-law might accuse her of inappropriate manners and a lack of traditional virtue, Qingjiao takes a chance and plays the victim's role in front of Chaoying. She complains to Chaoying about his mother's suspicion, insisting on her own innocence. This unsettling event leads to the onset of a series of conflicts between Qingjiao and her mother-in-law, who eventually leaves Shanghai and returns to Hangzhou.

Chaoying's mother regrets forcing Chaoying into this marriage with Hong Qingjiao, who enjoys spending money and seeking entertainment outside everyday marriage (23: 10). The city of Shanghai, where urban materialism prevails, is portrayed as 銷金窟 (*xiaojinku,* a gold-melting cave), which contains endless temptations for a shallow and fun-loving young woman like Qingjiao (see Yeh). After the couple moves from Hangzhou to Shanghai, the dispute between them escalates. Qingjiao's subversive attitude is revealed in a monologue in which she defends her love for material comfort. "Since ancient times the beauties have been cared for in golden chambers; / who would care to appreciate the songs of the poor and lowly born? / You should not blame me for having little affection for a husband of meager fortune, / for since the ancient times, those women who were commemorated with memorial portals have only enjoyed their fame of chastity in vain." She ponders on her young lover, the son of a rich merchant, and prefers his effeminate looks and cleverness in pleasing women. Nonchalant with the bookish husband who refuses to go out and enjoy the urban night life, Qingjiao can only imagine the hustle and bustle of the modern theater, where "men and women are mingled and seated side by side; the waft of cologne and fragrance is ample to stir one's spirit" (26: 6). In the entertainment halls, "the crowd is wide as a sea, shoulder by shoulder, the couples are countless in number. Since men and women can socialize in public and have little restraint, they talk and laugh in high spirits." This conjured mental linkage between Qingjiao with the urban sites of entertainment, such as halls and theaters, reveals her aspirations for the urban space, which is a site of pleasure and freedom in comparison with her constraining household. In a *tanci* song, 遊夜花園 ("*You yehuayuan*," "A Tour of the Night Garden"), Jiang strongly disapproves of the morally corrupting forces of decadent modern entertainment sites and discourages youth from becoming addicted to such imprudent pleasure (*Tanci kaipian ji* 14-15).

Qingjiao's boredom and melancholy are symptomatic of the individual trapped in an increasingly congested modern society. Emblematic of the modern girl in cosmopolitan Shanghai, she is the self-centered petit bourgeois who brings about her own downfall by having an illicit love affair. Qingjiao is one of the petty urbanites of Shanghai, who were in flux throughout the period covered in Jiang's *tanci*. She is a fallen imperial official's illicit daughter, a fashion girl whose education does nothing but keep her fashionable, a shrewd wife who lingers in dancing halls and does not return home.

Qingjiao's character as the antiheroine is illustrated in the title picture in chapter 24; she is portrayed as a woman leaving the house, while the husband looks on, not daring to complain. Knowing that her husband is sick and already suspecting her unfaithfulness, she still stays overnight with her lover. Her actions cause Chaoying's health to further deteriorate and almost cost him his life. Chaoying has nothing to do but play *ngaa pai*, listen to the radio, or read the newspaper, which consists of nothing other than accounts of people running into debt during a time of chaos and disorder and miscellaneous reports of rape and abduction (24: 9). Chaoying sacrifices his desire to live in Hangzhou and moves to Shanghai for a profession, his life and work completely dependent on his wife's family connections. His personal tragedy is echoed by a group of his friends who are elite intellectuals educated abroad but who find it hard to adapt to the social reality at home. Even if his father-in-law's connection provides a good possibility for Chaoying to practice his knowledge, he finds it difficult to apply that knowledge to anything. The name of the hero, Zhen Chaoying, indicates a "truly exceptional intellect." The name is ironic, however, as the story later reveals that he cannot make his own decisions in marriage and career due to family constraints and a conventional mentality. The differences and conflicts between the Western-educated Chaoying and Qingjiao, a descendant of the local elite, portray a time when modern intellectuals are disempowered by local warlords, corrupted imperial officials, opportunist bankers, and entrepreneurs who collaborate and dictate the development of China's socio-economy.

In contrast to Chaoying's frustration with his cosmopolitan ideals in the local reality, Qingjiao's character represents the shrewd, resourceful, and calculating aspects of the petite bourgeoisie woman. When she and her lover Zhou Shaowen are found out at a Shanghai hotel and blackmailed by a gang of hooligans, she reacts with unusual calmness and composure. When her lover is horrified by the exposure and does not know how to respond to the situation, Qingjiao adeptly bargains with the blackmailing villains, settles upon the price the lover should pay to keep their affair secret, and finds her way out of the hotel without paying a penny herself. The text depicts a woman who is in full command of the situation and who plays diverse roles. To her female lawyer friend, she impersonates the victimized wife dominated by a tasteless and uncaring husband; to her parents she is the obedient and understanding daughter; to Chaoying, she pretends to be the attractive companion who, although spoiled and headstrong, still unveils some true feelings for him when he is fatally ill.

In her *tanci*, Jiang's exploration of Chaoying's domestic life portrays the characters in an interior landscape of the city, where profound changes have been brought upon traditional family relationships through the process of urbanization.

This controversy between the modern and the traditional is remarkably reflected in the afflicted relationship between Qingjiao and her mother-in-law, a woman bound by old traditions. When the mother blames the daughter-in-law for not taking good care of Chaoying, Qingjiao retorts, "[My mother,] your reproach is really far-fetched. Even though we are a couple resting in the same bed, how on earth could I know his mindset?" (34: 2). Traditional values of fidelity, filial devotion, and chastity have been completely dismantled. This scenario also recalls contemporary social controversies about modern women who neglect traditional family values and are seduced by the sounds and sights of urban life. An article in 1924, for example, portrays a group of modern girls as 紅粉骷髏 (*hongfen kulou,* rouged skeletons) who, fully dressed in silk gowns, flowery hats, shining diamonds, and precious stones, spend their days strolling in the hustling markets and theaters or playing *majiang* day and night. The author laments, "In such fragrant and intoxicating dreams, they do not know what human being is, and what personality means. Half drunk in the cradle of material desires, they squander time and waste money" (Pu Nong 7). Qingjiao is a woman who, uneducated and lacking self-consciousness, easily falls into the traps and temptations of urban society. The author's attitude is profoundly critical and disapproving of this character, and by extension, of the social trend of fully embracing modern civilization and abandoning traditional familial virtues.

Qingjiao's character may represent the Modern Girl archetype who is a "mirror-gazing woman seeking to find herself" (Qian Qianwu 226-36). Portrayed as a femme fatale character, she evokes the image of a praying mantis devouring a befuddled urban man. The Confucian framework is also largely reflected in the book. Even though the author advocates for women exploring social roles, she is critical of the corrupting force of modern civilization. Qingjiao is symbolic of the many "fallen women" in 1920s and 1930s Shanghai who enjoyed the pleasures and conveniences of modern life and who were seduced by playboys and suffered failed marriages. Qingjiao's relationship with her lover leads to the incident of blackmail that, in turn, brings her husband to bankruptcy; however, Qingjiao herself emerges unscathed. Her defiance against Chaoying causes the resurgence of his illness that almost takes his life. Qingjiao represents the dangerously desirable femme fatale, whereas Tanhua represents an introspective female subject searching for her identity. Such descriptions of transgressive women are reminiscent of what David Der-wei Wang notes as signs of emotive excess in late Qing fiction, which not only "include transgression or mismatching of different categories of emotions but also the trivialization or exaggeration of subjects and forms all out of proportion" (Wang, David Der-wei 38-41).

The text, in addition to the vivid depiction of the progressive Tanhua and the modern girl Qingjiao, portrays many minor women characters. In comparison with Tanhua's image, which is endowed with narrative centrality and power, these minor female characters contribute to the collective representation of womanhood and jointly reflect the polemical question of femininity, its multiple manifestations in ordinary women's daily lives, and the dialectical relation between individual agency and social contingency. The life stories of these ordinary women refract the ideals of modern womanhood and unravel the gaps between imagined freedom and unsurpassable constraints, between progressive visions and regressive social customs. Like Qingjiao, Gu Tan's sister Xuefen is a calculating and dominant character. In the house she commands her brother; she is shrewd and responsible for the conspiracy with her brother to seduce Tanhua. However, her cleverness never goes beyond scheming and plotting in ordinary affairs. Although she went to women's school, her personal ambition is never comparable to Tanhua's ideal. Xuefen's scheme with Gu Tan is driven mostly by a desire for Tanhua's money, unveiling the callousness in her nature. A new-fashioned girl, Xuefen smokes cigarettes, plays piano, reads the evening news, and passes her leisure time playing *majiang*. However, she is incapable of sympathizing with women at the grassroots level. When an elderly maid at their house falls down the stairs and is wounded, Xuefen, who dislikes the aged maid, fires her for her clumsiness even though the maid has faithfully served their family for decades. Xuefen also schemes to replace the old servant with a girl who has served at Tanhua's family home in a plot to seduce Tanhua into becoming her brother's wife. Xuefen, though having enjoyed the benefits of good family upbringing and the comforts of modern life, represents a character equally as apathetic and selfish as Qingjiao.

The matchmaker Wang Sansao, who assists Gu Tan in the seduction of Tanhua, is another striking minor character. In order to become close to Tanhua, she pretends to be interested in learning to read and write characters. Tanhua, unsuspicious of Wang's intentions, happily agrees to become her teacher. The matchmaker's character recalls a series of notorious figures in late imperial fiction who exercise morally corrupting influences on women in the inner chambers. Descriptions of morally corrupting matchmakers in late imperial fiction can be found in *The Golden Lotus*, *The Water Margin*, and Illustrous Words to Instruct the World. Wang's daughter A Nan (阿囡) is also a lively person. A young, clever girl, A Nan first catches Gu Tan's attention with her artfulness in hair styling. Clever and worldly, she helps her mother welcome Gu Tan. However, seeing that her mother is occupied with matchmaking for others, she laments the meager circumstances that she is in: "It is no good to be born in a low family, / no matter how busy one is, his efforts are all for others' good" (3: 9). Living on her mother's flower-selling business, A Nan can barely make afford daily expenses. Silk garments are not attainable for a nameless girl like her; the coarse and cheap clothing she must wear makes her lose face. Thinking of her marriage, not knowing where and to whom she will be wed, is a nearly unbearable grievance for her. A Nan's monologue makes clear the author's sympathetic feelings toward women born in lower social classes. Like many uneducated women who do not even have formal written names, A Nan thinks only of finding the ideal marriage as her destiny, demonstrating her ultimate value. Minor women characters such as Wang Sansao and A Nan portray women at the bottom of the social classes, bereft of the possibilities of receiving education or of becoming self-sufficient with work.

A similar example of an ill-fated female character is a young woman at women's school who is attracted by the frivolous Gu Tan and is pregnant with his child before marrying him. After Gu Tan dies of syphilis due to his degenerative lifestyle, she is overwhelmed with grief and dies, together with the unborn baby, in Tanhua's hospital. Gu Tan's character represents intractable backward social customs and sets off the protagonist Tanhua, who bespeaks the ideals of new womanhood which are constantly being challenged by the old societal and cultural order. While modern education advocates women's freedom, financial independence, and conscious thinking, to Gu Tan, such changes only make women more attractive sexual objects to satisfy male fantasies.

This historical discrepancy between the traditional and the modern contributes to prominent gaps of agency, that is, the gaps between women's ideal of exercising their rights and utilizing their options, and the actual national policy framework and social circumstances that frame and condition the individuals' households and everyday lives. Tanhua's choice to leave the hospital and travel abroad reflects the difficulty for professional women in finding a feasible social space for survival. Social debates about professional women from 1922 to 1926, when Jiang composed this *tanci*, were part of the process of breaking down the old culture and establishing the new culture. Women's work, importantly, is conditioned by class: those of poor families have to work with their hands at home or work in the fields to support family. Because of their lower social economic status at home and in society, they really do not have any freedom (Keshi 25). Similar concerns are prevalent in translated essays on women and career introduced from the West (see the essay by German critic Madame Hannah in Han Na 543-49). In 1921, activists also introduced to China the history of the International Women's Labor Union and its relations with Chinese women (Se Lu, "*Guoji funü*" 1-5). The socially and economically oppressed women, as another critic of the time held, are opposite to the capitalists who control the economic power of the society. The author criticizes the limitations of China's feminist scholars, who belong to the third class, drawing examples from the Geneva International Labor Conference in 1922 and the insufficient representation of lower-class women by the China group on that conference.

Social debates about women's working conditions in the 1920s provide evidence that the majority of women did not have access to professional positions due to limited education, family restraints, and lack of opportunities. This retrospection of feminist cultural history in 1920s China resonates with Joan W. Scott's argument that feminist history ideally aspires not only to uncover women in history, but to argue for the primacy of gender in the symbolic formations of culture and the political arrangements shaping social life (1053-75). A reading of Tanhua, Qingjiao, and minor women characters in *Fengliu zuiren* representing specific forms of femininity invites a redefinition of republican women's roles as important social agents. Women's agency could be "imagined as continuous with unreflective forms of power that are simply transmitted by culturally embedded subjects" (Anderson, Amanda 44). In the text, the multiple images of women, progressive and conservative, elite and uneducated, traditional or modern, are what Amanda Anderson calls the "culturally embedded subjects" in the influx of modern Chinese history. This pluralistic view of multiple and coexistent forms of femininity and the broad array of women as agents of social change challenge the use of antithetical and polarized terms in defining women's gender roles. The elite heroine Tanhua and the author Jiang Yingqing both act as agents of power who mediate for and speak through themselves of China's social transformation toward modernity. Correspondingly, these fictional stories transformed a traditional genre in order to make a discussion of women's social roles enter into the discourse of the day and become an object for thought.

Jiang's reconfiguration of the *tanci* genre brings to the fore the vexed relationship between the historical legacy of women's self-empowerment and contemporary discourses of women's liberation, social freedom, and gender equality, and elicits new understandings of womanhood and gendered ambiguity during this historical period. During the New Culture Movement, a main controversy was the relation between traditional or classical fiction and modern fiction. The former more often conveys moral messages inserted in poetic forms within the text, while the latter endeavors to convey emancipatory messages. Jiang's use of the *tanci* explores a problematization of the ostensibly different trends of the old and new. Readers may find the long-lasting tradition of didacticism in late imperial *tanci* fiction in the title of Jiang's work The Valiant and The Culprit which may refer to the contradictory characters, courageous Jia Tanhua and degenerated Gu Tan and Hong Qingjiao. The chapter titles foreshadow moral messages, endorsing the upright and denouncing the corrupted. The story, nonetheless, ends with Tanhua looking for a life of freedom abroad, suggesting modern women's endeavor to search for achievements in a wider social terrain outside marriage. The author conceives female mobility as a form of intellectual sovereignty beyond social and moral constraints. Besides revealing Jiang's legacy of traditional literature, the text's use of didactic titles may also reflect her concern about moral censorship or her conscious choice to meet editorial demands. This stylistic multiplicity once again directs the audience's gaze toward Jiang's re-adaptation of *tanci* to tell new stories of the modern era.

Jiang's use of the traditional narrative form *tanci* as a vessel to mediate and reconfigure nascent ideals of feminine political and social identity is not a unique case. An important precursory example is the *tanci* author Li Guiyu, who composed the voluminous *tanci Liuhuameng* (Dream of the Pomegranate Flower). Li's *tanci* extensively portrayed the theme of war, which, mediated through the allegory of bloodshedding, is evoked as a metaphor to convey the author's understanding of the emotional impact of love (Hu, Siao-chen, "War, Violence"). Another prominent female *tanci* author is the Shanghai-based Peng Liangjuan 彭靚娟 (nineteenth century), who authored 四雲亭 (*Siyunting*, The Pavilion of the Four Clouds; preface dated 1899). Peng's *tanci*, though also containing conventional narrative elements such as cross-dressing, polygamy, and talented and virtuous heroines, portrays multiple subplots of war, violence, tyranny, and exile, mirroring the imminent political crisis of late Qing society (Hu, Siao-chen, *Xin lixiang*).

Following these earlier trends, at the turn of the twentieth century, some progressive male authors also took to writing short *tanci* tales to depict Western heroines to enlighten their native female audience. Among the most memorable characters in these *tanci* stories are the Russian anarchist Sophia Perofskaya and the French revolutionary Madame Roland, both of whom were not only held up as exemplary feminine models in the late Qing press, but who were even featured as characters in short *tanci* stories. Florence Nightingale (1820-1910) was also emulated for her pioneering work in the nursing profession. Western women in these stories oftentimes appeared as super-heroines endowed with remarkable power for delivering the author's message against the patriarchal social system. In a *tanci* tale, *Yanzhixue* (Rouge Blood, by Zhou Shoujuan, 1908), the male author's Joan of Arc is modeled upon the legendary Mulan, who rises when the nation is in peril and commands thousands of male soldiers in the battlefield, with no one able to find out she is a woman. Similar *tanci* tales by men include Tale of a French Woman Hero (1904) by Wanlan ciren (挽瀾詞人), the pen name of Yu Chenglai (1881-1937), and Twentieth-Century *Tanci*: Light of Civilization in the Women's World (1911) by Zhong Xinqing. These male authors' tales of heroic Western women enriched Chinese women's conception of a universal womanhood and endeavored to cultivate women's political consciousness through the appropriation and modification of traditional *tanci*. The foreignness of these stories of Western women was addressed by native authors who applied traditional narrative strategies in Chinese vernacular fiction in their writing. These *tanci* envisioned an intersubjective relationship between native Chinese women and their Western counterparts, and renarrated stories of Western women as instructive stories for Chinese readers.

The late imperial and republican authors' efforts to renarrativize foreign heroines for the native audience, and to tell new stories with the old narrative form, suggest the enduring vitality of *tanci* during the process of China's transition toward modernity. Critic Jin Feng suggests that May Fourth writers forged an ambiguous relationship with popular fiction of the time. Many of them vigorously criticized popular literature and excluded works by popular writers from the canon of modern Chinese literature. However, the commercial success of popular fiction suggests that despite their vow to educate the masses, May Fourth intellectuals could not match the efforts of their lowbrow rivals in conveying the point of their narrative to a wider audience (Feng, Jin 17). Jiang's *tanci* poses an important question about the function of popular literature in the formation of modern Chinese literary tradition. Jiang's reinvigoration of traditional *tanci* in order to tell stories of new Chinese women creates a multivocal textual chorus between the old and the new, and extends the reception of new ideals of modern womanhood to audiences of popular literature. Jiang's New Woman is a medium-specific one; she is seen through the veil of the traditional; her predicated identity is none other than an emblem of the hybrid modern subjectivity.

Jiang's *tanci* facilitates the exploration of the interwar culture of consumption and spectacle by depicting women's experience of modern social transitions and by projecting ways of remaking themselves as historical and gendered subjects. The *tanci* provides a panoramic vision of women of diverse social classes, containing vivid depictions of the youthful, educated, and professional new modern women, and minor women characters who stand in stark contrast with the idealized heroine. These minor heroines include the illiterate housemaid, the calculating matchmaker, the daughter of imperial officials, traditional housewives, concubines hanging out in hotels, and spoiled daughters of the rich who rely on fashion, tabloids, and shopping to pass time. Jiang's representation of the Western-educated Tanhua, when set against this backdrop of 1920s Shanghai, appeals to her contemporary audiences even more strongly. The union of the *tanci* genre and Jiang's profound social criticism grinds a realistic fictional lens which refracts contemporary discourses of women, modernity, and nation, as well as the tensions between these discursive explorations. While the old moral system collapses and makes way for the establishment of a new order, Jiang's characters demonstrate individual men and women, who, in searching for a new form of social existence, negotiate the distance between private acts and public culture. Sarah E. Stevens makes a distinction between the New Woman and the Modern Girl in the republican period. She notes, "The New Woman represents a positive view of linear modernity and hopes for a strong future China. The Modern Girl manifests in two distinct ways: as a self-absorbed woman searching for subjectivity and as a dangerous femme fatale who devours the urban male" (Stevens 83). Stevens argues that these archetypes of femininity reflect distinctively different and often opposing types of modernity. In the text, Tanhua's character is approximate to the New Woman, who represents the necessary transformation of the nation toward modernity. Qingjiao, by contrast, is close to the Modern Girl femme fatale image. The New Woman archetype is one "of revolutionary nature, devotion to the larger cause of nationalism, and a search to find self-identity which is inevitably bracketed within the larger nationalistic struggle" (Stevens 83). This archetype, however, does not fully represent the author Jiang Yingqing, nor her heroine Jia Tanhua, each of whom represents the strong legacy of the late imperial *cainü* writers.

Specifically, Jiang writes from the position of a modern professional woman author, educator, and activist, as well as from that of an accomplished traditional poet. Her subjective position is different from the positions of leftist writers who rose to power after the May Fourth Movement. Nor does she belong to a cadre of decadent writers such as *Xin ganjue pai* (新感覺派), or the New Perceptionists who portray the Modern Girl in order to express male disillusionment with modernity and their fears of alienation that accompany the urban, cosmopolitan world. The New Perceptionists represents an important school of fiction in the late 1920s and 1930s. Representative writers of this trend include Liu Na'ou (劉吶鷗, 1900 1940), Shi Zhecun (施蟄存, 1905-2004), and Mu Shiying (穆時英, 1912-1940). These authors, following their forerunners in Japan, demonstrate interest in exploring Freudian concepts of the unconscious, the dreamwish, and death drive (Larson 70; Wu Lichang 195). Different from female images in leftist and realist writings in the 1920s and 1930s, Tanhua's image resonates more resolutely with primordial *tanci* heroines such as Meng Lijun whose freedom comes from personal decision-making against encaging social circumstances. Jiang chooses traditional *tanci* as a vehicle for the portrayal of women's epochal feelings and China's urbanization process. Among her peers, Jiang redefines the traditional identity of 才女 (*cainü,* a talented woman) to her own advantage. Even through the so-called *cainü* were often described as knowing nothing more than writing sentimental poetry, it was precisely the *cainü* type of woman who became most active in the political and educational reforms of the late Qing period (Qian, Fong, and Smith 9).

A favorable external condition for learned women's activism in the public sphere is the male intellectual's increasing need to witness the presence of women in the public sphere since the 1898 reform period. A pragmatic concern for the reformists is to encourage women to make their own living so that they would not burden the nation and be a cause of its continued backwardness (Qian, Fong, and Smith, *Different Worlds* 9). Any examination of the relation between gender and genre in the reform era must give attention to the lives and works of those women, both past and present, who were designated, or who identified themselves, as traditional *cainü* (9). This historical context underlies current study of Jiang Yingqing's public identity as a woman author of *tanci*, a poet, a head of a women's school, and an educational and social reformist. The protagonist Tanhua was born in Hangzhou, a city at the heart of the late imperial culture of talented women and home to the famous *tanci* author Chen Duansheng. Tanhua's life departs from this traditional cultural habitat to travel abroad, and then to the cosmopolitan city of Shanghai. Jiang Yingqing revisions Hangzhou as an environment which nourished a culture of talented women in the story space, and thus connects the textual representation of the modern heroine to precursory fictional and historical women in the same space. Likewise, Joan Judge points out that "the Chinese women question can be understood as the product of China's own distinct history" (Judge, *Precious Raft* 7). The "women question—how, or whether, to redefine female virtue, talent, and heroism within the modern world order—epitomizes the tensions between past and present, Chinese principles and Western practices, and Confucian ritual teachings and new ideas (*Precious Raft* 7). Judge and Fong's criticism share the common viewpoint that Chinese women's subjectivity needs to be grounded in China's specific social, cultural, and historical contexts. The discourse of *cainü wenhua* (才女文化), as an ongoing, expanding, and constantly changing narrative, has interpolated into the social, cultural codes about modern women's freedom, agency, and identity.

Jiang depicts women as historical and gendered subjects through a panoramic view of women of diverse social classes, including professional women, an illiterate housemaid, and a calculating matchmaker, in addition to housewives, concubines, and fashion girls. In comparison with Tanhua's character, which is endowed with narrative centrality, minor women characters expose the polemical question of femininity and its multiple manifestations in ordinary women's lives. Jiang's modern woman, veiled in a traditional narrative medium, is an emblem of the hybrid modern subjectivity. The modern woman is an agent of social enlightenment, the one who is destined to liberate the many from the obscurity of themselves. Jiang's representation of the female national citizen opens up new transformative possibilities of women's agency and displays a vigilant search for a bottom-up solution for the meshing and reconciliation of women's personal subjectivity and their nationalistic ambition. The open ending of the heroine traveling overseas implies that the author might have directed her gaze toward searching for women's agency in transnational spheres outside China.

In conclusion, Jiang's portrayal of Jia Tanhua draws attention to the question of women's self-making and social agency, which is subjected to multiple social and historical discourses that are "different, changing . . . and even antipathetic to each other" (Dissanayake 10). The author's exploitation of modern print media to create a space for self-expression distinguishes her from earlier *tanci* writers, and transforms the traditional narrative genre of *tanci* into a form of profound social inquiry into women's careers, marriage, and social emancipation. Tanhua's pursuit of an independent life outside the family articulates an aspect of women's agency that is shared by contemporary women's activism, that is, that the formation of women's selfhood is shaped by their immediate historical and social conditions, and that women's social and political agency reflects their strategic self-making in response to such social conditions. Jiang's heroine Tanhua represents an ideal of individual agency achieved through her social commitment, self-sacrifice, and strategic identification with modern citizenship. Simultaneously, the author's exploration of multiple female subjectivities in the traditional *tanci* demonstrates proliferating understandings of modern womanhood, the possible linkages between feminist social activism instigated by the May Fourth cultural movement, and the foregoing late imperial protofeminist thinking. As Lydia Liu points out, "It is the incongruities, tensions, and struggles between selfhood and national identity, as well as their mutual implication and complicity, that give full meaning to the lived experience of Chinese modernity" (Liu, Lydia 10). The contrast, complexity, and coexistence of multiple female subjectivities in Jiang's *tanci*, as illustrated in this chapter, signal the contention and complicity of social discourses that influence and situate the various roles that individual women subsume. The vanguard heroine mirrors the author's understanding of female social mobility which lies beyond domestic spheres, and remains exempt from complete dependency on the master narratives of the nation and state in republican China.

Conclusion

This study reviewed five novel-length *tanci* works to highlight the theoretical themes in these narratives, including cross-dressing, portraits and self-portraits, authorial insertions, empathetic identification, and gendered citizenship. These narrative features link the genre of *tanci* to late imperial Chinese literature of other genres, manifesting women authors' strategic appropriation and reinvention of traditional narrative motifs for the sake of self-empowerment. Probing into selected *tanci* texts from the late imperial to the early twentieth century from a historically situated perspective, this book avoids imposing preconceived historical or genealogical structures onto the development of this evolving narrative form that have been co-opted by the authors of the five *tanci*. *Tanci* incorporates common features and gives expression to many key elements in women's writings in other genres such as poetry, fiction, drama, and travel accounts. Though this narrative form yields possibilities for women's freer expression in speech, women authors of *tanci* inexorably encountered the same historical and social norms as women writers of other genres. Instead of seeking to make a genre-based claim about women's expressed desires for a greater degree of agency, this book project endeavors to showcase the same anxieties, challenges, and yearnings for self-expression that *tanci* authors shared with late imperial women authors of other genres. The current project, therefore, seeks to contribute to a historically situated understanding of women's writing conditions in late imperial China.

The chapters of this book project the ongoing process in which *tanci* authors envisioned new forms of female subjectivities over the last three centuries. The first two chapters on *tanci* novels *Zaishengyuan* and *Bishenghua* considered the scenario of cross-dressing, which, in the fictional realm, both liberates women and allows them to explore the largely male social territory outside, and represents these disguised heroines as male substitutes whose agency is often limited and transitory. In chapter 1, my analysis considered the classic *tanci* work *Zaishengyuan* (Destiny of Rebirth) by the eighteenth-century author Chen Duansheng, and discussed the themes of self-portrait, cross-dressing, and authorial voice in this work. I compared two scenes in which the protagonist looks at her own image in the mirror, before and after she cross-dresses as a man. These textual examples show that in the fictional sphere, cross-dressing empowers the protagonist to pursue a life of autonomy outside the inner quarters and to explore her life as the equal of men in the social space. Lijun's subversive act challenges the Confucian ideological codes on women's gender roles and inspires women readers to conceive of an unconventional lifestyle. However, the author's appropriation of the cult of virtue and chastity also led to controversies among conservative readers, some of whom strongly disapproved of Lijun's unconventional acts, especially her refusal to revert back to a woman's life at the end. The author's dilemma in concluding the work reflects the incommensurable distance between the author's progressive vision of women's social autonomy and the unsympathetic social climate that constrained women's choices for alternatives outside the inner quarters.

Cross-dressing in Chen's *tanci* surfaces both as a central plot and a cause for narrative dilemma, as the cross-dressed woman inexorably faces the disclosure of her true identity and the pressure of marriage. In a later *tanci* by Qiu Xinru, *Bishenghua* (Blossom from the Brush), the author balances her narrative responsibility and the cross-dressed heroine's moral dilemma by resorting to supernatural elements, such as the fox spirit who synchronizes the heroine's transformation into a male identity, and the motif of female immortals who indicate an imaginative alternative for the traditional *tanci* tale. Despite this usage of the fantastic narrative, Qiu's claimed purpose is didactic, seeking to exempt the heroine Dehua from direct conflict with conventional social and familial relationships. Qiu's arrangement for Dehua to return to the inner chambers indicates a cautious reconceptualization of the domestic sphere as a space of female authority within the orthodox social system. Though Dehua's disguise as a man is exposed, the narrative itself proceeds and constructs a moralistic vision of feminine agency via negotiation with orthodox social systems. This moralistic imperative serves as an ancillary cover for authorial jurisdiction over women's pursuit of freedom and autonomy beyond social norms.

Such inspirational themes of authorial maneuvering and negotiation with moral and ethical principals constitute an important part of chapters 3 and 4, in which I explored the relationships between women's *tanci,* authorial ethics, visual representation, and orthodox discourses about feminine virtue. Author Chen Duansheng's anxiety about women's social space finds resonance in another *tanci* work: *Mengyingyuan* (Dream, Image, Destiny). This *tanci*, published a century after Chen's *Zaishengyuan*, shows a similar pursuit of a space for self-expression. My analysis of this *tanci* discussed how authorial insertions in the text establish a feminine voice, which invites the readers to establish a sympathetic relationship with the author. In her authorial statements, Zheng reflects on the difficulties of writing and her hardship in finding appreciative audiences. These difficulties further emphasize the social and ideological constraints on women's speech and writing activities during the period, which also resonated in the confessions and grievances of precursory women authors who suffered analogous hardships in writing and publishing their works. I proposed that Zheng's reflection on the ethical issues in writing reveals late imperial women authors' shared anxiety for bringing forth a voice that truly can speak for women writers and readers of the time.

Zheng Danruo's moralizing emphasis on feminine virtue and chastity is an effort to revise the male elite literati's discourses on feminine virtue. Her innovative interpretation of women's virtue might be oriented toward the female reading public of the time, many of whom had been under the influence of the prevailing social discourses about women's ethical duties. These abundant authorial insertions in Zheng's *tanci* provide evidence that Zheng's work appropriates and revises literati's discourses about feminine virtue to bring forth the author's distinctive voice. This voice expresses the writer's grievances against injustice and appeals to the readers' sympathetic identification with the narrator and the fictional character. The prevalent use of the first-person "I" in these authorial insertions further calls attention to the woman author's presence and self-construction in *tanci*. Compared with the cross-dressed Lijun, who is reborn with a new social identity by disguising herself as a man, Zheng justifies her literary authorship by appropriating elite discourses of virtue to validate her own purpose in writing. This authorial voice also finds enrichment in a dialogic relationship with the readers of the text, many of whom sympathize with the author about women's difficulty in acquiring social acknowledgement for their literary achievements. Unlike Destiny of Rebirth, Zheng's *tanci* concludes with the happy reunion of the flower goddesses, reincarnated in the immortal world. This utopian vision, however, is in stark contrast with the author's tragic personal life. Her suicide in the Taiping Rebellion serves to underscore the fact that space for a woman author was not yet obtainable in such a political and social climate.

Chapter 4 investigated the visual space in *Mengyingyuan* and discussed how literary portraiture in the text invites the reader to sympathize with the women characters and to establish an emotive association with the fictional women in the diegesis. Portraits of women in *tanci* invite reader sympathy and literally depict alternate possibilities for the self-actualization of women in the late imperial period. This chapter compared the presentation of women in portraiture by literati intellectuals with women's own tradition of making and writing about portraits. Zheng's text enriches traditions of portraiture; she presents the painted woman's power to interact with the viewers and to elicit sympathetic identification from them. In Zheng's text, women characters make portraits to display their resistance to marriage, their filial devotion to parents, and the preservation of their virginity. This gendered perspective underlying the portraiture of women draws attention to the fictional characters as empowered subjects who employ paintings to tell stories of filial devotion and chastity. Such a gendered perspective also evokes a sympathetic relationship with the women readers in the inner quarters of the time as well as with readers in the contemporary period. Readers interact and sympathize with the fictional women and are invited to explore their own places in the story's diegesis. Zheng's transformation of the portrait conventions makes an important contribution to the tradition of *tanci* and late imperial literature, drawing attention to the intense moral implications of women's painted images and their potential power to question and reconfigure dominant social discourses about womanhood.

The last two chapters study the tropes of itinerant women in modern *tanci* novels. I expanded the scope of study on women's *tanci* fiction into the early twentieth century, and offered enquiry on two long *tanci* works that inherit and resuscinate the narrative tradition of late imperial *tanci* in a modern historical context. First, chapter 5 revisited the tradition of women's cross-dressing in a 1905 text, *Xianü qunying shi* (A History of Women Warriors). Echoing previous discussions of the progressive potential of women cross-dressers, I considered multiple examples of cross-dressed women in this text, comparing its presentation of cross-dressing with precursor narratives about women disguised as men in *tanci* and other late imperial literature. In contrast with the cross-dressed heroines in the previous *tanci* works, most of the women cross-dressers in this later *tanci* do not revert back to their feminine identity, but continue to conduct their lives as men's social equals. These women's actions show the authors' reconfigurations of the Confucian ethical discourses about women's virtue and chastity. In the text, cross-dressers are depicted as heroic scholars and warriors who support the good, punish the evil, and rescue the country at times of national crisis. In their private lives, cross-dressed women manage to marry other women and are sometimes married to more than one wife. Their former male fiancés are depicted as "male widows" who wait for the cross-dressers' return in vain. Such a reconception of the gender hierarchy suggests that cross-dressed women of the time might have enjoyed more social tolerance to exercise their social and political power. The text also carries rich examples of homoerotic sensitivities between cross-dressers and other women, who may or may not be aware of the cross-dressers' real sexuality. The women's same-sex desire as depicted in this text resonates with similar scenes in previous *tanci*. In all, cross dressing and women's homoeroticism as protofeminist traits in late imperial women's writings critically reflect on their emancipating potentials (on late Qing women's same-sex love, see Xu Ke 38: 114).

The last chapter of the book explored the theme of female citizenship during the interwar period in Shanghai represented in *Fengliu zuiren* (The Valiant and the Culprit), written by professional female writer Jiang Yingqing. Jiang used the traditional *tanci* as a narrative vessel to construct new ideals of female citizenship during the interwar period. In her *tanci*, Jiang took on the relation between women and nation as a pivotal theme to reimagine modern women's social and political agency. Late Qing reformists, nationalists, and Social Darwinist scholars considered women's liberation to be an integral part of China's national reform and rejuvenation. Jiang's *tanci* invites an important reflection of these elite discourses on women's liberation and social identity and suggests that women's emancipation should be achieved through constructive relationships with one's self, community, and nation. Jiang's heroine Jia Tanhua, who is a social activist and reformer, commits herself to educating fellow women and promoting the rights of lower-class women. Like the feminist revolutionist Qiu Jin, who escaped the yokes of family and went to Japan to study, Tanhua travels to the United States to pursue knowledge after turning down the male protagonist's marriage proposal. Tanhua's political zeal and nationalistic passion fortify her social and political agency. Also, the author presents women's agency by constructing a pluralistic vision of women's gender roles. Her women characters, progressive or traditional, collectively illustrate the lives and aspirations of women as culturally embedded subjects in the flux of modern Chinese history.

The authorial introspection and self-reflection embedded within all of these texts are of women who proclaimed their competence to write in the male-dominated literary terrain. These authors' dilemmas and anxieties about writing are a possible reason for the unfinished quality of many *tanci.* The unfinished works offer textual margins, that is, conceptual areas which have been exiled from the center, and which invite readers to actively participate in continuing the narrative. In this space of the marginalia resides the nexus of reciprocating interpretation and communicative reproduction. Each *tanci* author assumes the role of a historian who not only cultivates appreciative readers of her work, but also leads the readers toward self-empowerment by disrupting extant narratives and by inviting them to live tales of their own.

Contextualized reading calls for a critical assessment of the oral traditions that nurtured the development of *tanci* in its beginning stage and of the literary writings by late imperial women authors which reflect women's shared hardship in partaking in literary activities. Also, contextualized study of *tanci* includes an overall review of the relation between *tanci* and the canonical literatures by male literati writers. The dialogue between *tanci* and these multifarious literary traditions and cultures contributes to a situated understanding of the literary status of this unique genre. A situated reading of *tanci* encompasses a social and historical study of women's gender roles in the patriarchal Confucian society. Social and ideological discourses about women's virtue and chastity constrained women's intellectual pursuits and restricted them to the domestic space. Such social and historical background lay behind women authors' anxiety to search for a space of self-expression through literary endeavors. Reading late imperial protofeminist stories in a contemporary context, specifically, requires a critical assessment of one's own critical language in writing and presenting these women authors and texts. The meanings of these pre-twentieth-century and early modern works are contingent upon specific social and cultural landscapes as well as the historical negotiation and inscription by women of their social presence. The contents of these texts express universal concerns of women regarding agency, autonomy, freedom, and self-expression, which are themes of enduring importance in feminist studies of contemporary materials in a range of cultural contexts.

Currently *tanci* works are extant in hand-copied editions, letterpress editions, engraved wood block editions, lead print editions, and lithographical editions. The theme of visuality in *tanci* texts demands exploration, especially by comparing and analyzing the different editions of illustrated *tanci* works in relation to the development of the printing technology of the late imperial period since the Ming dynasty. Classic *tanci* works such as Destiny of Rebirth; Dream, Image, Destiny; and Blossom from the Brush were usually published with woodblock illustrations depicting important scenes from the texts. These illustrations, inserted at the beginning of each chapter, provide evidence for the interconnectedness of *tanci* narratives and the Ming-Qing publishing enterprise, and the complex mechanism of readerly reception as affected by the correlations among literary texts, art, and print culture of the time. The nineteenth century also saw the advance of new printing technology (the mechanized lithographic press) in China, especially in Shanghai. This new technology led to more modern printing of *tanci* works in the late nineteenth and early twentieth centuries. A diachronic study of the various editions of the same *tanci* work could lead to valuable discoveries about the circulation of *tanci* among audiences across various historical periods.

Two other topics regarding *tanci* could be of import. One is the relation between protofeminist *tanci* stories and women's presses in early twentieth-century China. These progressive *tanci* works evolved from traditional *tanci* writings under the influence of modernization and the introduction of Western literature in translation. *Tanci* writers in the early twentieth century resorted to this traditional genre to advocate for women's enlightenment and education. Many such stories were published or cited in women's journals and magazines and thus were circulated to a wide audience. Several of these stories also reflect an aspiration toward an idealized womanhood inspired by women heroes in Europe and America and suggest a desire to achieve a spiritual solidarity with Western women peers. A study of these *tanci* stories may enrich the current study in Chinese women's social mobility and their desire for social change at a period of historical transition. Another meaningful research topic is related to the use of technology in disseminating traditional literary texts. In the late 1920s, with the introduction of the radio industry in the southern areas of China, especially in the cities of Shanghai, Suzhou, and Hangzhou, many *tanci* were adapted for radio programs and gained wide popularity among local audiences. These broadcasted *tanci* stories and introductory songs, thanks to the popularization of electronic media, consolidated their traditional readership and gained access to audiences in a wide range of social classes and geographical locations. The use of technology in the dissemination of *tanci* elicits questions about the expanded roles of the audience, who would not only be listeners or readers of the text, but also be inspired to sing and perform these narratives after hearing them on the radio. The expansion of the audience's roles would demand an enriched critical understanding of the literary, social, and cultural values of *tanci* narratives as they continuously evolve through shifting societal contexts. This ongoing evolution of *tanci* narratives provides an even greater impetus for critical evaluation of them as protofeminist works that broaden and deepen contemporary feminism's calls for greater empowerment of women in the global context.

Appendix

Chinese Characters for Authors' Names, Terms, and Titles of Works

This appendix offers a list of Chinese characters for the *pinyin* used in the manuscript in reference to authors' names, terms, and titles of works in Chinese. The purpose of this appendix is to assist readers and researchers to identify the original sources in Chinese, as well as names and terms in the book.

"Aihe bo" "愛河波"
"Baimei tu" "百美圖"
"Bingta de huigu" "病榻的回顧"
"Cainü shuo" "才女說"
"Ci shuxiang qinü shi" "辭蜀相妻女詩"
"Ciniao wangbu tu" "慈鳥望哺圖"
"Hongxiu tianxiang tu" "紅袖添香圖"
"Manjianghong" "滿江紅"
"Modeng nülang tan" "摩登女郎嘆"
"Shinian qian zhi wo" "十年前之我"
"Siyu" "私語"
"Suiyuan hulou qingye tu" "隨園湖樓請業圖"
"Tianwen" "天問"
"Tongxinshuo" "童心說"
"Xin xiaozi tu" "心孝子圖"
"Yinjiu dusao" "飲酒讀騷"
"You yehuayuan" "遊夜花園"
"Zixiao" "自笑"

A Nan 阿囡
Anbang zhi 安邦誌

baihuaban 百花班
Ban Biao 班彪
Ban Gu 班固
Ban Zhao 班昭
bei 悲
beigong ying 北宮嬰
beiruo 卑弱
Bihua xianshi 碧華仙史
Bimei Shuji 彼美淑姬
Bishenghua 筆生花
Bo Ya 伯牙

Cai Wenji 蔡文姬
cainü 才女
cainü wenhua 才女文化
caizi jiaren 才子佳人
Cao Xueqin 曹雪芹
Cao Yanniang 曹燕娘
Chen Changsheng 陳長生
Chen Duansheng 陳端生
Chen Fangsu 陳芳素
Chen Tongxun 陳同勛
Chen Wenshu 陳文述

Chen Wulou 陳午樓
Chen Xiefen 陳擷芬
Chen Yudun 陳玉敦
Chen Yuechan 陳月嬋
Chen Yun 陳雲
Chen Zhaolun 陳兆倫
Chen Zhensun 陳振孫
Chen Zuotong 陳佐彤
chizi zhi xin 赤子之心
Chu Chunyi 楚春漪
Chu Tinghui 楚廷輝
Chu Yuanfang 楚元方
chuanqi 傳奇
Chuci 楚辭
chuixiao yinfeng 吹簫引鳳
ci 詞

Daoguang 道光
De xiansheng 德先生
Delong wangshu 得隴望蜀
dianjing 點睛
Du Lanxiang 杜蘭香
Du Liniang 杜麗娘

Ershi shiji nüjie wenmingdeng tanci 二十世紀女界文明燈彈詞
Ershinian mudu zhi guai xianzhuang 二十年目睹之怪現狀
Ershiyi shi tanci 二十一史彈詞

Faguo nüyingxiong tanci 法國女英雄彈詞
Fan Tan 范菼
Fang Wanyi 方婉儀
Feng Menglong 馮夢龍
Feng Xiaoqing 馮小青
Fengliu Zuiren 風流罪人
Fengshen yanyi 封神演義
Fengshuangfei 鳳雙飛
fude 婦德
fugong 婦工
furong 婦容
Furong Zhuren 芙蓉主人
fuyan 婦言

Gan Bao 干寶
ganying 感應
Gao Yandi 高延第
gezhong ren 個中人
Gu Taiqing 顧太清
Gu Tan 古檀
Gu Xuefen 古雪芬
Guanju 關雎
Guanzi 管子
Gui Hengkui 桂恒魁
guikun 閨閫
guishu shi 閨塾師
guiwei 閨闈
guixiu 閨秀
Guiyuanshi 閨怨詩

Han Zigao 韓子高
Han Ziying 韓紫瑛
Hangzhou 杭州
Hanshu 漢書
Hong Qingjiao 洪青椒
hongfen kulou 紅粉骷髏
Hongloumeng 紅樓夢
Hou Zhi 侯芝
Hu Yuexian 胡月仙
huaben 話本
Huai'An 淮安
Huang Chonggu 黃崇嘏
Huang Shancong 黃善聰
Huang Yuanjie 黃媛介
Huangfu Shaohua 皇甫少華
Huangfu Zhanghua 皇甫長華
huanlei 還淚
Huazhongren 畫中人
hui 回
Huishengge ji 繪聲閣集
Huiyingge ji 繪影閣集
Huizui zhi dalue 悔罪之大略

Jia Baoyu 賈寶玉
Jia Tanhua 賈曇花
Jia Yucun 賈雨村
Jiajing 嘉靖
Jiang Dehua 姜德華
Jiang Jinren 姜近仁
Jiang Jisheng 姜繼生
Jiang Jixiu 蔣機秀
Jiang Junbi 姜峻璧
Jiang Wencai 姜文彩
Jiang Yan 江淹
Jiang Yingqing 姜映清
Jiang Zhu 江珠
jiangshilei tanci 講史類彈詞
Jiangzhu xiancao 絳珠仙草
Jiaoyuan shishe 蕉園詩社
Jiaqing 嘉慶
jie 節
Jinghuayuan 鏡花緣
Jingshanghua 錦上花
Jinguijie 金閨傑
jinguo ren 巾幗人
Jingwei 精衛
Jingweishi 精衛石
Jingzhongzhuan 精忠傳
Jinpingmei 金瓶梅
Jinshanghua 錦上花
Jinyu zhuyi 禁欲主義
Jinyuyuan 金魚緣
juan 卷
juren 舉人

Kang Aide 康愛德
Kuifang Xianzi 魁芳仙子

Lei 嫘
Li Bai 李白
Li Junyu 酈君玉
Li Mingtang 酈明堂
Li Qingzhao 李清照
Li Renlan 李紉蘭
Li Ruzhen 李汝珍
Li Sao 離騷
Li Xiuqing 李秀卿
Li Ye 李冶
Li Yin 李茵
Li Yü 李漁
Li Yutang 李雨堂
Li Zhi 李贄
li 理
Liang Hong 梁鴻
Liang Hongyu 梁紅玉
Liang Qichao 梁啟超
Liang Shanbo 梁山伯
Liang Shanbo yu Zhu Yingtai 梁山伯與祝英臺
Liang Suhua 梁素華
Liao Yunjing 廖雲錦
Liaozhai zhiyi 聊齋誌異
Lidai shilue shiduanjin cihua 歷代史略十段錦詞話
lie 烈
Lienü zhuan 列女傳
Lihuameng 梨花夢
Lin Daiyu 林黛玉
Lin Daoxuan 林道瑄
Lin Daoyu 林道腴
Lin Mengyun 林夢雲
Lin Wu 林武
Lin Xianyu 林纖玉
Lin Zhiyang 林之洋
Linglong 玲瓏
Linhuai 臨淮
Linyunju shicao 臨雲居詩草
Liu Bei 劉備
Liu Chen 劉晨
Liu Kuibi 劉奎璧
Liu Lingjuan 劉令娟
Liu Mengmei 柳夢梅
Liu Na'ou 劉吶鷗
Liu Qingyun 柳卿雲
Liu Shi 柳是
Liu Xiahui 柳下惠
Liu Xiang 劉向

Liu Yanyu 劉燕玉
Liu Yazi 柳亞子
Liuhuameng 榴花夢
Lü Bicheng 呂碧城
Lu Dan'An 陸澹安
Lü Kun 呂坤
Lunyu 論語
Lüyinlou shiyi 綠飲樓詩遺

Ma Rufei 馬如飛
Mao Qiling 毛奇齡
Mao Xiang 冒襄
Mei Fu 梅福
Meili 枚裏
meipi 眉批
meiren tu 美人圖
meiren 美人
Meng Guang 孟光
Meng Lijun 孟麗君
Mengjü 夢菊
Mengyin Zhenren 夢隱真人
Mengyingyuan 夢影緣
Mingji tanci 明紀彈詞
Mo Shi 莫氏
Mu Hualong 沐化龍
Mu Shiying 穆時英
Mudanting 牡丹亭
Mujiao 母教
Mulan ci 木蘭辭
Mulan 木蘭
Murong Chunniang 慕容純娘

Nan wanghou 男王後
nei 內
Neixun 內訓
ngaa pai 牙牌
Nü qingnian 女青年
Nü subao 女蘇報
Nübao 女報
Nü'er guo 女兒國
Nüfan jielu 女範捷錄
Nüjie 女誡
Nülunyu 女論語
Nüsheng 女聲
nüxian 女仙
nüyao 女妖
Nüyuhua 女獄花
*Nüzhuangyuan*女狀元
nüzongshi 女宗師

Pang Yulong 龐玉龍
Peng Liangjuan 彭靚娟
pigu 辟穀
pingtan 評彈
pipa 琵琶
Pu Songling 蒲松齡

Qi Hong 泣紅
Qian Qianyi 錢謙益
Qian Shurong 錢淑榮
Qiaoying 喬影
Qin Ao 秦鏊.
Qin Liangyu 秦良玉
Qin Ling 秦淩
Qin Shi 秦氏
Qing Shunxin 慶順馨
qing 情
Qinghai chongwen 情海重吻
Qingjiao 情教
Qingshi 情史
Qiu Guangye 邱廣業
Qiu Jin 秋瑾
Qu Yuan 屈原
quanqiu nüquan 全球女權
Quanxiao ge 勸孝歌

Rouputuan 肉蒲團
Ruan Lianqing 阮蓮清
Ruan Zhao 阮肇

Sai xiansheng 賽先生
sanshengshi 三生石
Shanghai zhonghua nüjie lianhe hui 上海中華女界聯合會

Shanyang 山陽
shanzhong xuezhe 善種學者
Shehui zhi hua 社會之花
Shen Fu 沈復
Shen Xiang 沈纕
Shen Xiangpei 沈湘佩
Shen Yixiu 沈宜修
Shenbao 申報
Shenxian zhuan 神仙傳
Shenying shizhe 神瑛侍者
sheshen chudi 設身處地
shexing quying 舍形取影
Shi Zhecun 施蟄存
shidizi 詩弟子
Shijing 詩經
shishi tanci 時事彈詞
Shitouji 石頭記
Shuihuzhuan 水滸傳
shuoshuren 說書人
Shuzhu 書竹
Siyunting 四雲亭
Song Renfang 宋紉芳
Songchuang zaji 松窗雜記
Soushen ji 搜神記
Su Daji 蘇妲己
Su Yingxue 蘇映雪
Su Yunxian 蘇韻仙
Su Zixiu 蘇子秀
suihan sanyou 歲寒三友
Suiyuan nüdizi 隨園女弟子
Sun Biwu 孫碧梧
Sun Deying 孫德英
Suzhou 蘇州

tan 嘆
Tanci kaipian ji 彈詞開篇集
tanci 彈詞
Tang Xianzu 湯顯祖
Tanghu yunyu nüshi 棠湖雲腴女士
Tanhua yixian 曇花一現
Tao Xianbi 陶纖碧
Tao Zhenhuai 陶貞懷

Tianyuhua 天雨花
tongxin 童心

wai 外
Wang Duan 汪端
Wang Duanshu 王端淑
Wang Dungen 王鈍根
Wang Jide 王驥德
Wang Miaoru 王妙如
Wang Miaoxiang 王妙想
Wang Ruyang 汪如洋
Wang Sansao 汪三嫂
Wang Sen 汪森
Wang Shangyu 汪上堉
Wang Shifu 王實甫
Wang Shouren 王守仁
Wang Xiang 王相
Wang Yangming 王陽明
Wang Yaofen 王瑤芬
Wang Zhaojun 王昭君
Wanhualou 萬花樓
Wanlan ciren 挽瀾詞人
wanzhen 玩真
Wei Yong'e 衛勇娥
Weiqingshuo 唯情說
Wen Peilan 文佩蘭
Wen Shanglin 文上林
Wen Shaoxia 文少霞
Wen Tingjun 溫庭筠
Wen Xiaxian 文霞仙
wenyan 文言
Wo Lianggui 沃良規
Wo Shi 沃氏
Wu Bing 吳炳
Wu Musu 吳穆蘇
Wu Zao 吳藻
wuchang 五常
Wulin zhongxiao duanhui gongzhu 武林忠孝端惠公主
Wumengtang ji 午夢堂集
Wusheng xi 無聲戲
Wuzhong shizi 吳中十子

Xi Peilan 席佩蘭
Xialang 霞郎
xiangcao 香草
Xiangxi 香溪
Xiangzhou nüshi 湘州女史
Xianü qunying shi 俠女群英史
xianü zhongchen 俠女忠臣
xiao 孝
Xiaojing 孝經
xiaojinku 銷金窟
Xiaojinqian 小金錢
Xiaonü bing 孝女兵
xiaxie xiaoshuo 狹邪小說
Xie Chunrong 謝春溶
Xie Xiang'e 謝湘娥
Xie Xiao'e 謝小娥
Xie Xucai 謝絮才
Xie Yuhui 謝玉輝
Xie Yujuan 謝玉娟
Xie Yunxian 謝韻仙
xieqing xiaoshuo 寫情小說
Xieyunlou shichao 寫韻樓詩鈔
Xin ganjue pai 新感覺派
Xin nüjie 新女界
Xin qingnian 新青年
Xin wenhua yundong 新文化運動
Xin wenxue 新文學
xing 性
Xinjiang 新疆
Xinshijie 新世界
Xiong Wenju 熊文舉
Xixiangji 西廂記
Xiyuan 西苑
Xu Yunlin 許雲林
Xu Yuxin 徐裕馨
Xue Tao 薛濤
Xun Yu 荀彧
xundao 訓導

Yan Jin 嚴謹
Yan Yonghua 嚴永華
Yang Buwei 楊步偉
Yang Guxue 楊古雪
Yang Shen 楊慎
yanqing xiaoshuo 言情小說
Yanzhixue 胭脂血
Ye Shaoyuan 葉紹袁
Ye Xiaoluan 葉小鸞
Ye Xiaowan 葉小婉
Yingmei'an yiyü 影梅庵憶語
Yonglan 詠蘭
Youmei 友梅
Yu Chenglai 俞承萊
Yu Xuanji 魚玄機
Yuan Mei 袁枚
Yuan 怨
Yuanguan 圓觀
Yuanyang hudie pai 鴛鴦蝴蝶派
Yuanyangmeng 鴛鴦夢
Yuchuanyuan 玉釧緣
Yue Fei 嶽飛
Yuedi yanjiu xiaojuan 月堤煙柳小卷
Yuhua 玉華
Yujingtai 玉鏡臺
Yulianhuan 玉連環
Yushi mingyan 喻世明言
Yutai huashi 玉臺畫史
Yuxuancao 娛萱草

Zaishengyuan 再生緣
Zaizaotian 再造天
zajü 雜劇
zhang 丈
zhang 章
Zhang Chang 張敞
Zhang Ouling 張藕玲
Zhang Sanyi 張三異
Zhang Xuecheng 章學誠
Zhang Zhonghuang 張仲璜
zhanghui xiaoshuo 章回小說
Zhao Yuanren 趙元任
Zhao Yueying 趙月英
Zhejiang 浙江
Zhen Baoyu 甄寶玉

Zhen Chaoying 甄超英
Zhen Shiyin 甄士隱
Zheng Danruo 鄭澹若
Zheng Guotai 鄭國泰
Zheng Hua 鄭華
Zheng Qiongzhi 鄭瓊芝
Zheng Ruzhao 鄭如昭
Zheng Zhenhua 鄭貞華
Zhengde 正德
zhenrong 真容
zhenzhen 真真
Zhong Xinqing 鐘心青
Zhong Ziqi 鐘子期
zhong 忠
Zhonghua nübao 中華女報
Zhou Miaohua 周妙華
Zhou Shoujuan 周瘦鵑
Zhou Yingfang 周穎芳
Zhoujintang ji 晝錦堂記
Zhu Suxian 朱素仙
Zhu Yingtai 祝英臺
Zhuang Mengyu 莊夢玉
Zhuang Yuan 莊淵
Zhuge Kongming 諸葛孔明
zifa de dushen 自發的獨身
ziyou lian'ai 自由戀愛
Zuo Weiming 左維明
Zuo Yizhen 左儀貞
zuoshuren 作書人

Works Cited

A Ying (阿英). 晚清小說叢鈔 (*Wanqing xiaoshuo congchao*, Late Qing Literature Series). Beijing: Zhonghua shujü, 1960.

A Ying. 小說閑談四種 (*Xiaoshuo xiantan sizhong*, Four Casual Discussions of the Novel). Shanghai: Shanghai guji chubanshe, 1985.

Altenburger, Roland. *The Sword or the Needle: The Female Knight-Errant (Xia) in Traditional Chinese Narrative*. Bern: Peter Lang, 2009.

Anderson, Amanda. "The Temptations of Aggrandized Agency: Feminist Histories and the Horizon of Modernity." *Victorian Studies* 43.1 (2000): 43-65.

Anderson, Benedict. *Imagined Communities: Reflections on the Origin and Spread of Nationalism*. London: Verso, 2006.

Anonymous. 安邦誌 (*Anbang zhi*, A Tale of Shielding the Nation). Shanghai: Xuehaitang, 1849.

Anonymous. *Book of Odes* (*Shi-King*). Trans. Launcelot Cranmer-Byng. London: John Murray, 1908.

Anonymous. 小金錢全傳 (*Xiaojinqian quanzhuan*, Little Gold Coins). Shanghai: Cuiying shuju, 1917.

Anonymous. 玉釧緣 (*Yuchuanyuan*, Jade Bracelets). Ed. Lin Yu and Song Bi. Harbin: Heilongjiang renmin chubanshe, 1987.

Ban, Gu (班固). 漢書 (*Hanshu*, History of the Han Dynasty). Beijing: Zhonghua shujü, 1962.

Ban, Zhao (班昭) 女誡 (*Nüjie*, Admonishment for Women). Chengdu: Sichuan renmin chubanshe, 1997.

Bao, Zhenpei. 清代女作家彈詞研究 (*Qingdai nüzuojia tanci yanjiu*, A Study of *Tanci* Narratives by Women in the Qing Dynasty). Tianjin: Tianjin shehui kexue, 2002.

Barwell, Ismay. "Feminist Perspective and Narrative Points of View." *Aesthetics in Feminist Perspective*. Ed. Hilde S. Hein and Carolyn Korsmeyer. Indianapolis: Indiana UP, 1993. 93-105.

Bender, Mark. *Plum and Bamboo: China's Suzhou Chantefable Tradition*. Champaign: U of Illinois P, 2003.

Bender, Mark. "Shifting and Performance in Suzhou Chantefable." *The Eternal Storyteller: Oral Literature in Modern China*. Ed. Vibeke Børdahl. Richmond: Curzon, 1999. 181-96.

Bender, Mark. *Zaisheng yuan and Meng Lijun: Performance, Context, and Form of Two* Tanci. Ph.D. Diss. Ohio State University, 1995.

Bender, Mark, and Victor Mair. "'I Sit Here and Sing for You' The Oral Literature of China." *The Columbia Anthology of Chinese Folk and Popular Literature*. Ed. Victor H. Mair and Mark Bender. New York: Columbia UP, 2011. 2-12.

Berg, Daria. "Female Self-Fashioning in Late Imperial China: How the Gentlewoman and the Courtesan Edited Her Story and Rewrote Hi/story." *Reading China: Fiction, History and the Dynamics of Discourse: Essays in Honour of Professor Glen Dudbridge*. Ed. Daria Berg. Leiden: Brill, 2007. 238-89.

Berg, Daria. *Women Writers and the Literary World in Early Modern China*. London: Routledge, 2013.

Bleeker, Maaike. *Visuality in the Theatre: The Locus of Looking*. New York: Palgrave Macmillan, 2008.

Børdahl, Vibeke, ed. *The Eternal Storyteller: Oral Literature in Modern China*. Richmond: Curzon, 1999.

Brinker, Helmut. *Zen in the Art of Painting*. New York: Penguin, 1988.

Brokaw, Cynthia J., and Kai-Wing Chow, eds. *Printing and Book Culture in Late Imperial China*. Berkeley: U of California P, 2005.

Brooks, Peter. *Body Work: Objects of Desire in Modern Narrative*. Cambridge: Harvard UP, 1993.

Brooks, Peter. *Psychoanalysis and Storytelling*. Oxford: Blackwell, 1994.

Butler, Judith. *Bodies That Matter: On the Discursive Limits of "Sex."* London: Routledge, 1993.

Butler, Judith. *Gender Trouble: Feminism and the Subversion of Identity*. London: Routledge, 1999.

Butler, Judith. *Undoing Gender*. London Routledge, 2004.

Cahill, James. "Paintings Done for Women in Ming-Qing China?" *Nan Nü* 8.1 (2006): 1-54.

Cai, Yuanpei (蔡元培). 中國新文學大系總序 (*Zhongguo xinwenxue daxi zongxu*, General Introduction to the Grand Anthology of Chinese New Literature). Shanghai: Liangyou tushu yinshua gongsi, 1936.

Cao, Xueqin. *The Dream of the Red Chamber*. Trans. Edwin Lowe. North Clarendon: Tuttle Publishing, 2010.

Cao, Xueqin (曹雪芹). 紅樓夢 (*Hongloumeng*, The Dream of the Red Chamber). Shanghai: Shanghai wenyi chubanshe, 2005.

Cao, Xueqin. *The Story of the Stone, or The Dream of the Red Chamber*. Translated by David Hawkes. Chicago: Penguin, 1974.

Carlitz, Katherine. "Desire, Danger, and the Body: Stories of Women's Virtue in Late Ming China." *Engendering China: Women, Culture, and the State*. Ed. Christina K. Gilmartin, Gail Hershatter, Lisa Rofel, and Tyrene White. Cambridge: Harvard UP, 1994. 101-25.

Chan, Ching-kiu Stephen. "The Language of Despair: Ideological Representations of the 'New Women' (*xin nüxing*) by May Fourth Writers." *Gender Politics in Modern China: Feminism and Literature*. Ed. Tani E. Barlow. Durham: Duke UP, 1993. 13-32.

Chang, Kang-I Sun. "Liu Shih and Hsü Ts'an: Feminine or Feminist?" *Voices of the Song Lyric in China*. Ed. Pauline Yu. Berkeley: U of California P, 1994. 170-91.

Chang, Kang-I Sun, and Haun Saussy, eds. *Women Writers of Traditional China: An Anthology of Poetry and Criticism.* Stanford: Stanford UP, 1999.

Chang, Shelley Hsueh-lun. *History and Legend: Ideas and Images in the Ming Historical Novels*. Ann Arbor: U of Michigan P, 1990.

Che, Zhenhua (車振華). "閨塾師的創意: 筆生花的隱秘訴求及其在女作家彈詞鏈條中的地位" ("Guishushi de chuangyi: *Bishenghua* de yinmi suqiu jiqi zai nüzuojia tanci liantiao zhong de diwei," "The Innovation of the Teachers of the Inner Chambers: the Private Desires in Blossom from the Brush and its Status in the Tradition of Women's *Tanci*"). *Journal of Shandong Normal University* 54.4 (2009): 97-101.

Chen, Duansheng, and Liang Desheng (陳端生, 梁德繩). 再生緣 (*Zaishengyuan*, Destiny of Rebirth). Ed. Guo Moruo. Beijing: Beijing guji chubanshe, 2002.

Chen, Duxiu. "文學革命論" ("Wenxue geming lun," "On Literary Revolution"). *Xin Qingnian* (New Youth). 2.6 (1917).

Chen, Fan Pen Li. *Chinese Shadow Theatre: History, Popular Religion, and Women Warriors*. Montréal: McGill-Queen's UP, 2007.

Chen, Pingyuan, and Xia Xiaohong (陳平原, 夏曉虹), eds. 二十世紀中國小說理論資料. (*Ershi shiji zhongguo xiaoshuo lilun ziliao*, Theories of the Novel in Twentieth-Century China). Beijing: Beijing daxue chubanshe, 1989.

Chen, Pingyuan. 中國小說敘事模式的轉變 (*Zhongguo xiaoshuo xushi moshi de zhuanbian*, The Evolvement of the Narrative Models in Chinese Fiction). Beijing: Peking UP, 2003.

Chen, Ruheng (陳汝衡). 說書小史 (*Shuoshu xiaoshi*, A Brief History of Storytelling Performance). Shanghai: Zhonghua shujü, 1936.

Chen, Tongxun. 序 (Xu, Preface). 筆生花 (*Bishenghua*, Blossom from the Brush). Qiu Xinru. Hong Kong: Yimei tushu gongsi, 1984. 1-2.

Chen, Toyoko Yoshida. *Women in Confucian Society: A Study of Three T'an-Tz'u Narratives*. Ph.D. Diss. Columbia U. Ann Arbor: UMI Dissertation Services, 2004.

Chen, Weike. "Going Public through Education: Female Reformers and Girls' Schools in Late Qing Beijing." *Late Imperial China* 21.1 (2000): 107-44.

Chen, Wenxuan (陳文璇). 邱心如筆生花研究 (*Qiu Xinru Bishenghua yanjiu*, A Study of Qiu Xinru's Blossom from the Brush). Yonghe: Huamulan chubanshe, 2008.

Chen, Wulou (陳午樓). "Some Topics in My Study of Yangzhou Storytelling." *The Eternal Storyteller: Oral Literature in Modern China*. Ed. Vibeke Børdahl. Surrey: Curzon, 1999. 210-17.

Chen, Xiefen (陳擷芬). 女報 (*Nübao*, Women's Journal). Shanghai: Nüxue baoguan bianji suo, 1902.

Chen, Yinke (陳寅恪). 論再生緣 (*Lun Zaishengyuan*, On Destiny of Rebirth). Jiulong, Hong Kong: Youlian chubanshe, 1959.

Chen, Yun (陳蕓). 陳孝女遺集 (*Chen Xiaonü yiji*, Collections of Surviving Poems by the Filial Daughter of the Chen Family). *pds.lib.harvard.edu* <http://pds.lib.harvard.edu/pds/view/2586444>.

Chen, Zhensun (陳振孫). 直齋書錄解題 (*Zhizhai shulu jieti*, Annotated Catalogue of the Zhizhai Studio). Guangzhou: Guangya shujü, 1899.

Cheng, Huiying (程蕙英). 鳳雙飛 (*Fengshuangfei*, Phoenixes Flying Together). 1899. Zhengzhou: Zhongzhou guji chubanshe, 1988.

Cheng, Zhanlu (程瞻廬). 同心梔彈詞 (*Tongxinzhi tanci*, Heartlocked Cape Jasmine). Shanghai: Shanghai shangwu yinshu guan, 1919.

Cixous, Hélène. "The Laugh of the Medusa." Trans. Keith Cohen and Paula Cohen. *Feminisms: An Anthology of Literary Theory and Criticism*. Ed. Robyn R. Warhol, and Diane Price Herndl. New Brunswick: Rutgers UP, 1991. 334-49.

Cixous, Hélène. *The Newly Born Woman*. Trans. Betsy Wing. Minneapolis: U of Minnesota P, 1986.

Cleary, Thomas, ed. and trans., *Immortal Sisters: Secrets of Taoist Women*. Boston: Shambhala, 1989.

Clunas, Craig. *Fruitful Sites: Garden Culture in Ming Dynasty China*. Durham: Duke UP, 1996.

Confucius. *The Analects of Confucius: A Philosophical Translation*. Translated by Roger T. Ames. New York: Random House, 1998.

Dan, Shen. "Defense and Challenge: Reflections on the Relation between Story and Discourse." *Narrative* 10.3 (2002): 222-41.

Davis, Richard L. "Chaste and Filial Women in Chinese Historical Writings of the Eleventh Century." *Journal of the American Oriental Society* 121.2 (2001): 204-19.

Delmar, Rosalind. "What is Feminism?" *Theorizing Feminism*. Ed. Anne C. Hermann, and Abigail J. Stewart. Boulder: Westview, 2001. 5-28.

Deng, Xiang (鄧翔), ed. 詩經繹參 (*Shijing yican*, Book of Odes with Annotations and Comments). Guangzhou: Yangcheng kongshi, 1867.

Di, Xianting, and Chao Rui (狄嫺婷, 晁瑞). "筆生花韻腳字所反映的語音問題" ("*Bishenghua* yunjiaozi suo fanying de yüyin wenti," "A Study of Rhyming Words in Blossom from the Brush and Their Pronunciations"). *Journal of Huaiyin Normal University* 2 (2013): 249-53.

Ding, Zhi'An (丁誌安). "筆生花作者邱心如家世考" ("*Bishenghua* zuozhe Qiu Xinru jiashi kao," "A Study of the Family Background of Qiu Xinru, the Author of Blossom from the Brush"). 中華文史論叢 (*Zhonghua wenshi luncong*, Journal of Chinese Literature and History) 22 (1982): 299-300.

Dissanayake, Wimal, ed. *Narratives of Agency: Self-Making in China, India, and Japan*. Minneapolis: U of Minnesota P, 1996.

Dong, Lan. *Mulan's Legend and Legacy in China and the United States*. Philadelphia: Temple UP, 2010.

Dong, Lan. *Cross-Cultural Palimpsest of Mulan : Iconography of the Woman Warrior from Premodern China to Asian America*. Ph.D. Diss. Amherst: University of Massachusetts, Amherst, 2006.

Dong, Naibin (董乃斌), ed. 中國文學敘事傳統研究 (*Zhongguo wenxue xushi chuantong yanjiu*, A Study of Narrative Traditions of Chinese Literature). Beijing: Zhonghua shujü, 2012.

Dooling, Amy. *Women's Literary Feminism in Twentieth-Century China*. New York: Palgrave MacMillan, 2005.

Du, Xunhe (杜荀鶴). 松窗雜集 (*Songchuang zaji*, Pine Window Miscellany). Ed. Liu Shixian. Shanghai: Shanghai shudian chubanshe, 1994.

Edwards, Louise. *Gender, Politics, and Democracy: Women's Suffrage in China*. Stanford: Stanford UP, 2008.

Edwards, Louise. "Policing the Modern Woman in Republican China." *Modern China* 26.2 (2000): 115-47.

Edwards, Louise. "Transformations of the Woman Warrior Hua Mulan: From Defender of the Family to Servant of the State." *Nan Nü* 12.2 (2010): 175-214.

Elman, Benjamin A., John B. Duncan, and Herman Ooms, eds. *Rethinking Confucianism: Past and Present in China, Japan, Korea and Vietnam*. Los Angeles: U of California Los Angeles P, 2002.

Elsaesser, Thomas. "Tales of Sound and Fury: Observations on the Family Melodrama." *Monogram* 4 (1972): 2-15.

Elvin, Mark. "Female Virtue and the State in China." *Past and Present* 104 (1984): 111-52.

Epstein, Maram. *Competing Discourses: Orthodoxy, Authenticity, and Engendered Meanings in Late Imperial Chinese Fiction*. Cambridge: Harvard Asia Center, 2001.

Epstein, Maram. "Patrimonial Bonds: Daughters, Fathers, and Power in *Tianyuhua*." *Late Imperial China* 32.2 (2011): 1-33.

Fang, Bao (方苞). 方望溪全集 (*Fang Wangxi quanji*, The Complete Collection of Fang Wangxi's Works). Shanghai: Shijie shuqu, 1965.

Feng, Jin. *The New Woman in Early Twentieth-Century Chinese Fiction*. West Lafayette: Purdue UP, 2004.

Feng, Menglong (馮夢龍). 情史 (*Qingshi*, A History of Qing). Hunan: Yuelu shushe, 2003.

Feng, Menglong. *Stories Old and New: A Ming Dynasty Collection* (Complete Translation of *Illustrious Words to Instruct the World.*) Trans. Shuhui Yang and Yunqin Yang. Seattle: U of Washington P, 2000.

Feng, Menglong. 燕居筆記 (*Yanju biji*, A Journal of the Swallow House). *Guben xiaoshuo jicheng* (Collection of Ancient Editions of Fiction). Shanghai: Shanghai guji chubanshe. Vol. 98 (1990): 534-41.

Feng, Menglong. 喻世明言 (*Yushi mingyan*, Illustrious Words to Instruct the World). 1620. Taipei: Guiguan chubanshe, 2001.

Fong, Grace S. "Engendering the Lyric: Her Image and Voice in Song." *Voices of the Song Lyric in China*. Ed. Pauline Yu. Berkeley: U of California P, 1994. 107-44.

Fong, Grace S. "Female Hands: Embroidery As A Knowledge Field in Women's Everyday Life in Late Imperial and Early Republican China." *Late Imperial China* 25.1 (2004): 1-58.

Fong, Grace S. *Herself an Author: Gender, Agency, and Writing in Late Imperial China*. Honolulu: U of Hawai'i P, 2008.

Fong, Grace S. "Signifying Bodies: The Cultural Significance of Suicide Writings by Women in Ming-Qing China." *Nan Nü* 3.1 (2001): 105-42.

Fong, Grace S, Nanxiu Qian, and Harriet T. Zurndorfer, eds. *Beyond Tradition and Modernity: Gender, Genre, and Cosmopolitanism in Late Qing China*. Leiden: Brill, 2004.

Furong, Zhuren (芙蓉主人). 癡婆子傳 (*Chipozi zhuan,* Memoirs of a Crazy Old Woman*)*. Taipei: Shuangdi guoji chubanbu, 1994.

Furong, Zhuren. "*Memoirs of a Crazy Old Woman*." *Of Woman by Woman: Two Erotic Novellas from Ming China*. Trans. R. W. L. Guisso and Lenny Hu. Bern: Peter Lang, 2011. 75-121.

Gan, Bao. *In Search of the Supernatural: The Written Record*. Trans. Kenneth J. Dewoskin and J. I. Crump. Stanford: Stanford UP, 1996.

Gan, Bao (干寶). 搜神記 (*Soushen ji*, *In Search of the Supernatural*). Taipei: Taiwan shufang, 2010.

Gao, Yandi (高延第). 光緒淮安府志 (*Guangxu huai'an fuzhi*, Huai'an Prefecture Gazetteer during the Reign of Emperor Guangxu). Shanghai: Jiangsu guji chubanshe, 1991.

Garber, Marjorie. *Vested Interests: Cross-Dressing & Cultural Anxiety*. London: Routledge, 1992.

Gardiner, Ellen. *Regulating Readers: Gender and Literary Criticism in the Eighteenth-Century Novel*. Newark: U of Delaware P, 1999.

Ge, Hong (葛洪). 神仙傳 (*Shenxian zhuan*, Biographies of the Immortals). Ed. Mengsu Li. Beijing: Neimenggu renmin chubanshe, 2003.

Genette, Gérard. *Narrative Discourse: An Essay in Method*. Trans. Jane E. Lewin. Ithaca: Cornell UP, 1980.

Genette, Gérard. *Paratexts: Thresholds of Interpretation*. Trans. Jane E. Lewin. New York: Cambridge UP, 1997.

Goodman, Bryna, and Wendy Larson, eds. *Gender in Motion: Divisions of Labor and Cultural Change in Late Imperial and Modern China*. Lanham: Rowman & Littlefield, 2005.

Grant, Beata. *Eminent Nuns: Women Chan Masters of Seventeenth-Century China*. Honolulu: U of Hawai'i P, 2008.

Grant, Beata. "Patterns of Female Religious Experience in Qing Dynasty Popular Literature." *Journal of Chinese Religious Studies* 23 (1995): 29-58.

Greiner, Rae. "Sympathy Time: Adam Smith, George Eliot, and the Realist Novel." *Narrative* 17.3 (2009): 291-311.

Gu, Ming Dong. *Chinese Theories of Reading and Writing: A Route to Hermeneutics and Open Poetics*. Albany: State U of New York P, 2005.

Guan, Zhong. *Guanzi: Political, Economic, and Philosophical Essays from Early China: A Study and Translation by W. Allyn Rickett*. Trans. W. Allyn Rickett. Boston: Cheng & Tsui, 2001.

Guo, Maoqian (郭茂倩), ed. 樂府詩集 (*Yuefu shiji*, Anthology of "Music Bureau" Poetry). Beijing: Zhonghua shujü, 1979.

Han, Na (漢娜). "德國婦女工作平等的要求" ("Deguo funü gongzuo pingdeng de yaoqiu," "German Women's Request for Equality in Work"). Trans. Zhong Yun. 婦女雜誌 (*Funü zazhi*, Lady's Journal) 3 (1924): 543-49.

Hanan, Patrick. *The Chinese Vernacular Story*. Cambridge: Harvard UP, 1981.

Hanan, Patrick. "The Missionary Novels of Nineteenth-Century China." *Harvard Journal of Asiatic Studies* 60.2 (2000): 413-43.

Harvey, Matthew. *Sex, Law, and Society in Late Imperial China*. Stanford: Stanford UP, 2000.

Hawkes, David. *The Songs of the South*. New York: Penguin Books, 1985.

Hegel, Robert E. *The Novel in Seventeenth-Century China*. New York: Columbia UP, 1981.

Hegel, Robert E. *Reading Illustrated Fiction in Late Imperial China*. Stanford: Stanford UP, 1988.

Hegel, Robert E., and Katherine Carlitz. *Writing and Law in Late Imperial China: Crime, Conflict, and Judgment*. Seattle: U of Washington P, 2007.

Hinsch, Bret. "Male Honor and Female Chastity in China." *Nan Nü* 13.2 (2011): 169-204.

Hodes, Nancy. *Strumming and Singing the "Three Smiles Romance": A Study of the Tanci Text*. Ph.D. Diss. Ann Arbor: UMI Dissertation, 2004.

Hou, Zhi (侯芝). 金閨傑 (*Jinguijie*, Heroines in the Golden Chambers). Ms. 1824. Shanghai: Shanghai Municipal Library.

Hou, Zhi. 再造天 (*Zaizaotian*, Remaking Heaven). Ms. 1869. Nanjing: Nanjing Library.

Hsiung, Ping-chen. "Female Gentility in Transition and Transmission: Mother-Daughter Ties in Ming/Qing China." *The Quest for Gentility in China: Negotiations beyond Gender and Class*. Ed. Daria Berg and Chloë Starr. London: Routledge, 2007. 97-116.

Hu, Bingwen (胡炳文). 純正蒙求 (*Chunzheng mengqiu*, Accounts of Enlightenment and Pursuit of the Pure and Upright). Taipei: Shangwu yinshu guan, 1980.

Hu, Shi (胡適). 嘗試集 (*Changshi ji*, Experiments). Beijing: Peking UP, 1920.

Hu, Siao-chen. 才女徹夜未眠:近代中國女性敘事文學的興起 (*Cainü cheye weimian: jindai zhongguo nüxing xushi wenxue de xingqi*, Burning the Midnight Oil: The Rise of the Female Narrative in Early Modern China). Taipei: Maitian chubanshe, 2008.

Hu, Siao-chen. "The Daughter's Vision of National Crisis: *Tianyuhua* and A Woman Writer's Construction of the Late Ming." *Dynastic Crisis and Cultural Innovation: From Late Ming to the Late Qing and Beyond*. Ed. David Wang and Sheng Wei. Cambridge: Harvard Asia Center, 2005. 200-31.

Hu, Siao-chen (胡曉真). "Hou Zhi and the Transformation of the *Tanci* Narrative in Form and Ideology in the Mid Qing." *Journal of the Institute of Literature and Philosophy* 12 (1998): 41-90.

Hu, Siao-chen. *Literary Tanci: A Woman's Tradition of Narrative in Verse*. Ph.D. Diss. Ann Arbor: UMI Dissertation, 1994.

Hu, Siao-chen. "祕密花園：論清代女性彈詞小說中的幽閉空間與心靈活動" ("Mimi huayuan: lun qingdai nüxing *tanci* xiaoshuo zhong de youbi kongjian yu xinling huodong," "Secret Garden: Polysemantic Spaces in Qing Women's *Tanci* Narratives"). 欲掩彌彰：中國歷史文化中的"私"與"情"：私情篇 (*Yugai mizhang: zhongguo lishi wenhua zhong de "Si" yu "Qing,"* "Concealing to reveal": An International Scholarly Conference on "the Private" and "Sentiment" in Chinese History and Culture). Ed. Siao-chen Hu, Bingzhen Xu, Ayling Wang. Taipei: Institute of Sinology, 2003. 279-315.

Hu, Siao-chen. "Qiu Xinru." *The Oxford Encyclopedia of Women in World History*. Ed. Bonnie G. Smith. Oxford: Oxford UP, 2008. 539.

Hu, Siao-chen. "Unorthodox Female Figures in Zhu Suxian's *Linked Rings of Jade*." *Text, Performance, and Gender in Chinese Literature and Music: Essays in Honor of Wilt Idema*. Ed. Maghiel van Crevel, Tian Yuan Tan, and Michel Hockx. Leiden: Brill, 2009. 311-24.

Hu, Siao-chen. "晚清前期女性彈詞小說試探：　非政治文本的政治解讀" ("Wanqing qianqi nüxing tanci xiaoshuo shitan: feizhengzhi wenben de zhengzhi jiedu," "Exploring Women's *Tanci* Fiction in the Initial Stage of Late Qing: A Political Reading of Apolitical Texts"). 中國文哲研究集刊 (*Zhongguo wenzhe yanjiu jikan*, Bulletin of the Institute of Chinese Literature and Philosophy) 11 (1997): 89-113.

Hu, Siao-chen. "War, Violence, and the Metaphor of Blood in *Tanci* Narratives by Women Authors." *The Inner Quarters and Beyond: Women Writers from Ming through Qing*. Ed. Grace S. Fong and Ellen Widmer. Leiden: Brill, 2010. 249-83.

Hu, Siao-chen. 新理想、舊體例與不可思議之社會:清末民初上海「傳統派」文人與閨秀作家的轉型現象 (*Xin lixiang, jiu tili yu buke siyi zhi shehui: qingmo minchu Shanghai chuantongpai wenren yu guixiu zuojia de zhuanxing xianxiang,* New Ideals, Old System, and the Inconceivable Society: Transformation of Traditional Scholars and Talented Women Writers in Late Qing and Early Republic Shanghai). Taipei: Academia Sinica, 2010.

Hu, Siao-chen. "酗酒，瘋癲與獨身：清代女性彈詞小說中的極端女性人物" ("Xujiu, fengdian yu dushen: qingdai nüxing tanci xiaoshuo zhong de jiduan nüxing renwu," "The Alcoholic Mother, the Mad Wife and the Celibate Daughter: Extreme Female Figures in Women's *Tanci* Narrative"). 中國文哲研究集刊 (*Zhongguo wenzhe yanjiu jikan*, Bulletin of the Institute of Chinese Literature and Philosophy) 28 (2006): 51-80.

Hu, Siao-chen. "由彈詞編訂家侯芝談清代中期彈詞小說的創作形式與意識型態轉化" ("You tanci biandingjia Hou Zhi tan qingdai zhongqi tanci xiaoshuo de chuangzuo xingshi yu yishi xingtai zhuanhua," "Hou Chih and the Transformation of the *Tanci* Narrative in Form and Ideology in the Mid-Qing"). 中國文哲研究集刊 (*Zhongguo wenzhe yanjiu jikan*, Bulletin of the Institute of Chinese Literature and Philosophy) 12 (1998): 41-90.

Hu, Siao-chen. "閱讀反應與彈詞小說的創作：清代女性敘事文學傳統建立之一隅" ("Yuedu fanying yu tanci xiaoshuo de chuangzuo: qingdai nüxing xushi wenxue chuantong jianli zhi yiyu," "Reading Network and the Writing of Literary *Tanci*: A Cornerstone of Late Qing Women's Narrative Tradition"). 中國文哲研究集刊 (*Zhongguo wenzhe yanjiu jikan*, Bulletin of the Institute of Chinese Literature and Philosophy) 8 (1996): 305-64.

Hu, Siao-chen. "秩序追求與末世恐懼：由彈詞小說《四雲亭》看晚清上海婦女的時代意識" ("Zhixu zhuiqiu yu moshi kongju: you *tanci* xiaoshuo *Siyunting* kan wanqing Shanghai funü de shidai yishi," "Pursuit of Order and Fin-de-Siècle Phobia: *Siyunting* Tanci and the Sense of Decline of Late Qing Women in Shanghai"). 近代中國婦女史研究 (*Jindai zhongguo funü shi yanjiu*, Research on Women in Modern Chinese History) 8 (2000): 89-128.

Hu, Wanchuan (胡萬川). 話本與才子佳人小說之研究 (*Huaben yu caizi jiaren xiaoshuo zhi yanjiu*, A Study on the Relation between Huaben Fiction and Scholar-Beauty Romances). Taipei: Da'An chubanshe, 1994.

Hu, Wenkai (胡文楷). 歷代婦女著作考 (*Lidai funü zhuzuo kao*, Bibliography of Works Written by Women through the Ages). Shanghai: Shanghai guji chubanshe, 1985.

Hu, Ying. "'How Can a Daughter Glorify the Family Name?' Filialty and Women's Rights in the Late Qing." *Nan Nü* 11 (2009): 234-69.

Hu, Ying. *Tales of Translation: Composing the New Woman in China, 1899-1918*. Stanford: Stanford UP, 2000.

Hu, Ying. *Toward a Social History of Women in Seventeenth Century China*. Doctoral dissertation. Stanford, Ann Arbor: U Microfilms International, 1990.

Hua, Erxi (華爾西). "婦女與工作" ("Funü yu gongzuo," "Women and Work"). Trans. Kenjie Bo. 婦女雜誌 (*Funü zazhi*, Lady's Journal) 8 (1924): 1249-57.

Hua, Wei. "From Private Life to Public Performances: The Constituted Memory and (Re)writings of the Early-Qing Woman Wu Zong'ai." *The Inner Quarters and Beyond: Women Writers from Ming through Qing*. Ed. Grace Fong and Ellen Widmer. Leiden: Brill, 2010. 141-75.

Hua, Wei. "How Dangerous Can the Peony Be? Textual Space, *Caizi Mudanting*, and Naturalizing the Erotic." *Journal of Asian Studies* 65.4 (2006): 741-62.

Hua, Wei. "The Lament of Frustrated Talents: An Analysis of Three Women's Plays in Later Imperial China." *Ming Studies* 32 (1994): 28-42.

Hua, Wei. "On Feminine Consciousness in *Caizi Mudanting*." *Theatre Arts* 1 (2001): 90-101.

Hua, Wei, and Jiang Jurong (華瑋, 江巨榮), eds. 才子牡丹亭 (*Caizi Mudanting*, The Genius Peony Pavilion). Taipei: Xuesheng shuju, 2004.

Hua, Wei, and Ayling Wang (華瑋, 王璦玲), eds. 明清戲曲國際研討會論文集 (*Mingqing xiqü guoji yantaohui lunwen ji*, Collected Papers from the International Conference on Ming-Qing Drama). Taipei: Academia Sinica, 1998.

Huang, Martin W. *Desire and Fictional Narrative in Late Imperial China*. Cambridge: Harvard East Asian Monographs, 2001.

Huang, Martin W. "Sentiments of Desire: Thoughts on the Cult of Qing in Ming-Qing Literature." *Chinese Literature: Essays, Articles, Reviews* (*CLEAR*) 20 (1998): 153-84.

Huffer, Lynne. "'There Is No Gomorrah': Narrative Ethics in Feminist and Queer Theory." *differences* 12.3 (2001): 1-32.

Huntington, Rania. *Alien Kind: Foxes and the Late Imperial Narrative*. Cambridge: Harvard East Asian Monographs, 2003.

Huntington, Rania. "Ghosts Seeking Substitutes: Female Suicide and Repetition." *Late Imperial China* 26.1 (2005): 1-40.

Idema, Wilt L. *Chinese Vernacular Fiction: The Formative Period*. Leiden: Brill, 1974.

Idema, Wilt L. "Female Talent and Female Virtue: Xu Wei's *Nü Zhuangyuan* and Meng Chengshun's *Zhenwenji*."明清戲曲國際研討會論文集 (*Mingqing xiqü guoji yantaohui lunwen ji*, Collected Papers from the International Conference on Ming-Qing Drama). Ed. Wei Hua and Ayling Wang. Taipei: Academia Sinica, 1998. 549-71.

Idema, Wilt L., trans. *Meng Jiangnü Brings Down the Great Wall: Ten Versions of a Chinese Legend*. Seattle: U of Washington P, 2008.

Idema, Wilt L. *Personal Salvation and Filial Piety: Two Precious Scroll Narratives of Guanyin and Her Acolytes*. Classics in East Asian Buddhism. Honolulu: U of Hawai'i P, 2008.

Idema, Wilt L., and Beata Grant eds. *The Red Brush: Writing Women of Imperial China*. Cambridge: Harvard U, Asia Center, 2004.

Ji, Yougong (計有功). 唐詩紀事 (*Tangshi jishi*, About Tang Poets and Poetry). Taipei: Taiwan Zhonghua shujü, 1981.

Jiang, Yingqing (姜映清). 風流罪人 (*Fengliu zuiren*, The Valiant and the Culprit). Shanghai: Dalu tushu gongsi, 1926.

Jiang, Yingqing. 彈詞開篇集 (*Tanci kaipian ji*, Collections of *Tanci* Introductory Songs). Shanghai: Jiating chubanshe, 1936.

Jin, Tianhe (金天翮). 女界鐘 (*Nüjie zhong*, *The Women's Bell*, 1903). Shanghai: Shanghai guji chubanshe, 2003.

Jin, Tianhe. "The Women's Bell." Trans. Michael Gibbs Hill. *The Birth of Chinese Feminism: Essential Texts in Transnational Theory*. Ed. Lydia He Liu, Rebecca E. Karl, and Dorothy Ko. New York: Columbia UP, 2013. 207-86.

Jing, Li, ed. 國家圖書館藏珍本雜劇傳奇地方戲曲藝插圖全集 (*Guojia tushuguan cang zhenben zajü chuanqi difangxi quyi chatu quanji*, The National Library

Collections of Illustrations in Rare Texts, Drama, and Folk Opera). Beijing: Quanguo tushuguan wenxiansuowei fuzhi zhongxin, 2006.

Johnson, Linda Cooke. *Cities of Jiangnan in Late Imperial China.* Herndon: State U of New York P, 1993.

Ju Daoren. 娛萱草彈詞 (*Yuxuancao tanci*, A Tanci to Please My Mother-in-Law). Shanghai: Shangwu yinshuguan, 1931.

Judge, Joan. "Blended Wish Images: Chinese and Western Exemplary Women at the Turn of the Twentieth Century." *Beyond Tradition and Modernity: Gender, Genre, and Cosmopolitanism in Late Qing China*. Ed. Grace S. Fong, Nanxiu Qian, and Harriet T. Zurndorfer. Leiden: Brill, 2004. 102-35.

Judge, Joan. "'Citizens or Mothers of Citizens?' Gender and the Meaning of Modern Chinese Citizenship." *Changing Meanings of Citizenship in Modern China*. Ed. Merle Goldman and Elizabeth J. Perry. Cambridge: Harvard UP, 2002. 23-44.

Judge, Joan. *The Precious Raft of History: The Past, the West, and the Woman Question in China.* Stanford: Stanford UP, 2008.

Judge, Joan. "A Translocal Technology of the Self: Biographies of World Heroines and the Chinese Woman Question." *Journal of Women's History* 21.4 (2009): 59-83.

Kang, Wenqing. *Obsession: Male Same-Sex Relations in China, 1900-1950*. Hong Kong: Hong Kong UP, 2009.

Karl, Rebecca E. "Journalism, Social Value, and a Philosophy of the Everyday in 1920s China." *Positions* 16.3 (2008): 539-66.

Keshi (克士). "婦女與工作" ("Funü yu gongzuo," "Women and Work"). 婦女雜誌 (*Funü zazhi*, Lady's Journal). *juan* 8, 1922.

Kilroe, Patricia. "The Dream as Text, The Dream as Narrative." *Dreaming: Journal of the Association for the Study of Dreams* 10.3 (2000): 125-37.

Ko, Dorothy. "The Body as Attire: The Shifting Meanings of Footbinding in Seventeenth-Century China." *Journal of Women's History* 8.4 (1997): 8-27.

Ko, Dorothy. *Cinderella's Sisters: A Revisionist History of Footbinding*. Berkeley: U of California P, 2005.

Ko, Dorothy. *Every Step a Lotus: Shoes for Bound Feet*. Berkeley: U of California P, 2001.

Ko, Dorothy. *Teachers of the Inner Chambers: Women and Culture in Seventeenth-Century China*. Stanford: Stanford UP, 1994.

Ko, Dorothy, JaHyun Kim Haboush, and Joan R. Piggott, eds. *Women and Confucian Cultures in Premodern China, Korea, and Japan*. Berkeley: U of California P, 2003.

Kong, Xiangwo (孔襄我). "獨身的我見" ("Dushen de wojian," "My View on Celibacy"). 婦女雜誌 (*Funü zazhi*, Lady's Journal) 8.10 (1923): 10-11.

Kwa, Shiamin, and Wilt L. Idema, eds. *Mulan: Five Versions of a Classic Chinese Legend with Related Texts*. Indianapolis: Hackett Publishing, 2010.

Lacan, Jacques. "The Mirror Stage as Formative of the Function of the I as Revealed in Psychoanalytic Experience." *Ecrits: A Selection*. By Jacques Lacan. Trans. Alan Sheridan. New York: Norton, 1977. 1-7.

Lai, Sufen. "From the Cross-Dressing Daughter to the Lady-Knight Errant: The Origin and Evolution of Women Warriors in Medieval China." *Presence and Presentation: Women in the Chinese Literati Tradition*. Ed. Sherry J. Mou. New York: St. Martins, 1999. 77-107.

Lanling Xiaoxiaosheng (蘭陵笑笑生). 古本金瓶梅 (*Guben Jinpingmei*, Ancient Edition of *The Golden Lotus*). Taipei: Wenhua tushu gongsi, 1966.

Lanling Xiaoxiaosheng. *The Golden Lotus*. Trans. Clement Egerton. Rockville: Silk Pagoda, 2008.

Larson, Wendy. *From Ah Q to Lei Feng: Freud and Revolutionary Spirit in 20th Century China*. Stanford: Stanford UP, 2009.

Lee, Haiyan. *Revolution of the Heart: A Genealogy of Love in China 1900-1950*. Stanford: Stanford UP, 2007.

Li, Fang (李昉), ed. 太平廣記 (*Taiping guangji*, The Extensive Records of the Taiping Era). Beijing: Zhonghua shujü, 2003.

Li, Fang (李昉). 太平御覽 (*Taiping yulan*, Imperial Overview of the Era Taiping Great Peace). Taipei: Taiwan shangwu yinshuguan, 1967.

Li, Guiyu (李桂玉). 榴花夢 (*Liuhuameng*, Dream of the Pomegranate Flower). Beijing: Zhongguo wenlian chubanshe, 1998.

Li, Kaixuan (李凱旋). 寄宿在自己的一間閨房裏:再生緣研究 (*Jisu zai ziji de yijian guifang li: Zaishengyuan yanjiu*, A Guest in One's Own Boudoir: A Study of Destiny of Rebirth). M.A. Thesis. Guangxi: Guangxi Normal U, 2006.

Li, Ruzhen. *Flowers in the Mirror*. Trans. Lin Tai-Yi. Berkeley: U of California P, 1965.

Li, Ruzhen (李汝珍). 鏡花緣 (*Jinghuayuan*, *Flowers in the Mirror*). Shanghai: Shanghai guji chubanshe, 1991.

Li, Siu Leung. *Cross-Dressing in Chinese Opera*. Hong Kong: Hong Kong UP, 2003.

Li, Wai-Yee. "Heroic Transformations: Women and National Trauma in Early Qing Literature." *Harvard Journal of Asiatic Studies* 59. 2 (1999): 363-443.

Li, Wai-Yee. "The Late Ming Courtesan: Invention of a Cultural Ideal." *Writing Women in Late Imperial China*. Ed. Ellen Widmer and Kang-I Sun Chang. Stanford: Stanford UP, 1997. 47-74.

Li, Xiaorong. "Who Are the Most Beautiful Women of China?—The 'One Hundred Beauties' Genre in the Qing and Early Republican Eras." *Frontier of Literary Studies in China* 7.4 (2013): 617-53.

Li, Xiaorong. *Women's Poetry of Late Imperial China: Transforming the Inner Chambers*. Seattle: U of Washington P, 2012.

Li, Xuyu (李栩鈺). 午夢堂集:女性作品研究 (*Wumengtang ji: nüxing zuopin yanjiu*, Works from the Hall of Meridian Dreams: A Study of Women's Writings). Taipei: Liren shujü, 1999.

Li, Yanshou (李延壽). 南史 (*Nanshi*, The History of the Nan Dynasty). Beijing: Zhonghua shujü, 1975.

Li, Yü. *The Carnal Prayer Mat*. Trans. Patrick Hanan. Honolulu: U of Hawaii P, 1996.

Li, Yü (李漁). 李笠翁十種曲 (*Li Liweng shizhong qu*, Ten Categories of Operas by Li Liweng). Shanghai: Chaoji shuzhuang, 1918.

Li, Yü. 肉蒲團 (*Rouputuan*, *The Carnal Prayer Mat*). Xianggang: Lianhe chubanshe, 1976.

Li, Yü. *Silent Operas*. Trans. Patrick Hanan. Hong Kong: Renditions, 1990.

Li, Yü. 無聲戲 (*Wushengxi*, Silent Operas). Shanghai: Shanghai guji chubanshe, 1990.

Li, Yü. 閑情偶寄 (*Xianqing ouji*, Sparse Notes of an Inquiring Mind). 1671. Yanji: Yanbian renmin chubanshe, 2004.

Li, Zhi. 焚書·續焚書 (*Fenshu· xu Fenshu,* A Book to Burn, and A Book to Burn Continued). Beijing: Zhonghua shujü, 1974.

Li, Zhi (李贄). "司馬相如" ("Sima Xiangru," "On Sima Xiangru"). 藏書 (*Cangshu*, Books Collection). Beijing: Zhonghua shujü, 1959. 624-26.

Liang, Qichao (梁啟超). "變法通義: 論女學" ("Bianfa tongyi: lun nüxue," "General Discussions of Reform: On Women's Education"). 飲冰室合集 (*Yinbingshi heji*, Collected Writings from the Ice-Drinker's Studio). 1897. Shanghai: Zhonghua shujü, 1936.

Liang, Qichao. "記江西康女士" ("Ji Jiangxi Kang nüshi," "A Record of Miss Kang from Jiangxi 1897"). Liang Qichao. 飲冰室合集 (*Yinbingshi heji*, Collected Writings from the Ice-Drinker's Studio 1897). Shanghai: Zhonghua shujü, 1936. 119-20.

Liang, Xiaoping (梁曉萍). 明清家族小說的文化與敘事 (*Mingqing jiazu xiaoshuo de wenhua yu xushi*, On the Culture and Narration of the Family and Clan Novels of the Ming and Qing Dynasties). Tianjin: Nankai daxue chubanshe, 2008.

Liao, Wen (廖雯). "閨閣畫與新閨閣畫: 中國婦女繪畫逃不出的藩籬" ("Guigehua yu xin guigehua: zhongguo funü huihua tao buchu de fanli," "Boudoir Paintings and New Boudoir Paintings: Inescapable Constraints of Women's paintings in China"). 大藝術 (*Da yishu*, Great Arts) 1 (2004): 31-35.

Ling, Mengchu (凌濛初). 二刻拍案驚奇 (*Erke pai'an jingqi*, Striking the Table with Amazement). Taipei: Guiguan chubanshe, 2001.

Lingis, Alphonso. *Foreign Bodies*. London: Routledge, 1994.

Liu, An (劉安). 淮南子 (*Huai'nan zi*, Book of the Master of Huai'nan). Taipei: Taiwan Zhonghua shujü, 1965.

Liu, Guo (劉果). 三言性別話語研究: 以話本小說的文獻比勘為基礎 (*Sanyan xingbie huayu yanjiu: yi huaben xiaoshuo de wenxian bikan wei jichu*, A Study of the Gender Discourse in *Three Collections of Words*: Based on a Comparison of Archives of the Huaben Fiction). Beijing: Zhonghua shujü, 2008.

Liu, Huiying (劉慧英). "女權啟蒙中塑造的救國女子形象" ("Nüquan qimeng zhong suzao de jiuguo nüzi xingxiang," "Images of Women National Saviors in the Feminist Enlightenment"). 中國現代文學研究叢刊 (*Zhongguo xiandai wenxue yanjiu congkan*, Modern Chinese Literature Research Series) 2 (2002): 156-80.

Liu, Kwang-Ching, ed. *Orthodoxy in Late Imperial China*. Berkeley: U of California P, 1990.

Liu, Lydia. "Translingual Practice: The Discourse of Individualism between China and the West." *Narratives of Agency: Self-Making in China, India, and Japan*. Ed. Wimal Dissanayake. Minneapolis: U of Minnesota P, 1996. 1-34.

Liu, Meijun (柳眉君). "婦女回家運動" ("Funü huijia yundong," "Women's Movement of Returning Home"). 女聲 (*Nüsheng*, Women's Voice) 1 (1934): 6.

Liu, Wenjia. *The Tanci Fengshuangfei: A Female Perspective on the Gender and Sexual Politics of Late-Qing China*. Ph.D. Diss. Ann Arbor: UMI Dissertation Services, 2010.

Liu, Xiang. *Exemplary Women of Early China: The Lienü Zhuan of Liu Xiang*. Trans. Anne Behnke Kinney. New York: Columbia UP, 2014.

Liu, Xiang (劉向). 列女傳 (*Lienü zhuan*, The Biographies of Exemplary Women). Ed. Shao Zhengkui (邵正魁). Taipei: Zhonghua shujü, 1966.

Liu, Xiang. 戰國策 (*Zhan'guoce*, Intrigues of the Warring States). Annotated by Gao You (高誘) and Huang Pilie (黃丕烈). Shanghai: Feiyingguan, 1887.

Liu, Xiang. 續列女傳 (*Xu Leinü zhuan,* Sequel to The Biographies of Exemplary Women). 列女傳 (*Lienü zhuan*, The Biographies of Exemplary Women). Ed. Shao Zhengkui (邵正魁). Taipei: Zhonghua shujü, 2. 8 (1966): 10a-b.

Liu, Yazi (柳亞子). 柳亞子選集 (*Liu Yazi xuanji*, Selected Works by Liu Yazi). Beijing: Renmin chubanshe, 1989.

Lou, Yulie (樓宇烈). "湯顯祖哲學思想初探" ("Tang Xianzu zhexue sixiang chutan," "A Preliminary Study of Tang Xianzu's Philosophical Thoughts"). 湯顯祖研究論文集 (*Tang Xianzu yanjiu lunwen ji*, Collections of Studies on Tang Xianzu). Ed. Jiangxi sheng wenxue yishu yanjiu suo (江西省文學藝術研究所). Beijing: Zhongguo xiju chubanshe, 1984. 152-73.

Lowry, Kathryn. "Duplicating the Strength of Feeling: The Circulation of Qingshu in the Late Ming." *Writing and Materiality in China: Essays in Honor of Patrick Hanan*. Ed. Judith Zeitlin, Lydia H. Liu, and Ellen Widmer. Cambridge: Harvard Asia Center, 2003. 239-72.

Lu, Dan'An (陸澹安). 滿江紅 (*Manjianghong*, River Washed in Red). Shanghai: Shanghai xinsheng chubanshe, 1935.

Lu, Huitzu. "Women's Ascetic Practices during the Song." *Asia Major* 15.1 (2002): 73-108.

Lü, Kun (呂坤). 呂新吾先生閨範圖說 (*Lü Xinwu xiansheng Guifan tushuo*, Illustrated Notes on Women Exemplars by Lü Xinwu). 1600. 四庫全書存目叢書 (*Siku quanshu cunmu congshu*, Anthologies of Siku Imperial Library Existing Titles). Jinan: Qilu shushe, 1995.

Lu, Tina. *Persons, Roles and Minds, Identity in Peony Pavilion and Peach Blossom Fan*. Stanford: Stanford UP, 2001.

Lu, Weijing. "Abstaining from Sex: Mourning Ritual and the Confucian Elite." *Journal of the History of Sexuality* 22.2 (2013): 230-52.

Lu, Wenjing. *True to Her Word: The Faithful Maiden Cult in Late Imperial China*. Stanford: Stanford UP, 2008.

Lu, Xun. "What Happens After Nora Leaves Home?" *Silent China: Selected Writings of Lu Xun*. Ed. and trans. Gladys Yang. Oxford: Oxford UP, 1973. 148-54.

Mair, Victor. "The Prosimetric Form in the Chinese Literary Tradition." *Prosimetrum: Cross-Cultural Perspectives on Narrative in Prose and Verse*. Ed. Joseph Harris and Karl Reichl. Cambridge: Brewer, 1997. 365-85.

Mair, Victor H. *Tang Transformation Texts: A Study of the Buddhist Contribution to the Rise of Vernacular Fiction and Drama in China*. Cambridge: Harvard UP, 1989.

Mair, Victor H., and Mark Bender. "Professional Storytelling Traditions of the North and South." *The Columbia Anthology of Chinese Folk and Popular Literature*. Ed. Victor H. Mair and Mark Bender. New York: Columbia UP, 2011. 309-13.

Mann, Susan. "The Lady and the State: Women's Writings in Times of Trouble during the Nineteenth Century." *The Inner Quarters and Beyond: Women Writers from Ming through Qing*. Ed. Grace S. Fong and Ellen Widmer. Leiden: Brill, 2011. 283-314.

Mann, Susan. *Precious Records: Women in China's Long Eighteenth Century*. Stanford: Stanford UP, 1997.

Mann, Susan. "The Virtue of Travel for Women in the Late Empire." *Gender in Motion: Divisions of Labor and Cultural Change in Late Imperial and Modern China*. Ed. Bryna Goodman and Wendy Larson. Lanham: Rowman & Littlefield, 2005. 55-74.

Mann, Susan. "Widows in the Kinship, Class, and Community Structures of Qing Dynasty China." *The Journal of Asian Studies* 46.1 (1987): 37-56.

Mann, Susan. "Women in the Life and Thought of Zhang Xuecheng." *Chinese Language, Thought, and Culture: Nivision and His Critics*. Ed. P. J. Ivanhoe. Chicago: Carus Publishing, 1996. 94-120.

Mann, Susan, and Yu-Yin Cheng, eds. *Under Confucian Eyes: Writings on Gender in Chinese History*. Berkeley: U of California P, 2001.

Mao, Qiling (毛奇齡). 明武宗外紀 (*Ming Wuzong waiji*, A Supplementary History of Emperor Wuzong). Ed. Chen Yansheng. Shanghai: Shenzhou guoguangshe, 1941.

Mao, Wenfang. 物•性別•觀看: 明末清初文化書寫新探 (*Wu, xingbie, guankan: mingmo qingchu wenhua shuxie xintan*, Object, Gender, Gaze: A New Interpretation of the Late Ming and Early Qing Cultural Inscription). Taiwan: xuesheng shujü, 2001.

Mao, Wenfang (毛文芳). "一個清代閨閣的視角: 顧太清1799－1877 畫像題詠析論" ("Yige qingdai guige de shijiao: Gu Taiqing 1799-1877 huaxiang tiyong xilun," "A Perspective from the Qing Inner Chambers: A Study of Gu Taiqing 1799-1877 and the Poetry Inscriptions on Her Portraits"). 文與哲 (*Wenyuzhe*, Literature and Philosophy) 8 (2006): 417-74.

Masuda, Wataru (増田涉). "「話本」という ことについて一通説(あるいは定説)への疑問" ("Notes on *huaben*: Doubt about the Prevailing Opinion"). 人文研究 (*Jinbun kenkyu*, The Journal of Humanities) 16.5 (1965): 22-33.

Menegon, Eugenio. *Ancestors, Virgins, and Friars: Christianity as a Local Religion in Late Imperial China*. Cambridge: Harvard Asia Center, 2010. 76-89.

Meyer-Fong, Tobie. *What Remains: Coming to Terms with Civil War in 19th-Century China*. Stanford: Stanford UP, 2013.

Mingmo, Shilong (明莫是龍). 明人畫學論著23 種 (*Mingren huaxue lunzhu 23 zhong*, Twenty Three Essays on the Art of Painting in the Ming Period). Taipei: Shijie shujü, 2008.

Mulvey, Laura. "Visual Pleasure and Narrative Cinema." *Film Theory and Criticism: Introductory Readings*. Ed. Leo Braudy and Marshall Cohen. Oxford: Oxford UP, 1999. 833-44.

Ng, Vivian. "Homosexuality and the State in Late Imperial China." *Hidden from History: Reclaiming the Gay and Lesbian Past*. Ed. Martin Bauml Duberman, Martha Vicinus, and George Chauncey. New York: Plume, 1989. 76-89.

Ouyang, Xiu (歐陽修), and Song Qi (宋祁) eds. 新唐書 (*Xintangshu*, The New History of the Tang Dynasty). Beijing: Zhonghua shujü, 1975.

Pearce, Lynne. & Sara Mills. *Feminist Readings/ Feminists Reading*. New York: Prentice Hall, 1996.

Pearson, Roberta E. *Eloquent Gestures: The Transformation of Performance Style in the Griffith Biography Films*. Berkeley: U of California P, 1992.

Peng, Dingqiu (彭定求), ed. 全唐詩 (*Quantangshi*, The Complete Collection of Tang *shi* Poems). 1707. Beijing: Zhonghua shujü, 1960.

Phelan, James. *Narrative as Rhetoric: Technique, Audiences, Ethics, Ideology*. Columbus: Ohio State UP, 1996.

Pickowicz, Paul G. "Framing the 'Modern Marriage' in Shanghai Silent-era Films of the 1920s." Presentation at the Annual Meeting of the Association for Asian Studies. Hawaii, 2011.

Ping, Yao. "The Status of Pleasure: Courtesan and Literati Connections in T'ang China (618-907)." *Journal of Women's History* 14.2 (2002): 26-53.

Plaks, Andrew H. "Allegory in *Hsi-Yu Chi* and *Hung-Lou Meng*." *Chinese Narrative: Critical and Theoretical Essays*. Ed. Andrew H. Plaks. New Jersey: Princeton UP, 1977.

Pu, Nong (蒲農). "紅粉骷髏" ("Hongfen kulou," "Rouge Skeletons"). 婦女周刊 (*Funü zhoukan*, Women's Weekly) 2 (1924): 7.

Pu, Songling (蒲松齡). 聊齋誌異 (*Liaozhai zhiyi*, Strange Tales from a Chinese Studio). Ed. Youhue Zhang. Shanghai: Shanghai guji chubanshe, 1978.

Pu, Songling. *Strange Tales from a Chinese Studio*. Trans. John Minford. New York: Penguin Classics, 2006.

Qi, Hong (泣紅). "胭脂血彈詞" ("Yanzhixue tanci," "Rouge Blood"). *Wanqing wenxue congchao* (Late-Qing Literature Series). Ed. A Ying. Beijing: Zhonghua shujü, 1908. 223-52.

Qian, Nanxiu, Grace S. Fong, and Richard Joseph Smith, eds. *Different Worlds of Discourse: Transformations of Gender and Genre in Late Qing and Early Republican China*. Leiden: Brill, 2008.

Qian, Qianwu (錢謙吾). "丁玲" ("Ding Ling"). 1931. 丁玲研究資料 (*Ding Ling yanjiu ziliao*, Research Materials on Ding Ling). Ed. Yuan Liangjun (袁良駿). Tianjin: Tianjin renmin chubanshe, 1982. 226-36.

Qian, Yi (錢宜), Chen Tong (陳同) and Tan Ze (談則). 吳吳山三婦合評牡丹亭 (*Wuwushan sanfu heping Mudanting*, Three Wives' Commentary on *The Peony Pavilion*). 1694. Shanghai: Shanghai guji chubanshe, 2008.

Qiu, Jin (秋瑾). "精衛石" ("Jingweishi," "Pebbles of the Jingwei Bird"). 1905. 秋瑾集 (*Qiu Jin ji*, Collections of Qiu Jin's Works). Shanghai: Shanghai guji chubanshe, 1991. 125-70.

Qiu, Jin (秋瑾). "勉女權" ("Mian nüquan," "Song for Women's Rights"). 中國女報 (*Zhongguo nübao*, Chinese Women's Periodical) 2 (1907): 48.

Qiu, Xinru (邱心如). 筆生花 (*Bishenghua*, Blossom from the Brush). 1857. Hong Kong: Yimei tushu gongsi, 1984.

Qu, Yuan 屈原. *The Li Sao* (*An Elegy on Encountering Sorrows*). Translated by Boon Keng Lim. Commercial Press, 1935.

Raphals, Lisa Ann. *Sharing the Light: Representations of Women and Virtue in Early China*. Albany: State U of New York P, 1998.

Robertson, Maureen. "Changing the Subject: Gender and Self-inscription in Authors." *Writing Women in Late Imperial China*. Ed. Ellen Widmer and Kang-I Sun Chang. Stanford: Stanford UP, 1997. 171-221.

Robertson, Maureen. "Literary Authorship by Late Imperial Governing-Class Chinese Women and the Emergence of a 'Minor Literature.'" *The Inner Quarters and Beyond: Women Writers from Ming through Qing*. Ed. Grace S. Fong and Ellen Widmer. Leiden: Brill, 2010. 375-87.

Robertson, Maureen. "Voicing the Feminine: Constructions of the Gendered Subject in Lyric Poetry by Women of Medieval and Late Imperial China." *Late Imperial China* 13.1 (1992): 63-110.

Rolston, David L., ed. *How to Read the Chinese Novel*. Princeton: Princeton UP, 1990.

Rolston, David L. "'Points of View' in the Writings of Traditional Chinese Fiction Critics." *Chinese Literature: Essays, Articles, Reviews* 15 (1993): 113-42.

Ropp, Paul S. "Between Two Worlds: Women in Shen Fu's *Six Chapters of a Floating Life*." *Woman and Literature in China*. Ed. Anna Gerstlacher and Ruth Keen. Bochum: Brockmeyer, 1985. 98-140.

Ropp, Paul S. "Love, Literacy, and Laments Themes of Women Writers in Late Imperial China." *Women's History Review* 2.1 (1993): 107-41.

Ropp, Paul. "Qiu Xinru." Trans. Zhongguang Zhang. *Biographical Dictionary of Chinese Women: The Qing Period, 1644-1911*. Ed. Clara Wing-chung Ho. Hong Kong: Hong Kong UP, 1999. 132.

Ropp, Paul S., Paola Zamperini, and Harriet T. Zurndorfer, eds. *Passionate Women: Female Suicide in Late Imperial China*. Leiden: Brill, 2001.

Rosenlee, Li-Hsiang Lisa. *Confucianism and Women: A Philosophical Interpretation*. Albany: State U of New York P, 2006.

Sang, Tze-lan Deborah. *The Emerging Lesbian: Female Same-Sex Desire in Modern China*. Chicago: U of Chicago P, 2003.

Scott, Joan W. "Gender: A Useful Category of Historical Analysis." *The American Historical Review* 91.5 (1986): 1053-75.

Se, Lu (瑟廬). "國際婦女勞工會與中國婦女" ("Guoji funü laogonghui yu zhongguo funü," "International Women's Labor Union and Chinese Women"). 婦女雜誌 (*Funü zazhi*, Lady's Journal) 7.11 (1921): 1-5.

Se, Lu. "文明與獨身" ("Wenming yu dushen," "Civilization and Celibacy"). 婦女雜誌 (*Funü zazhi*, Lady's Journal) 10 (1922): 1-5.

Shen, Dan. "Defense and Challenge: Reflections on the Relation between Story and Discourse." *Narrative* 10.3 (2002): 222-43.

Shen, Fu (沈復). 浮生六記 (*Fusheng liuji*, Six Records of a Floating Life). 1808. Nanchang: Jiangxi renmin chubanshe, 1980.

Shen, Fu. *Six Records of a Floating Life*. Trans. Leonard Pratt. New York: Penguin, 1983.

Shen, Tai (沈泰). 盛明雜劇 (*Shengming zajü*, Zajü of the High Ming). Beijing: Zhongguo xijü chubanshe, 1958.

Shen, Xiang (沈纕). "題柳蘼芜小影" ("Ti Liu Miwu xiaoying," "On the Miniature of Liu Miwu"). 翡翠樓集 (*Feicui louji*, Collection of the Emerald Pergola). Ed. Ren Zhaolin (任兆麟) and Zhang Zilan (張滋蘭). 吳中女士詩鈔 (*Wuzhong nüshi shichao*, Poetry of Suzhou Ladies): <http://digital.library.mcgill.ca/mingqing/search/details-poem.php?poemID=6198&language=eng>.

Sheng, Zhimei (盛誌梅). 清代彈詞研究 (*Qingdai tanci yanjiu*, A Study of *Tanci* in the Qing Dynasty). Jinan: Qilu shushe, 2008.

Shi, Naian (施耐庵). 水滸傳 (*Shuihuzhuan*, *The Water Margin*). Changsha: Yuelu shushe, 2006.

Shi, Naian. *The Water Margin: Outlaws of the Marsh*. Trans. J. H. Jackson. North Clarendon: Tuttle Publishing, 2011.

Shikibu, Murasaki. *The Tale of Genji: A Novel*. Trans. Arthur Waley. Boston: Houghton Mifflin, 1936.

Sieber, Patricia. "Corporal Transactions: New Perspectives on Traditional Practices in China, India, and Africa." *Journal of Women's History* 17.4 (2005): 142-47.

Silverman, Kaja. *The Threshold of the Visible World*. London: Routledge, 1996.

Stanzel, Franz. *A Theory of Narrative*. Cambridge: Cambridge UP, 1986.

Stevens, Sara. "Figuring Modernity: The New Woman and the Modern Girl in Republican China." *NWSA Journal* 15.3 (2003): 82-103.

Stone, Jacqueline. "When Disobedience Is Filial and Resistance Is Loyal: The Lotus Sutra and Social Obligations in the Medieval Nichiren Tradition." *A Buddhist Kaleidoscope: Essays on the Lotus Sutra*. Ed. Gene Reeves. Tokyo: Kosei Publishing, 2002. 261-81.

Sung, Marina H. *The Narrative Art of Tsai-sheng-yüan: A Feminist Vision in Traditional Confucian Society.* San Francisco: Chinese Materials Center Publications, 1994.

Tan, Zhengbi (譚正璧). 評彈通考 (*Pingtan tongkao*, A Comprehensive Research of Storytelling and Storysinging). Beijing: Zhongguo quyi chubanshe, 1985.

Tan, Zhengbi. 中國女性的文學生活 (*Zhongguo nüxing de wenxue shenghuo*, The Literary Lives of Chinese Women). Shanghai: Guangming shujü, 1931.

Tan, Zhengbi. 中國女性文學史 (*Zhongguo nüxing wenxueshi*, The History of Chinese Women's Literature). Shanghai: Guangming shuju, 1935.

Tan, Zhengbi (譚正璧), and Tan Xun (譚尋), eds. 彈詞敘錄 (*Tanci xulu*, *Tanci* outlines). Shanghai: Guji chubanshe, 1980.

Tanghu yunyu nüshi (棠湖雲腴女士). "敘" ("Xu," "A Note," 1872). 筆生花 (*Bishenghua*, Blossom from the Brush). Qiu Xinru. Hong Kong: Yimei tushu gongsi, 1984. 1-2.

Tang, Xianzu (湯顯祖). 牡丹亭 (*Mudanting*, *The Peony Pavilion*). Beijing: Beijing renmin chubanshe, 1997.

Tang, Xianzu. *The Peony Pavilion*. Trans. Cyril Birch. Bloomington: Indiana UP, 2002.

Tao, Xisheng (陶希盛). "新舊商品與新舊婦女" ("Xinjiu shangpin yu xinjiu funü," "New and Old Merchandise vs New and Old Women"). 婦女雜誌 (*Funü zazhi*, Lady's Journal) 17.2 (1930): 2-5.

Tao, Zhenhuai (陶貞懷). 天雨花 (*Tianyuhua*, Heaven Rains Flowers). Ed. Ping Li (李平). Zhengzhou: Zhongzhou guji chubanshe, 1984.

Tetsuzō, Henshūsha Tsukamoto, ed. 古列女傳:女四書 (*Gu Lienü zhuan: nü sishu*, Ko Retsujoden. Onna shisho Ancient *Biographies of Exemplary Women* and "Women's Four Books"). Tōkyō: Yūhōdō, Taishō, 1920.

Theiss, Janet. *Disgraceful Matters: The Politics of Chastity in Eighteenth-Century China.* Berkeley: U of California P, 2004.

Tian, Min. *The Poetics of Difference and Displacement: Twentieth-Century Chinese-Western Intercultural Theatre*. Hong Kong: Hong Kong UP, 2008.

Tian, Rukang. *Male Anxiety and Female Chastity: A Comparative Study of Chinese Ethical Values in Ming-Ch'ing times*. Leiden: Brill, 1988.

Tong, Lijun (童李君). "鳳雙飛對女作家彈詞小說的寫作模式的創新" ("*Fengshuangfei* dui nüzuojia tanci xiaoshuo de xiezuo moshi de chuangxin,"

"The Renovation of Women *Tanci* Writers' Writing Models in Phoenixes Flying Together"). 明清小說研究 (*Mingqing xiaoshuo yanjiu*, Mingqing Fiction Studies) 4 (2010): 217-25.

Tötösy de Zepetnek, Steven. "From Comparative Literature Today toward Comparative Cultural Studies." *Comparative Literature and Comparative Cultural Studies*. Ed. Steven Tötösy de Zepetnek. West Lafayette: Purdue UP, 2003. 235-67.

Van Zoonen, Liesbet. *Feminist Media Studies*. New York: Sage Publications, 1994.

Volpp, Sophie. "Classifying Lust: The Seventeenth Century Vogue for Male Love." *Harvard Journal of Asiatic Studies* 61.1 (2001): 77-118.

Wan, Maggie C. K. "Building an Immortal Land: The Ming Jiajing Emperor's West Park." *Asia Major* 22.2 (2009): 65-99.

Wang, David Der-Wei. *Fin-de-Siècle Splendor: Repressed Modernities of Late Qing Fiction, 1849-1911*. Stanford: Stanford UP, 1997.

Wang, Duanshu (王端淑). 名媛詩緯初編 (*Mingyuan shiwei chubian*, Classical Poetry of Famous Women: An Initial Collection): <http://digital.library.mcgill.ca/mingqing/search/results-work.php?workID=120&language=eng>.

Wang, Dungen (王鈍根), ed. 社會之花 (*Shehui zhi hua*, Flower of the Society). Shanghai: Dalu tushu gongsi, 1924-1925.

Wang, Jide (王驥德). 男王後 (*Nan wanghou*, The Male Queen) 盛明雜劇 (*Shengming zajü*, Zajü Drama of the High Ming 1629). Ed. Sheng Tai. Song Fen Studio edition. Beijing: Guji chubanshe, 1958. 1-28.

Wang, Lijian (王力堅). 清代才媛文學之文化考察 (*Qingdai caiyuan wenxue zhi wenhua kaocha*, A Cultural Exploration of the Talented Woman Literary Trend of Qing Dynasty). Taipei: Wenjin chubanshe, 2006.

Wang, Lingzhen. *Personal Matters: Chinese Women's Autobiographical Practices in Twentieth-Century China.* Stanford: Stanford UP, 2004.

Wang, Oushang (汪藕裳). 子虛記 (*Zixu ji*, A Tale of Illusions). 1883. Shanghai: Shijie fanhua baoguan, 1901.

Wang, Qinghua (王慶華). 話本小說文體研究 (*Huaben xiaoshuo wenti yanjiu*, A Study of the Style of Huaban Fiction). Shanghai: Huadong shifan daxue chubanshe, 2006.

Wang, Renyu (王仁裕). 開元天寶遺事 (*Kaiyuan tianbao yishi*, Stories of the Kaiyuan and Tianbao Periods). Shanghai: Shanghai guji chubanshe, 1985.

Wang, Robin. *Images of Women in Chinese Thought and Culture: Writings from the Pre-Qin Period through the Song Dynasty.* Indianapolis: Hackett Publishing, 2003.

Wang, Yangming (王陽明). 王陽明全集 (*Wang Yangming quanji*, Complete Works of Wang Yangming). Ed. Guang Wu (吴光). Shanghai: Shanghai guji chubanshe, 1992.

Wang, Yanning. "Qing Women's Poetry on Roaming as a Female Transcendent." *Nan Nü* 12.1 (2010): 65-102.

Wang, Zheng. *Women in the Chinese Enlightenment: Oral and Textual Histories*. Berkeley: U of California P, 1999.

Webster-Cheng, Stephanie J. *Composing, Revising, and Performing Suzhou Ballads: a Study of Political Control and Artistic Freedom in* Tanci*, 1949-1964*. Ph.D. Diss. University of Pittsburgh, 2009.

Wei, Ruzhi (魏如芝). "我之獨身主義觀" ("Wo zhi dushen zhuyi guan," "My View on Celibacy"). 婦女雜誌 (*Funü zazhi*, Lady's Journal) 9.2 (1923): 25.

Wei, Yuzhang (衛瑜章). 離騷集釋 (*Li Sao jishi*, Collected Annotations to *An Elegy on Encountering Sorrows*) Shanghai: Shangwu yinshuguan, 1937.

Widmer, Ellen. *The Beauty and the Book: Women and Fiction in Nineteenth-Century China*. Cambridge: Harvard U, Asia Center, 2006.

Widmer, Ellen. "Gentility in Transition: Travels, Novels, and the New *Guixiu*." *The Quest for Gentility in China: Negotiations Beyond Gender and Class*. Ed. Daria Berg and Chloe Starr. New York: Routledge, 2007. 21-44.

Widmer, Ellen. "Ming Loyalism and the Women's Voice in Fiction after *Hong lou meng*." *Writing Women in Late Imperial China*. Ed. Ellen Widmer and Kang-I Sun Chang. Stanford: Stanford UP, 1997. 366-96.

Widmer, Ellen. "Xiaoqing's Literary Legacy and the Place of the Woman Writer in Late Imperial China." *Late Imperial China* 13.1 (1992): 139-42.

Widmer, Ellen, and Kang-I Sun Chang, eds. *Writing Women in Late Imperial China*. Stanford: Stanford UP, 1997.

Wu, Bing (吳炳). 畫中人 (*Huazhongren*, The Beauty in the Painting). 粲花齋五種 (*Caihuazhai wuzhong*, Five Plays from the Canhua Studio). Yangzhou: Yangzhou guji shudian faxing, 1990.

Wu, Cuncun, ed. *Homoerotic Sensibilities in Late Imperial China*. London: Routledge, 2004.

Wu, H. Laura. "Through the Prism of Male Writing: Representation of Lesbian Love in Ming-Qing Literature." *Nan Nü* 4.1 (2002): 1-34.

Wu, Hung. "Beyond Stereotypes: The Twelve Beauties in Qing Court Art and the 'Dream of the Red Chamber.'" *Writing Women in Late Imperial China*. Ed. Ellen Widmer and Kang-I Sun Chang. Stanford: Stanford UP, 1997. 306-66.

Wu, Lichang (吳立昌). 精神分析與中西文學 (*Jingshen fenxi yu zhongxi wenxue*, Psychoanalysis and Sino-Western Literature). Shanghai: Xuelin chubanshe, 1987.

Wu, Qingyun. *Female Rule in Chinese and English Literary Utopias*. Syracuse: Syracuse UP, 1995.

Wu, Zao (吳藻). 喬影 (*Qiaoying*, The Image in Disguise). 續修四庫全書 (*Xuxiu siku quanshu*, Siku Imperial Library Continued). Volume 1768. Shanghai: Shanghai guji chubanshe, 2002. 131-37.

Xi, Peilan (席佩蘭). 長真閣集 (*Changzhenge ji*, A Collection of Poems in the Pergola of Everlasting Truth): <http://digital.library.mcgill.ca/mingqing/search/results-work.php?workID=51&language=eng>.

Xinyuege Zhuren. 修月閣主人. 繡像錦上花全傳 (*Xiuxiang jingshanghua quanzhuan*, Illustrated Edition o the Complete Account of Flower on the Brocade) Xueyutang. Original text held at Beijing Normal University Library, 1874.

Xu, Ke. (徐珂). 清稗類鈔 (*Qingbai leichao*, Classified Notes of Qing-Dynasty Unofficial Historical Material). Shanghai: Shangwu yinshu guan, 1917.

Xu, Wei (徐渭). 雌木蘭替父從軍 (*Ci Mulan tifu congjun*, Maid Mulan Joins the Army in Her Father's Stead). 續修四庫全書 (*Xuxiu siku quanshu*, Siku Imperial Library Continued). Vol. 1766 (2002): 219-24.

Xu, Wei. 女狀元 (*Nüzhuangyuan*, The Female Top Candidate). 續修四庫全書 (*Xuxiu siku quanshu*, Siku Imperial Library Continued). Vol. 1766 (2002): 224-39.

Xu, Xin (徐熙). 勸孝歌 (*Quanxiao ge*, A Song to Persuade People to Be Filial). 威信文史資料選輯 (*Weixin wenshi ziliao xuanji*, Weixin Literary and Historical Records Collections). Weixin: Weixin xian zhengxie wenshi ziliao bangongshi. Vol. 9, 1990.

Xu, Zhen (徐震). 女才子書 (*Nücaizi shu*, Book of Talented Women Scholars). 1658. 古本小說集成 (*Guben xiaoshuo jicheng*, Collections of Ancient Fiction Works). Vol. 1. Shanghai: Shanghai guji chubanshe, 1991. 5-31.

Yan, Yonghua (嚴永華). "寄祝鄭澹若夫人生日" ("Jizhu Zheng Danruo furen shengri," "For the Celebration of Lady Zheng Danruo's Birthday"). 紉蘭室詩鈔 (*Renlanshi shichao*, Poetry Collections of the Renlan Studio) 1:10a: <http://digital.library.mcgill.ca/mingqing/search/details-poem.php?poemID=12623&language=eng>.

Yang, Buwei (楊步偉). 一個女人的自傳 (*Yige nüren de zizhuan*, A Woman's Biography). Xinbei: Chuanji wenxue chubanshe, 1967.

Yang, Fuji (楊復吉). 三婦合評牡丹亭雜記跋 (*Sanfu heping Mudanting zaji ba*, Afterword to *The Three Wives' Commentary Miscellany*). 昭代叢書 (*Zhaodai congshu*, Collection of Volumes in the Present Age 1876). Wujiang: Shenshi shihaitang, 1833. 165.

Yang, Haihong. *Hoisting One's Own Banner: Self-Inscription in Lyric Poetry by Three Women Writers of Late Imperial China*. Ph.D. Diss. Ann Arbor, Michigan: UMI Dissertation Services, 2010.

Ye, Chang-Hai (葉長海). "理無情有說湯翁" ("Liwu qingyou shuo Tang weng," "On Tang Xianzu the Playwright Pursuing Sensibilities and Opposing Rationalism"). 湯顯祖與牡丹亭 (*Tang Xianzu yu Mudanting*, Tang Xianzu and *Mudanting*). Ed. Wei Hua and Ayling Wang Taipei: Academia Sinica, 2005. 105-36.

Ye, Dejun (葉德均). 戲曲小說叢考 (*Xiqu xiaoshuo congkao*, Collected Studies in Drama and Fiction). Beijing: Zhonghua shujü, 1979.

Ye, Shaoyuan, ed. 午夢堂全集 (*Wumengtang quanji*, Complete Works from the Hall of Meridian Dreams). Shanghai: Beiye Shanfang, 1935.

Yeh, Catherine Vance. *Shanghai Love: Courtesans, Intellectuals, and Entertainment Culture, 1850-1910.* Seattle: U of Washington P, 2006.

Yong Lan (詠蘭), Shu Zhu (書竹), You Mei (詠梅). Ed. Mengjü (夢菊). 俠女群英史 (*Xianü qunying shi*, A History of Women Warriors). Shanghai: Fudan daxue tushuguan, 1905.

Youtong (友彤). "倡母性尊重論的愛倫凱女士為什麼獨身?" ("Chang muxing zunzhong lun de Ai Lunkai nüshi wei shenme dushen?" "Why Does the Advocate of Respect for Motherhood Ms. Ellen Key Live a Single Life?"). 婦女雜誌 (*Funü zazhi*, Lady's Journal) 8.10 (1923): 12-15.

Yu, Anthony C. *Rereading the Stone: Desire and the Making of Fiction in* Dream of Red Mansions. Princeton, New Jersey: Princeton UP, 1997.

Yu, Dan (于丹). "花神形象的流變:兼探清代小說中的花神意蘊" ("Huashen xingxiang de liubian: jiantan qingdai xiaoshuo zhong de huashen yiyun," "The Evolvement of Flower Goddesses: A Study of the Implications of the Images of Flower Goddesses in Qing Fiction"). 學術交流 (*Xueshu jiaoliu*, Research Exchange) 160.7 (2007): 30-33.

Yuan, Jiao (袁郊). 甘澤謠 (*Ganze yao*, Ballads of Timely Rainfall). Shanghai: Shangwu yinshu guan, 1936.

Yuan, Mei (袁枚). 隨園女弟子詩選 (*Suiyuan nüdizi shixuan*, Collections of Poems by the Women Disciples of Sui Garden). Nanjing: Suiyuan, 1796.

Yuan, Mei. 隨園詩話 (*Suiyuan shihua*, Sui Garden Remarks on Poetry). Ed. Gu Xuejie (顧學頡). Beijing: Renming wenxue chubanshe, 1982.

Yue, Daiyun (樂黛雲). "無名、失語中的女性夢幻: 十八世紀中國女作家陳端生和她對女性的看法" ("Wuming, shiyu zhong de nüxing menghuan: shiba shiji zhongguo nüzuojia Chen Duansheng he ta dui nüxing de kanfa," "Loss of Name, Loss of Language: Female Imagination, an Eighteenth Century Chinese Female Author Chen Duansheng"). 中國文化 (*Zhongguo wenhua*, Chinese Culture) 10 (1994).

Zamperini, Paola. "Elective Affinities: Literary Soul Mates and the Marketplace in Late Qing Fiction." *Late Imperial China* 28.1 (2007): 62-91.

Zamperini, Paola. "Untamed Hearts: Eros and Suicide in Late Imperial Chinese Fiction." *Passionate Women: Female Suicide in Late Imperial China*. Ed. Paul S. Ropp, Paola Zamperini, and Harriet T. Zurndorfer. Leiden: Brill, 2001. 77-105.

Zarrow, Peter. *China in War and Revolution: 1895-1949*. London: Routledge, 2005.

Zeitlin, Judith. "Embodying the Disembodied: Representations of Ghosts and the Feminine." *Writing Women in Late Imperial China*. Ed. Ellen Widmer and Kang-I Sun Chang. Stanford: Stanford UP, 1997. 242-63.

Zeitlin, Judith. *Historian of the Strange: Pu Songling and the Classical Chinese Tale*. Stanford: Stanford UP, 1993.

Zeitlin, Judith, Lydia H. Liu, and Ellen Widmer, eds. *Writing and Materiality in China: Essays in Honor of Patrick Hanan*. Cambridge: Harvard Asia Center, 2003.

Zhang, Dejun (張德均). "陳端生的母親對她在文學成就上的影響" ("Chen Duansheng de muqin dui ta zai wenxue chengjiu shang de yingxiang," "Chen Duansheng's Mother and Her Influence on Chen Duansheng's Literary Achievements"). 光明日報 (*Guangming ribao*, The Guangming Daily), July 25, 1961.

Zhang, Jing'er (張靜二). "畫中人故事系列中的畫與情" ("*Huazhongren* gushi xilie zhong de hua yu qing," "Portrait and Desire in the stories about the Painted Person"). 明清戲曲國際研討會論文集 (*Mingqing xiqu guoji yantaohui lunwenji*, Collected Papers from the International Conference on Ming-Qing Drama). Ed. Wei Hua and Ayling Wang. Taipei: Academia Sinica, 1998. 485-512.

Zhang, Ruoming. "Vanguard Women." *Women in Republican China: A Sourcebook*. Ed. Hua R. Lan, Vanessa L. Fong, and M. E. Sharpe. New York: East Gate, 1999. 197-206.

Zhang, Xuecheng (章學誠). 文史通義校註 (*Wenshi tongyi jiaozhu*, The General Meaning of Literature and History with Annotations). 1832. Annotated by Ye Ying (葉瑛). Beijing: Zhonghua shujü, 1994.

Zhang, Yu. *The Female Rewriting of Grand History: The Tanci Fiction Jing Zhong Zhuang*. Ph.D. Diss. Ann Arbor: UMI Dissertation Services, 2013.

Zhao, Yongbing (趙詠冰). "帶著腳鐐的生命之舞: 從《再生緣》看傳統中國女性寫作的困境" ("Daizhe jiaoliao de shengming zhi wu: cong *Zaishengyuan* kan chuantong zhongguo nüxing xiezuo de kunjing," "Dancing in Shackles: *Zaishengyuan* and the Challenge of Writing for Women in China"). 明清小說研究 (*Mingqing xiaoshuo yanjiu*, Ming Qing Fiction Studies) 2 (2005): 244-54.

Zheng, Danruo (鄭澹若). 夢影緣 (*Mengyingyuan*, Dream, Image, Destiny). 1843. Taipei: Wenhai chubanshe, 1971.

Zheng, Danruo (鄭澹若). "序" ("Xu," "Author's Preface.") 夢影緣 (*Mengyingyuan*, Dream, Image, Destiny). Zheng Danruo. Taipei: Wenhai chubanshe, 1971.

Zheng, Zhenduo (鄭振鐸). 中國俗文學史 (*Zhongguo suwenxue shi*, A History of Chinese Popular Culture). Changsha: Shangwu yinshuguan, 1938.

Zhong, Xinqing (鐘心青). 二十世紀女界文明燈彈詞 (*Ershi shiji nüjie wenmingdeng tanci*, Twentieth Century *Tanci*: Light of Civilization in the Women's World). Shanghai: Mingming xueshe, 1911.

Zhou, Jianren (周建人). "中國女子的覺醒與獨身" ("Zhongguo nüzi de juexing yu dushen," "Chinese Women's Awakening and Celibacy"). 婦女雜誌 (*Funü zazhi*, Lady's Journal) 8.10 (1922): 7-15.

Zhou, Jun (周鈞), and Duan Chaorui (段朝瑞), eds. 續纂山陽縣志 (*Xuzuan shanyang xianzhi*, A Supplementary Gazette of Shanyang County). Haikou: Hainan chubanshe, 2001.

Zhou, Liang (周良). 蘇州評彈舊聞鈔 (*Suzhou pingtan jiuwen chao*, Old Anecdotes from Suzhou Tanci Narratives). Nanjing: Jiangsu renmin chubanshe, 1983.

Zhou, Yiqun. "The Hearth and the Temple: Mapping Female Religiosity in Late Imperial China, 1550-1900." *Late Imperial China* 24.2 (2003): 109-55.

Zhou, Zuyan. *Androgyny in Late Ming and Early Qing Literature*. Honolulu: U of Hawai'i P, 2003.

Zimmerman, Bonnie. *Lesbian Histories and Cultures: An Encyclopedia.* New York: Routledge, 1999.

Zou, Ying (鄒穎). "從對牡丹亭的回應看再生緣的女性書寫及其文學史意義" ("Cong dui *Mudanting* de huiying kan *Zaishengyuan* de nüxing shuxie jiqi wenxueshi yiyi," "Responding to *The Peony Pavilion*: On Feminine Writing in *Zaisheng yuan* and its Significance in Literary History"). 西南民族大學學報 (*Xi'Nan minzu daxue xuebao*, Journal of Southwest University for Nationalities) 4 (2014): 176-84.

Zou, Ying. "Cross-Dressing and Other Disguises in *Zaisheng yuan*." *Late Imperial China* 33.2 (2012): 119-53.

Zou, Ying. "再生緣中的時間經驗與文體特征" ("*Zaishengyuan* zhong de shijian jingyan yu wenti tezheng," "Time Experience and Generic Characterizations in *Zaishengyuan*"). 南昌大學學報 (*Nanchang daxue xuebao*, Journal of Nanchang University) 4 (2014): 113-24.

Zou, Zizhen (鄒自振). 湯顯祖綜論 (*Tang Xianzu zonglun*, A Comprehensive Study of Tang Xianzu). Chengdu: Bashu shushe, 2001.

Index